BUGIALLI
ON PASTA

REVISED AND ENLARGED

BUGIALLI

PHOTOGRAPHS BY ANDY RYAN

ILLUSTRATIONS BY GLENN WOLFF

ON PASTA

Giuliano Bugialli

STEWART, TABORI & CHANG
NEW YORK

EDITOR • H. D. R. CAMPBELL
DESIGNER • ALEXANDRA MALDONADO

Published in 2000 by
STEWART, TABORI & CHANG
A division of U.S. Media Holdings, Inc.
115 West 18th Street
New York, NY 10011

Distributed in Canada by
General Publishing Company Ltd.
30 Lesmill Road
Don Mills, Ontario, Canada M3B 2T6

LIBRARY OF CONGRESS CATALOGING-IN-PUBLICATION DATA

Bugialli, Giuliano.
        Bugialli on pasta / Giuliano Bugialli ; photographs by Andy Ryan ;
illustrations by Glenn Wolff.— Rev. and enl.
        p. cm.
    Includes index.
    ISBN 1-55670-984-6
        1. Cookery (Pasta) 2. Cookery, Italian. I. Title.

    TX809.M17 B84   2000
    641.8'22—dc21

For additional information about Giuliano Bugialli, contact the Web site:
www.bugialli.com

COVER: *Nidi de capelli d'angelo con filetti di pomodoro (Birds' Nests of Angel-Hair Pasta with Tomato Fillets), see page 108*
ENDPAPERS: *Ambrogio Lorenzetti, Allegory of Good Government. Effects of Good Government in the City, 1338-39. Palazzo Publico, Siena, Italy. Photograph © Scala/ Art Resource, NY, NY*

Printed in Singapore

10 9 8 7 6 5 4 3 2 1

FIRST PRINTING

TO
AUDREY

introduction 8

contents

introduction

Pasta has been basic to the Italian diet for at least a century and a half, and many pasta dishes have origins that go back much further. The enormous growth in pasta's popularity outside of Italy has been phenomenal. The discovery of its healthful qualities has led to a burst of innovation and creativity in its pairing with other ingredients.

The purpose of this book is to provide a model of traditional Italian pasta dishes that have stood the test of centuries in Italy. I hope these give you some guidelines for classic combinations and proper blending of ingredients so you can avoid the trial and error of undirected "creativity." Innovation without such guidelines has produced some bizarre combinations that may have temporary shock value, but which won't endure for an educated palate. As in all cooking—or any creative work—a foundation of basic techniques, methods, and information must be established. Some combinations now being touted as new and innovative were in fact rejected ages ago in Italy. For example, although goat cheese has existed in Italy for thousands of years, there is not a single traditional dish that uses it cooked. This is not because no one has ever thought of cooking it, but because the change in taste and strong smell of the heated cheese has been consciously rejected. It is my opinion that cooked goat cheese is a culinary travesty, with or without pasta.

I cite the example of a more positive guideline. Just about all dishes that combine pasta with zucchini alone require that the vegetable be fried first. Certainly this is the result of centuries of trial and error. Another idea worth pondering is that all dishes combining shrimp with pasta seem to be from the last sixty years. Why was there a traditional aversion to this combination? Why have a few such dishes come to be accepted in recent regional cooking?

In this book I concentrate on some pasta dishes that are still especially relevant to current gastronomy ten years after the original edition was published—pasta and beans, pasta and vegetables, pasta with fish, and so on—and I compare the various preparations of such combinations in different regions. For example, the diverse ways of combining pasta with eggplant is interesting in itself and provides a fair number of quite different and equally valid recipes. The same is true of other vegetables, beans, fish, and like ingredients. Many fine Italian cheeses are now available in the United States and this prompted me to include a new chapter on pasta and cheese in this revised and enlarged edition.

This is the first of my books in which I emphasize dried pasta recipes and give recipes incorporating a large selection of them. Fresh pasta is not overlooked, however, and here you will find many special regional examples with illustrated techniques, though that is not the main thrust of this book.

Arriving at an authentic version of a recipe with a long tradition requires work. The dish as prepared at one regional restaurant or by one family from an area is not necessarily an authentic version of that region's preparation. It is important to compare many different sources, printed and oral, especially the oldest available ones. Local restaurant versions are often unreliable, and a single family's version may not be typical. Let us not forget that not every Italian grandmother is an excellent cook. Most of all, I have avoided idiosyncratic versions of dishes made by myself and others.

Several other grain dishes, such as *gran farro*, Italian couscous, and *gnocchi*, are included because, aside from being wonderful dishes, they help us understand the evolution of pasta from ancient Roman times.* (As I discuss in chapter 1, Marco Polo did not introduce pasta to Italy from China.) If this book helps you understand some general principles of pasta selection, or assists you in matching various types of pasta with sauces and knowing which ingredients form appropriate pairs, I will feel I have accomplished my goal and have helped you move on to make your own creations that rest on an intelligent, solid basis. The recipes themselves form a collection of wonderful dishes and need no other justification. I hope you enjoy them.

CHOOSING THE SHAPES OF DRIED PASTA

It is fun and enlightening to match the exact regional type of dried pasta with its traditional sauce. But how does one find order among the hundreds of named pasta shapes? To add to the confusion, the same shape may have different names in different regions, and may differ even from one manufacturer of dried pasta to another. And then, the slightest difference in length or twist may give the pasta yet another name.

And what if it is not possible to find the exact pasta you need? What criteria should you use in choosing a substitute? Can we find some general categories to guide us? Here I attempt to show the main functional types of dried pasta to remove some of the mystique. I help you choose substitutes by creating basic categories by general shape, with a brief guide as to how each is used. Except for regional specialties, Italians do not hesitate to interchange the pastas within each of these categories.

LONG PASTA

Among the many different names are *spaghetti*, *vermicelli*, *bigoli*, *ciriole*, *bavette*, *linguine*, *fidelini*, *spaghettini*, and *capellini*. Formerly, some of these were defined by their length. *Spaghetti* was longer than it is today, and *bigoli* were extremely long. But, with the standardization in box size for shelf marketing, now all long pastas tend to be of the same length. The few differences that remain are in thickness and whether they are rounded or flattened. (Apropos of nothing, it is interesting to note that flattened *linguine* have achieved an importance outside of Italy that they never had at home.)

All of these types of traditional regional pastas are associated with specific sauces, and except for their varied thicknesses, they take the sauce in basically the same way. Naturally, the delicate *capellini* require a lighter sauce than the thick *ciriole*. The most commonly used pasta of this type, *spaghetti*, is now generally less thick than it used to be and is closer to *spaghettini*.

Medium-thick, long pastas can be substituted one for another if you can't find a specific one. If you can't find *capellini*, use the thinnest substitute; for *ciriole*, use the thickest.

LONG PASTA WITH A HOLE

Perciatelli or *bucatini* are a bit thicker than *spaghetti*, but their main characteristic is an almost imperceptible hole through their entire length. The first name is Neapolitan, the second Roman, for the same pasta. There are many other such instances of the same pasta parading under different regional names. Don't let this confuse you. And, of course, do not take a manufacturer's name for a type as holy writ.

WIDE PASTA

Long, flat pasta from ¼ inch to several inches wide include *tagliatelle* (*fettuccine*, the same), *pappardelle*, *trenette*, *laganelle*, *reginelle*, *lasagnette*, and *lasagne*. They may have straight or curled sides. Most of these appear more often as fresh pasta, and some manufacturers' versions of *tagliatelle* or *trenette* may not resemble the traditional fresh versions very much. Some of these appear at times as dried egg pasta. The main differences are in their widths, and, to a lesser degree, their thickness. These qualities should determine the closest substitute.

SHORT TUBULAR PASTA

Ranging from about 2 to 3 inches long, with a hole from ½ inch to 1 inch wide, these pastas include *penne*,

sedanini, *denti di cavallo*, *rigatoni*, and so on. They may have smooth or ridged surfaces, but this difference is not as important as you might think in the traditional pairing with a sauce. Both smoothed and ridged *penne* are used with the same sauces in Tuscany. *Mezzani* is a pasta between normal and small. In Italy, we say "*mezzo*."

SHORT PASTA—OTHER

Included here are bow- or butterfly-shaped *farfalle*, ring-shaped Sicilian *anellini*, twisted *fusilli*, shell-shaped *chiocciole*, and the like. Their shapes retain the sauce just as the hole does in tubular pasta, and they are often used interchangeably with that type.

PASTA PRIMARILY FOR BROTHS OR MINESTRONI

In this category are all the very small *pastine*, such as *grandinine*, *stelline*, and so forth; the very short tubular ones, *ditalini*, *avemarie*, *paternostri*; and smaller versions of the above-mentioned butterflies (*farfalle*) or of shells (*chiocciole*).

The word *maccherone* (not spelled "macaroni" in Italian) is sometimes used as a generic term for pasta, especially in the Naples area and in ancient cookbooks. Most commercial producers use the term to refer to a medium-length tubular pasta with ridges, in length between *penne* and *rigatoni*. The elbow shape for *maccherone* is less used. The spelling "macaroni" has existed in English, however, since the eighteenth century.

USE OF CHEESE ON PASTA

Cheese, grated or occasionally sliced very thinly, is often added to pasta before serving. However, in Italy it is not added all the time; it is used less often than many people think. Generally cheese is not used with fish, game, or mushroom sauces—though there are a few exceptions—and rarely in dishes with hot red pepper. And on many other dishes, cheese should not be sprinkled mindlessly, since often they are better without it.

Depending on the region, there is much variety in the cheeses used. The incomparable Parmigiano is used all over Italy, but numerous pecorinos, *bitto* from Valtellina, *latteria* from Friuli, *caciocavallo*, and others are preferred locally for regional dishes. One should not indiscriminately sprinkle Parmigiano over everything if all dishes are not to melt into an unappealing sameness.

There is no basis, however, to the recently developed misconception that Parmigiano is rarely used in recipes employing olive oil. It and other cheeses are combined with butter or oil, depending on the region.

I have added a new chaper featuring recipes that specifically combine pasta and cheese (chapter 7).

A NOTE ON RICOTTA

Since most containers of ricotta sold in markets have a net weight of 15 ounces rather than 1 pound, it is more convenient to use that amount.

A NOTE ON OLIVE OIL

First-pressing, extra-virgin olive oil and even some good ones with a little extra acidity are now available from many regions. Use the olive oil of a specific region in preparing a regional dish: Liguria, Tuscany, Umbria, Lazio, Apulia, Calabria, and Sicily are the principal olive oil producing regions. The production from other regions is negligible and their dishes reflect this; they usually employ butter rather than oil.

A special exception is Campania, around the Naples area, which though surrounded by other olive oil regions produces little of its own olive oil. The trees of Gaeta in Campania produce wonderful olives for eating. Cooks in Campania traditionally have used lard as the shortening in local recipes, but recently in southern Italy, there has been a tendency to lighten some dishes by substituting oil for the lard, or occasionally to use lighter oil from central Italy instead of their own excellent but fuller-bodied oil.

*In the early days of the Roman Empire, wheat was imported into Italy from Egypt and the northwestern African coast. By the end of the empire, Sicily had become the granary of the Mediterranean world. Wheat cultivation transformed that green, wooded island into the starker landscape and climate of today. Most authorities now feel that pasta originated in Sicily where the milled wheat was preserved by mixing it with water and drying it in the sun. Fresh egg pasta is documented in central and northern Italy from at least the Middle Ages. Factory-made pasta came into being in the early nineteenth century, and dried pasta started its triumphant march northward during the following century. The journey continues as pasta becomes a staple elsewhere in the world, across the Alps and the oceans.

basic technique for making fresh pasta

HOW TO PREPARE THE DOUGH AND KNEAD IT

1. Place the flour in a mound on a pasta board. Use a fork to make a well in the center.

2. Put the eggs, and other ingredients specified in the recipe, in the well.

3. With a fork, first mix together the eggs and other ingredients,

4. then begin to incorporate the flour from the inner rim of the well, always incorporating fresh flour from the lower part, pushing it under the dough that is forming to keep it from sticking to the board. Remove pieces of the dough attached to the fork.

5. Put the pieces of the dough together with your hands.

6. Scrape the board with a pastry scraper, gathering together all the unincorporated flour as well as the pieces of dough coated with flour.

7. Place this flour with the pieces of dough in a sifter. Resting the sifter on the board and using one hand, "clean" the flour by moving the sifter back and forth.

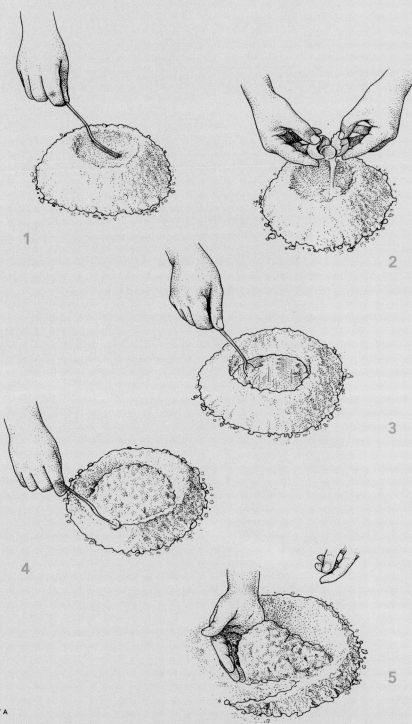

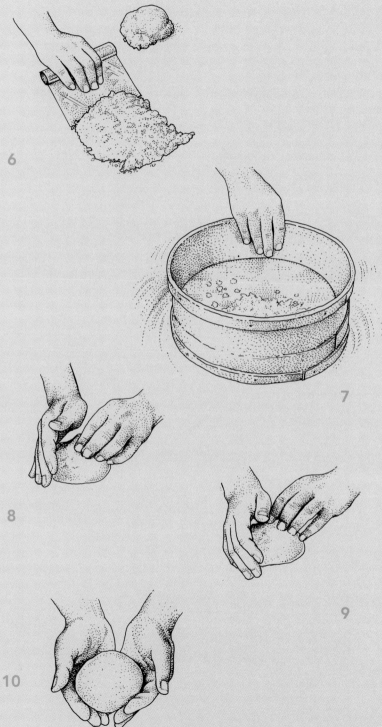

The globules of dough will remain in the sifter screen and will not filter through. Discard them because, being already coated with flour, they will not integrate into the wet dough and will cause lumps, which will make holes when the dough is stretched.

8. Start kneading the dough using the palm of the hand,

9. and folding the dough over with the other hand, absorbing the leftover flour from the board. Do not sprinkle the flour over the dough. Continue kneading, for about 5 minutes, absorbing the flour until the dough is no longer wet and all but 4 or 5 tablespoons have been incorporated (the remaining flour will be used for a second kneading of the dough). If you intend to stretch the dough by machine, knead for only 2 to 3 minutes. The amount of flour left over will remain about the same.

10. A ball of elastic and smooth dough should be the result of kneading the dough for this length of time. You can now do the additional kneading and stretching of the dough either by hand or with a pasta machine. (See pages 14-17 and 18-19.)

HOW TO STRETCH THE DOUGH BY HAND WITH A ROLLING PIN

Take the ball of dough that has been kneaded for 5 minutes and continue kneading for about 10 minutes longer, incorporating some, but not all, of the flour that remained from before.

The following drawings demonstrate the technique of using the long Italian-style rolling pin. The American ball-bearing rolling pin may also be used.

1. Place the center of the long rolling pin over the ball of dough. Rest the palms of your hands a bit from the ends (if using the ball-bearing type, do not grasp the rolling pin by the handles).

2. Gently roll the pin forward,

3. then backward. This is the basic motion, and should be repeated until the dough is elastic; that is, until the dough springs back when pulled. To stretch to an even thickness,

4. fold the edge over the rolling pin,

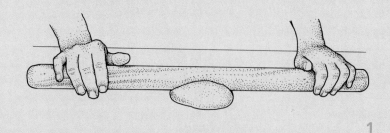

1

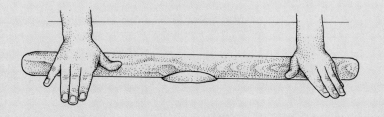

2

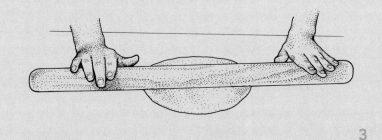

3

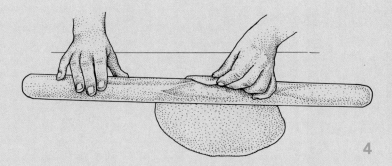

4

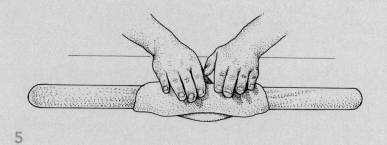

5. and roll up the sheet of dough around the pin, moving the fingers of your hands outward along the edge of the pasta sheet to even the edges out.

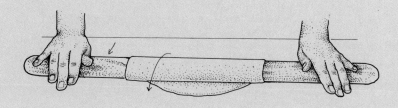

6. Move your hands outward almost to the edges of the pin. With a quick jerky movement, roll the pin away from you so that the edge of the pasta sheet slaps against the board. This movement stretches the edge of the sheet as thin as the rest.

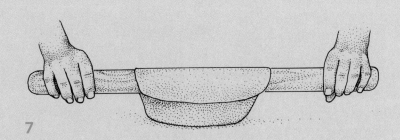

7. Flip the rolling pin over so that the edge of the pasta sheet is facing toward you rather than away from you.

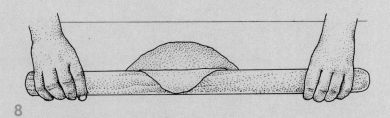

8. Unroll the sheet away from you, so that the underside will now be on top. To stretch the pasta evenly, it is important to alternate back-and-forth motion with side-to-side motion. This can be accomplished by first

9. turning your body sideways. Let one end of the long rolling pin overlap the end of the pasta board. Loosely hold this end with one hand. Rest the palm of the other hand, as before, on the rolling pin, but closer to the center. With this hand, roll the pin from side to side until the layer of pasta is stretched out to a little less than ⅛ inch thick.

10. Roll up the sheet in order to reverse it again. However, in this position, it is not possible to make the slapping movement. Simply flip the pin over and unroll the sheet on the other side.

Keep alternating the two kinds of movement until the pasta is stretched large and less than 1/16 inch thick.

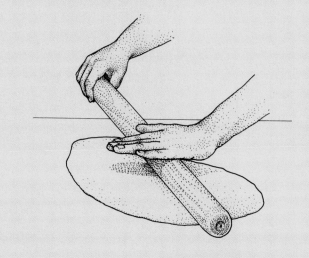

9

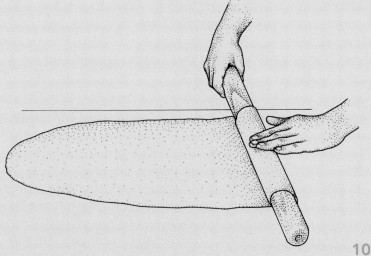

10

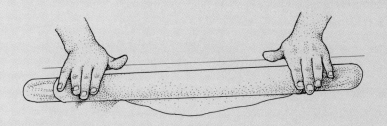

11. This is the rolled-up sheet of pasta, larger and thinner than before. Again, move the fingers outward along the edge to even out the sheet.

12. This is the largest sheet of pasta being unrolled and reversed.

13. The pasta stretched evenly to its final thickness, less than ⅟₁₆ inch thick.

11

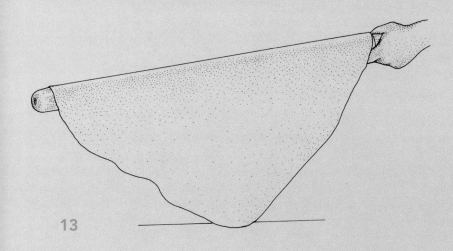

12

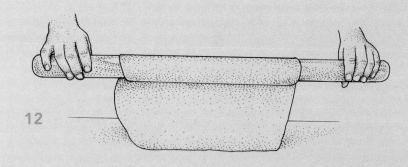

13

HOW TO STRETCH THE DOUGH WITH A HAND PASTA MACHINE

The machine has two parts (detachable or in one piece), one for rolling and stretching the dough in layers, the other for cutting.

The different brands of pasta machines vary in the number of settings controlling the rollers for stretching. They even vary in the final thinness achieved. On some, the last setting produces such a thin sheet (close to $\frac{1}{32}$ inch) that it is impossible to use without breaking the pasta. Get to know your machine and whether the last or next to the last produces the slightly less than $\frac{1}{16}$-inch thickness desirable for most pasta.

Note: If the pasta dough is made with more than 2 eggs, divide the dough into 1-cup portions before you flatten it in preparation for putting it between the rollers.

1. With the palm of your hand, flatten the ball of dough so it can fit between the rollers (about $\frac{1}{2}$ inch thick).

2. Set the wheel for the rollers at the widest setting. Turning the handle, pass the dough through the rollers.

3. With your hand, remove the layer of dough from underneath the pasta machine.

4. Holding the layer of dough with both your hands, gently flour one side of the dough by drawing it across the flour on the board.

5. Fold the dough into thirds,

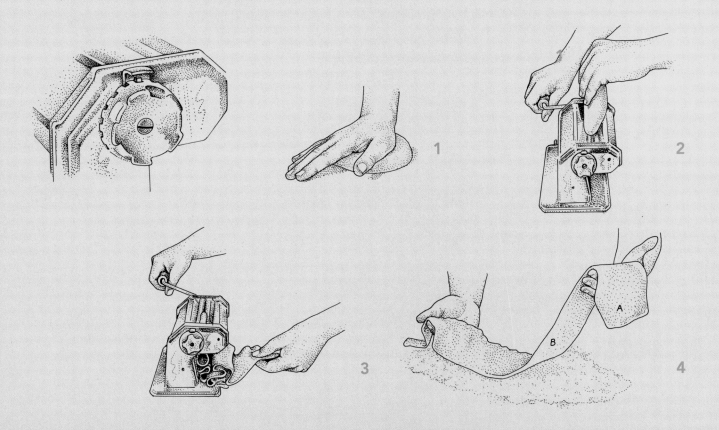

6. and press down with your fingers, starting from one open side toward the opposite open side, so that the three layers will be melded together and no air will remain inside between the three layers of dough.

Using the same wide setting of the rollers, insert the open end of the folded layer of dough through the rollers. Repeat the rolling and folding 8 to 10 times, until the dough is very smooth and elastic.

It is now ready to be stretched. Move the rollers to a narrower setting, following the manufacturer's instructions for the particular type of machine. Roll out a layer of pasta.

7. Flour the layer of pasta on both sides by drawing it across the flour on the board.

8. When feeding the layer of pasta into the machine, the position of your body is very important. Stand sideways in relation to the table, holding the handle of the machine with your right hand. Hold the other hand up sideways, keeping the four fingers together and holding the thumb out. Let the sheet of pasta rest over your hand between the first finger and outstretched thumb.

Pass the dough through the rollers once; do not fold any more. Move the wheel to the next notch, passing the dough through the rollers just once. Each time after passing, sprinkle the layer of pasta with a little flour. Each successive notch will produce a thinner layer of pasta. Repeat this procedure until the layer reaches the thickness desired. The specific thickness required for each kind of pasta is indicated in the individual recipes.

9. Still letting the pasta hang over one hand, pull it out to its full length. It is now ready to be cut into different shapes using the pasta machine.

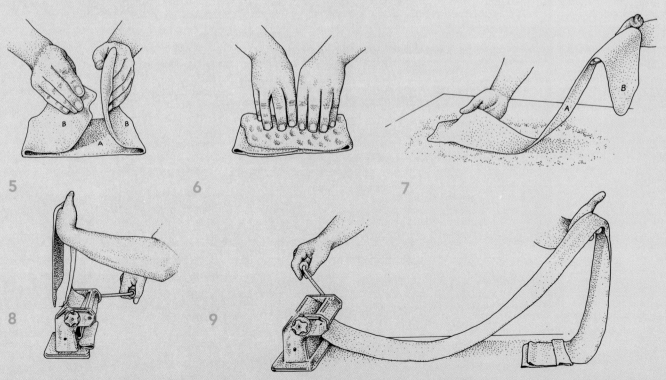

5

6

7

8

9

pasta an

d beans

Every part of Italy has its pasta and beans, *minestre* and *minestroni,* soups and full-bodied soups. Today we are reaffirming the wisdom of this combination, for it provides an almost balanced diet in itself, containing protein and carbohydrates without cholesterol or fat. This was understood through folk wisdom many centuries ago, and it may be that these dishes were among the first uses of pasta. Giacomo Devoto, Italy's leading modern etymologist, traces the origin of the word *maccherone* from "macco," the ancient dish *macco di fave*, with which we begin this book. In any case, attempts have been made to trace the origins of *maccherone* from a word in Venetian dialect, spelled with a single *c*. (The difference between single and double consonants in Italian is very basic etymology.) It makes more sense to expect the word to come from southern Italy, where pasta originated, rather than from the North, where it arrived much later.

The combination of fava beans with pasta uses one of the very few bean types that is indigenous to the Eastern Hemisphere, most beans having come to Europe from Latin America via the colonists. Dishes using fava beans, along with those using legumes such as chick-peas and lentils, are probably the oldest of this type. Dried peas were once used extensively in an analogous way, but when fresh peas came to be used in cooking during

Previous pages: The Church of San Martino in Lucca.

the Renaissance—probably for the first time in Europe—they changed the function of that vegetable in the *cucina* as a whole. The great diversity in approach to this basic combination yields an opportunity to see at a glance the regional variety in Italian cooking. We see this diversity also in other chapters showing combinations of pasta with various categories of ingredients.

IMPORTANT NOTE: Apparently, methods of drying beans have changed in the past decade. I have noticed from my own experience that cooking times seem to be drastically shorter, though even now these times vary considerably. Do not be surprised if my suggested cooking times are shorter than in earlier books written by me or by others. Of course, variation still depends on the source of the beans and the time of year they are used, since beans picked in early autumn continue to dry through the year. For all these reasons, it is best to test the beans from time to time during cooking to be sure the suggested time is correct for that particular batch. Also, bear in mind that Italians like beans a little firm, even a bit al dente.

If you wish to speed up the soaking process, a tablespoon of flour added to the water introduces some fermentation, which hastens the softening a bit.

macco di fave

FAVA BEAN SOUP WITH *MACCHERONI*

SERVES 8 TO 10

1 pound dried fava beans

Coarse-grained salt

1 very large ripe, fresh tomato; or 4 ounces canned tomatoes, preferably imported Italian, drained and seeded

2 ½ quarts cold water

2 medium-sized red onions, peeled and thinly sliced

1 pound dried *spaghetti*, preferably imported Italian

¼ cup olive oil

Salt and freshly ground black pepper to taste

TO COOK THE PASTA

Coarse-grained salt

TO SERVE

6 to 8 tablespoons freshly grated pecorino romano cheese (optional)

Macco, *or purée of dried or fresh fava beans, survives in different regions: Pescia in Tuscany, in Apulia, in Raffadali in Sicily with home-made* pasta di casa, *onions, cabbage, and ground pork (it is sometimes made with lentil rather than fava purée), and in Sardinia, where it is even more elaborate than in Sicily. But it is Calabria that is the center of this ancient dish, where it appears in the classically simple version that follows.*

Fava beans (Vicia faba l.) *are now considered to have originated in the Middle Eastern Mediterranean. The bean was domesticated about 5000 B.C. From Mesopotamia, it traveled across the northern coast of the Mediterranean as far as Italy and Provence. Interestingly, from Egypt, it crossed North Africa and went from there to Spain. This route from Africa to Spain was established millennia before the Arab conquests, and many foodstuffs thought by some to have been introduced by the Arabs in fact reached Europe by the time of the Roman Empire. Fava beans reached India from the West, one of a group of important foods that went from west to east.*

Dried fava beans are available year-round. They have tough outer skins that must be peeled off after soaking. Fresh fava beans—called baccelli *when still in the pod, small and tender—are eaten raw, with their skins, dipped in salt or with pecorino cheese.*

The vernacular phrase "cacio e baccelli" (cheese and fresh fava beans), is used to mean "perfectly matched."

Soak the dried beans in cold water overnight. The next morning, rinse the beans very well; remove the skins, placing the peeled beans in a bowl of fresh cold water. Let beans soak while you blanch the fresh tomato in salted boiling water, then peel and seed it. Drain and rinse many times under cold running water. Place the beans in a medium-sized stockpot, add the 2½ quarts cold water, then add the tomatoes. Add the onions to the stockpot along with coarse salt to taste. Place over medium heat; when the water reaches a boil, cover and simmer for 1 hour.

When the beans are almost done (almost dissolved), bring a large quantity of cold water to a boil, add coarse salt to taste, then add the *spaghetti*, broken in thirds. Cook the pasta for 8 to 11 minutes depending on the brand; that is, 1 minute less than for normal al dente. Drain the pasta and add it to the simmering soup along with the oil. Let cook for 1 minute more, then taste for salt and pepper. Let the soup rest off the heat for a few minutes before serving. If using cheese, sprinkle a little on each portion.

minestrone con fave

MINESTRONE WITH FAVA BEANS

Minestrone con fave *is on the border between a* pasta e fagioli *dish and a minestrone. It contains only Swiss chard in addition to its two main ingredients. A minestrone is a soup of vegetables and beans, usually with pasta, sometimes with rice, and occasionally without either. Most minestroni contain both beans and pasta, but they are not the main ingredients. Vegetables are the primary feature and so, with this one exception, I have not included this large category of recipes in the book. This soup is really a simpler version of the very elaborate* macco *of Sardinia called* favata, *which contains fresh meat from several parts of the pig, cut into strips and pieces, as well as ground and cured pork. Sausages,* pancetta, *and* guanciale *(cheek) are among the possibilities. Like the Sicilian* macco, *this dish has cabbage and onions along with the fava purée. Instead of pasta, Sardinian bread,* carta di musica *(music paper), is used.*

Soak the fava beans in cold water overnight. The next morning, drain and peel them; rinse the beans in cold water and drain again. Cut the *prosciutto* or *pancetta* into small pieces and put in a large stockpot. Add the oil and place the stockpot over low heat; sauté for 5 minutes. Coarsely chop the chard and parsley together on a board. Thinly slice the onion. Add the chopped ingredients and onion to the pot, mix well, and put in the cold water, tomatoes, and beans. When the soup reaches a boil, simmer, uncovered, for 1 hour, mixing with a wooden spoon every so often.

Season soup with salt and pepper to taste, then add the pasta, stir well, and cook for 9 to 12 minutes depending on the brand, or until al dente. Taste for salt and pepper, remove from stove, and let rest for 10 minutes before serving.

SERVES 8

1 pound dried fava beans

6 ounces very fatty *prosciutto* or *pancetta,* in 1 piece

3 tablespoons olive oil

12 ounces Swiss chard, large stems removed

15 large sprigs Italian parsley, leaves only

1 medium-sized red onion, peeled

3 quarts plus 1 cup cold water

5 large, ripe, fresh tomatoes, peeled and seeded; or 7 canned tomatoes, seeded

Salt and freshly ground black pepper

½ pound dried short tubular pasta, preferably imported Italian

pasta e lenticchie
PASTA WITH LENTILS

SERVES 6 TO 8

FOR THE LENTILS

1 ½ cups dried lentils

2 ½ quarts cold water

5 tablespoons olive oil

½ teaspoon hot red pepper flakes

Salt and freshly ground black pepper

FOR THE PASTA

1 pound dried *orecchiette*

or

2 cups unbleached all-purpose flour

1 cup semolina flour

1 cup cold water

Pinch of salt

TO COOK THE PASTA

Coarse-grained salt

TO SERVE

6 to 8 teaspoons olive oil

Lentils (Lens culinaris or esculenta) have been found at archaeological sites 7,000 years old, in the Middle East. In the Bible, Esau sold his birthright to Jacob for a plate of lentils. The symbolism is that the lentils were worth only a pittance, because they were so common.

Lentils usually develop two to a pod and are usually eaten dried. Their convex shape has caused the word lens *to be applied to eyeglasses. Lentils are rarely puréed in Italy today. But centuries ago the purées were more common in Italy, and do still survive in a few dishes, such as this one. An enormous number of lentil dishes were developed in Italy during the Second World War to substitute for many foodstuffs that were impossible to obtain. I recall as a child eating not only lentil soups and sauces but even lentil bread, main dishes, and desserts, in which sugar beets provided the sweetener. Toasted lentils were even used in place of coffee. It has taken Italians decades to be able to face lentils again.*

Nothing could be simpler than this dish, containing just pasta and lentils, flavored with only a little olive oil and hot pepper—a holding to basics which is typical of Apulia.

Soak the lentils in a bowl of cold water for 1 hour. Discard the lentils floating on top, then drain and rinse the rest. Put the lentils with the 2 ½ quarts cold water in a flameproof casserole over medium heat. Cover the casserole and when the water reaches a boil, simmer until the lentils are soft but still whole, about 45 minutes. Drain, saving the cooking water.

If using fresh pasta, prepare it with the ingredients and quantities listed, following the directions on page 12. Shape into *orecchiette* following the accompanying illustrations. Let rest on cotton dish towels until ready to use.

Pass the lentils through a food mill, using the disc with the smallest holes, into a medium-sized bowl. Bring the casserole with the cooking water back to a boil. Heat the oil in a large skillet over medium heat, and when the oil is warm, add the lentil purée, then the pepper flakes, and salt and pepper to taste. Sauté for 5 minutes, stirring very well to be sure that the lentils do not stick to the pan. When the water reaches a boil, add coarse salt to taste, then add the pasta. Cook the dried pasta for 9 to 12 minutes depending on the brand, or fresh pasta for 5 to 10 minutes depending on dryness. Drain the pasta and add to the skillet with the puréed lentils, mix very well, and sauté for 30 seconds. Serve, adding 1 teaspoon of oil to each portion.

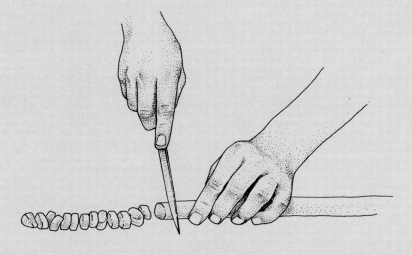

ORECCHIETTE

1. When the ball of dough is prepared, divide it into 3 or 4 pieces. Roll each piece with four fingers of both hands, moving both hands gradually apart from the center. Roll these large pieces of dough into a long cord about ½ inch in diameter. Cut the cord into ½-inch pieces.

2. Flatten each piece into a small disc.

3. By pressing your thumb into it, make the central depression more round and deep by turning your thumb a bit in place clockwise.

1

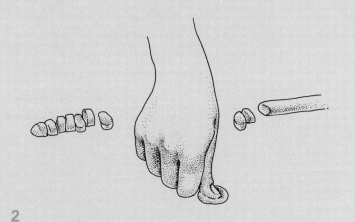

2

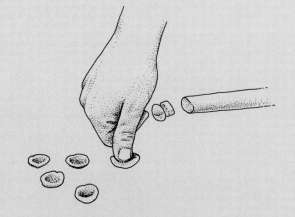

3

pasta e ceci alla romana
PASTA WITH CHICK-PEAS, ROMAN STYLE

SERVES 8

FOR THE CHICK-PEAS

2 cups dried chick-peas

2 ½ quarts cold water

1 medium-sized sprig fresh rosemary; or 1 heaping tablespoon rosemary leaves, tied into a small cheesecloth bag

Coarse-grained salt

FOR THE SAUCE

½ cup olive oil

2 large cloves garlic, peeled but left whole

1 tablespoon rosemary leaves, fresh or preserved in salt

3 tablespoons tomato paste

Salt and freshly ground black pepper

FOR THE PASTA

½ pound dried *tagliatelle*, preferably imported Italian

Ceci (Cicer arietinum), *or chick-peas, probably originated in southeastern Turkey, but there are no known survivors of the original, wild form of the plant. The varieties presently known likely are domesticated mutations. The Mediterranean chick-pea is larger and is white to dark yellow in color, while the type used in India and Persia is smaller and brown.*

Following are four recipes for pasta e ceci: *from Rome, Naples, Tuscany, and Lecce (Apulia), all seats of ancient Greek and Roman culture. The Tuscans, famous in Italy as "bean eaters," have in addition to their many* Phaseolus vulgaris *bean dishes quite a few using chick-peas.*

The first, Roman version of pasta with chick-peas shares certain traditional ingredients of the Tuscan dish, but here the rosemary taste is much stronger, tomato paste is used instead of tomatoes, and the pasta is dried tagliatelle *instead of the very short tubular* avemarie, paternostri, *or* ditalini.

Soak the chick-peas in cold water overnight. The next morning, drain and rinse them under cold running water. Place a medium-sized stockpot with the chick-peas, 2 ½ quarts cold water, and rosemary over medium heat. When the water reaches a boil, cover and cook chick-peas for 1 to 2 hours depending on their dryness; they should be cooked but still firm. Add coarse salt to taste, cover again, and simmer for 15 minutes more.

Prepare the sauce. Heat the oil with the garlic and rosemary leaves in a small saucepan over medium heat for 5 minutes. Remove 1 cup of the chick-pea broth, dissolve the tomato paste in it, and add the mixture to the pan. Season with salt and abundant black pepper, and cook over high heat for 10 minutes. Pass the sauce through a wire strainer into the stockpot, discarding the garlic and rosemary. Also remove and discard the rosemary from the broth. Add pasta and simmer, uncovered, until done—about 5 minutes depending on the brand. Taste for salt and pepper, and let the soup rest for 5 minutes off the heat before serving.

VARIATIONS

1. The garlic for the sauce can be finely chopped instead of left whole.
2. Cut 4 ounces of *guanciale* (cured pork cheek) or *pancetta* into small pieces and sauté it with the garlic when making the sauce.

pasta e ceci di magro, *or* lampi e tuoni

PASTA WITH CHICK-PEAS, NEAPOLITAN STYLE

The Neapolitan dish—called, with the local earthy humor, Lampi e tuoni *(lightning and thunder)—is flavored with parsley and hot red pepper. The pasta is* laganelle, *a form of* lasagnette, *or narrow* lasagne, *that resembles* tagliatelle *but is made without eggs. The dialect form "lagane" * comes from* laganum, *the Latin word for* lasagne, *another indication that pasta existed in Italy when Latin was spoken, before Marco Polo.*

Soak the chick-peas in cold water overnight. The next morning, drain the chick-peas and put them in a flameproof casserole with the 2 ½ quarts cold water. Set casserole over medium heat, cover, and bring to a boil.

Meanwhile, finely chop the garlic and coarsely chop the parsley on a board, then mix them together. Warm the oil in a small saucepan over medium heat, add the chopped ingredients, and sauté for 3 minutes.

When the water in the casserole reaches a boil, add the sautéed garlic and parsley, cover, and simmer until the chick-peas are cooked but still firm—1 to 2 hours depending on the dryness of the beans.

Remove the casserole from the heat. Scoop out 1 cup of the cooked beans and pass them through a food mill, using the disc with the smallest holes, into a small bowl. Add some of the cooking water if necessary to help purée the beans more easily. Pour the purée back into the casserole and return to medium heat. Taste for salt and pepper, and add the red pepper flakes. When the broth returns to a boil, add the pasta and cook for 9 to 12 minutes depending on the brand. When the pasta is cooked, cover the casserole, remove from the heat, and rest it for at least 15 minutes before serving.

NOTE

Fresh *laganelle* can be made using the ingredients and quantities for *Pasta e fagioli alla monferrina* (page 39), and then cutting it into *tagliatelle*. The cooking time for fresh pasta is the same as for that recipe.

*Laganelle is, of course, a diminutive form.

SERVES 6 TO 8

1 ½ cups dried chick-peas

2 ½ quarts cold water

3 large cloves garlic, peeled

15 large sprigs Italian parsley, leaves only

5 tablespoons olive oil

Salt and freshly ground black pepper

½ teaspoon hot red pepper flakes

½ pound dried *laganelle* or *lasagnette*

pasta e ceci alla toscana

PASTA AND CHICK-PEAS, TUSCAN STYLE

SERVES 4 TO 6

1 cup dried chick-peas

3 quarts cold water

4 large cloves garlic, peeled

1 tablespoon fresh rosemary leaves

8 tablespoons extra-virgin olive oil

Coarse-grained salt

4 large fresh sage leaves

1 medium-sized red onion, cleaned

1 stalk celery

10 sprigs Italian parsley, leaves only

1 medium-sized carrot, scraped

½ teaspoon hot red pepper flakes

1½ pounds ripe, fresh tomatoes; or 1½ pounds drained canned tomatoes, preferably imported Italian, drained

Salt and freshly ground black pepper

TO COOK THE PASTA

4 cups completely defatted chicken or meat broth, preferably homemade

8 ounces dried *paternostri* or *avemarie* pasta or broken-up *spaghetti*

TO SERVE

4 to 6 teaspoons extra-virgin olive oil

Sprigs of rosemary or sage, leaves only

Tuscan cooking is known for its simplicity and few ingredients, but this version of Pasta e ceci *breaks all the rules. It combines the ingredients from the other versions and is generous in its use of garlic and hot pepper. This recipe may reflect the tastes of Tuscany's main seaport, Livorno, especially its love for hot pepper.*

This dish, which is really a thick soup, may be prepared several hours in advance and served at room temperature, especially in the summer.

Soak the chick-peas in a bowl of cold water overnight. The next morning drain the chick-peas and put them in a medium-sized stockpot with the 3 quarts of cold water over medium heat. When the water reaches a boil, add 2 cloves of the garlic, ½ tablespoon of the rosemary, 2 tablespoons of the olive oil, and coarse salt to taste. Cover and simmer until the chick-peas are cooked and very soft, about 1 hour. Drain the chick-peas and transfer them to a crockery or glass bowl, saving the poaching broth.

Place a wet cotton dish towel over the beans. Finely chop the remaining garlic and rosemary along with the sage, onion, celery, parsley, carrot, and hot pepper all together on a board.

Heat the remaining oil in the medium-sized stockpot over medium heat. When the oil is warm, add the chopped ingredients and sauté for 2 to 3 minutes, stirring constantly with a wooden spoon. If using fresh tomatoes, cut them into 1-inch pieces. Pass fresh or canned tomatoes through a food mill, using the disc with the smallest holes, into a crockery or glass bowl. Add the tomatoes to the stockpot with the vegetables, season with salt and pepper, then cover and cook for 15 minutes, stirring every so often with a wooden spoon.

Meanwhile, bring the broth to a boil in a large pot over medium heat, add the pasta, and cook for 4 minutes. In the meantime, add the poaching broth to the stockpot and bring to a boil. Drain the pasta, add it to the stockpot, taste for salt and pepper, and simmer for 4 minutes more, or until the pasta is cooked completely. Cover the stockpot and let the soup rest for 10 minutes before serving. Ladle the soup into individual bowls, then drizzle a little oil over each portion and serve with a sprig of rosemary or sage. Serve from the pot or from a hollowed-out Tuscan bread.

Pasta e ceci alla toscana in hollowed-out Tuscan bread.

pasta e ceci alla leccese

PASTA AND CHICK-PEAS, LECCE STYLE

SERVES 6 TO 8

FOR THE CHICK-PEAS

1 ½ cups dried chick-peas

3 quarts cold water

1 large stalk celery

1 medium-sized red onion, peeled and left whole

1 large carrot, scraped and left whole

2 large cloves garlic, peeled and left whole

2 bay leaves

Salt and freshly ground black pepper

FOR THE PASTA

1 scant cup semolina flour

1 scant cup unbleached all-purpose flour

½ cup lukewarm water

Pinch of salt

TO FRY THE PASTA

1 quart vegetable oil, preferably mixed corn and sunflower oil

FOR THE SOUP

2 medium-sized red onions, peeled

6 tablespoons olive oil

Salt and freshly ground black pepper

½ teaspoon hot red pepper flakes

TO SERVE

6 to 8 teaspoons olive oil

In Lecce, the chick-peas are cooked with vegetables and aromatic herbs. It is traditional to use fresh, short tagliatelle, *and in another unique touch, half the pasta is fried before adding it to the* minestra.

Soak the chick-peas in cold water overnight. The next morning, drain and rinse them under cold running water. Put the 3 quarts cold water in a large stockpot and add the chick-peas along with the celery, onion, carrot, garlic, and bay leaves. Cover the pot, place it over medium heat, and simmer until chick-peas are cooked but still firm—1 to 2 hours depending on dryness. Season with salt and pepper. Drain the chick-peas, saving the cooking broth and discarding the aromatic vegetables. Transfer to a crockery or glass bowl and cover.

While the chick-peas are cooking, prepare the pasta with the ingredients and quantities listed following instructions on page 12. Stretch the layer to ¹⁄₁₆ inch thick—on the pasta machine, take it to next to last setting, following the techniques on page 18-19. With a knife, cut the sheet of pasta into strips about 3 inches wide, then cut each strip into ½-inch pieces. Spread out pasta on cotton dish towels and let rest until needed.

Heat the vegetable oil in a deep-fat fryer over medium heat. When the oil is hot (about 375 degrees), fry a few pieces of pasta at a time until lightly golden, about 30 seconds. Continue frying until half the pasta is cooked; leave the other half uncooked. Put the fried pasta on paper towels to drain off any excess grease.

Prepare the soup. Finely slice the onions and place them in a bowl of cold water for 15 minutes. Warm the oil in the stockpot over medium heat; drain the onions and add them to the pot. Lower the heat and sauté onions until translucent, about 15 minutes. Add salt, pepper, and the red pepper flakes, then pour in the reserved cooking broth from the chick-peas. Bring the soup to a boil. Add the chick-peas, and when the soup returns to a boil, add the unfried pasta; after 1 minute more, add the fried pasta. Cook for 1 to 3 minutes. Remove from the heat, cover the pot, and let rest 5 minutes before serving. Pour a teaspoon of olive oil on each portion just before serving.

VARIATION

Use 4 large cloves of garlic, peeled and coarsely chopped, in the soup instead of the onions.

minestrone di ceci alla marchigiana

CHICK-PEA SOUP, MARCHES STYLE

Bean or chick-pea soups are often flavored with pancetta *or* prosciutto *but in Marche and Calabria, both regions along the coast, the preferred flavoring for* minestroni *is spare ribs. Once cooked, these precious ribs are not discarded, but served to lucky guests along with the soup.*

Soak the chick-peas in a bowl of cold water overnight. The next morning, rinse them under cold running water and place them in a heavy stockpot.

If you are using the oven method, preheat the oven to 400° F. Coarsely chop the parsley, celery, onion, garlic, and escarole all together on a board and add to the stockpot. Coarsely grind the *prosciutto* using a meat grinder or pulse it in a food processor, then add it to the stockpot. If using fresh tomatoes, blanch them in a medium-sized pot of salted boiling water, then remove the skins and seeds, and cut them into 1-inch squares. If using canned tomatoes, pass them through a food mill, using the disc with smallest holes, into a crockery or glass bowl. Add the tomatoes, spare ribs, and the oil to the

stockpot. Pour 3 quarts of cold water in, cover the pot, and set it over medium heat or in the preheated oven. Let simmer for 1 hour; by that time, the chick-peas should be cooked and soft, but should still retain their shape.

Remove 1½ cups of the solids, mainly the chick-peas, and pass them through a food mill, using the disc with the smallest holes, directly into the pot. Season with salt and pepper and cook for 5 minutes more on the stovetop, stirring every so often with a wooden spoon so none of the ingredients sticks to the bottom of the pot.

Meanwhile, put the broth in a medium-sized casserole and bring to a boil, add coarse salt to taste, then add the pasta and cook for 8 to 11 minutes depending on the brand; that is, 1 minute less than for normal al dente. Drain the pasta, add it to the stockpot containing the chick-pea mixture, and simmer for 1 minute more. Let the soup rest for a few minutes before serving with abundant grated cheese over each portion.

SERVES 8 TO 10

- 1 ½ cups dried chick-peas
- 20 large sprigs Italian parsley, leaves only
- 2 medium-sized stalks celery
- 1 medium-sized red onion, peeled
- 2 medium-sized cloves garlic, peeled
- 3 or 4 escarole leaves
- 3 ounces *prosciutto*, in 1 piece
- 4 medium-sized ripe but not overripe fresh tomatoes; or 4 canned tomatoes, preferably imported Italian, drained
- 4 very small pork spare ribs
- 4 tablespoons extra-virgin olive oil
- Salt and freshly ground black pepper

FOR THE PASTA

- 3 quarts completely defatted chicken broth, preferably homemade, or 3 quarts cold water
- Coarse-grained salt
- 8 ounces dried short wide tubular pasta, such as *mezzi ditalini or paternostri*, preferably imported Italian

TO SERVE

- Freshly grated pecorino romano cheese

TAGLIATELLE

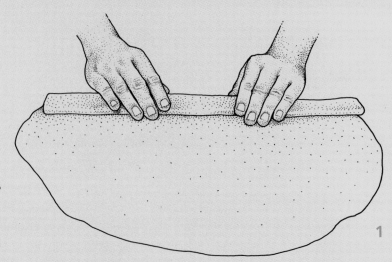

1. Roll up the sheet of pasta.

2. The sheet completely rolled.

3. With a knife, cut roll into *tagliatelle* about $\frac{1}{4}$ inch wide.

4. Unroll the strands of pasta to their full length before allowing them to dry.

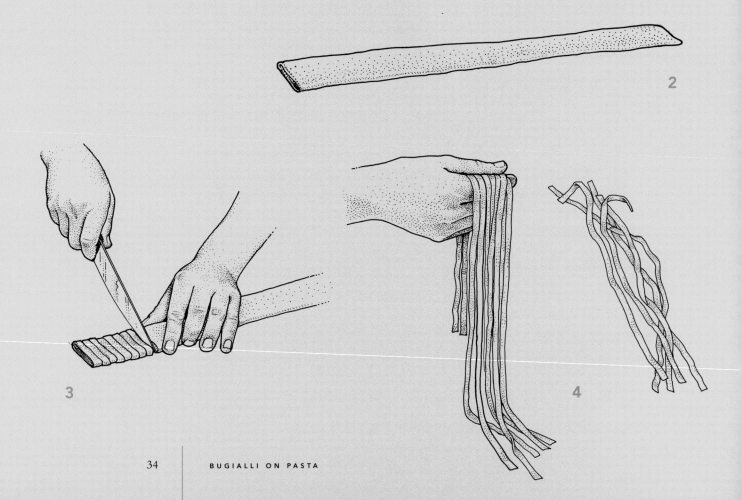

1

TAGLIATELLE OR TAGLIERINI

1. With a scalloped pastry cutter, cut the layer of pasta into pieces about 15 inches long. Let pieces rest on cotton dish towels until a thin film forms on the surface.

2. For *tagliatelle*, insert the layer of pasta into the wider cutter.

3. For *taglierini*, insert the layer of pasta into the narrower cutter.

4. *Tagliatelle* and *taglierini*.

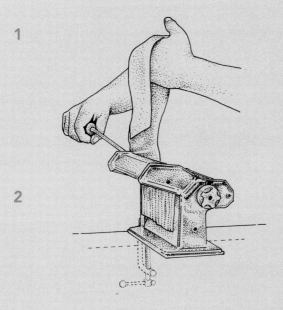

2

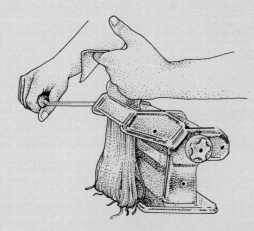

3

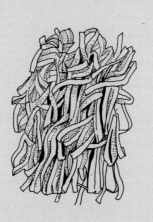

4

beans

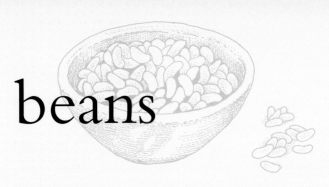

With the colonization of the New World, the bean repertory of Europe expanded enormously. *Cannellini* (white kidney beans), red kidney beans, *borlotti*, navy beans, great Northern beans, cranberry beans, Michigan beans, Lamon beans—all belong to the species *Phaseolus vulgaris*. Spanish beans, similar to but larger and flatter than *cannellini*, are from the related *Phaseolus coccineus*. Because one does not find classifications that specify the differences among all the beans belonging to this same large category, in practical terms it is sometimes difficult to know if two beans called by different names, but which resemble one another very much, are really the same. For example, *borlotti*, Roman beans, and cranberry beans are different, yet they have the same red streaks on a white-to-yellow background and turn dark red when cooked, as the others do. When you look them up in a reference work, both are called simply *Phaseolus vulgaris*.

All this becomes a real problem when you must decide what to substitute for *borlotti* outside Italy, as even the dried ones are difficult to obtain, though they are more available in Hispanic markets today. (The special Venetian type of *borlotti* called Lamon are still more difficult to find, if not impossible.) Let us hope that this will change, because this particular bean adds much to the character of each local *pasta e fagioli* dish. Dried *cannellini* are exported and are widely available.

passato di fagioli alla fiorentina

PURÉED BEAN SOUP WITH PASTA

This Passato di fagioli alla fiorentina *differs from the Tuscan puréed bean soup in my book* The Fine Art of Italian Cooking *in that the beans here are baked with flavorings rather than boiled before being puréed. This dish is additionally flavored with sage, along with the rosemary, and with tomato paste (there are no tomatoes at all in the other version). In this Florentine version, the pasta is smaller and is cooked before being added to the soup. It's a good example of how two bean purées from the same locality can differ a great deal in flavor. It is well worth making both of them.*

Soak the beans in cold water overnight. The next morning, preheat the oven to 375° F. Drain the beans and place them in a medium-sized casserole, preferably terra-cotta or enamel, along with the sage, rosemary, garlic, olive oil, and cold water. Cover the casserole and bake until the beans are very soft, about 2 hours.

When the beans are ready, prepare the sauce. Coarsely chop the garlic. Place the oil in a small saucepan over medium heat; when the oil is warm, add the garlic and sauté for 2 minutes. Add the tomato paste, red pepper flakes, rosemary, and salt and pepper to taste. Meanwhile, transfer the casserole of beans from the oven to the top of the stove over medium heat. Remove cover, taste for salt and pepper, and mix well. Add the prepared sauce and simmer for 10 minutes more.

Remove as many rosemary leaves as possible from the bean mixture, then pass the contents of the casserole through a food mill, using the disc with the smallest holes, into a second casserole. Place this casserole over low heat to simmer for 15 minutes more, tasting for salt and pepper.

Bring a large pot of cold water to a boil. When the water reaches a boil, add coarse salt to taste, then add the pasta and cook until al dente—9 to 12 minutes depending on the brand. Drain the pasta, then add it to the casserole and cook for 1 minute more before serving. (The bean purée can be prepared in advance and the pasta added at the last moment. If so, then add some broth to thin the purée, since it will thicken as it stands.)

Serve with a twist of black pepper and, if you wish, a teaspoon of olive oil over each portion.

SERVES 6 TO 8

FOR THE BEANS

- 1 pound dried *cannellini* (white kidney beans)
- 5 large leaves sage, fresh or preserved in salt
- 1 heaping teaspoon rosemary leaves, fresh or preserved in salt
- 2 large cloves garlic, peeled but left whole
- 3 tablespoons olive oil
- 6 cups cold water

FOR THE SAUCE

- 2 medium-sized cloves garlic, peeled
- 6 tablespoons olive oil
- 2 tablespoons tomato paste
- ½ teaspoon hot red pepper flakes
- 1 teaspoon rosemary leaves, fresh or preserved in salt
- Salt and freshly ground black pepper
- ½ pound dried short tubular pasta, such as *ditalini*, *paternostri*, or *avemarie*, preferably imported Italian

TO COOK THE PASTA

- Coarse-grained salt

TO SERVE

- Freshly ground black pepper
- 6 to 8 teaspoons olive oil (optional)

pasta e fagioli alla bolognese

PASTA WITH *BORLOTTI* BEANS, BOLOGNA STYLE

SERVES 6 TO 8

- 1 ½ cups dried *borlotti* or cranberry beans

- 2 quarts cold water

- 4 ounces unsmoked pork rind or *prosciutto*, in one piece

- 8 large sage leaves, fresh or preserved in salt

- 2 large cloves garlic, peeled

- 10 sprigs Italian parsley, leaves only

- 1 medium-sized red onion, peeled

- 6 tablespoons olive oil

- Salt and freshly ground black pepper

- 6 ounces any dried short tubular pasta about 1 inch long and ¼ to ½ inch wide, such as *mezze maniche, mezze penne, paternostri,* or *ditaloni*

TO SERVE

- 6 to 8 heaping tablespoons freshly grated Parmigiano

Both this Bolognese recipe and the one from Monferrato (Piedmont) that follows employ borlotti *beans (from the Milanese dialect word* borlot*), which are light in color and streaked with red. They are also called Roman beans, and are sometimes available fresh in some localities. Cranberry beans, fresh or dried, are available in most places and can be substituted; though not identical in taste, they are close.*

Neither of these northern versions includes tomatoes. It is possible that tomatoes are added to some versions in small amounts to add color, though borlotti *beans lend their own dark red coloring to the soup. The Bologna version of pasta and beans, though made with different beans, does share some ingredients with the earlier Tuscan recipe—pork rind, onions with the garlic—but here the sage and parsley are added. As in the Tuscan version, the beans are not puréed; the soup is not even thickened with potato.*

Soak the beans in cold water overnight. The next morning, rinse and drain the beans, then place them in a medium-sized heavy casserole with the 2 quarts of cold water over medium heat. Meanwhile, cut the pork rind or *prosciutto* into cubes smaller than ½ inch. When the water reaches a boil, add the pork cubes and cover the casserole. Simmer until the beans are cooked but still quite firm—45 minutes to 1 hour, depending on the dryness of the beans.

Finely chop the sage, garlic, parsley, and onion all together on a board. Warm the oil in a small saucepan and add the chopped ingredients; sauté for 5 minutes.

When the beans are done, drain them over a large pot, then set the beans aside. Place the pot over medium heat, and when the cooking water reaches a boil, add the sautéed vegetables; simmer for 15 minutes, then taste for salt and pepper. Add the pasta and cook until al dente—9 to 12 minutes depending on the brand. Five minutes before the pasta is cooked, add the beans to the pot and stir very well. When the pasta is ready, cover the casserole and let the soup rest for 15 minutes before serving. Serve, and sprinkle Parmigiano over each serving.

pasta e fagioli alla monferrina

PASTA WITH BEANS, MONFERRATO STYLE

This very interesting Monferrato pasta-and-bean soup includes smoked pancetta, *an ingredient usually restricted to the far north of Italy. A small amount of beans is puréed with the potato and basil, and added to the parsley, sage, and celery. Most pasta-and-beans soups employ dried pasta, but this is one of the few in which fresh pasta is preferred, though dried may be used in a pinch.*

Soak the beans in cold water overnight. The next day, if you are using fresh pasta, prepare the dough with the ingredients and quantities listed, following the directions on page 12, then stretch the layer to slightly less than 1/16 inch thick—take it to the last setting on most machines. Cut into *tagliatelle* (see page 35) and let rest on a floured cotton dish towel until needed.

Finely chop the bacon, basil, parsley, sage, garlic, onion, and celery all together on a board. Peel the potatoes and put them in a bowl of cold water. Place a medium-sized flameproof casserole with the butter and oil over medium heat, and, when the butter is melted, add the chopped ingredients; sauté for 5 minutes. Bring 2 quarts cold water to a boil in a large pot. Drain and rinse the beans, and add them to casserole along with the boiling water and the sautéed ingredients. Cut the potatoes in half and add to casserole. Simmer, covered, for 45 minutes to 1 hour depending on the dryness of the beans; the beans should be cooked but still firm.

Remove the casserole from the heat. Pass the potatoes and 1 cup of the beans through a food mill, using the disc with medium-sized holes, into a bowl, then add to casserole. Return the casserole to medium heat, taste for salt and pepper, and stir very well. When the soup returns to a boil, add the pasta. Cook the fresh pasta for 30 to 45 seconds depending on dryness; if using dried pasta, cook 9 to 12 minutes depending on the brand. When the pasta is cooked, remove the casserole from heat, cover, and let rest for 15 minutes before serving. This pasta with beans is also very good eaten at room temperature after a few hours or reheated the next day.

SERVES 6 TO 8

1 ½ cups dried *borlotti* or cranberry beans

FOR THE PASTA

1 ½ cups unbleached all-purpose flour

½ cup lukewarm water

Pinch of salt

or

½ pound dried egg *tagliatelle*

FOR THE SOUP

2 ounces bacon, or smoked *pancetta*

4 large basil leaves, fresh or preserved in salt

10 large sprigs Italian parsley, leaves only

4 large sage leaves, fresh or preserved in salt

1 large clove garlic, peeled

1 medium-sized red onion, peeled

1 large celery stalk

2 medium-sized potatoes (not new potatoes), about 12 ounces

2 tablespoons (1 ounce) sweet butter

4 tablespoons olive oil

2 quarts cold water

Salt and freshly ground black pepper

A small sample of the many types of beans used in Italian cookery.

pasta e fagioli alla vicentina

PASTA AND BEANS, VICENZA VERSION

The Veneto is particularly celebrated for its pasta-and-bean dishes; and Venice, Padua, and other cities in the region each have famous versions, but older printed sources point to Vicenza as the origin for the Veneto type. A special kind of borlotti *from the locality of Lamon is the pride of the bean lovers of this area, who feel it is the best of all beans. Veneto pasta-and-beans dishes usually employ fresh pasta.*

Soak the beans in cold water overnight. The next morning, put the 2½ quarts cold water in a medium-sized flameproof casserole, drain the beans, and add them to the casserole. Peel the potato and put it whole into the casserole. Cut the *pancetta* into tiny pieces, and finely chop the celery, garlic, sage, parsley, and onion all together on a board. If using fresh tomatoes, cut them into pieces. Pass the fresh or canned tomatoes through a food mill, using the disc with the smallest holes, and add them, together with the chopped ingredients, to the casserole. Cover the casserole and place it over medium heat; let the mixture simmer until the beans are cooked but still firm, about 1 hour.

Prepare the pasta with the ingredients and quantities listed, following the directions on page 12. Stretch the layer to less than ⅟₁₆ inch thick—on the pasta machine, take it to the last setting— then cut into short *tagliatelle* (see page 34), about 4 inches long. Let pasta rest on a cotton dish towel until needed.

Season beans to taste with salt and pepper. Take out the potato and ¾ cup beans, and pass them together through a food mill, using the disc with smallest holes, into a bowl. Return the purée to the casserole, still over medium heat. Mix well and taste for salt and pepper.

Add the pasta to the casserole and cook for 2 to 4 minutes depending on dryness. Let the soup rest for 5 minutes before serving, then pour a teaspoon of oil over each portion.

VARIATIONS

1. A pinch of ground cinnamon can be added to the casserole. For a thicker soup, dissolve 2 tablespoons of flour in a cup of broth and add it to the casserole.
2. Twenty sprigs of Italian parsley can be chopped together with 2 medium-sized cloves garlic, and the resultant *buttuto* sprinkled over the soup when it is finished cooking.
3. Freshly grated Parmigiano cheese can be sprinkled over each serving. All but ½ cup of the beans can be puréed along with the potato to make a thicker soup.

SERVES 8

FOR THE SOUP

½ pound dried *borlotti* (Roman beans) or cranberry beans (substitutes for Lamon beans)

2½ quarts cold water

1 large potato (not new potato), about ½ pound

4 ounces *pancetta*

3 medium celery stalks

2 large cloves garlic, peeled

5 large sage leaves, fresh or preserved in salt

15 large sprigs Italian parsley, leaves only

1 large yellow onion, peeled

4 ounces ripe, fresh tomatoes; or 4 ounces canned tomatoes, preferably imported Italian, drained

Salt and freshly ground black pepper

FOR THE PASTA

1½ cups unbleached all-purpose flour

2 extra-large eggs

Pinch of salt

TO SERVE

8 teaspoons olive oil

pasta e fagioli con l'occhio
PASTA WITH BLACK-EYED PEAS

SERVES 6 TO 8

1 ½ cups dried black-eyed peas

2 quarts cold water

2 ounces *pancetta* or *prosciutto*, in one piece

2 tablespoons olive oil

1 tablespoon rosemary leaves, fresh or pre-served in salt

½ pound very ripe, fresh tomatoes; or ½ pound canned tomatoes, preferably imported Italian, drained

Salt and freshly ground black pepper

½ pound dried *ditali* or any other short tubular pasta about 1 inch long and ¼ inch wide

A literal translation of fagioli con l'occhio is "beans with the eye," quite similar to our black-eyed peas,* which are native to Central Africa and have found their way to both Europe and America. They are particularly appreciated in "bean-eating" Tuscany as well as the southern United States. In this Tuscan dish, black-eyed peas are flavored with pancetta, rosemary, and a little tomato (no garlic or onion), and 1 cup of the beans are puréed to thicken the soup.

Soak the peas in cold water overnight. The next morning drain and rinse them. Put the peas in a flameproof casserole with the 2 quarts cold water and place over medium heat, cover, and simmer until they are cooked but still very firm, 45 minutes to 1 hour depending on the dryness of the beans.

Meanwhile, cut the *pancetta* or *prosciutto* into small pieces on a board. Warm the oil in a small saucepan over low heat; add the rosemary leaves and sauté for 5 minutes. If using fresh tomatoes, cut them into 1-inch pieces. Pass fresh or canned tomatoes through a food mill, using the disc with the smallest holes, into a small bowl.

Use a slotted spoon to remove the rosemary from the oil, and discard it. Immediately add the *pancetta* to the oil and sauté for 3 minutes. Add the tomatoes, lower the heat, and simmer for 10 minutes. Season with salt and pepper.

While the beans are still simmering, add the tomato sauce and simmer for 1 minute more. Remove the casserole from the heat, take out 1 cup of the beans, and pass them through a food mill, using the disc with the smallest holes, into a small bowl. Put the puréed beans back into the casserole, and place it back over medium heat. Taste for salt and pepper. When the broth in the casserole returns to a boil, add the pasta and cook it in the bean broth for 9 to 12 minutes depending on the brand. Remove the casserole from the heat, cover, and let rest for 15 minutes before serving.

*Technically, the plant is called cowpeas (*Vigna unguiculata*) and the seeds are called black-eyed peas.

millecosedde

MIXED BEANS WITH PASTA, CALABRIAN STYLE

We end this chapter, appropriately, with a minestra combining five different types of legumes. A Calabrian dish, its most unusual feature aside from the mixed beans is the flavoring from dried wild mushrooms. This is among the pasta-and-bean dishes that also feature vegetables—here, cabbage and celery as well as the more usual onions. I consider this dish to be in the pasta-and-bean category rather than a minestrone because its beans are so much more central than its vegetables. Long pasta is used, broken into thirds.

Soak the lentils, beans, and chick-peas separately in 5 different bowls of cold water overnight. The next morning, soak the mushrooms in a bowl of lukewarm water for 30 minutes. Rinse the beans, remove and discard the skins from the fava beans, and put all the beans in a large stockpot. Slice the cabbage into ½-inch strips, coarsely chop the onions and celery, and add the vegetables to the pot. Drain the mushrooms, making sure no sand is attached to the stems, and add them to the pot. Add the 4 quarts cold water, cover, and place the pot over medium heat. When the water reaches a boil, simmer for 1 hour.

When all the vegetables and legumes are almost cooked, add coarse salt to taste, then add the oil, mixing very well. When the soup reaches a boil again, add the pasta, broken into thirds, and cook for 9 to 12 minutes depending on the brand. As the pasta cooks, stir the mixture several times to prevent it from sticking to the bottom of the pot. Taste for salt and pepper. When the pasta is cooked, even the least tender beans will be completely cooked and others will be puréed to form a quite thick *minestra*. Remove the pot from heat and let the mixture rest for 10 minutes before serving. Pour 1 teaspoon of olive oil over each serving.

This *minestra* may be eaten at room temperature or prepared in advance and reheated.

SERVES 12

½ cup dried lentils

½ cup dried *cannellini* (white kidney beans)

½ cup dried *borlotti* or cranberry beans

½ cup dried fava beans

½ cup dried chick-peas

½ ounce dried *porcini* mushrooms

1 pound savoy cabbage, cleaned

2 medium-sized red onions, peeled

2 medium-sized stalks celery

4 quarts cold water

Coarse-grained salt

4 teaspoons olive oil

1 pound dried long pasta, such as *spaghetti* or *linguine*, preferably imported Italian

Salt and freshly ground black pepper

TO SERVE

12 teaspoons olive oil

pasta and

vegetables

If I may reveal my own personal taste, I would say that a dish made with pasta and vegetables is the most satisfying thing I can eat. It is just the right combination of taste, texture, nourishment, and lightness. I feel completely satisfied afterward, and any dishes that might follow are simply an embellishment.

Strangely, this feeling does not come out of my own Tuscan background, although such dishes do exist there; it was the rich contribution of southern Italy that opened my eyes to the wide repertory of these combinations. And what a joy to be able to make, for example, artichokes with pasta in four or five different ways, each reflecting its own region and yielding a completely new flavor.

Let us begin with that incomparable ingredient, garlic.

pasta aglio e olio

PASTA WITH GARLIC AND OIL

The most basic dressing for pasta is that of olive oil with garlic. Aglio e olio is the simplest of vegetable or herb dressings for pasta, and it is still the most used, in many slight variations, all over Italy. It seems reasonable to regard it as possibly the oldest of all dressings. We can see that many other dressings evolved from it. The addition of parsley, basil, rosemary, oregano, mint, black pepper, and hot red pepper flakes all contribute to manifold small variations on the theme. I cannot state strongly enough that grated cheese is never *added to any aglio–olio preparation.*

Here are the fundamental recipe and six variations, including the most classic of herbs—parsley, rosemary, and basil.

Coarsely chop the garlic on a board. Bring a large pot of cold water to a boil, add coarse salt to taste, then add the pasta and cook it until al dente—9 to 12 minutes depending on the brand.

Meanwhile, place a small saucepan with the oil over low heat; when the oil is warm, add the chopped garlic and sauté for 2 minutes. Add the red pepper flakes and salt and black pepper to taste, and sauté until the garlic is golden, about 2 minutes. Coarsely chop the parsley on a board.

When the pasta is ready, drain and transfer it to a large, warmed serving dish; pour the oil with the garlic over the top, toss very well, add the parsley, and serve immediately.

VARIATIONS

1. Garlic can be chopped and sautéed, but removed before the oil is added to pasta.
2. Garlic can be left whole, sautéed, then removed or left in the serving dish.
3. Rather than sautéing the garlic, it can be grated raw over the pasta already tossed with oil, salt, pepper, and red pepper flakes in the serving dish.
4. Parsley can be left out.
5. Garlic can be left whole, sautéed with 1 heaping tablespoon of rosemary leaves, fresh or preserved in salt. Discard garlic and rosemary and toss pasta with the oil.
6. Ten large leaves of fresh basil, torn into thirds, can be added to either of the first two variations.

SERVES 4 TO 6

- 2 large cloves garlic, peeled
- 1 pound dried *spaghetti*, preferably imported Italian
- ¾ cup extra-virgin olive oil
- ½ teaspoons hot red pepper flakes
- Salt and freshly ground black pepper
- 25 large sprigs Italian parsley, leaves only

TO COOK THE PASTA

- Coarse-grained salt

pasta aglio olio e basilico
PASTA WITH UNCOOKED GARLIC AND BASIL

SERVES 4 TO 6

24 large cloves garlic, peeled but left whole

24 large fresh basil leaves, left whole

1 pound dried *spaghetti*, preferably imported Italian

¾ cup extra-virgin olive oil

½ teaspoon hot red pepper flakes

Salt and freshly ground black pepper

TO COOK THE PASTA

Coarse-grained salt

We have seen the addition of fresh, uncooked basil in two variations of the fundamental recipe. There are, in addition, two separate treatments with basil that deserve to be regarded as separate recipes.

A wonderful treatment that always evokes a tremendous response from my guests is the use of a very large amount of both garlic and basil, both uncooked and mixed with the oil and pasta. The fresh flavors suffuse the oil in a remarkably light way. This treatment is related to the Tuscan method of preparing Pasta alla puttanesca, *in which uncooked tomatoes are also added with the garlic and basil. But as with* Maccheroni alla marinara *(page 105), the tomatoes were likely added to a previous* aglio e olio *recipe.*

Wash and dry the garlic and basil, place on a large serving platter, and set aside until needed.

Bring a large pot of cold water to a boil, add coarse salt to taste, then add the pasta and cook until al dente—9 to 12 minutes depending on the brand. Meanwhile, place a small saucepan with the oil over low heat; when the oil is warm, add the red pepper flakes and salt and pepper to taste, then let the oil become very hot. When the pasta is ready, drain and transfer it to the prepared serving platter, placing it over the uncooked garlic and basil. Pour the still-hot oil over the top, toss very well, and serve immediately.

herbs

Three recipes here are dominated by the flavor of a single herb or a combination of them. *Rigatoni al basilico* stresses sautéed whole basil leaves. Such leaves are most often eaten uncooked or used to flavor tomatoes, thus the flavor of the sautéed leaves used in this dish is really unique.

A sauce that does use the basil in the normal way is the beloved *Pesto alla genovese.* However, *pesto* does not refer only to the sauces made with basil, but really applies to any combination of herbs ground with a mortar and pestle, in Liguria and elsewhere. Even in Liguria there are other pestos, such as this favorite made with mint leaves. (See also the Sicilian pesto based on uncooked tomatoes and basil, page 112.)

rigatoni al basilico
RIGATONI WITH SAUTÉED BASIL

Here we shift the emphasis from the garlic to the basil, so that we really have a basil sauce flavored with garlic. This shift of emphasis is accomplished by sautéing the basil, thereby emphasizing its flavor, and also by reducing the amount of garlic.

In the early nineteenth century, when ripe, red tomatoes exploded on the southern Italian scene, they were added to the funda-mental aglio e olio *to form the so-called* marinara *preparation, which in its classic form does not necessarily have to do with fish or seafood. See the discussion of its real meaning in the introduction to* Maccheroni alla marinara *(page 105).*

Place the oil in a large skillet over low heat. Meanwhile, coarsely chop the garlic and place the basil leaves in a bowl of cold water. Bring a large pot of cold water to a boil.

When the oil is warm, add the chopped garlic and sauté for 2 minutes, then drain the basil and add it to the skillet. Season with salt and abundant pepper, and sauté for 15 minutes more over very low heat.

When the water reaches a boil, add coarse salt to taste, then add the pasta and cook it for 8 to 11 minutes depending on the brand; that is, 1 minute less than for normal al dente. Drain the pasta, add it to the skillet, raise the heat to medium, and sauté, continuously mixing with a wooden spoon, for another minute. Taste for salt and pepper, stir again, and remove from the heat. Transfer the pasta to a warmed serving dish and serve immediately.

SERVES 4 TO 6

¾ cup olive oil

2 medium-sized cloves garlic, peeled

40 large fresh basil leaves, left whole

Salt and freshly ground black pepper

1 pound dried *rigatoni*, preferably imported Italian

TO COOK THE PASTA

Coarse-grained salt

tagliatelle verdi alla menta
GREEN TAGLIATELLE WITH MINT PESTO

SERVES 4 TO 6

FOR THE PASTA

3 ½ cups unbleached all-purpose flour

3 extra-large eggs

2 heaping tablespoons cooked, drained, and finely chopped spinach

Pinch of salt

or

1 pound dried green *tagliatelle*, preferably imported Italian

FOR THE MINT PESTO

15 large sprigs Italian parsley, leaves only

5 large fresh basil leaves

15 large fresh mint leaves

1 teaspoon coarse-grained salt

5 tablespoons (2 ½ ounces) sweet butter, at room temperature

1 ½ cups heavy cream

¼ cup freshly grated Parmigiano cheese

Salt and freshly ground black pepper

TO COOK THE PASTA

Coarse-grained salt

TO SERVE

4 tablespoons (2 ounces) sweet butter, cut into pieces

15 large fresh mint leaves

Perhaps it is not generally known abroad how much fresh mint is used in Italy. The mint flavor here is combined with small amounts of parsley and basil, and is accentuated by the butter, cream, and Parmigiano, in lieu of the creamy local ricotta prescinsus, *while the more usual garlic and nuts are omitted.*

If fresh pasta is to be used, prepare it with the ingredients and quantities listed, following the directions on page 12. Stretch layer to a little more than 1⁄16 inch—on the pasta machine, take it to the next to the last setting. Cut into *tagliatelle*, as on page 34. Let the pasta rest on a cotton dish towel until needed.

Prepare the pesto. Place the parsley, basil, mint, and coarse salt in a stone mortar and use a marble pestle to coarsely grind all the ingredients together. Transfer the mixture to a crockery or glass bowl, then add the butter, cream, and Parmigiano; mix very well with a wooden spoon and season with salt and pepper. Place the bowl, covered, in the refrigerator until needed.

Bring a large pot of cold water to a boil, add coarse salt to taste, then add the fresh pasta and cook for 30 seconds to 1 minute depending on dryness; if dried pasta is used, cook it until al dente—9 to 12 minutes depending on the brand. Drain and transfer the pasta to a large, warmed serving platter, toss it with the butter, then pour the prepared sauce over the top, toss again, and sprinkle with the mint leaves. Serve immediately.

troffie al pesto di montagna

GENOESE PASTA WITH MOUNTAIN PESTO

Not all pesto sauces are based on basil. The word pesto *refers to a sauce created by grinding ingredients with a mortar and pestle to achieve a creamy consistency. This pesto from the border mountains between Emilia-Romagna and Liguria includes elements from both regions. The pesto is made from boiled potataoes, walnuts, and Parmigiano ground together, and the liquid binder is not oil or butter, but milk or broth. Basil is used in the flavoring—a Ligurian touch—but the leaves are torn into thirds rather than ground. The* troffie *pasta used is also from Liguria.*

Boil the potatoes with their skins on in salted boiling water until very soft, about 30 minutes, depending on their size. Peel the potatoes while still very hot, then pass them through a potato ricer, using the disc with the smallest holes, into a crockery or glass bowl.

Finely chop the garlic and the walnuts together on a board or in a blender or food processor. Add the Parmigiano (and chopped ingredients, if chopped by hand) to the blender or food processor and gradually add the riced potatoes and lukewarm milk or broth, blending until a very smooth paste forms. Season with salt and pepper. Transfer the pesto to a crockery or glass bowl and let rest, covered, in the refrigerator until needed.

Bring a large pot of cold water to a boil over medium heat, add coarse salt to taste, then add the pasta and cook until al dente—9 to 12 minutes depending on the brand.

Meanwhile, put the butter in a large serving casserole, and melt it over boiling water. Remove the pesto from the refrigerator and add ½ cup to 1 cup of the boiling pasta water; mix very well, tasting for salt and pepper.

Drain the pasta, add it to the casserole with the melted butter, and toss very well. Then add the pesto and the basil leaves, mix very well, and serve hot with additional black pepper over each serving.

SERVES 4 TO 6

FOR THE PESTO

1 pound all-purpose potatoes

Coarse-grained salt

1 ounce garlic, peeled and any greenish cores removed

4 ounces shelled walnuts

4 ounces freshly grated Parmigiano cheese

1½ cups lukewarm milk or completely defatted chicken broth, preferably homemade

Salt and freshly ground black pepper

FOR THE PASTA

1 pound dried *troffie* pasta or a short twisted pasta like *tortiglioni*, preferably imported Italian

TO COOK THE PASTA

Coarse-grained salt

TO SERVE

6 tablespoons (3 ounces) sweet butter

40 large fresh basil leaves, torn into thirds

Freshly ground black pepper

nastri alla borraccina

RIBBONS OF PASTA WITH SIX-HERB SAUCE

SERVES 8 TO 10

FOR THE SAUCE

2 medium-sized cloves garlic, peeled

2 tablespoons rosemary leaves, fresh or preserved in salt; or 2 tablespoons rosemary leaves, dried and blanched

10 large sage leaves, fresh or preserved in salt

10 large fresh mint leaves

1 teaspoon dried marjoram

2 cups dry white wine

4 bay leaves

Coarse-grained salt

2 pounds fresh spinach, leaves only, carefully washed

½ cup olive oil

10 tablespoons (5 ounces) sweet butter

Salt and freshly ground black pepper

2 cups beef broth, preferably homemade

FOR THE PASTA

4 cups unbleached all-purpose flour

4 extra-large eggs

4 teaspoons vegetable or olive oil

Pinch of salt

TO COOK THE PASTA

Coarse-grained salt

Borraccina *sauce is a "moss" made by chopping many herbs extremely fine so they emit an incredible fresh perfume, like the woods after a rain. Body is added to this delicate Tuscan sauce by including some cooked spinach.* Borraccina *sauce should be used with fresh pasta only.*

Prepare the sauce. Finely chop the garlic, rosemary, sage, mint, and marjoram on a board. Place the chopped ingredients in a crockery or glass bowl, then add the wine along with the bay leaves. Let the ingredients marinate for 2 hours.

Prepare the pasta with the ingredients and quantities listed, following the instructions on page 12. Stretch layer to ⅟₁₆ inch thick—on the pasta machine, take it to the next to the last setting, then, with a scalloped pastry wheel, cut the layers of dough into strips 4 inches long and 1 inch wide (see the illustration on page 34). Let the pasta rest on a dry cotton dish towel until needed.

Bring a large quantity of cold water to a boil, add coarse salt to taste, then add the spinach and cook for 10 minutes. Drain the spinach and rinse under cold running water until cool, squeeze dry, and finely chop on a board.

Place a heavy saucepan with the oil and 6 tablespoons of the butter over medium heat. When the butter is melted, add the chopped spinach and sauté for 2 minutes. Discard the bay leaves from the marinated mixture and add the remaining contents of the bowl to the pan. Cook for 20 minutes, stirring and mixing all ingredients together. Taste for salt and pepper.

Heat the broth in a small saucepan, and, when it is hot, add it to the pan with the herb sauce; reduce it over medium heat for 25 minutes.

Bring a large quantity of cold water to a boil, add coarse salt to taste, then add the pasta and cook for 30 seconds to 1 minute depending on dryness. Drain the pasta, transfer it to a warmed serving platter, and toss well with the remaining butter. Add the sauce, mix very well, and serve immediately.

mollica

Bread with the crust removed, or the inside of the bread, is called the "crumb" of the bread in English and *mollica* in Italian. It is, of course, not the same thing as bread crumbs. Both of these played an enormous role in medieval cooking and continue to be used as an ingredient in some traditional Italian dishes. Bread crumbs, or *pangrattato*, are understood to be grated bread, therefore considerably hardened. In Italy today, it is also understood that the crumbs are toasted after grating. Most of the time these crumbs remain unseasoned, to allow for greatest versatility in combination with other ingredients.

Pasta sauced with oil and bread crumbs or *mollica* is probably as old and as fundamental a combination as pasta with garlic. The simplest form of this is *Spaghetti con briciolata*, a combination of pasta, oil, and bread crumbs, sometimes with a little fresh parsley added at the end. The recipe that follows, a Tuscan dish with bread crumbs, and its Sicilian counterpart that uses *mollica* as a starting point—uses garlic and abundant parsley. Both versions are therefore combinations of oil with both garlic and bread crumbs. These recipes may sound old-fashioned to you, but try them. They remain very appropriate.

Bread crumbs were used in medieval recipes as a thickener in place of modern grated cheese or flour, which only emerged in the fifteenth century. *Mollica* was much used in stuffings, and to a lesser degree, still is.

pasta con pangrattato
PASTA WITH GARLIC AND BREAD CRUMBS

SERVES 4 TO 6

2 large cloves garlic, peeled

1 pound dried short tubular pasta, such as *penne* or *penne rigate*, preferably imported Italian

¾ cup extra-virgin olive oil

3 tablespoons unseasoned bread crumbs, preferably homemade

Salt and freshly ground black pepper

25 large sprigs Italian parsley, leaves only

TO COOK THE PASTA

Coarse-grained salt

Coarsely chop the garlic on a board. Bring a large pot of cold water to a boil, add coarse salt to taste, then add the pasta and cook until al dente—9 to 12 minutes depending on the brand.

Meanwhile, place a small saucepan with the oil over low heat, and, when the oil is warm, add the garlic and sauté for 2 minutes. Add the bread crumbs, season to taste with salt and pepper, and sauté until the bread crumbs are slightly golden, about 1 minute. Coarsely chop the parsley on a board.

When the pasta is ready, drain and transfer it to a large, warmed serving dish; pour the oil with the garlic and bread crumbs over the top, toss very well, add the parsley, and serve.

VARIATIONS

1. The 2 cloves of garlic can be peeled and left whole, sautéed, then discarded.
2. Parsley can be omitted.

NOTE

The Sicilian dish *pasta cu la muddica* (in Italian, *pasta con la mollica*) is similar to this Tuscan one. However, the *mollica*, or "crumb"—bread inside only, without crust—is baked in the oven with oil poured over it until very crisp. Then it is made into bread crumbs, which are sautéed in oil as in the Tuscan version. (More complicated Sicilian versions also use tomatoes and anchovies.)

The Tuscan recipe *Spaghetti con briciolata* in my book *The Fine Art of Italian Cooking* does not contain garlic. That particular bread-crumb sauce is always paired with *spaghetti*.

pasta col coniglio scappato

PASTA WITH MOCK RABBIT SAUCE

"Scappato" *dishes are those made with all the ingredients of a classic dish, minus a single central ingredient—in this case, the rabbit. The name comes from the Italian word* scappare, *to escape. The combination of ingredients that remains produces a valid dish, though a different one.*

Finely chop and combine the garlic, rosemary, salt, and pepper all together on a board or in a food processor or blender. Bring a large pot of cold water to a boil, add coarse salt to taste, then add the pasta and cook until al dente—9 to 12 minutes depending on the brand.

Meanwhile, place a small pan with the oil over low heat, and, when the oil is warm, add the garlic mixture and lightly sauté for 1 minute, then add the bread crumbs and taste for salt and pepper. Cook for 1 minute more, stirring constantly with a wooden spoon. Add the broth and simmer for 1 minute longer.

Drain the pasta, transfer it to a large, warmed bowl, pour the sauce over the top, and mix very well. Transfer the pasta to a warmed serving platter, sprinkle with the parsley, and serve.

SERVES 4

3 large cloves garlic, peeled

1½ tablespoons fresh rosemary leaves

¼ tablespoon fine salt

⅛ tablespoon freshly ground black pepper

8 tablespoons extra-virgin olive oil

6 tablespoons fine unseasoned bread crumbs, preferably homemade

1 cup completely defatted chicken broth or vegetable broth, preferably homemade

¾ pound dried short tubular pasta, such as *penne, penne rigate,* or *denti di cavallo,* preferably imported Italian

TO COOK THE PASTA

Coarse-grained salt

TO SERVE

15 large sprigs Italian parsley, leaves only, coarsely chopped

The fruit and vegetable market in San Gimignano, the famous town of one hundred towers.

mushrooms

In Italy it is assumed that "mushrooms" (*funghi*) means wild mushrooms, of many different types, varying according to the locale. Pasta is happily combined with different kinds of fresh mushrooms when they are in season. However, dried wild mushrooms, especially *porcini*, are even more commonly used—in sauces in which they are the dominant ingredient as well as in many dishes in which they are merely a flavoring for the main ingredients.

The following two mushroom sauces, from Tuscany and Liguria respectively, are based on dried *porcini*; as elsewhere their differing treatments give insight into the varying approaches in those regions.

Fresh porcini mushrooms with nipitella.

pasta ai funghi alla chiantigiana

PASTA WITH MUSHROOMS, CHIANTI STYLE

This Tuscan mushroom sauce employs olive oil, wine, and a touch of tomato paste, with parsley as the herb. The aromatic vegetables are simply chopped. Typically Tuscan is the dry Vinsanto from the Chianti, which when unavailable can be replaced with a dry Marsala.

Prepare the sauce. Soak the mushrooms in lukewarm water for 30 minutes. Drain the mushrooms, saving 2 cups of the soaking water, then clean them very well to remove all sand attached to the stems. Strain the mushroom water by passing it through several layers of paper towels. Finely chop the mushrooms, onion, garlic, and parsley all together on a board. Heat the oil in a medium-sized saucepan over medium heat, and, when the oil is warm, add the chopped ingredients. Sauté for 15 minutes, mixing every so often with a wooden spoon. Then add the wine and let it evaporate for 5 minutes. Meanwhile, dissolve the tomato paste in the 2 cups of reserved mushroom water and add them to pan. Cover and cook over low heat for 1 hour, mixing occasionally with a wooden spoon. Season to taste with salt and pepper, raise the heat, and reduce the sauce by half, about 10 minutes more.

If using fresh pasta, prepare it with the ingredients listed, following the directions on page 12. Stretch layer to ⅛ inch, and cut into *spaghetti* (see below). Let rest on cotton dish towels until ready to use.

Bring a large pot of cold water to a boil, add coarse salt to taste, then add the pasta. If using dried *spaghetti*, cook it for 8 to 11 minutes depending on the brand; that is, 1 minute less than normal for al dente. If using fresh *spaghetti*, cook it for 1 to 3 minutes depending on dryness. Drain and transfer the pasta to a large bowl with the butter, mix well, then place in a large skillet together with the sauce and sauté over high heat for 1 minute more. Place pasta on a warmed serving dish and serve immediately.

SPAGHETTI

To cut *spaghetti*, insert the thick pasta layer into the *taglierini* cutter (narrower cutter).

SERVES 6

FOR THE SAUCE

2 ounces dried *porcini* mushrooms

1 medium-sized red onion, peeled

2 medium-sized cloves garlic, peeled

20 medium-sized sprigs Italian parsley, leaves only

4 tablespoons olive oil

½ cup dry Vinsanto or dry Marsala

5 tablespoons tomato paste

Salt and freshly ground black pepper

FOR THE PASTA

1 pound dried *spaghetti*

or

3 cups unbleached all-purpose flour

4 extra-large eggs

Pinch of salt

TO COOK THE PASTA

Coarse-grained salt

TO SERVE

2 tablespoons (1 ounce) sweet butter

pasta con intingolo di funghi alla genovese

PASTA WITH MUSHROOM PESTO

SERVES 4 TO 6

FOR THE SAUCE

1 ounce dried *porcini* mushrooms

1 medium-sized red onion, peeled

2 medium-sized cloves garlic, peeled

3 tablespoons pine nuts (*pignolis*)

1 tablespoon rosemary leaves, fresh or preserved in salt

4 tablespoons (2 ounces) sweet butter

8 tablespoons olive oil

1 pound ripe, fresh tomatoes; or 1 pound canned tomatoes, preferably imported Italian, drained

Salt and freshly ground black pepper

2 anchovies in salt, or 4 anchovy fillets in oil, drained

1 pound flat dried pasta such as *tagliatelle* or *lasagnette*

TO COOK THE PASTA

Coarse-grained salt

This Ligurian sauce is a real pesto in which the mushrooms, vegetables, herbs—in this case rosemary—and pignolis *are ground with a mortar and pestle, combined with tomatoes, and flavored with anchovies. Butter is used with the oil, a northern touch. Especially Ligurian is the combination of rosemary with mushrooms, which is not done in central Italy.*

Prepare the sauce. Soak the mushrooms in lukewarm water for 30 minutes, then drain and clean them thoroughly to remove all sand attached to the stems; discard the soaking water. Finely chop the mushrooms, onion, garlic, pine nuts, and rosemary all together on a board (or with a mortar and pestle, or a food processor). Place the butter and 5 tablespoons of the oil in a medium-sized flameproof casserole over medium heat. When the oil is warm but the butter not yet completely melted, add the chopped ingredients and sauté for 15 minutes, stirring every so often with a wooden spoon.

Meanwhile, if using fresh tomatoes, cut them into pieces. Pass fresh or canned tomatoes through a food mill, using the disc with smallest holes, into a crockery or glass bowl. Add the tomatoes to the casserole, season to taste with salt and pepper, and simmer for 15 minutes more. Every so often be sure to stir so the mushrooms do not stick to the bottom of the casserole.

Bring a large pot of cold water to a boil, add coarse salt to taste, then add the pasta and cook it for 9 to 12 minutes depending on the brand.

While the pasta cooks, put a small saucepan with the remaining oil over low heat. If using anchovies in salt, clean and fillet them under cold running water. When the oil is warm, remove the pan from heat, add the anchovy fillets, and use a fork to mash them into the oil. Add this paste to the casserole, and mix well over high heat for 1 minute.

When the pasta is ready, drain and transfer it to a large bowl, pour the sauce over the top, and mix well again. Transfer to a large, warmed dish and serve immediately.

minestrone o zuppa di funghi alla contadina

TUSCAN WILD MUSHROOM MINESTRONE OR SOUP

This wonderful mushroom dish made with fresh pasta is Minestrone o zuppa di funghi alla contadina, *though it is not a true* minestrone *because it has no beans. The soup is thickened instead with riced potatoes. When croutons are added instead of pasta, you have a* zuppa.

Soak the mushrooms in the lukewarm water for 30 minutes. Meanwhile, bring a medium-sized pot of cold water to a boil, add coarse salt to taste, then add the potatoes and cook until very soft, 30 to 45 minutes depending on size. Drain the mushrooms, saving the soaking water. Clean the mushrooms well, removing all the sand attached to the stems. Strain the soaking water by passing it several times through layers of paper towels.

Cut the *prosciutto* or *pancetta* into small pieces. Heat the oil in a medium-sized stockpot over low heat, and, when the oil is warm, add the *prosciutto* or *pancetta* and the garlic, then sauté for 5 minutes. Pour in the mushroom water and enough additional cold broth to total 3 quarts liquid; bring to a boil and simmer, uncovered, for 30 minutes.

Meanwhile, peel the potatoes and pass them through a food mill, using the disc with smallest holes (rather than a potato ricer), into a small bowl. Add the mushrooms to the stockpot and simmer for another 30 minutes, tasting for salt and pepper. Add the potatoes and stir well with a wooden spoon to dissolve them completely in the broth. Stir in the tomato paste and simmer for 30 minutes, tasting again for salt and pepper.

If using fresh pasta, prepare it with the ingredients and quantities listed, following the directions on page 12. Stretch layer to about $\frac{1}{16}$ inch thick—on the pasta machine, take it to the next to the last setting. Using a pastry cutter, cut the sheets into 3-inch-long pieces, then with the machine cut them into 3-inch-long *tagliatelle* (see page 34). When the broth is ready, add the pasta and cook for 1 to 3 minutes depending on dryness. With the addition of the pasta, the soup is a *minestrone* without beans.

If using croutons, ladle the soup into individual bowls and place the croutons on top.

SERVES 10 TO 12

FOR THE MINESTRONE

1 ½ ounces dried *porcini* mushrooms

6 cups lukewarm water

Coarse-grained salt

1 ½ pounds potatoes (not new potatoes)

4 ounces *prosciutto* or *pancetta*, in one piece

¼ cup olive oil

3 large cloves garlic, peeled and finely chopped

About 7 cups cold chicken or beef broth, preferably homemade

Salt and freshly ground black pepper

2 tablespoons tomato paste

FOR THE PASTA

2 cups unbleached all-purpose flour

3 extra-large eggs

Pinch of salt

FOR THE ZUPPA

2 cups homemade croutons, fried or toasted

minestrone di verdura alla genovese

GENOESE VEGETABLE MINESTRONE

SERVES 8 TO 10

1 cup dried *cannellini* (white kidney beans)

3½ quarts cold water

2 tablespoons extra-virgin olive oil

2 all-purpose potatoes, about ¾ pound, peeled and left whole

Coarse-grained salt

2 small carrots, scraped and cut into ½-inch-thick discs

1 medium-sized red onion, peeled and cut into less-than-1-inch squares

2 medium-sized cloves garlic, peeled and coarsely chopped

1 small zucchini, cleaned and cut into ½-inch pieces

1 cup spinach or Swiss chard, or a combination stemmed, cleaned, and chopped

1 cup cleaned and chopped string beans, cleaned and cut into 1-inch pieces

1 large, ripe, fresh tomato, about 8 ounces; or 8 ounces canned tomatoes, preferably imported Italian, drained

½ pound savoy cabbage, cleaned and chopped into 1-inch-thick strips

Every region of Italy has its own minestrone, *a soup that incorporates a variety of favorite regional vegetables, the preferred type of beans, and a pasta or rice. Usually,* minestrone *is thickened by puréeing a portion of the beans and leaving the potatoes, if they are among the ingredients, simply cut in large pieces. The Genoese version, however, is thickened by ricing the potatoes and leaving the beans whole. It should come as no surprise that the main flavoring is pesto, the signature of Ligurian cooking, added at the last moment.*

Soak the beans in cold water overnight. The next morning, put the 3½ quarts of cold water in a medium-sized stockpot over medium heat, and bring to a boil. Drain the beans and add them to the pot along with the olive oil. Simmer for 15 minutes, then add the whole potatoes and coarse salt to taste and cook for 20 minutes more. Meanwhile, soak the carrots, red onion, garlic, zucchini, spinach, and string beans in a bowl of cold water for 20 minutes, then drain and add them to the stockpot. Simmer for 1½ hours, stirring every so often with a wooden spoon to be sure none of the ingredients stick to the bottom of the pot.

In the meantime, prepare the pesto using the ingredients and quantities listed above, following the directions on page 112. Refrigerate the pesto, covered, until needed.

Season the soup with salt and pepper, keeping in mind that the pesto will be added later. Remove the potatoes from the soup and pass them through a potato ricer directly back into the stockpot. Taste again for salt and pepper and mix very well.

Put about 3 quarts of cold water or chicken broth in a casserole over medium heat. Bring to a boil, add coarse salt to taste, then add the pasta and cook it until al dente—9 to 12 minutes depending on the brand. Drain the pasta, add it to the stockpot, and mix very well, then add the pesto and mix again. Let the *minestrone* rest for a few minutes before serving.

1 cup fresh seasonal vegetables, such as fresh peas or asparagus

10 large sprigs Italian parsley, leaves only

5 basil leaves, fresh or preserved in salt, torn into thirds

Freshly ground black pepper

FOR THE PESTO

1 cup fresh basil leaves, loosely packed

2 medium-sized cloves garlic, peeled

½ cup extra-virgin olive oil

2 heaping tablespoons freshly grated Parmigiano

Salt and freshly ground black pepper

FOR THE PASTA

½ pound short tubular pasta, such as elbow macaroni, preferably imported Italian

TO COOK THE PASTA

About 3 quarts water or chicken broth

Coarse-grained salt

Long zucchini, the blossoms of which are not used in cooking, and round zucchini, waiting to be stuffed.

spaghetti alla nursina
SPAGHETTI WITH BLACK TRUFFLES

SERVES 4 TO 6

1 ounce black truffles, fresh or canned

¾ cup olive oil

1 large clove garlic, peeled but left whole

2 anchovies preserved in salt; or 4 anchovy fillets packed in oil, drained

Salt and freshly ground black pepper

1 pound dried *spaghetti,* preferably imported Italian

TO COOK THE PASTA

Coarse-grained salt

TO SERVE

20 large sprigs Italian parsley, leaves only

Umbria is the home of Italian black truffles, and Norcia is the center. While white truffles are characteristically eaten raw, the black ones are most often cooked for a long time in order to bring out their nutty flavor, as in various galantines. However, when black truffles are combined with anchovies, which strongly heighten their flavor, it is not necessary to have such a long cooking time.

If working with fresh truffles, use a small brush to clean them very well. Finely chop the truffles on a board. Place a small saucepan with the oil over low heat. When the oil is warm, add the garlic and sauté until golden brown, about 5 minutes. Meanwhile, bring a large pot of cold water to a boil.

If anchovies in salt are used, clean them under cold running water, removing bones and excess salt. When the garlic is done, discard it, remove the saucepan from the heat, and add the anchovy fillets to the hot oil, using a fork to mash them into the oil. Add the chopped truffles and mix very well. Taste for salt and pepper.

When the water reaches a boil, add coarse salt to taste, then add the pasta and cook until al dente—9 to 12 minutes depending on the brand. As the pasta cooks, coarsely chop the parsley on a board. Just 1 minute before the pasta is ready, put the pan with the sauce over medium heat. Drain the pasta; transfer to a large, warmed serving platter, pour the sauce over the top, and toss very well. Sprinkle the parsley all over and serve immediately.

Black and white fresh truffles.

pasta alla panzanella

PASTA IN THE MANNER OF PANZANELLA

Pasta alla panzanella *belongs to a type of dish much more appreciated in Italy than the cold pasta salads popular elsewhere. Here, a cold sauce is used with hot pasta. Cold sauces are also combined in Italy with hot main courses and even desserts. Panzanella is the traditional Tuscan bread salad, mixing the crumbled bread with fresh tomatoes, basil, and onions, and dressed with olive oil and vinegar. In Siena, the uncooked sauce has been adapted to pasta and fresh arugula is added.*

Arugula is not typically Tuscan, but because Siena is close to the border of Lazio, the green is better known there than in Florence.

Prepare the sauce. Coarsely chop the onion and put it in a bowl of cold water for 30 minutes. Cut the tomatoes into 1-inch pieces without removing the seeds and put them in a crockery or glass bowl. Drain the onion and place it over the tomatoes. Finely chop the garlic on a board, and scatter it over the onion. Top with olive oil and season to taste with salt and pepper. Cover the bowl and refrigerate for at least 1 hour.

If fresh pasta is to be used, prepare it with the ingredients and quantities listed, following the directions on page 12. Stretch the layer to ⅛ inch thick. Cut it into *spaghetti* (see illustration on page 59).

Use 2 bunches of arugula to make a bed on each of the individual serving plates. Bring a large pot of cold water to a boil, add coarse salt to taste, and add the pasta. Cook fresh pasta 1 to 3 minutes depending on the dryness; cook dried pasta for 9 to 12 minutes depending on the brand.

Remove the sauce from the refrigerator and mix well. Arrange the remaining arugula and the basil leaves on a large platter. When the pasta is ready, drain it and place it on the greens. Immediately distribute the cold sauce over the pasta. Mix everything and serve, placing the mixed pasta on the prepared plates over the beds of arugula.

SERVES 4 TO 6

FOR THE SAUCE

1 large red onion, cleaned

1 ½ pounds ripe (but not overripe) fresh tomatoes

1 medium-sized clove garlic, peeled

¾ to 1 cup olive oil

Salt and freshly ground black pepper

FOR THE PASTA

3 cups unbleached all-purpose flour

4 extra-large eggs

Pinch of salt

or

1 pound dried *penne* or any other tubular pasta 2 inches long and ¼ inch wide, preferably imported Italian

TO SERVE

4 bunches arugula (rocket), about 1 pound, large stems removed and leaves thoroughly washed

15 large fresh basil leaves

TO COOK THE PASTA

Coarse-grained salt

orecchiette con ruchetta e patate

PASTA WITH ARUGULA AND POTATOES

Here is the first of two recipes in this book in which the arugula* is cooked. The other, on page 301, is the Apulian Cavatieddi con la rucola. Arugula is best known as a salad green, but it is also excellent when cooked and often used that way in Apulia. The dried orecchiette are firm and form an interesting texture with the cooked green and the potatoes. The dish is flavored with garlic and hot red pepper flakes, but no tomatoes.

Peel the potatoes and cut them into ¾-inch cubes. Place the potatoes and arugula in a bowl of cold water and set aside for 30 minutes.

Bring a large pot of cold water to a boil, add coarse salt to taste, then drain the vegetables and add them to the pot. When the water returns to a boil, add the pasta, mix very well, and cook until al dente—9 to 12 minutes depending on the brand. By then the potatoes also should be completely cooked but still firm.

Coarsely chop the garlic on a board. Place the oil in a small saucepan over medium heat, and when the oil is warm, add the garlic and sauté until lightly golden, about 1 minute. Add salt, pepper, and the red pepper flakes. Drain the pasta and vegetables, then transfer to a large, warmed serving platter. Pour the sauce over, toss very well, and serve immediately.

*The Italian word is *rucola* or *ruchetta*. The Italian slang word, "*arugula*" has come into current use, but the older English word is "rocket."

SERVES 6

1 pound potatoes (not new potatoes)

1 pound arugula (rocket), cleaned

1 pound dried *orecchiette*, preferably imported Italian

TO COOK THE VEGETABLES AND PASTA

Coarse-grained salt

FOR THE SAUCE

2 large cloves garlic, peeled

¾ cup olive oil

Salt and freshly ground black pepper

1 teaspoon hot red pepper flakes

combined vegetable sauces

Combined vegetable sauces are prepared in two different ways. In the first, very contemporary mode, each vegetable is cooked separately and then they are all combined with the pasta. The obvious advantage is that each can receive its optimum cooking time. Each vegetable also retains its own flavor and there is a minimum of blending, which may be a disadvantage. The second and older method is to cook all the vegetables together in order to achieve a new flavor that none could produce individually. One must be more careful about the vegetables selected in this second method, because not all necessarily blend well with others. The best blends—indeed, those most used in combination, even as the basis for meat sauces—include carrots, celery, and onions. Spinach and chard do not create problems, nor do peas, zucchini, and artichokes. Much care must be taken with the cabbage family and with fennel, because of their strong, dominant personalities. Of the cabbage family, I would select only cauliflower for blending; cabbage itself and broccoli I would avoid. Broccoli is much used in combination when it can be cooked separately, as in the first method, but it will not produce a good result when cooked with other vegetables.

Neither of the two mixed-vegetable sauces that follow attempts to preserve the perfect cooking time of each individual vegetable, and certainly they do not take an Asian-style al dente approach to the vegetables.

spaghetti con salsa di verdure
SPAGHETTI WITH TUSCAN DICED VEGETABLE SAUCE

This modern diced vegetable sauce combines artichokes, zucchini, celery, onions, and carrots, cooking them all for the same amount of time so that the tender zucchini will become almost a purée while the artichokes and carrots will remain firm. This is exactly as should be, as you will agree when you taste it. Unusual flavoring for this Tuscan dish is the oregano mixed with the hot red pepper flakes.

Place the artichoke in a bowl of cold water with the lemon halves; put the zucchini and celery in a second large bowl of cold water and soak both for 30 minutes.

Finely chop the onion, carrot, and parsley on a board. Place the oil in a heavy, medium-sized flameproof casserole over low heat, and, when the oil is warm, add the chopped ingredients and sauté for 10 minutes.

Clean the artichoke following the directions on page 70 and cut it into 1-inch pieces. Cut the zucchini lengthwise into quarters, then into ½-inch pieces. Cut the celery into similar-sized pieces. Add the vegetables to the casserole, sauté for 2 minutes, then cover and cook over medium heat for 20 minutes, stirring every so often with a wooden spoon.

If using fresh tomatoes, cut them into pieces. Pass fresh or canned tomatoes through a food mill, using the disc with the smallest holes, into a crockery or glass bowl. Add tomatoes to the casserole and season with salt, pepper, red pepper flakes, and oregano. Cover and cook for 20 minutes more. Add the broth, cover, reduce heat, and simmer for 15 minutes. Uncover, raise the heat, and cook for 15 minutes; taste for salt and pepper. (The sauce may be prepared a day in advance, refrigerated in a covered crockery or glass bowl, and reheated before using.)

Bring a large pot of cold water to a boil, add coarse salt to taste, then add the pasta and cook for 9 to 12 minutes depending on the brand. As the pasta cooks, warm a large serving dish and ladle some of the sauce onto it. Drain the pasta, transfer it to the prepared platter, add the remaining sauce, mix well, and serve hot.

SERVES 6

- 1 large artichoke
- 1 large lemon, cut in half
- 2 medium-sized zucchini
- 1 large stalk celery
- 1 medium-sized red onion, peeled
- 1 medium-sized carrot, scraped
- 20 large sprigs Italian parsley, leaves only
- 6 tablespoons olive oil
- 1 pound ripe, fresh tomatoes; or 1 pound canned tomatoes, preferably imported Italian, drained
- Salt and freshly ground black pepper
- ¼ teaspoon hot red pepper flakes
- ½ teaspoon dried oregano
- ½ cup chicken or beef broth, preferably homemade
- 1 pound dried *spaghetti*, preferably imported Italian

TO COOK THE PASTA
Coarse-grained salt

ARTICHOKES

1. Trim off all of the darker outer ring. The inner core is the best part because it has the real taste of the artichoke.

2. Remove as many rows of the outer leaves as necessary to arrive at those tender inner rows where you can clearly see the separation between the green at the top and the light yellow at the bottom. Then remove the top green part. Press your thumb on the bottom of each leaf, the white part, to hold it in place, and with the other hand, tear off the top green part. As each new row is uncovered the tender yellow part of the leaves will be bigger. When you reach the rows in which only the very tips of the leaves are green, cut off all the tips together with a knife.

3. It is best to cut the artichoke into quarters lengthwise, in order to remove the choke. Draw the tip of the knife blade across just below the choke to draw it out.

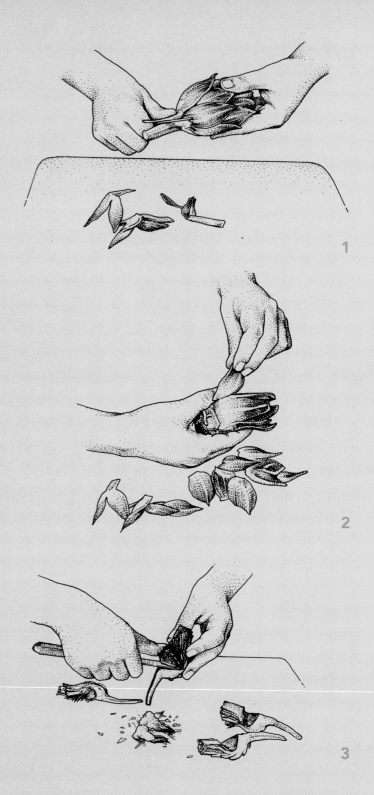

pasta alle erbe
SPAGHETTI WITH SPRING VEGETABLES

Spaghetti *with Spring Vegetables comes from a Renaissance Florentine cookbook, and it combines many seasonal vegetables: small peas, thin asparagus, and spring onions or scallions—all flavored with the* pancetta *so popular in Michelangelo's Florence. This really was a* pasta primavera, *and remains very valid alongside its modern counterparts. The vegetables are not miniaturized, nor are they undercooked or very crisp.*

Place the artichokes in a bowl of cold water with the lemon halves; set aside for 30 minutes. Place the chard and asparagus in 2 separate bowls of cold water; set aside for 30 minutes. Shell the peas and place them in a fourth bowl of cold water together with the flour; set aside for 30 minutes.

Cut off and discard the very green parts of the scallions. Cut the white portions into pieces less than ½-inch long. Cut the *pancetta* or *prosciutto* into ½-inch cubes. Clean the artichokes according to instructions on page 70, cutting them into quarters, then cutting each quarter into thirds. Place artichoke pieces back in the lemon water. Cut the green leaves of chard into 1-inch strips. Trim off and discard the white parts of the asparagus, and cut the green parts into 1-inch pieces. Drain and rinse the peas under cold running water.

Place the *pancetta* or *prosciutto* in a medium-sized saucepan with the oil over medium heat; sauté for 5 minutes; add the scallions; sauté for 5 more minutes. Drain. Add all of the vegetables; cook, covered, for 30 minutes, adding broth as needed, and stirring every so often with a wooden spoon. Taste for salt and pepper. The vegetables should all be cooked, some softer than others.

If fresh pasta is used, prepare it with the ingredients and quantities listed, following the directions on page 12. Stretch layer to ⅛ inch thick and cut into *spaghetti* (see the illustration on page 59). Bring a large pot of cold water to a boil, add coarse salt to taste, add the pasta, stir with a wooden spoon, and cover the pot to bring the water back to a boil. Cook the fresh pasta for 1 to 3 minutes depending on dryness, or dried pasta for 9 to 12 minutes depending on the brand.

Coarsely chop the parsley on a board. When the pasta is ready, drain and transfer it to the pan with the sauce. Mix very well and cook for 20 more seconds. Transfer to a large, warmed serving platter. Serve with the chopped parsley sprinkled over the individual servings. (No cheese should be added.)

SERVES 6

FOR THE SAUCE

2 large artichokes

1 large lemon, cut in half

½ pound Swiss chard, large stems removed

1 pound very thin asparagus

1 pound unshelled peas

1 tablespoon unbleached all-purpose flour

10 scallions

4 ounces *pancetta* or *prosciutto*, in 1 piece

½ cup olive oil

About 1 cup chicken broth, preferably homemade

Salt and freshly ground black pepper

FOR THE PASTA

3 cups unbleached all-purpose flour

4 extra-large eggs

Pinch of salt

or

1 pound dried *spaghetti*, preferably imported Italian

TO COOK THE PASTA

Coarse-grained salt

TO SERVE

15 large sprigs Italian parsley, leaves only

spaghetti al limone
SPAGHETTI WITH LEMON CREAM SAUCE

SERVES 4 TO 6

FOR THE PASTA

3 cups unbleached all-purpose flour

3 extra-large eggs

3 teaspoons vegetable or olive oil

Pinch of salt

or

1 pound dried *spaghetti*, preferably imported Italian

TO COOK THE PASTA

Coarse-grained salt

FOR THE SAUCE

12 tablespoons (6 ounces) sweet butter

2 cups heavy cream

Grated peel of 2 large lemons with thick skin

Salt and freshly ground white pepper

Pinch of freshly grated nutmeg

1 cup freshly grated Parmigiano cheese

TO SERVE

15 large sprigs Italian parsley, leaves only

The flavor of lemon, so versatile it enhances so many different kinds of dishes, even has its application to pasta. Lately, in the search for new varieties of flavored fresh pasta, it has become popular to put grated lemon peel into the dough itself. One must be careful in doing this with thin tagliatelle *dressed with a butter-cream sauce, because the extremely tart taste that develops when the lemon peel is cooked is not balanced by the delicate butter and cream and does not succeed in combining with them. With this pasta and sauce, it is better if the grated lemon peel is placed in the butter-cream sauce itself, pleasantly flavoring the* alla panna, *which absorbs the oil of the lemon skin. In this way the sauce can be used with plain fresh pasta or even with dried pasta to produce a good result. (See page 362 for Fiocchietti al pomodoro, a pasta made with lemon peel. The dish works because the pasta is thick and short; nutmeg as well as lemon flavors the pasta, and the two recommended sauces are hearty enough to absorb and stand up to the lemon oils.)*

If using fresh pasta, prepare the pasta with the ingredients and quantities listed, following the directions on page 12. Stretch layer to ⅛ inch thick and cut into *spaghetti*, (see illustration on page 59). Let the pasta rest on cotton dish towels until needed.

Bring a large pot of cold water to a boil, and put a large skillet with the butter in it over the pot so that the butter melts as the water heats. When the water reaches a boil and the butter is melted, remove the skillet and add coarse salt to taste to the pot. Then add the pasta and cook fresh pasta for 1 to 3 minutes depending on the dryness or dried pasta for 9 to 12 minutes depending on the brand. Drain pasta and add to the skillet. Immediately put the skillet over medium heat, and add the cream, lemon peel, salt and pepper to taste, and nutmeg. Mix very well and let the sauce reduce for 2 minutes. Add the Parmigiano, mix very well, and transfer to a warmed serving platter. Sprinkle with parsley leaves and serve immediately.

asparagus

Asparagus has a very limited spring season in Italy, and the use of those grown in hothouses is rare. Though only available for a short period, Italian asparagus has a very distinctive flavor and appears in a variety of forms. Cultivated asparagus is preferred almost pencil-thin and young. In addition, wild asparagus may still be found, even thinner and with an aggressive flavor. Subtly flavored white asparagus is grown in a number of areas. And finally, there is the rare and exquisite snow asparagus, which peeps out from the snow covering the pre-Alpine hills and mountains. When the season comes, one eats asparagus every day and then relishes the memory of it for a year until it reappears. Asparagus is used with both risotto and pasta, imparting a distinctive flavor.

pasta con asparagi
PASTA WITH ASPARAGUS

SERVES 4 TO 6

2 ½ pounds pencil-thin asparagus, yielding about 6 ounces tips plus ½ pound stems

Coarse-grained salt

1 ½ pounds ripe, fresh tomatoes; or 1 pound canned tomatoes, preferably imported Italian, drained

½ cup olive oil

Salt and freshly ground black pepper

1 pound dried *spaghetti*, preferably imported Italian

TO SERVE

4 to 6 tablespoons freshly grated pecorino sardo or pecorino romano cheese (optional)

This version of Pasta with Asparagus from Umbria also employs tomatoes; the northern versions do not, relying on the distinctive flavor of the vegetable itself. With the cultivated asparagus, often raised in hothouses, one finds the version with tomatoes is perhaps preferable. Should you have the good fortune to obtain wild or snow asparagus, I suggest you omit the tomatoes.

Place a large pot of cold water for the pasta over medium heat.

Prepare the sauce. Cut off the asparagus tips and place them in a bowl of cold water and put the tender green stems in a second bowl, letting both soak until needed. Put the remaining white sections of asparagus in the pot of water for the pasta. When the pasta water reaches a boil, add coarse salt to taste and cook the asparagus ends for 20 minutes.

If using fresh tomatoes, blanch them in a small pot of salted boiling water, then remove the skins and seeds, and cut them into 1-inch squares. If using canned tomatoes, pass them through a food mill, using the disc with the smallest holes, into a glass or crockery bowl.

Place a large skillet with the oil over medium heat, and, when the oil is warm, drain the green asparagus stems, add them to the skillet, and sauté for 4 minutes. Then drain and add the asparagus tips, and sauté for 2 minutes more. Add the tomatoes, lower the heat, season to taste with salt and pepper, cover, and cook for 10 minutes, stirring every so often with a wooden spoon.

Meanwhile, remove the white asparagus ends from the boiling pasta water, using a strainer-skimmer, and discard them. Add the pasta to the asparagus-flavored water, and cook it for 8 to 11 minutes depending on the brand; that is, 1 minute less than for normal al dente. Drain the pasta, add it to the skillet containing the sauce, mix gently but thoroughly, and let the pasta absorb the sauce for 1 minute. Remove from heat, transfer to a warmed serving platter, and serve with or without the cheese.

NOTE

In Italy, wild asparagus is preferred for this dish.

eggplant

Pasta combined with eggplant is exclusively associated with southern Italy and especially with Sicily, where a whole series of dishes called *Pasta alla norma* developed. This category is said to have originated in Catania, the birthplace of the composer Bellini, whose popular opera *Norma* is widely assumed to have given its name to the dish. In fact, *norma* is spelled with a small *n* and the word is taken from the Sicilian language, not from Italian. It actually means "pasta in the normal way." And so we can see from this how important the combination is to the Sicilians.

There are many, many dishes throughout Sicily using eggplant as the base for a pasta sauce. In an area in which beef is not much used, it is as though eggplant sauce plays the role that meat sauce does in such areas as Emilia-Romagna, where meat is more abundant.

I have included three versions of *Pasta alla norma*. In the first, not containing tomatoes, the peeled eggplant is sautéed until it almost dissolves into a purée. In the second, the eggplant discs are fried and then placed over the pasta with a tomato sauce. In the third, the very thin slices or discs of eggplant are broiled and combined with the tomato sauce and pasta. The three preparations result in very different dishes.

Note that Italian eggplants are smaller than regular eggplants but not as small as Japanese or miniature eggplants.

pasta alla norma I
PASTA WITH EGGPLANT, FIRST VERSION

SERVES 4 TO 6

2 pounds Italian eggplant

Coarse-grained salt

¼ cup olive oil

2 large cloves garlic, peeled

Salt and freshly ground
  black pepper

½ cup cold water

1 pound dried *rigatoni* or
  spaghetti, preferably
  imported Italian

TO COOK THE PASTA

Coarse-grained salt

TO SERVE

15 large sprigs Italian parsley, leaves only

Peel the eggplants and slice them cross-wise into discs less than ½ inch thick. Place the eggplant in a bowl, lightly sprinkling coarse salt on each layer. Let stand for 30 minutes, with a weight on them (such as a plate with a can of tomatoes on top).

Rinse the eggplant very well and pat dry with paper towels. Heat the oil in a medium-sized flameproof casserole over medium heat; add the garlic and sauté for 2 minutes. Add the eggplant and sauté for 15 minutes. Taste for salt and pepper. Pour in cold water, cover, and cook for 20 minutes more, stirring every so often with a wooden spoon.

Bring a large pot of cold water to a boil. When the water reaches a boil, add coarse salt to taste, then add the pasta and cook until al dente—9 to 12 minutes depending on the brand. Coarsely chop the parsley on a board. Remove the garlic from the eggplant and discard. Drain the pasta, transfer to a large, warmed serving dish, and pour the eggplant sauce over the top. Toss very well, sprinkle with the parsley, and serve with more freshly ground black pepper. (Do not add any cheese.)

pasta alla norma II
PASTA WITH EGGPLANT, SECOND VERSION

Peel the eggplants and slice them crosswise into discs less than ½ inch thick. Place the eggplant in a bowl, lightly sprinkling coarse salt on each layer. Let stand for 30 minutes, with a weight on them (such as a plate with a can of tomatoes on top).

Start the sauce. Heat ⅓ cup olive oil in a medium-sized saucepan over medium heat; add the garlic and sauté for 3 minutes. If using fresh tomatoes, cut them into 1-inch pieces. Add fresh or canned tomatoes to saucepan and simmer for 25 minutes, stirring every so often with a wooden spoon. Taste for salt and pepper. Pass the contents of pan through a food mill, using the disc with the smallest holes, into a medium-sized crockery or glass bowl. Return the tomato purée to the saucepan and reduce for 5 minutes.

Heat the vegetable oil and ¼ cup olive oil together in a deep-fat fryer over medium heat. Rinse the eggplant very well and pat dry with paper towels. When the oil is hot (about 400° F), add some of the eggplant and cook until lightly golden on each side, about 2 minutes. Using a strainer-skimmer, transfer the cooked eggplant to a serving dish lined with paper towels. Fry the rest of the eggplant in the same way.

Bring a large pot of cold water to a boil. When the water reaches a boil, add coarse salt to taste, then add the pasta and cook until al dente—9 to 12 minutes depending on the brand. Reheat the tomato sauce and add the basil leaves. Drain the pasta, transfer to a large serving dish, and pour the sauce over the top. Toss very well, add the eggplant, and serve with grated *ricotta salata* sprinkled over each portion.

SERVES 4 TO 6

2 pounds Italian eggplant

Coarse-grained salt

1 quart vegetable oil

¼ cup olive oil

1 pound dried *rigatoni* or *spaghetti*, preferably imported Italian

FOR THE SAUCE

⅓ cup olive oil

2 medium-sized cloves garlic, peeled

1 ½ pounds ripe, fresh tomatoes; or 1 ½ pounds canned tomatoes, preferably imported Italian, drained

Salt and freshly ground black pepper

10 large basil leaves, fresh or preserved in salt, torn into thirds

TO COOK THE PASTA

Coarse-grained salt

TO SERVE

4 to 6 tablespoons freshly grated *ricotta salata*

pasta alla norma III
PASTA WITH EGGPLANT, THIRD VERSION

SERVES 4 TO 6

1 ½ pounds Italian eggplants

2 medium-sized cloves garlic, peeled

½ cup olive oil

Salt and freshly ground black pepper

1 pound dried *rigatoni* or *spaghetti*, preferably imported Italian

FOR THE SAUCE

1 medium-sized red onion, peeled

½ cup olive oil

1 ½ pounds ripe, fresh tomatoes, or 1 ½ pounds canned tomatoes, preferably imported Italian, drained

Salt and freshly ground black pepper

10 large basil leaves, fresh or preserved in salt, torn into thirds

TO COOK THE PASTA

Coarse-grained salt

TO SERVE

4 to 6 tablespoons freshly grated *ricotta salata*

Wash the eggplants well but do not peel them. Slice the eggplants crosswise into discs less than ¼ inch thick. Place the eggplant in a crockery or glass bowl. Coarsely chop the garlic on a board and sprinkle it over the eggplant, then add ¼ cup of the oil and salt and pepper to taste. Mix very well and let rest for 5 minutes.

Preheat the broiler. Using tongs, transfer the eggplant directly from the bowl to the broiler rack; broil for about 20 minutes or more if eggplants are very large and tough. Transfer slices back to the same bowl. Pour over the remaining oil and mix well.

Prepare the sauce. Finely chop the onion on a board. Place the oil in a medium-sized saucepan over medium heat, and when the oil is warm, add the chopped onion and sauté for 5 minutes. If using fresh tomatoes, cut them into 1-inch pieces. Add fresh or canned tomatoes to the saucepan and simmer for 25 minutes, mixing every so often. Season with salt and pepper. Pass the contents of the saucepan through a food mill, using the disc with the smallest holes, into a crockery or glass bowl.

Bring a large quantity of cold water to a boil, add coarse salt to taste, then add the pasta and cook until al dente—9 to 12 minutes depending on the brand.

Transfer the tomato sauce to a large skillet, add the basil, and reduce over low heat until the pasta is ready. Drain the pasta, add the sauce, mix well, then add the broiled eggplant. Mix and transfer to a warmed serving dish. Serve with the grated *ricotta salata* sprinkled over the top.

pasta alle melanzane
PASTA WITH EGGPLANT SAUCE

The recipe from Apulia, Pasta alle melanzane, combines eggplant cubes and sweet pepper rings with the pasta, flavored with onion, garlic, and hot red pepper flakes. Apulia sometimes has quite peppery dishes, like its neighbor, Calabria. This is in contrast to Sicily, where—contrary to some assumptions— dishes are preferred more on the sweet side than on the hot. It is not usual for Sicilian recipes to employ hot red pepper flakes.

Clean the peppers, but do not cut into their sides; remove stems, cores, and seeds through the stem end. Cut the peppers into rings less than 1 inch wide, and soak them in a bowl of cold water for 30 minutes. Clean the eggplants and remove their stems; cut them, unpeeled, into 1-inch cubes and soak them in a bowl of cold water with a little coarse salt for 10 minutes. Coarsely chop the onion and garlic together on a board.

Pour the oil into a medium-sized flameproof casserole, add the chopped onion and garlic, then drain the pepper rings and place them on top. Drain and rinse the eggplant cubes very well under cold running water, pat them dry with paper towels, and arrange them over the peppers. Cover the casserole and put it over medium heat; cook for 15 minutes without stirring. Add the ½ cup cold water, salt and pepper to taste, and red pepper flakes, then cover again and cook for 20 minutes more, stirring every so often with a wooden spoon.

Bring a large pot of cold water to a boil, add coarse salt to taste, then add the pasta and cook until al dente—9 to 12 minutes depending on the brand. Drain the pasta, transfer it to a warmed serving platter, pour the sauce over the top, mix, and serve. (Cheese is not used with this dish.)

SERVES 4 TO 6

2 sweet bell peppers, any color

2 medium-sized Italian eggplants (about 1 pound total)

Coarse-grained salt

1 medium-sized red onion, peeled

1 large clove garlic, peeled

⅓ cup olive oil

½ cup cold water

Salt and freshly ground black pepper

½ teaspoon hot red pepper flakes

1 pound dried short tubular pasta, such as *rigatoni* or *penne rigate*

TO COOK THE PASTA

Coarse-grained salt

melanzane ripiene di pasta
EGGPLANT STUFFED WITH PASTA

SERVES 8

FOR THE TOMATO SAUCE

1 medium-sized carrot, scraped

1 small red onion, peeled

1 large stalk celery

1 medium-sized clove garlic, peeled

1 ½ pounds fresh, ripe tomatoes; or 1 ½ pounds canned tomatoes, preferably imported Italian, drained

¼ cup olive oil

Salt and freshly ground black pepper

10 large basil leaves, fresh or preserved in salt

FOR THE SHELLS

8 small, round white Sicilian or purple eggplants (about 10 ounces each)

Coarse-grained salt

FOR THE FILLING

6 ounces dried *cavatappi* (twisted tubular pasta), preferably imported Italian

4 tablespoons freshly grated pecorino sardo or Parmigiano

1 cup cold water

Salt and freshly ground black pepper

TO COOK THE PASTA

Coarse-grained salt

The fascinating Melanzane ripiene di pasta, *also from Sicily, consists of small eggplants, preferably the whitish purple ones, emptied of their pulp to make a container for pasta and sauce. The stuffed eggplants are baked in a tomato sauce. The presentation is attractive and appropriate for a fancier dinner.*

Begin the sauce. Cut the carrot, onion, celery, garlic, and tomatoes into large pieces; put them in a medium-sized nonreactive saucepan. Add the oil, place the pan over medium heat, cover, and cook for 45 minutes, stirring with a wooden spoon every so often. Pass the contents of the pan through a food mill, using the disc with the smallest holes, into a medium-sized flameproof casserole. Return the sauce to the pan, season with salt and pepper, and reduce over medium heat for 30 minutes.

Wash the eggplants, slice 1 inch off the stem ends, and cut off enough of the bottom ends to flatten them. Use a melon baller to scoop out the pulp, making a "container" ½ inch thick. Save 1 pound (about 2 cups) of the pulp. Soak the eggplant shells in a bowl of cold water for 10 minutes.

Bring a large pot of cold water to a boil, add coarse salt to taste, then add the eggplant and simmer for 8 minutes. Transfer the eggplant to a bowl of cold water; let stand for a few minutes, then invert them on paper towels to drain completely.

Finish the sauce. Cut the reserved pulp into small pieces; put it in the casserole with the tomato sauce and the basil. Place the casserole over medium heat; cook for 35 minutes, then season with salt and pepper. Pass the mixture through a food mill, using the disc with the smallest holes, into a medium-sized saucepan. Place the pan over medium heat; reduce until you have about 4 cups of sauce, about 10 minutes.

Preheat the oven to 375°F. Bring a medium-sized stockpot of cold water to a boil. Add coarse salt to taste, then add the pasta; cook it for 4 to 7 minutes depending upon the brand—5 minutes less than for pasta cooked normal al dente. Drain the pasta. Mix with 3 cups of the sauce and the grated cheese. Use a tablespoon of oil to coat a 13½-by-8¾-inch glass baking dish; add the cold water to the sauce and pour it into the dish. Arrange the eggplant in the dish, sprinkle the insides with a little salt and pepper, and fill each shell with the sauced pasta and a good amount of sauce. Cover with aluminum foil and bake for 1 hour. Remove from the oven and serve. Each portion consists of 1 stuffed eggplant and some more sauce poured over the top.

trenette avvantaggiate con melanzane

PASTA WITH EGGPLANT AND PESTO SAUCE

The Ligurian term for whole-wheat trenette *is "trenette avvantaggiate." Since all* avvantaggiate trenette *dishes include a vegetable, some assume that the term refers to the enrichment of the dish with the vegetable, but my Genoese friends assure me that* avvantaggiate *refers only to the whole-wheat* trenette.

Linguistics aside, this dish reveals a wonderful discovery: boiled eggplant, so plain by itself, becomes delicious when dressed with pesto.

Peel the eggplants, remove the stems, and cut them into 1½-inch cubes. Place the eggplant on a serving platter, sprinkle with the coarse salt, and place a second serving platter over the eggplant as a weight. Let stand for 1 hour.

Meanwhile, prepare the pesto. Place the basil and garlic in a mortar or in a blender or food processor and grind until quite fine. Transfer the sauce to a crockery or glass bowl, add salt and pepper to taste, then incorporate the oil a little at a time, always mixing with a wooden spoon. Add the cheese, mix very well, then cover and refrigerate until needed.

Drain the eggplant and rinse it under cold running water, then pat dry with paper towels.

Put the 3 quarts of cold water in a large pot over medium heat; bring to a boil and add coarse salt to taste, and the garlic. When the water reaches a boil again, add the eggplant and simmer for 5 minutes, then add the pasta and cook until al dente—9 to 12 minutes depending on the brand.

Reserve about ½ cup of the pasta-cooking water, drain the pasta and eggplant, discard the garlic, and transfer the pasta and eggplant to a large serving platter. Pour the pesto over the top and mix very well. If the pesto seems too thick, add a few tablespoons of the pasta cooking water. Sprinkle the basil on top and serve immediately. (No extra cheese is used for serving.)

SERVES 4 TO 6

- **2 pounds small but not miniature eggplant**
- **1 tablespoon coarse-grained salt**
- **1 pound dried whole-wheat *trenette (trenette avvantaggiate)* or white *trenette*; or 1 pound dried whole-wheat flat long pasta, such as *bavette* or *linguine*, preferably imported Italian**

FOR THE PESTO

- **1 cup loosely packed fresh basil leaves, stems removed**
- **1 large clove garlic, peeled**
- **Salt and freshly ground black pepper**
- **½ cup extra-virgin olive oil**
- **2 heaping tablespoons freshly grated Parmigiano**

TO COOK THE PASTA

- **3 quarts cold water**
- **Coarse-grained salt**
- **1 large clove garlic, peeled**

TO SERVE

- **Sprigs of basil leaves**

peppers

Pasta is combined with peppers in as many different ways as it is with eggplant, and each region of the south has one or more treatments of its own. Bell peppers are most commonly used in a variety of colors: green, red, yellow, and orange. Green peppers are common and fortunately, the yellow and orange peppers so popular in Italy have become widely available outside the peninsula. They add variety in color, flavor, and texture as they are more delicate than green peppers. Sweet red peppers found in Italy, as elsewhere, are not pimientos. They are slightly less sweet, so be sure to use red peppers, not pimientos, for these dishes.

THE BEST METHOD OF REMOVING THE SKINS is to roast them, ideally over an open flame—until the skins are charred, and peel easily when cool. I personally avoid frying or broiling; the fried peppers absorb too much fat, and the broiled ones retain a smoky taste.

For cooked dishes, preheat the oven to 375° F. Place a baking dish half full of cold water on a lower shelf of the oven. After a few minutes, put the whole peppers on the oven rack above the steaming water. Roast the peppers for about 40 minutes, turning them 3 or 4 times. Remove the peppers from the oven and put them in a plastic bag. Let them stand until they are cool enough to handle (approximately 15 minutes). Peel the peppers in a large bowl of cold water, removing the skins, stems, and seeds.

For every combination of pasta and peppers, one really begins by preparing a *peperonata* to use as the sauce. *Peperonata* is a pepper stew that exists in many versions all over Italy, including the northern regions, which do not combine peppers with pasta.

The first two versions from Sicily and Calabria have several points of interest. They reverse the normal roles of the two regions regarding hot red pepper flakes. The Sicilian version employs them while the Calabrian does not. Also, the Sicilian version uses no tomatoes. This is much more characteristic of the Naples region, and even our Calabrian recipe is influenced more by Naples than by Sicily. The Sicilian recipe without tomatoes is expressed in its purest, simplest form, using only olive oil and black pepper and not even garlic. There are other versions without tomatoes from other areas of Italy, but none as pure.

The Calabrian dish, Pasta in *Peperonata* Sauce, is traditionally served with a second dish, the Sweet Bell Pepper *Frittata*. After cooking, the peppers are removed from the sauce and reused in the Italian omelet, or *frittata*, which is eaten after the pasta course; this is unusual in Italy. (A more typical approach is taken in *Lasagne* with Duck; the duck is cooked in the sauce and removed to be eaten at another meal.) The Neapolitan recipe employs tomatoes, bell peppers, onion, and basil. Other versions use peppers, garlic, and basil. The Calabrian recipe, mentioned earlier, contains parsley and garlic.

From these alterations, we are reminded how carefully each ingredient is weighed in Italian regional cooking and how much the flavor differs among these small variations. Each ingredient has its role and its reason. There are no arbitrary improvisations or substitutions in these recipes; they have been developed over a century of trial and error.

pasta e peperoni alla calabrese

PASTA IN PEPERONATA SAUCE, WITH SWEET BELL PEPPER FRITTATA

SERVES 6 TO 8

8 large sweet bell peppers of different colors

1 medium-sized red onion, peeled

10 large sprigs Italian parsley, leaves only

1 large clove garlic, peeled

5 tablespoons olive oil

1 ½ pounds ripe, fresh tomatoes; or 1 ½ pounds canned tomatoes, preferably imported Italian, drained

Salt and freshly ground black pepper

1 pound dried *rigatoni*, preferably imported Italian

TO COOK THE PASTA

Coarse-grained salt

FOR THE *FRITTATA*

6 extra-large eggs

Salt and freshly ground black pepper

1 scant tablespoon olive or vegetable oil

TO SERVE

Sprigs of fresh basil leaves

Roast the peppers following directions on page 82, and remove the skins, seeds, and stems. Cut the peppers into ½-inch strips and put them between layers of paper towels to dry.

Finely chop the onion, parsley, and garlic all together on a board. Heat the oil in a large skillet over medium heat; add the chopped ingredients and sauté for 5 minutes. If using fresh tomatoes, cut them into 1-inch pieces. Pass fresh or canned tomatoes through a food mill, using the disc with the smallest holes, into a crockery or glass bowl. Add tomatoes to the skillet and sauté for 5 minutes more. Taste for salt and pepper. Add the peppers, cover the skillet, and simmer for 20 minutes, stirring every so often with a wooden spoon. Pour the mixture into a colander and set over a large bowl; drain well and reserve juices. Set peppers aside. Transfer the pepper juices to the skillet and put it over low heat.

Bring a large pot of cold water to a boil. When the water reaches a boil, add coarse salt to taste, then add the pasta and cook until al dente—9 to 12 minutes depending on the brand. While the pasta is cooking prepare the *frittata*. Set aside. (see Note).

Drain the pasta, add it to the skillet with the sauce, and mix very well to incorporate all the sauce with the pasta. Transfer to a warmed serving platter and serve immediately with fresh basil leaves.

NOTE: TO PREPARE *FRITTATA*

Break the eggs into a large bowl. With a fork, break the yolks of the eggs; beat them lightly so no air bubbles or foam can form. Season with salt and pepper. Place a 10-inch omelet pan over medium heat. Add the oil to the pan. When the oil is hot, add the beaten eggs and reserved pepper mixture.

Keep puncturing the bottom with a fork as the eggs set to allow the liquid on top to move through to the bottom.

When the eggs are well set and the *frittata* is well detached from the bottom of the pan, about 2 minutes, put a plate, upside down, over the pan. Holding the plate firmly, invert the pan and turn the *frittata* out onto the plate. Return the pan to the heat and carefully slide the *frittata* into the pan and cook the other side. When the eggs are well set (about 1 minute), invert the *frittata* onto a serving dish. Serve the *frittata* at room temperature as a second course. Top with fresh basil leaves.

perciatelli ai peperoncini verdi
PERCIATELLI WITH "ITALIAN" PEPPERS

SERVES 4 TO 6

1 ½ pounds small or 2 pounds large, light green "Italian" (frying) peppers

¾ cup olive oil

1 ¾ pounds fresh, ripe tomatoes; or 1 ¾ pounds canned tomatoes, preferably imported Italian, drained

2 large cloves garlic, peeled but left whole

Salt and freshly ground black pepper

5 large basil leaves, fresh or preserved in salt

1 pound dried *perciatelli*, *bucatini*, or *spaghetti*, preferably imported Italian

TO COOK THE PASTA

Coarse-grained salt

In Campania, the Naples area, there exists a special, smaller light green pepper, sometimes referred to as an Italian pepper, which is marvelous combined with pasta. Longer and thinner than those of the bell shape, they are also less meaty and perhaps more delicate than green bell peppers. Classic recipes do exist for dishes in which the peppers are used with their skins. The Neapolitan or Italian peppers have delicate skins that do not separate in cooking.

If using small peppers, put them in a bowl of cold water, without removing seeds and stems, for 30 minutes. If using large peppers, remove stems and larger seeds before soaking them.

Place a large skillet with the oil over medium heat; when the oil is warm, drain the peppers and add to the skillet. Cover the skillet and sauté for 15 minutes, turning peppers over 2 or 3 times until they are cooked but still firm. Use a strainer-skimmer to transfer the peppers to a crockery or glass bowl. If using fresh tomatoes, cut into pieces. Add the fresh or canned tomatoes and the garlic to the pan juices. Simmer the tomatoes for 25 minutes, stirring every so often with a wooden spoon.

Pass the contents of the skillet through a food mill, using the disc with the smallest holes, into a crockery or glass bowl. Pour the purée back into the skillet and place over medium heat. Put the peppers back in, taste for salt and pepper, and add the basil leaves. Simmer the sauce for 10 minutes more.

Meanwhile, bring a large pot of cold water to a boil, add coarse salt to taste, then add the pasta and cook for 8 to 11 minutes depending on the brand; that is, 1 minute less than for normal al dente. Drain the pasta, add it to the skillet with the sauce, mix well, and sauté for 1 minute more. Transfer to a warmed serving platter and serve.

Peppers after roasting.

pasta ai peperoni

PASTA WITH SWEET BELL PEPPERS

Roast the peppers, following the directions on page 82, and remove the skins, stems, and seeds. Cut the peppers into 1-inch strips. Heat the oil in a large skillet over medium heat, add the peppers, and sauté for 2 minutes. Add salt, pepper, and red pepper flakes, mix very well, cover, and cook over low heat for 20 minutes, stirring every so often with a wooden spoon.

Bring a large pot of cold water to a boil, add coarse salt to taste, then add the pasta and cook until al dente—9 to 12 minutes depending on the brand. Drain pasta and add to the peppers. Mix very well, incorporating the peppers, which by now should have a very creamy texture. Transfer to a warmed serving dish and serve immediately.

SERVES 4 TO 6

6 very large or 8 medium-sized sweet bell peppers of different colors

½ cup extra-virgin olive oil from southern Italy

Salt and freshly ground black pepper

¾ teaspoon hot red pepper flakes

1 pound dried tubular pasta, such as *rigatoni*, preferably imported Italian

TO COOK THE PASTA

Coarse-grained salt

Bologna's central fruit and vegetable market.

pasta con la peperonata alla napoletana

PASTA WITH SWEET BELL PEPPERS, NAPLES STYLE

SERVES 4 TO 6

8 medium-sized sweet
  bell peppers of different
  colors

1 medium-sized red onion,
  peeled

1 pound very ripe, fresh
  tomatoes; or 1 pound
  canned tomatoes, preferably imported Italian,
  drained

4 tablespoons olive oil

5 large basil leaves, fresh or
  preserved in salt, torn
  into thirds

Salt and freshly ground
  black pepper

1 pound dried *conchiglie,
  fusilli,* or any short pasta,
  not tubular

TO COOK THE PASTA

Coarse-grained salt

Roast the peppers, following directions on page 82, and remove their skins, stems, and seeds. Cut the peppers into 1-inch strips. Place the strips between layers of paper towels and pat them dry.

Coarsely chop the onion and place it in a small bowl of cold water for 30 minutes. If using fresh tomatoes, cut them into 1-inch pieces. Pass fresh or canned tomatoes through a food mill, using the disc with the smallest holes, into a crockery or glass bowl. Place a flameproof casserole with the oil over medium heat; when the oil is warm, drain the onion and add it to the casserole. Sauté for 4 minutes, then cover and cook for 15 minutes more. Add the tomatoes and basil leaves. Cover and cook for 20 minutes, stirring every so often. Taste for salt and pepper. Add the peppers, mix very well, and cook, uncovered, for 10 minutes more.

Meanwhile, bring a large pot of cold water to a boil. When the water reaches a boil, add coarse salt to taste, then add the pasta and cook until al dente—9 to 12 minutes depending on the brand. Drain the pasta and add it to the casserole. Mix all the ingredients very well. Let the sauce be absorbed by the pasta for 30 seconds, then transfer from the casserole to a large, warmed serving dish and serve immediately.

broccoli and cauliflower

Broccoli means "hard flower" in Italian and is used in the area south of Rome to mean any vegetable with a hard flower top, such as white, green, or purple cauliflower. Most often, in Sicily and southern Italy, the word refers to some type of cauliflower. The word is used so interchangeably, however, that dishes that most often involve cauliflower might just as well have broccoli itself, if that should be more available. There are, in addition, species of *broccoli* (in the Italian sense of the word) that exist locally and are not available outside of the region. These would be used locally when available in place of other types of *broccoli*. *Cime di rape* (*broccolirab,* in dialect) is also known as *broccoletti.*

pasta e broccoli
PASTA AND BROCCOLI

SERVES 4 TO 6

1 large bunch broccoli, with at least 4 stems

Coarse-grained salt

1 pound dried pasta, such as *cavatappi* or *fusilli*, preferably imported Italian

2 large cloves garlic, peeled

¾ cup olive oil

Salt and freshly ground black pepper

½ to ¾ teaspoon hot red pepper flakes

4 heaping tablespoons capers packed in wine vinegar, drained

TO SERVE

20 large sprigs Italian parsley, leaves only, coarsely chopped

In this version of pasta and broccoli, found all over southern Italy, the anchovy is omitted in favor of capers, garlic, and parsley, and is made with short pasta rather than spaghetti. However, the main difference in preparation is that the vegetable stems and flowers are cooked together with the pasta, rather than before. As in the other versions, the pasta and vegetables here are then sautéed with their seasonings. The classic Spaghetti with Broccoli is flavored with anchovy and red pepper flakes.

Clean the broccoli, discarding the tough bottom stems, and separate the stems from the florets; place them in 2 different bowls of cold water for 30 minutes.

Bring a large pot of cold water to a boil, add coarse salt to taste, then add the pasta and immediately afterward add the broccoli stems. The pasta should be cooked al dente—9 to 12 minutes depending on the brand. Two minutes after adding the stems, add the florets. All three—pasta, stems, and florets—should emerge properly cooked at the end of the pasta cooking time.

Meanwhile, mince the garlic. Place the oil in a small saucepan over medium heat; when the oil is warm, add the garlic and sauté until lightly golden, about 1 minute. Season with salt, pepper, and the red pepper flakes. Add the capers and sauté for 2 minutes more. By that time, the pasta and broccoli should be cooked.

Drain the contents of the stockpot, transfer to a large warmed serving dish, pour the sauce over the top, mix well, sprinkle with the parsley, and serve immediately.

pasta con broccoli saltati
PASTA WITH SAUTÉED CAULIFLOWER

It should not surprise you to see the recipe here, Pasta con broccoli saltati, *translated as Pasta with Sautéed Cauliflower. In Sicily,* "broccoli" *usually means cauliflower.*

Clean the cauliflower, detach all the florets, and discard everything else. Soak them in a bowl of cold water for 30 minutes. Peel the potatoes, cut them into 1-inch cubes, and put them in a second bowl of cold water.

Bring a large pot of cold water to a boil, add coarse salt to taste, then drain the cauliflower and add it to the pot. Cook for 3 minutes, then use a strainer-skimmer to transfer the florets to a platter. Place a towel dampened with cold water over the cauliflower. Drain the potatoes, add them to the boiling cauliflower water, and cook for 5 minutes. Again use a strainer-skimmer to transfer them to the platter with the cauliflower. Save the cooking water.

Prepare the sauce. If using fresh tomatoes, cut them into pieces. Put the fresh or canned tomatoes in a medium-sized saucepan along with the garlic and oil, and place the pan over medium heat; cook for 15 minutes. Season with salt and pepper and cook for 5 minutes more. Pass the contents of the saucepan through a food mill, using the disc with the smallest holes, into a second saucepan. Set aside.

Reheat the cauliflower-potato cooking water to a boil, taste for salt, then add the pasta and cook until al dente—9 to 12 minutes depending on the brand. As the pasta cooks, heat the oil in a large skillet over medium heat, and, when the oil is hot, add the whole cloves of garlic together with the potatoes and cauliflower. Season with salt and pepper, and sauté, mixing every so often with a wooden spoon.

Reheat the tomato sauce. When the pasta is ready, drain it and transfer it to a large bowl, pour the sauce over the top, sprinkle with the cheese, and mix very well. Then transfer the pasta and sauce to a large, warmed serving platter. Use a strainer-skimmer to transfer the sautéed vegetables from the skillet onto the platter of pasta. Serve very hot.

SERVES 4 TO 6

- 1 medium-sized cauliflower, to yield 1 ½ pounds florets
- ½ pound potatoes (not new potatoes)
- Coarse-grained salt
- 1 pound dried pasta, such as *spaghetti*, preferably imported Italian
- ½ cup olive oil
- 2 medium-sized cloves garlic, peeled but left whole
- Salt and freshly ground black pepper
- ½ cup freshly grated pecorino Siciliano or romano cheese

FOR THE SAUCE

- 1 ½ pounds ripe, fresh tomatoes; or 1 ½ pounds canned tomatoes, preferably imported Italian, drained
- 1 medium-sized clove garlic, peeled but left whole
- ½ cup olive oil
- Salt and freshly ground black pepper

TO COOK THE PASTA

- Coarse-grained salt

pasta al cavolfiore
PASTA AND CAULIFLOWER

SERVES 4 TO 6

1 medium-sized cauliflower

Coarse-grained salt

1 pound dried pasta, such as *orecchiette*, or any short tubular pasta

FOR THE SAUCE

1 ½ pounds ripe, fresh tomatoes; or 1 ½ pounds canned tomatoes, preferably imported Italian, drained

20 large sprigs Italian parsley, leaves only

2 large cloves garlic, peeled

½ cup olive oil

Salt and freshly ground black pepper

½ cup freshly grated pecorino romano or pecorino sardo cheese

Dishes made with cauliflower demonstrate perfectly how to use almost the same ingredients and, by varying the treatments, change the entire flavor of a dish. Both the Sicilian and Apulian versions of pasta with cauliflower use tomatoes, garlic, olive oil, and black pepper. But the Sicilians sauté the cauliflower with potatoes, which don't exist in this version, in the oil and garlic before adding it to the tomato sauce. In the Apulian version, the boiled cauliflower is simply added to the tomato sauce, along with the parsley. The difference is accentuated by using two different kinds of pasta and two different sheep's milk cheeses.

Remove all the leaves from the cauliflower. Use a knife to detach all the florets, discarding the rest. Soak them in a bowl of cold water for 30 minutes. Bring a large pot of cold water to a boil, add coarse salt to taste, then add the cauliflower and cook until done but still very firm, 10 to 15 minutes. Use a strainer-skimmer to transfer the cauliflower to a crockery or glass bowl; save the cooking water. Cover the bowl and let stand until needed.

Begin the sauce. If using fresh tomatoes, cut them into pieces. Pass fresh or canned tomatoes through a food mill, using the disc with the smallest holes, into a crockery or glass bowl. Finely chop the parsley and garlic together on a board. Heat the oil in a large skillet over low heat, and, when warm, add the chopped ingredients and sauté for 5 minutes. Add the tomatoes, season with salt and pepper, and simmer for 10 minutes.

Meanwhile, bring the cauliflower water back to a boil. Add the pasta and cook for 8 to 11 minutes depending on the brand; that is, 1 minute less than for normal al dente. When the pasta is ready, place the cauliflower in the skillet with the sauce, still on low heat. Drain the pasta, raise the heat, and add the pasta to the skillet. Mix gently but thoroughly. Taste for salt and pepper, and add the grated cheese. Mix well and let cook for 1 minute more, mixing constantly with 2 spoons. Transfer the pasta to a warmed serving dish and serve immediately.

VARIATIONS

1. One-half cup dry white wine can be added to the sauce and evaporated away.
2. Parsley or cheese can be omitted.
3. Green or purple cauliflower can be used instead of white.
4. A large pinch of hot red pepper flakes can be added.

pasta chi vruccoli arriminata
MACCHERONI WITH CAULIFLOWER AND SAFFRON

This recipe, Pasta chi vruccoli arriminata, *also from Sicily, combines the pasta and cauliflower with onions, raisins, saffron, and pine nuts to make one of the classics of the island. This dish is as typical of Sicily as* Pasta con le sarde.

Place the cauliflower in a bowl of cold water and soak for 30 minutes. Bring a large pot of cold water to a boil, add coarse salt to taste, and, when the water returns to a boil, add the cauliflower and cook for 5 minutes. Transfer the cauliflower, whole, to a bowl of cold water to cool for 30 minutes. Detach the individual florets from the head, and place them on paper towels to drain well. Discard the rest of the cauliflower.

Soak the raisins in a small bowl of lukewarm water for 30 minutes. Meanwhile, slice the onion into thin rings. Heat the oil in a heavy saucepan over low heat, and, when warm, add the onion and sauté for 5 minutes. Then add the saffron along with the broth. Season with salt and pepper to taste and simmer for 10 minutes.

Bring a stockpot of cold water to a boil; add coarse salt to taste. While the water is heating, transfer the onion-saffron mixture to a large skillet and put it over medium heat. If you are using whole anchovies packed in salt, fillet them under cold running water. Add anchovy fillets to the skillet along with the cauliflower and pine nuts. Drain the raisins and pat them dry with paper towels, then add them to the skillet and cook for 5 minutes, stirring all the ingredients together.

When the stockpot of water is boiling, add the pasta and cook until al dente—9 to 12 minutes depending on the brand. Drain and transfer pasta to the skillet. Mix very well over medium heat for 1 minute, then transfer contents to a large, warmed serving platter. Sprinkle the cheese and basil leaves over the top and serve immediately.

VARIATIONS
1. Saffron can be omitted.
2. Four large cloves of garlic, finely chopped, can be substituted for the red onion. Saffron can be used or omitted here as well.

SERVES 6

1 large cauliflower, cleaned and left whole

Coarse-grained salt

4 tablespoons raisins

1 large red onion, peeled

¾ cup olive oil

½ teaspoon ground saffron

1 cup hot chicken or beef broth, preferably home-made

Salt and freshly ground black pepper

4 anchovies preserved in salt; or 8 anchovy fillets packed in oil, drained

4 tablespoons pine nuts (*pignolis*)

1 pound dried *maccheroni*, preferably imported Italian

TO COOK THE PASTA

Coarse-grained salt

TO SERVE

½ cup freshly grated pecorino siciliano or Parmigiano cheese

10 large fresh basil leaves, torn into thirds

pasta e verza
PASTA WITH SAVOY CABBAGE

SERVES 4 TO 6

1 medium-sized savoy cabbage, about 2 pounds, cleaned

Coarse-grained salt

4 ounces *prosciutto* or *pancetta*, in 1 piece

2 tablespoons extra-virgin olive oil

8 tablespoons (4 ounces) sweet butter

3 bay leaves

4 quarts chicken or beef broth, preferably home-made

Salt and freshly ground black pepper

1 pound dried *gramigna* pasta or broken-up *spaghetti* or *vermicelli*, preferably imported Italian

5 tablespoons freshly grated Parmigiano

TO SERVE

Freshly grated Parmigiano

Freshly ground black pepper

Wrinkly savoy cabbage is more popular in Italy than the smooth type, which is known as "lasagnino" because its smooth leaves are aligned in layers that resemble lasagne. Lasagnino is more tender than savoy and is often used raw, much like cole slaw, but dressed with olive oil rather than mayonnaise. For most cooked cabbage dishes, Italians use the much more flavorful savoy, which requires a rather long cooking time, both to become tender and to lose its strong smell.

Stewing the savoy with pancetta, olive oil, and butter creates a thick, sweetly flavored pasta sauce that is enriched with the flavor of bay leaves.

Remove the tough outer leaves from the cabbage and the large middle ribs from the remaining leaves and discard. You should have more than 1½ pounds of cabbage. Soak the cabbage leaves in a bowl of cold water for 30 minutes. Bring a large pot of cold water to a boil, add coarse salt to taste, drain the cabbage, slice it into ½-inch strips, and add it to the pot. Boil for 5 minutes. Drain the cabbage and cool it under cold running water.

Meanwhile, using a meat grinder or a food processor, finely grind the *prosciutto*. Place the oil and half of the butter in a medium-sized casserole over very low heat. Add the *prosciutto* and the bay leaves

and sauté for 1 minute. Place the cabbage over the sautéed meat without mixing it in. Pour in half of the broth, season with salt and pepper, cover, and cook for 35 minutes. Mix very well and taste for salt and pepper. Continue to cook over low heat, covered, for 15 more minutes. The cabbage should be quite thick—almost a purée. If not, cook for 10 more minutes, uncovered.

Bring the remaining broth to a boil over medium heat in a large casserole, taste for salt, add the pasta, and cook for 8 to 11 minutes depending on the brand; that is, 1 minute less than for normal al dente.

In the meantime, place a large serving platter over a pot of boiling water and add the remaining butter; this process will heat the serving platter while melting the butter.

Add half of the cabbage sauce to the platter, then drain the pasta and mix it on the serving platter with the cabbage and butter. Transfer the contents of the serving platter plus the remaining cabbage sauce to the casserole and warm over low heat. Sprinkle the cheese over the top, mix very well, discard the bay leaves, and serve directly from the casserole, with additional cheese and freshly ground black pepper sprinkled over each serving.

pasta e carciofi
PASTA AND ARTICHOKES

In this Sicilian recipe, the artichokes are cut into thin slices so that they almost dissolve into the sauce. A special feature is the use of white wine. It is often asserted that artichokes kill the bouquet of wine, yet there exist a number of traditional recipes in which this vegetable is cooked in white wine. While no herb is used in the cooking, parsley, which goes so well with artichokes, is added uncooked at the end, along with small cubes of provolone, blending in its distinct flavor and replacing the usual grated cheese.

Place the artichokes and the lemon halves in a bowl of cold water and set aside for 30 minutes. Meanwhile, finely chop the garlic on a board.

Clean the artichokes, following the instructions on page 70, cutting them into quarters, and cutting each quarter into thin slices. Put them back in the lemon water. Heat the oil in a medium-sized flameproof casserole over medium heat; when the oil is warm, add the garlic and sauté for 2 minutes. Drain the artichokes, add them to the casserole, and sauté for 5 minutes. Pour in the wine and boil, letting it evaporate for 10 minutes. Season to taste with salt and pepper, then add the water, cover the pan, and cook for 20 minutes, stirring every so often with a wooden spoon.

Bring a large pot of cold water to a boil. Preheat the oven to 375°F. When the water reaches a boil, add coarse salt to taste, then add the pasta and cook for 8 to 11 minutes depending on the brand; that is, 1 minute less than for normal al dente.

Use the 2 tablespoons of butter to heavily coat a 13½-by-8¾-inch glass baking dish. Coarsely chop the parsley on a board, and cut the cheese into cubes smaller than ½ inch. Drain the pasta, transfer it to a large bowl, add the artichokes with their juice, then sprinkle on the chopped parsley and the provolone cubes. Mix gently but thoroughly, then transfer to the prepared baking dish and bake for 10 minutes. Remove from the oven and serve immediately.

SERVES 4 TO 6

3 large artichokes

1 large lemon, cut in half

2 medium-sized cloves garlic, peeled

½ cup olive oil

½ cup dry white wine

Salt and freshly ground black pepper

1 cup lukewarm water

1 pound dried *rigatoni*, preferably imported Italian

TO COOK THE PASTA

Coarse-grained salt

TO BAKE

2 tablespoons (1 ounce) sweet butter

15 large sprigs Italian parsley, leaves only

4 ounces *provolone* cheese

pasta ripiena di carciofi
PASTA STUFFED WITH ARTICHOKES

This stuffed pasta from the Veneto, alone among these artichoke recipes, requires fresh pasta, since it is a type of lasagne with only top and bottom layers of pasta. The artichoke stuffing becomes almost a purée, with eggs, cheese, and some of the balsamella added to the vegetable, then flavored with nutmeg. The rest of the balsamella is placed on top, along with a small amount of tomato sauce. This wonderful dish is well suited to a formal presentation.

Prepare the pasta with the ingredients and quantities listed, following the instructions on page 12. Stretch layer to $\frac{1}{16}$ inch thick—on the pasta machine, take it to the next to the last setting. Cut the pasta into squares as for *lasagne*. Preboil the squares in a large amount of salted boiling water for 2 seconds. Transfer the pasta to a large bowl of cold water to which the oil has been added. Cool the pasta in the water, then transfer to wet cotton dish towels until needed.

Prepare the stuffing. Soak the artichokes in a bowl of cold water with the lemon halves for 30 minutes. Clean the artichokes (page 70), and cut them into pieces no larger than an almond. Place the artichoke pieces back in the acidulated water until needed. Coarsely chop the parsley and finely chop the garlic separately on a board. Place a medium-sized saucepan with the oil and butter over medium heat. When the butter is melted, add the chopped ingredients and sauté for 2 minutes. Drain the artichokes and add to saucepan, season with salt and pepper, cover, and cook for 15 minutes. Add the cold water, cover again, and cook artichokes for 10 more minutes, by which time they should be very soft. Transfer to a large dish and let rest until completely cooled, about 30 minutes.

As the artichokes cool, prepare the *balsamella* with the ingredients and quantities listed (see Note), but do not season the sauce yet.

Prepare the tomato sauce. If fresh tomatoes are used, cut them into 1-inch pieces. Place fresh or canned tomatoes in a small saucepan with 4 tablespoons of the butter and the basil over medium heat; cook for 20 minutes. Pass tomatoes through a food mill, using the disc with the smallest holes, into a bowl, then return the sauce to the pan, season with salt and pepper, and simmer until the sauce is quite thick, about 15 minutes. Let rest until needed.

Assemble the dish. Preheat the oven to 375°F. With the remaining tablespoon of butter, heavily butter the bottom and sides of a jelly roll pan.

Finish the stuffing. Transfer artichokes to a large bowl, add the eggs, then the Parmigiano, and mix very well; add half the *balsamella,* taste for salt and pepper, season with nutmeg, and mix again. Line the jelly roll pan with half the pasta and let the squares hang over the sides 2 inches all around. Pour the stuffing into the pan, level it, then cover with the remaining pasta squares. Fold the overlapping pieces of pasta inward, spread the remaining *balsamella* over the top, and pour the tomato sauce on top of that.

Bake for 25 minutes. Allow to cool for a few minutes before serving.

NOTE: TO PREPARE *BALSAMELLA*

Melt the butter in a heavy saucepan, preferably copper or enamel, over low heat. When the butter reaches the frothing point, add the flour all at once. Mix very well with a wooden spoon.

Cook until the flour is completely incorporated (1 to 3 minutes). If any lumps form, dissolve them by crushing them against the side of the pan with the wooden spoon. Remove the pan from the heat and let stand for 10 to 15 minutes.

While the butter–flour mixture is standing, heat the milk in another pan until it is very close to the boiling point. Put the saucepan with the butter–flour mixture over low heat and add all of the hot milk at once. Stir until the sauce is smooth.

When the sauce reaches the boiling point, add the salt and continue to stir gently while the sauce cooks slowly for about 10 minutes longer. Remove from the heat and transfer the sauce to a crockery bowl, pressing a piece of buttered wax paper directly over the surface to prevent a skin from forming. Let the sauce cool completely.

FOR THE *BALSAMELLA* (BÉCHAMEL)

8 tablespoons (4 ounces) sweet butter

¼ cup unbleached all-purpose flour

3 ½ cups milk

Salt, freshly ground black pepper, and freshly grated nutmeg

FOR THE TOMATO SAUCE

1 ½ pounds ripe, fresh tomatoes; or 1 ½ pounds canned tomatoes, preferably imported Italian, drained

5 tablespoons (2½ ounces) sweet butter

4 large basil leaves, fresh or preserved in salt

Salt and freshly ground black pepper

pasta con i carciofi
PASTA WITH ARTICHOKES AND EGGS

SERVES 4 TO 6

1 large lemon, cut in half

3 large artichokes

1 medium-sized red onion, peeled

½ cup olive oil

Salt and freshly ground black pepper

1 cup lukewarm water

2 extra-large eggs

2 tablespoons freshly grated pecorino siciliano or romano cheese

1 pound dried *rigatoni*, preferably imported Italian

TO COOK THE PASTA

Coarse-grained salt

In Pasta with Artichokes and Eggs, as in the other Sicilian version, the vegetable is cut into small pieces which almost dissolve. They are sautéed together with onions. Two eggs are mixed with the grated pecorino (as in Pasta alla carbonara) then mixed gently with the hot pasta before the cooked artichokes are added.

Squeeze the lemon into a bowl of cold water and drop in the lemon halves. Add the artichokes to soak for 30 minutes. Meanwhile, finely chop the onion on a board. Clean the artichokes, following the instructions on page 70, and cut them into quarters. Then cut each quarter into thin slices and return them to the lemon water.

Heat the oil in a medium-sized flameproof casserole over medium heat; when the oil is warm, add the onion and sauté for 5 minutes. Drain the artichokes and add to the casserole, mix very well, and sauté for 4 minutes more. Season to taste with salt and pepper, and add the water. Cover the casserole and cook for 30 minutes, stirring every so often with a wooden spoon. When finished, the liquid should be completely absorbed and the artichokes very soft.

Bring a large pot of cold water to a boil. Mix the eggs with the cheese and salt and pepper to taste in a large serving bowl. When the water reaches a boil, add coarse salt to taste, then add the pasta and cook until al dente—9 to 12 minutes depending on the brand. Drain the pasta, transfer to the bowl with the egg mixture, mix gently but thoroughly, then add the artichokes with their juice. Mix again and serve with a few twists of black pepper.

pasta alla patate
PASTA WITH POTATOES

In Tuscany, pasta is combined with potatoes in several ways. Pasta has some protein and potatoes have valuable vitamins and minerals, and so we are not faced with a completely unbalanced dish.

If the potatoes are boiled, as in the basic recipe for the Pasta alla patate, *the pasta is then cooked in the potato water and the two are sautéed together with olive oil and garlic; fresh parsley and red pepper flakes are added at the end. The result is a warming and most satisfying dish. In one variation, the potatoes can be sautéed without boiling; in another, the potatoes are mashed before being incorporated.*

Peel the potatoes, then cut them into ½-inch slices, placing them in a bowl of cold water until needed. Bring a large quantity of cold water to a boil, add coarse salt to taste, then drain the potatoes, add them to the boiling water, and cook for 2 minutes. Use a strainer-skimmer to transfer the potatoes to a serving dish; reserve the potato water.

Finely chop the garlic on a board. Place the oil in a large skillet over medium heat. When the oil is warm, add the garlic and sauté for 2 minutes, then add the potatoes; season with salt, pepper, and red pepper flakes; and sauté for 5 minutes, mixing every so often with a wooden spoon.

Meanwhile, bring the potato water back to a boil, add the pasta, and cook for 8 to 11 minutes depending on the brand; that is, 1 minute less than for normal al dente. As the pasta cooks, finish the potato sauce. Add the cold water to the skillet with the potatoes, cover, and cook for 10 minutes more. Coarsely chop the parsley on a board. When pasta is ready, drain and place it in the skillet with the potatoes. Raise the heat to high, mix well, and sauté for 1 minute more. Sprinkle the parsley over the top, mix well again, then transfer to a large, warmed platter and serve immediately.

VARIATIONS

1. The sliced potatoes can be added to the skillet raw instead of parboiled. In this case, ¼ cup of lukewarm chicken or beef broth should be added to the skillet after 2 minutes to help cook the potatoes. The ¼ cup cold water is still added later, and the pasta is then cooked in fresh water rather than the potato water.

2. With either the original recipe or the above variation, once cooked, the potatoes can be passed through a food mill.

SERVES 4 TO 6

1 pound potatoes (not new potatoes)

Coarse-grained salt

2 large cloves garlic, peeled

½ cup olive oil

Salt and freshly ground black pepper

½ teaspoon hot red pepper flakes

1 pound dried *spaghetti*, preferably imported Italian

¼ cup cold water

30 large sprigs Italian parsley, leaves only

spaghetti al finocchio
SPAGHETTI WITH FRESH FENNEL

SERVES 4 TO 6

1 medium-sized bulb fennel
  (about 1 ¼ pounds), with
  green top leaves

1 ½ pounds ripe, fresh tomatoes; or 1 ½ pounds
  canned tomatoes, preferably imported Italian,
  drained

1 cup lukewarm water

Salt

6 tablespoons olive oil

½ teaspoon hot red pepper
  flakes

½ teaspoon dried oregano

Freshly ground black pepper

1 pound dried *spaghetti*,
  preferably imported
  Italian

TO COOK THE PASTA

Coarse-grained salt

Recipes for fennel bulbs with pasta are very rare, but here is a wonderful one from Sicily, in which the fennel is cooked in tomato with oil, oregano, and red pepper flakes, and then puréed. The result is a tomato sauce flavored with lightly sautéed, puréed fennel. It is interesting to speculate as to why fennel is not traditionally used more in combination with pasta. Is there something in the texture that was not favored, and is this overcome by purée-ing the fennel?

Clean the fennel, discarding the tough outer leaves and the dark green stems but not the feathery leafy parts; you should have about ¾ pound. Cut fennel into 1-inch pieces and put in a bowl of cold water for 30 minutes. If using fresh toma-toes, cut them into small pieces. Put fresh or canned tomatoes in a medium-sized flameproof casserole; drain the fennel and add it to the casserole along with the water and a little salt. Place casserole over medium heat and cook for 30 minutes.

Pass casserole contents through a food mill, using the disc with medium-sized holes, into a crockery or glass bowl. Place a medium-sized skillet with the oil, red pepper flakes, and oregano over low heat, and sauté for 1 minute. Add the puréed sauce, taste for salt and pepper, and reduce liquid for 10 minutes.

Bring a large pot of cold water to a boil, add coarse salt to taste, then add the pasta and cook for 8 to 11 minutes depending on the brand; that is, 1 minute less than for normal al dente. Drain the pasta, transfer it to the skillet, raise the heat, and sauté for 1 minute more, mixing with 2 forks to incorporate all the sauce. Transfer to a warmed serving platter and serve hot.

penne alle cipolle
PASTA WITH ONION SAUCE

A simple onion sauce is a favorite both in Tuscany and around Naples. The sweetness of the red onions is accentuated by white wine and, in Tuscany, by mixing some butter with the olive oil. In the Naples area, the traditional lard is used instead.

Cut the onions into quarters and soak them in a bowl of cold water for 30 minutes. Drain and coarsely chop the onions on a board. Place a large skillet with the onions, butter, and oil over medium heat. Cover and sauté for 10 minutes. Stir very well, lower the heat, add the first cup of wine, cover, and simmer for 1½ hours, stirring every so often with a wooden spoon. Add the remaining cup of wine and finally the cold water, ½ cup at a time, every 30 minutes. When all the liquid is added, season to taste with salt and abundant black pepper.

Bring a large pot of cold water to a boil, add coarse salt to taste, then add the pasta and cook until al dente—9 to 12 minutes depending on the brand.

As the pasta cooks, coarsely chop the parsley on a board. Drain the pasta, add it to the skillet with the sauce, and sauté for 30 seconds, mixing constantly and incorporating all the sauce with the pasta. Transfer to a large, warmed serving platter, sprinkle with more black pepper, then add the parsley and serve immediately.

NOTE

In Campania, lard is used instead of butter, along with a small amount of oil; *perciatelli* is used rather than *penne.*

SERVES 4 TO 6

- 2 pounds red onions, peeled
- 8 tablespoons (4 ounces) sweet butter
- 2 tablespoons olive oil
- 2 cups dry white wine
- 1 cup cold water
- Salt and freshly ground black pepper
- 1 pound dried tubular pasta, such as plain or ridged *penne*, preferably imported Italian

TO COOK THE PASTA

Coarse-grained salt

TO SERVE

25 large sprigs Italian parsley, leaves only

Freshly ground black pepper

sedanini al sedano
PASTA WITH CELERY

SERVES 4 TO 6

2 large bunches celery
   (2 cups)

Coarse-grained salt

1 large clove garlic, peeled

½ cup olive oil

Salt and freshly ground
   black pepper

½ teaspoon hot red
   pepper flakes

1 pound dried *sedanini*
   (ridged tubular pasta
   similar to *rigatoni*,
   but smaller, also called
   fischiotti)

TO SERVE

20 large sprigs Italian
   parsley, leaves only

Another combination that appeals to the aesthetic Tuscans is celery cut into pieces the same size and shape as the dried pasta called sedanini *(which in fact means "small celery pieces") and combined with that same pasta. With or without pasta, the frequent use of cooked celery as a vegetable is particularly Tuscan.*

Clean the celery, removing and discarding the tough outer stalks. Cut the tender white inner stalks into pieces the same length and width as the pasta. Weigh out 1 pound (see Note) of the cut-up celery and place it in a bowl of cold water to soak for 30 minutes.

Bring a large pot of cold water to a boil, add coarse salt to taste, then add the celery and boil until the vegetable is fully cooked but still firm, about 5 to 8 minutes. Use a strainer-skimmer to transfer the celery pieces to a crockery or large glass bowl; reserve the cooking water.

Coarsely chop the garlic on a board. Place the oil in a large skillet over medium heat, and, when the oil is warm, add the garlic and sauté for 30 seconds. Add the celery, then season with salt, pepper, and the red pepper flakes; mix very well and sauté for 5 minutes more.

Return the celery water to a boil, add the pasta, and cook 7 to 10 minutes depending on the brand; that is, 2 minutes less than for normal al dente. As the pasta cooks, coarsely chop the parsley on a board. Drain the pasta, transfer it to the skillet with the celery, and sauté over medium heat for 2 minutes more, mixing very well. Transfer to a warmed platter, add the parsley, toss very well, and serve.

NOTE

If you do not have a kitchen scale, 1 pound of the cut-up celery is approximately 2 cups.

sedanini alla crudaiola
PASTA WITH UNCOOKED VEGETABLE SAUCE

From Apulia we have the refreshing Sedanini alla crudaiola, *in which the pasta is combined with uncooked celery and herbs; again, a cold sauce combined with a hot pasta.*

Blanch the tomatoes in salted boiling water, then remove the skins and seeds, leaving the tomato fillets whole. Place tomatoes in a crockery or glass bowl with the garlic and hot red pepper flakes, if desired. Pour the lemon juice over the top. Cut the celery into pieces the same size as the pasta and put them in the bowl with the tomatoes. Add the oil. Season with salt to taste and abundant black pepper, but do not mix. Cover the bowl and refrigerate for at least 1 hour, or until needed.

Bring a large pot of cold water to a boil over medium heat, add coarse salt to taste; add the pasta, and cook it for 9 to 12 minutes depending on the brand. Meanwhile, mix the tomatoes with the other ingredients and coarsely chop the parsley. When the pasta is ready, drain and transfer it to a large serving platter, then pour the sauce over the top. Mix the pasta and sauce together very well; sprinkle the parsley and basil all over. Mix again and serve.

SERVES 4 TO 6

1 ½ pounds ripe, fresh tomatoes

Coarse-grained salt

2 medium-sized cloves garlic, peeled

½ teaspoon hot red pepper flakes, to be added to marinade (optional)

Juice of a medium-sized lemon

4 medium-sized celery stalks from the white, inner part of the bunch, well scraped

½ cup olive oil

Salt and freshly ground black pepper

1 pound dried *sedanini* pasta, preferably imported Italian

TO COOK THE PASTA

Coarse-grained salt

TO SERVE

20 large sprigs Italian parsley, leaves only

15 large fresh basil leaves, left whole

Pots of aromatic herbs at the market.

tomatoes

The pairing of pasta and tomatoes is legendary, yet it has existed only since the nineteenth century. The earliest printed recipe I have found is *Maccheroni all' Ultima Moda 1841 alla Napoletana*. Only fried green tomato dishes existed before that in the 1600's in Florence.

The most classic tomato sauces are *Pommarola* (Summer Tomato Sauce) and *Sugo scappato* (Winter Tomato Sauce) made with aromatic vegetables and herbs. The summer sauce simply simmers the vegetables in fresh tomatoes. The winter sauce is made with canned tomatoes and the vegetables are sautéed first.

A classic Neapolitan tomato sauce includes onions, basil, and lard. Today, olive oil is substituted for the lard, but you may want to try it. The favorite Neapolitan pasta is *vermicelli*, but *spaghetti* can be used. Cheese is usually grated over the finished dish. In the Neapolitan version of *alla puttanesca*, garlic is substituted for onions and the piquant ingredients—olives, capers, anchovies, and hot pepper flakes—are added. A little tomato paste is also authentic. In Tuscany, *alla puttanesca* is characterized by tomatoes, garlic, and basil, uncooked, and simply marinated in olive oil, chilled, and tossed with hot pasta to release their incredible flavors.

Penne alla pizza, also from Naples, uses the *Pommarola* tomato sauce; the pasta, sauce, and olives are spread on a baking dish, mixed with mozzarella and baked.

The special pesto from Trapani is made with fresh tomatoes, garlic, basil, and typical Sicilian almonds. Piedmont's secret ingredient in their tomato sauce is egg mixed with Parmigiano.

maccheroni alla marinara

PASTA MARINARA STYLE

"Alla marinara" is a very popular treatment, though some versions have strayed very far from the original. Fundamentally, alla marinara simply means to add tomatoes to the basic garlic and olive oil, aglio e olio. This must have originated sometime in the nineteenth century, when ripe tomatoes came to play a dominant role in Neapolitan cooking, before spreading north. In Italy, even pizza alla marinara still means only tomatoes, garlic, and oil. The phrase refers to sailors or to fishermen, and, like "alla pescatora," means made in a quick and simple way, with just the few ingredients easily available to them. Because this basic sauce became popular to use with mussels, clams and pasta, some mistakenly think the phrase means "with seafood."

Another variation, the popular red sauce for spaghetti with clams, which is simply "marinara" with the addition of the delicious "fruit of the sea" will be found on page 140. In Italy, no one ever refers to "marinara sauce," because it never appears independently. The sauce is always prepared quickly, together with the dish it is adorning. The greatest distortion of "alla marinara" is to add cheese, whether grated Parmigiano or pecorino or mozzarella, coarsely grated or in slices. In Italy, it is always understood that when you order "alla marinara," whether pasta or pizza, cheese is not an ingredient. And, of course, grated cheese should not be served with any dish in this category.

Finely chop the garlic and coarsely chop the parsley separately on a board, then combine them. Place the oil in a medium-sized flameproof casserole over medium heat; when the oil is warm, add the chopped ingredients and sauté for 2 minutes. If using fresh tomatoes, cut them into 1-inch pieces. Add fresh or canned tomatoes to the casserole and cook for 25 minutes more, stirring every so often with a wooden spoon. Pass the contents of the casserole through a food mill, using the disc with the smallest holes, into a crockery or glass bowl. Then return sauce to the casserole, season with salt and pepper, and reduce over medium heat for 10 minutes.

Meanwhile, bring a large pot of cold water to a boil, add coarse salt to taste, then add the pasta and cook until al dente—9 to 12 minutes depending on the brand. As the pasta cooks, reheat the sauce. Drain the pasta, transfer it to a warmed serving dish, pour the sauce over the top, toss well, and serve.

SERVES 4 TO 6

- 2 large cloves garlic, peeled
- 20 large sprigs Italian parsley, leaves only
- ½ cup olive oil
- 2 pounds ripe, fresh tomatoes; or 2 pounds canned tomatoes, imported Italian, drained
- Salt and freshly ground black pepper
- 1 pound dried *vermicelli* or *perciatelli*, preferably imported Italian

TO COOK THE PASTA

Coarse-grained salt

spaghetti all'arrabbiata
SPAGHETTI WITH VERY SPICY TOMATO SAUCE

SERVES 4 TO 6

1 ½ pounds ripe, fresh tomatoes; or 1 ½ pounds canned tomatoes, preferably imported Italian, drained

4 tablespoons olive oil

Salt and freshly ground black pepper

½ teaspoon to ¾ teaspoon hot red pepper flakes

1 pound dried *spaghetti*, preferably imported Italian

TO COOK THE PASTA

Coarse-grained salt

TO SERVE

20 large sprigs Italian parsley, leaves only

Tomato sauce with only olive oil and lots of hot red pepper flakes exists under a variety of names, one of the most picturesque being this Spaghetti all'arrabbiata, *which means "angry" spaghetti. Pasta sauces that are dominated by hot red pepper also often contain meat, such as* pancetta *or* prosciutto.

If fresh tomatoes are used, cut them into pieces. Place fresh or canned tomatoes with the oil in a medium-sized saucepan over medium heat and cook for 25 minutes, stirring every so often with a wooden spoon. Season to taste with salt and pepper. Pass the mixture through a food mill, using the disc with the smallest holes, into a second saucepan. Return the tomatoes to medium heat, add the red pepper flakes, and simmer for 15 more minutes.

Bring a large pot of cold water to a boil, add coarse salt to taste, then add the pasta and cook until al dente—9 to 12 minutes, depending on the brand.

Coarsely chop the parsley on a board. Drain the pasta, transfer to a warmed serving platter, pour the sauce over the top, mix very well, sprinkle with the parsley, and serve immediately.

VARIATION

Use 15 large fresh basil leaves, torn into thirds, instead of parsley.

capelli d'angelo al pomodoro e basilico

ANGEL-HAIR PASTA WITH TOMATO SAUCE AND BASIL

The flavor of ripe, fresh tomatoes in season is so satisfying that it is possible to add very little else to make a wonderful pasta dish. This simple treatment, incorporating a little olive oil and basil, and a bit of butter melted onto the hot pasta, works well with many kinds of pasta, but best of all with the thinnest of all, capelli d'angelo. *This "angel-hair" pasta has become very popular and, like* tortellini, *is put into all kinds of dishes where it does not belong. (The difference between* capellini *and* capelli d'angelo *is that the latter are arranged in small nests, while* capellini *are simply very fine long pasta.) In Italy, this fine pasta is used very little; indeed, one must really search to find a traditional regional dish that employs it. Again, it is important to ponder why this is so. Surely its use must have occurred to cooks and it must have been tried and rejected many times over the last two centuries.*

Prepare the fresh tomato sauce *alla toscana* (see Note). Cut fresh tomatoes into medium-sized pieces. Put them in a non-reactive flameproof casserole with the oil and basil leaves. Place the tomato casserole over medium heat and simmer, stirring every so often with a wooden spoon, for 25 minutes. Pass contents of casserole through a food mill, using the disc with the smallest holes, into a crockery or glass bowl. Pour the sauce back into the casserole and reduce over low heat for 5 minutes more. Taste for salt and pepper.

Bring a large pot of cold water to a boil, add coarse salt to taste, then add the pasta and cook for 3 to 5 minutes depending on the brand. Pour half the sauce into a warmed crockery or glass bowl. Drain the pasta, transfer it to the bowl containing the sauce, pour the remaining sauce over the top, then mix very well. Serve immediately, placing ½ tablespoon of the butter and a basil leaf over each serving. Serve with cheese, if desired.

NOTE

A slightly different *Sugo di pomodoro fresco* is given in my book *The Fine Art of Italian Cooking.*

SERVES 4

- 1¼ pounds ripe, fresh tomatoes
- 2 tablespoons olive oil
- 2 large basil leaves, fresh or preserved in salt
- Salt and freshly ground black pepper
- ½ pound dried *capelli d'angelo* or *capellini* (made with or without eggs), preferably imported Italian

TO COOK THE PASTA

- Coarse-grained salt

TO SERVE

- 2 tablespoons (1 ounce) sweet butter, in 4 pieces
- 4 large fresh basil leaves
- 4 tablespoons freshly grated Parmigiano (optional)

nidi de capelli d'angelo con filetti di pomodoro

BIRDS' NESTS OF ANGEL-HAIR PASTA WITH TOMATO FILLETS

1½ pounds fresh tomatoes, ripe, but not overripe

Coarse-grained salt

6 tablespoons extra-virgin olive oil

3 large cloves garlic, peeled and left whole

Salt and freshly ground black pepper

Several large fresh basil leaves

¾ pound nests of angel-hair pasta (*capelli d'angelo*), preferably imported Italian

TO COOK THE PASTA

Coarse-grained salt

TO SERVE

Freshly ground black pepper

Sprigs of fresh basil leaves

Angel-hair pasta is always dried, not fresh pasta, and is generally formed into nests. It has never been as popular in Italy as it has become abroad. However, it works very well with a light dressing of fresh tomatoes or simply topped with some butter and grated cheese or served with good-quality olive oil and a lot of freshly ground black pepper. In Italy, angel-hair pasta is most often used in a clear broth or, especially in Tuscany, served as fried whole nests with a rich meat sauce and generous amounts of grated pecorino or Parmigiano cheese.

Blanch the tomatoes in salted boiling water for a few minutes, transfer to a bowl of cold water, and immediately remove the skins. Cut the tomatoes into quarters and discard the seeds. If the tomatoes are very large, cut each piece in half.

Bring a large pot of cold water to a boil over medium heat, add coarse-grained salt to taste, then add the pasta and cook for 4 to 6 minutes, depending on the brand. Meanwhile, heat the oil in a medium skillet over medium heat; when the oil is warm, add the whole cloves of garlic and sauté until lightly golden, about 1 minute. Discard the garlic,

add the tomatoes, season with salt and pepper, and cook for a maximum of 2 minutes—tomatoes should still be in large pieces and not reduced to sauce. Add the basil leaves and mix well. Drain the pasta, transfer to a bowl, add the juice of the tomatoes from the skillet, and toss very well. Transfer the pasta to a large serving platter, season with pepper, then arrange the tomato pieces and the basil sprigs over the pasta and serve immediately.

vermicelli con salsa di pomodoro alla napoletana

VERMICELLI WITH NEAPOLITAN TOMATO SAUCE

Cut the onion into quarters. Place the lard or oil in a medium-sized flameproof casserole over medium heat; when the lard is melted or the oil is warm, add the onion and sauté until the outer layers are translucent, about 5 minutes. If using fresh tomatoes, cut them into 1-inch pieces. Add fresh or canned tomatoes to the casserole and cook for 25 minutes, seasoning to taste with salt and pepper. Remove and discard the onion, then pass the contents of the casserole through a food mill, using the disc with the smallest holes, into a second flameproof casserole. Place the second casserole over low heat and reduce sauce for 10 minutes.

Bring a large pot of cold water to a boil, add coarse salt to taste, then add the pasta and cook for 9 to 12 minutes depending on the brand (see Note.). As the pasta cooks, tear the basil leaves into thirds and add them to the sauce. Drain the pasta and transfer it to a large, warmed serving platter; add the sauce, toss well, and serve hot, sprinkling cheese over each serving.

NOTE

In Naples, pasta is eaten very al dente, cooked about 2 minutes less than indicated here.

SERVES 4 TO 6

- 1 medium-sized red onion, peeled
- 8 tablespoons lard or olive oil
- 1 ½ pounds ripe, fresh tomatoes; or 1 ½ pounds canned tomatoes, preferably imported Italian, drained
- Salt and freshly ground black pepper
- 1 pound dried *vermicelli* or *spaghetti*, preferably imported Italian
- 10 large fresh basil leaves

TO COOK THE PASTA

Coarse-grained salt

TO SERVE

Freshly grated pecorino romano or Parmigiano cheese

spaghetti alla puttanesca alla napoletana

SPAGHETTI ALLA PUTTANESCA, CAMPANIA STYLE

SERVES 4 TO 6

1 ½ pounds ripe, fresh tomatoes; or 1½ pounds canned tomatoes, preferably imported Italian, drained

Coarse-grained salt

2 medium-sized cloves garlic, peeled

½ cup olive oil

½ pound large Gaeta olives in brine

3 anchovies in salt; or 6 anchovy fillets packed in oil, drained

4 heaping tablespoons capers in wine vinegar, drained

2 tablespoons tomato paste

Salt and freshly ground black pepper

½ teaspoon hot red pepper flakes

1 pound dried *spaghetti*, preferably imported Italian

TO COOK THE PASTA

Coarse-grained salt

If using fresh tomatoes, blanch them in boiling salted water, remove the skins, and cut them into pieces. Pass fresh or canned tomatoes through a food mill, using the disc with the smallest holes, into a crockery or glass bowl.

Coarsely chop the garlic on a board. Heat the oil in a medium-sized saucepan over medium heat; when the oil is warm, add the garlic and sauté until lightly golden, about 10 minutes. Meanwhile, pit the olives and quarter them. If using anchovies preserved in salt, fillet them under cold running water, discarding bones and washing away excess salt. Cut anchovy fillets into 1-inch pieces. Add the tomatoes to the pan, then the olives, anchovies, capers, and tomato paste. Mix well and season to taste with salt, pepper, and the red pepper flakes. Cook for 15 minutes over medium heat, stirring every so often with a wooden spoon.

Meanwhile, bring a large pot of cold water to a boil, add coarse salt to taste, then add the pasta and cook until al dente—9 to 12 minutes depending on the brand. Drain the pasta, place it in a large bowl, pour the sauce over the top, and mix well. Transfer to a warmed serving dish and serve immediately.

penne alla pizza
PASTA IN THE STYLE OF PIZZA

Coarsely chop the celery, onion, garlic, parsley, carrots, and 5 of the basil leaves all together on a board. Put chopped ingredients in a medium-sized saucepan. If using fresh tomatoes, cut them into pieces. Add fresh or canned tomatoes to pan, cover, and cook over low heat for 1 hour, stirring every so often with a wooden spoon. Pass the contents of the pan through a food mill, using the disc with the smallest holes, into a second saucepan. Add salt and pepper to taste and the oil; cook for 10 minutes more.

Meanwhile, bring a large pot of cold water to a boil and preheat the oven to 375°F. When the water reaches a boil, add coarse salt to taste, then add the pasta and cook it for 8 to 11 minutes depending on the brand; that is, 1 minute less than for normal al dente.

Use the tablespoon of oil to heavily coat a 13½-by-8¾-inch glass baking dish. Drain the pasta and place it in a large bowl. Add the still-hot tomato sauce, the mozzarella, oregano, olives, remaining basil leaves torn into thirds, and salt and pepper to taste. Gently but thoroughly mix all the ingredients, then place in the oiled dish. Spread the butter pieces over the pasta, cover the dish with aluminum foil, and bake 15 minutes. Serve hot directly from the dish.

SERVES 6 TO 8

- 1 medium-sized stalk celery
- ½ medium-sized red onion, peeled
- 1 large clove garlic, peeled
- 10 large sprigs Italian parsley, leaves only
- 2 medium-sized carrots, scraped
- 20 large basil leaves, fresh or preserved in salt
- 2 pounds ripe, fresh tomatoes; or 2 pounds canned tomatoes, preferably imported Italian, drained
- Salt and freshly ground black pepper
- 3 tablespoons olive oil
- 1 pound dried *penne*, preferably imported Italian

TO COOK THE PASTA

Coarse-grained salt

TO BAKE

- 1 tablespoon olive oil
- 8 ounces mozzarella cheese, cut about ¼ inch thick cubes
- 1 teaspoon dried oregano
- 30 Gaeta olives in oil, drained and pitted
- Salt and freshly ground black pepper
- 2 tablespoons (1 ounce) sweet butter, cut into small pieces

pasta con pesto alla trapanese
PASTA WITH SICILIAN PESTO

SERVES 4 TO 6

Coarse-grained salt

1 ½ pounds ripe, fresh
   tomatoes

4 ½ ounces blanched
   almonds

4 medium-sized cloves
   garlic, peeled

25 large basil leaves

Salt and freshly ground
   black pepper

½ cup olive oil

FOR THE PASTA

1 pound dried *bucatini*,
   linguine, or *spaghetti*,
   preferably imported
   Italian

or

3 cups unbleached
   all-purpose flour

4 extra-large eggs

Pinch of salt

TO COOK THE PASTA

Coarse-grained salt

Bring a medium-sized saucepan of cold water to a boil, add coarse salt to taste, then add the tomatoes. Blanch them, then remove the skins and seeds and put the tomatoes in a crockery or glass bowl until needed.

With a mortar and pestle, finely grind the almonds with the garlic; when the texture is very creamy, add the basil and grind until the basil is completely incorporated. Transfer the mixture to a large crockery or glass bowl. Pass the tomatoes through a food mill, using the disc with the smallest holes, into the bowl containing the mixture. Season to taste with salt and pepper, add the olive oil, and mix all the ingredients with a wooden spoon. Cover the bowl and refrigerate until needed. (The pesto sauce can be prepared several hours before serving and kept, covered, in the refrigerator.)

If using fresh pasta, prepare it with the ingredients listed and follow the directions on page 12. Stretch layer to ⅛ inch thick and cut into *spaghetti* (see the illustration on page 59). Let pasta rest on cotton dish towels until needed.

Bring a large pot of cold water to a boil, add coarse salt to taste, then add the pasta and cook until al dente—9 to 12 minutes depending on the brand. (If using fresh pasta, cook for 1 to 3 minutes depending on dryness.) Drain the pasta, and transfer it to a large, warmed serving platter; pour the sauce over the top, mix very well, and serve immediately.

NOTE

The pesto can be made in a food processor. Place the almonds, garlic, and olive oil in the bowl and, using the metal blade, grind until very fine. Then add the basil, salt, and pepper, and grind again until the texture is very creamy.

spaghetti alla piemontese
SPAGHETTI, PIEDMONT STYLE

If using fresh tomatoes, cut them into 1-inch pieces. Pass fresh or canned tomatoes through a food mill, using the disc with the smallest holes, into a crockery or glass bowl. Place a saucepan with the butter and oil over medium heat, and, when the butter is melted, add the tomatoes and simmer for 15 minutes. Taste for salt and pepper.

Bring a large pot of cold water to a boil. Meanwhile, mix the eggs and Parmigiano very well in a small crockery or glass bowl and set aside until needed.

When the water reaches a boil, add coarse salt to taste, then add the pasta and cook until al dente—9 to 12 minutes depending on the brand.

As the pasta cooks, place 1 cup of the tomato sauce in a large serving dish and set it over the boiling water, partially covering the top of the pot. Drain the pasta, transfer it to the heated serving dish, and pour the remaining sauce over the top. Mix very well, then add the egg mixture, toss thoroughly, and serve immediately.

SERVES 4 TO 6

- 1 pound very ripe, fresh tomatoes; or 1 pound canned tomatoes, preferably imported Italian, drained
- 8 tablespoons (4 ounces) sweet butter
- 1 tablespoon olive oil
- Salt and freshly ground black pepper
- 3 extra-large eggs
- 1 cup freshly grated Parmigiano
- 1 pound dried *spaghetti*, preferably imported Italian

TO COOK THE PASTA

Coarse-grained salt

penne alla bettola
PENNE WITH SPICY TOMATO-CREAM SAUCE

SERVES 4 TO 6

2 medium-sized cloves garlic, peeled

5 tablespoons olive oil

1 ½ pounds ripe, fresh tomatoes; or 1½ pounds canned tomatoes, preferably imported Italian, drained

Salt and freshly ground black pepper

½ teaspoon hot red pepper flakes

1 pound dried *penne*, preferably imported Italian

15 large sprigs Italian parsley, leaves only

2 tablespoons vodka

1 cup heavy cream

TO COOK THE PASTA

Coarse-grained salt

Coarsely chop the garlic on a board. Heat the oil in a medium-sized saucepan over medium heat, and, when the oil is warm, add the chopped garlic and sauté for 3 minutes. If using fresh tomatoes, cut them into 1-inch pieces. Add fresh or canned tomatoes to the pan and cook for 20 minutes. Season to taste with salt and pepper, then add the red pepper flakes. Pass the contents of the pan through a food mill, using the disc with the smallest holes, into a large skillet.

Bring a large pot of cold water to a boil. Meanwhile, place the skillet over low heat and simmer the sauce as you cook the pasta. Add coarse salt to the boiling water, then add the pasta and cook for 8 to 11 minutes depending on the brand; that is, 1 minute less than for normal al dente.

Meanwhile, coarsely chop the parsley on a board. Drain the pasta and add it to the skillet with the tomato sauce. Add the vodka, mix very well, and raise the heat to medium. Sauté for 1 minute, stirring the pasta vigorously with a wooden spoon. Add the cream; taste for salt and pepper. Mix for 30 seconds to allow the cream to get well absorbed into the pasta, then sprinkle with the parsley, transfer pasta to a warmed serving dish, and serve immediately.

trenette al pomodoro
PASTA WITH LIGURIAN TOMATO SAUCE

SERVES 4 TO 6

1 large red onion, cleaned

7 tablespoons extra-virgin olive oil

2 stalks celery

2 medium-sized carrots, scraped

10 sprigs Italian parsley, leaves only

5 large fresh basil leaves

5 large cloves garlic, peeled and left whole

1 ½ pounds ripe, fresh tomatoes; or 1½ pounds canned tomatoes, preferably imported Italian, drained

Salt and freshly ground black pepper

1 pound dried *trenette* or any other long flat pasta, such as *bavette* or *linguine*, preferably imported Italian

1 teaspoon fresh oregano leaves; or a large pinch of dried oregano

TO COOK THE PASTA

Coarse-grained salt

TO SERVE

Fresh basil leaves

To make this Ligurian tomato sauce, first sauté the onion by itself. The other chopped vegetables and aromatic herbs are added along with whole garlic cloves. As a result, they do not become completely incorporated with the onions and the resulting texture is not typical. Although oregano is usually associated with southern Italian cooking, it is used in Liguria more than in other northern regions.

Thinly slice the onion on a chopping board. Place a large nonreactive casserole with 5 tablespoons of the olive oil over medium heat and, when the oil is warm, add the onion and sauté for 2 or 3 minutes, or until translucent, mixing every so often with a wooden spoon.

Meanwhile, finely chop the celery, carrots, parsley, and 5 leaves of the basil together on a board, then add them to the casserole along with the garlic. Sauté for 2 minutes more. Meanwhile, if using fresh tomatoes, cut them into pieces. Pass the fresh or canned tomatoes through a food mill, using the disc with the smallest holes, into a crockery or glass bowl. Add the tomatoes to the casserole and season with salt and pepper. Cover and simmer for 1 hour, stirring every so often with a wooden spoon and seasoning with salt and pepper. The sauce is ready when it is rather thick.

Bring a large stockpot of cold water to a boil, add coarse salt to taste, then add the pasta and cook until al dente—9 to 12 minutes depending on the brand. As the pasta finishes cooking, add the remaining 2 tablespoons of oil to the sauce, season with the oregano, and remove and discard the garlic.

Drain the pasta. Transfer it to a large bowl, pour the sauce over the top, then mix very well. Transfer to a large, warmed serving dish, sprinkle with the basil leaves and serve immediately.

NOTE

The fresh regional pasta *trenette* from Liguria is discussed on page 256, but *trenette* can also be obtained as a dried pasta.

zucchini

Most zucchini-and-pasta recipes come from southern Italy, and I have not found a single one from those regions in which the zucchini are not cut into discs and fried in olive oil. Included here are two Sicilian recipes with their variations, as well as one from Calabria— all three of which are typical of the treatment in the southern regions.

In the first version from Sicily, the fried zucchini are tossed together with the pasta and sprinkled with grated cheese. In this recipe, as in the previous one, some of the oil suffused with the zucchini flavor serves as the sauce. In the next version, first a pasta with bread crumbs is prepared, and then the fried zucchini discs are arranged either on top or on the side. No cheese is added. In the recipe from Calabria, ricotta is used, and the flavor of basil is added. The zucchini are fried in the lighter vegetable oil and only the olive oil used to brown the garlic is added. Again, it is unlikely that it never occurred to cooks over the course of several centuries that zucchini might be sautéed or boiled when combined with pasta. Clearly, these methods were eliminated as a consensus was reached that zucchini worked best when fried.

In Lucca (Tuscany), *ravioli* are dressed with a sauce in which coarsely grated zucchini are cooked together with tomatoes and olive oil. The *ravioli* and sauce are alternated in layers to make a most attractive presentation. Butter, basil, and Parmigiano are added at the end.

pasta con le zucchine
PASTA WITH ZUCCHINI, CALABRIAN STYLE

SERVES 4 TO 6

1 pound small, thin zucchini (not miniature), cleaned

Coarse-grained salt

1 quart vegetable oil

½ cup olive oil

4 large cloves garlic, peeled but left whole

1 pound dried *vermicelli*, preferably imported Italian

4 ounces whole-milk ricotta

Salt and freshly ground black pepper

10 large leaves fresh basil, torn into thirds

TO COOK THE PASTA

Coarse-grained salt

Slice the zucchini into discs about ¼ inch thick and place them on a large platter. Sprinkle 2 tablespoons of coarse salt over the slices and let stand for 30 minutes.

Rinse the zucchini under cold running water and pat dry with paper towels to drain off excess salt. Heat the vegetable oil in a large skillet over medium heat. When the oil is hot, add the zucchini and fry until lightly golden on both sides, about 4 minutes total. Meanwhile, bring a large pot of cold water to a boil over medium heat.

With a slotted spoon, transfer the cooked zucchini to a platter lined with paper towels to drain off excess oil. Discard all but ¼ cup of the cooking oil, add the olive oil to the skillet, and sauté the garlic until lightly golden, about 5 minutes.

Add coarse salt to the boiling water, then add the pasta and cook it until al dente—9 to 12 minutes depending on the brand. Drain the pasta and place it in a large bowl. Add the ricotta and salt and pepper to taste, then add the hot oil (discard the garlic) and mix very well. Arrange the fried zucchini over the top, sprinkle with the basil leaves, and serve very hot.

pasta e zucchini
PASTA AND ZUCCHINI

Cut off and discard the ends of the zucchini, then soak the zucchini in a bowl of cold water for 30 minutes. Place a large pot of cold water over high heat and a large skillet with the oil over medium heat. Remove the zucchini from the water, pat very dry with paper towels, then cut into ¼-inch-thick discs. When the oil is hot (about 400°F), raise the heat, add the zucchini, and cook until golden on both sides, about 3 minutes total, mixing frequently with a strainer-skimmer.

When the water reaches a boil, add coarse salt to taste, then add the pasta and cook until al dente—9 to 12 minutes depending on the brand. Use the strainer-skimmer to transfer the zucchini to a serving dish lined with paper towels to drain off excess oil. Season with salt and pepper to taste and cover the dish to keep the zucchini warm.

Remove ¾ cup of the hot oil from the zucchini pan, pour it into a small saucepan, and let it cook for 2 minutes. Add the bread crumbs, put the pan over low heat, season with salt and pepper, and sauté the bread crumbs until lightly golden, about 1 minute. Transfer the bread crumbs with strainer-skimmer to a dish, saving the oil.

Drain the pasta and arrange it on a large, warmed serving dish, pour the reserved hot oil over the top, toss well, place the zucchini over the pasta, then sprinkle with the bread crumbs and serve hot.

VARIATIONS

1. Use 1 pound of zucchini instead of 2.
2. Instead of placing the fried zucchini over the pasta, serve a portion separately on the same plate.

SERVES 4 TO 6

- **2 pounds small, thin zucchini (not miniature)**
- **2 cups extra-virgin olive oil, preferably from southern Italy**
- **Salt and freshly ground black pepper**
- **1 pound dried *spaghetti*, preferably imported Italian**
- **4 to 6 tablespoons unseasoned bread crumbs, preferably homemade**

TO COOK THE PASTA

Coarse-grained salt

pasta alle zucchine
PASTA WITH ZUCCHINI, SICILIAN STYLE

SERVES 4 TO 6

1 pound small, thin
   zucchini (not miniature)

2 cups extra-virgin,
   full-bodied olive oil,
   preferably from
   southern Italy

1 pound dried *spaghetti*,
   preferably imported
   Italian

Salt and freshly ground
   black pepper

½ cup freshly grated
   pecorino romano or
   Parmigiano cheese

TO COOK THE PASTA

Coarse-grained salt

Cut off and discard the ends of the zucchini, and soak the zucchini in a bowl of cold water for 30 minutes. Bring a large pot of cold water to a boil, and place a large, heavy skillet with the oil over medium heat. Remove the zucchini from the water, pat dry with paper towels, then cut into ¼-inch-thick discs. When the oil is hot (about 400°F), raise the heat, add the zucchini, and cook until golden on both sides, about 3 minutes total, mixing frequently with a strainer-skimmer.

When the water reaches a boil, add coarse salt to taste, and then add the pasta and cook until al dente—9 to 12 minutes depending on the brand. When the zucchini are ready, use the strainer-skimmer to transfer them to a serving dish lined with paper towels to drain off excess oil. Take ¾ cup of the hot oil from the zucchini and pour it into a large serving bowl. Add salt and pepper to taste. At that point the pasta should be ready; drain it and place it in the bowl with the oil. Sprinkle the cheese over the top, then add the zucchini, toss thoroughly but gently, and serve immediately.

VARIATIONS

1. Cheese can be omitted.
2. Leaves of 20 sprigs of Italian parsley, coarsely chopped, can be added to the bowl with the zucchini and tossed together with the other ingredients.
3. A large clove of peeled garlic can be added whole while frying the zucchini and discarded, or chopped and sautéed in the oil used to dress the pasta. This is not a very typical preparation.
4. Any combination of the above.

NOTE

Olive oil is no longer exclusively used for frying in Italy; most cooks have switched to the lighter vegetable oils, and use a little olive oil for flavor in sautéing. But this dish really depends on the flavor of olive oil-permeated zucchini. The flavor need not be heavy if the oil is fresh, and not reused, as was once the custom. The zucchini should be completely cooked, not half cooked, and crisp.

vermicelli e fiori di zucca all'abruzzese

VERMICELLI WITH ZUCCHINI BLOSSOMS, ABRUZZI STYLE

The special touches in this vegetable sauce include zucchini blossoms added to other already sautéed chopped vegetables; the typically Abruzzese saffron, which is among the best in Italy; and tempered egg added to the sauce at the end. Although many dishes from Abruzzi are spicy from hot red pepper (peperoncino), there are some at the other extreme, such as this recipe, which are very delicate and sweet.

Coarsely cut up the zucchini blossoms and set aside. Finely chop the onion, parsley, celery, and carrot together on a board. Heat the oil in a medium-sized casserole over medium heat and, when the oil is lukewarm, add the onions,

The blossom of the male zucchini, which is used in cooking.

parsley, celery, and carrot but reserve the zucchini blossoms. Lightly sauté for 2 or 3 minutes, or until the onion is translucent, mixing every so often with a wooden spoon. Add the blossoms and cook for 1 minute more. Season with salt and pepper. Add the saffron, mix very well, then add ½ cup of the broth to the sauce. Keep adding the broth, ½ cup at a time, stirring constantly with a wooden spoon, until all the broth is used up and the sauce has a thick but smooth texture.

Bring a large pot of cold water to a boil, add coarse salt to taste, then add the pasta and cook for 8 to 11 minutes depending on the brand; that is, 1 minute less than for normal al dente. As the pasta cooks, put the egg yolk in a small crockery or glass bowl, whisk in ¼ cup of lukewarm water, and mix very well; this tempers the egg yolk so it will not curdle when it is added to the hot sauce.

Place the sauce over medium heat again, add the egg mixture, mix very well, then add the pasta, mix again, and cook for 30 seconds more. Transfer to a warmed serving platter, sprinkle the cheese over the top, arrange the whole zucchini blossoms on top, and serve hot.

SERVES 4 TO 6

- **12** large zucchini blossoms, cleaned, stems and pistils removed
- **1** medium-sized red onion, cleaned
- **15** large sprigs Italian parsley, leaves only
- **1** small stalk celery
- **1** small carrot, scraped
- **5** tablespoons extra-virgin olive oil
- Salt and freshly ground black pepper
- Large pinch of powdered saffron, preferably from Abruzzo
- **2** cups chicken broth, preferably homemade
- **1** pound dried *vermicelli* or another long and rather thick pasta, preferably imported Italian
- **1** extra-large egg yolk

TO COOK THE PASTA

Coarse-grained salt

TO SERVE

- ½ cup freshly grated pecorino romano cheese
- Several whole zucchini blossoms

ravioli alle zucchine
RAVIOLI WITH ZUCCHINI SAUCE

SERVES 6 TO 8

FOR THE STUFFING

15 ounces whole-milk ricotta

2 extra-large egg yolks

4 tablespoons freshly grated Parmigiano

Salt and freshly ground black pepper

FOR THE PASTA

4 cups unbleached all-purpose flour

5 extra-large eggs

Pinch of salt

FOR THE SAUCE

1 ½ pounds thin zucchini

1 large lemon

1 pound ripe, fresh tomatoes; or 1 pound canned tomatoes, preferably imported Italian, drained and seeded

Coarse-grained salt

½ cup olive oil

Salt and freshly ground black pepper

TO COOK THE PASTA

Coarse-grained salt

TO SERVE

4 tablespoons (2 ounces) sweet butter

6 large fresh basil leaves

6 to 8 tablespoons freshly grated Parmigiano

Freshly ground black pepper

Prepare the stuffing. Use a cheesecloth to drain the ricotta very well, then place the ricotta in a crockery or glass bowl. Add the egg yolks, Parmigiano, and salt and pepper to taste, and mix with a wooden spoon. Cover the bowl and refrigerate until needed.

Prepare the pasta with the ingredients and quantities listed, following the directions on page 12. Stretch layer to less than 1⁄16 inch thick—on the pasta machine take it to the last setting. Prepare *ravioli* with a rectangular shape (2 by 3 inches; see illustrations, page 123), and use ½ tablespoon of the stuffing for each. Let the *ravioli* rest on cotton dish towels until needed.

Prepare the sauce. Clean and wash the zucchini well, then use a hand grater to coarsely grate them into a crockery or glass bowl. Squeeze the lemon and add 2 tablespoons of the juice to the bowl; mix well and let rest for 5 minutes. Meanwhile, if using fresh tomatoes, bring a small saucepan of cold water to a boil, add coarse salt to taste, then add the tomatoes. Blanch for 2 minutes, then remove from the water. Peel and seed the tomatoes. Heat the oil in a medium-sized saucepan over medium heat. Drain and rinse the zucchini under cold running water. When the oil is warm, add the zucchini along with the fresh or canned tomatoes without cutting them up. Sauté for 2 minutes, stirring every so often.

Bring a large pot of cold water to a boil and add coarse salt to taste. Melt the butter in a small saucepan set over the pot of boiling water. Raise the heat on the zucchini sauce, and season it with salt and pepper. Add the *ravioli* to the boiling water and cook for 1 to 3 minutes depending on dryness. Use a strainer-skimmer to transfer the cooked *ravioli* to a warmed serving dish.

Make a layer of *ravioli* on the serving dish, then pour one-third of the melted butter and one-third of the zucchini sauce over them. Sprinkle with 2 basil leaves torn into thirds. Repeat the same order—pasta, butter, sauce, and basil—2 more times. Serve, sprinkling each individual portion with some Parmigiano and a twist of black pepper.

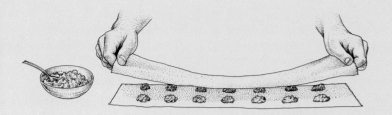

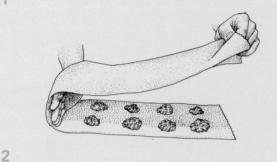

1

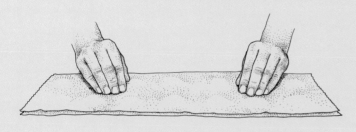

2

3

4

5

1. *Tortelli* may be squares, rounds, rectangles or half-moons of two layers of pasta filled with a little stuffing and sealed. They are sometimes called *ravioli*. After pasta is made, stretch the layer to the thickness required by the recipe. Place dots of the filling on the bottom layer and fit a second layer of pasta over the first.

2. It is also possible to place the dots of filling on half of one layer of pasta and fold the other half over.

3. With the tips of your fingers, press down the edges along the center of the two overlapped layers of pasta to remove the air.

4. Then, for square or rectangular shaped *tortelli or ravioli*, use a scalloped pastry cutter to cut them into these shapes.

5. If you want round *tortelli* or *ravioli*, use a large or small *ravioli* cutter.

pasta w

th fish

pesce azzurro

The category of fish known as *pesce azzurro*, literally "blue fish," which has no connection with the North Atlantic bluefish, includes mackerel and two smaller fish, sardines and anchovies. These two small types traditionally were preserved in salt and used to flavor many dishes. This practice probably originated with that ancient pungent Roman fish sauce called *garum*, which we find in Apicius, a very early Roman food writer. Sardines in their salted form were once used as much as anchovies, but they have all but disappeared. Flavoring pasta with these fish, filleted and crushed into a paste, may well have been the original wedding of fish with pasta. Indeed, when the Milanese adopted the original Venetian salted sardine dish and substituted fresh sardines, it was a noteworthy enough event that the use of fresh sardines with pasta is known as *alla milanese* to this day in parts of Sicily, where the dish still flourishes. (See page 237 for the Venetian *Bigoli scuri in salsa*, using the salted sardines or anchovies, and the Milanese version with fresh sardines.)

Fresh anchovies are abundant in the Mediterranean, but are not usually available in most areas of the Atlantic. However, even in Italy, fresh anchovies are not traditionally combined with pasta. They are eaten marinated, as an appetizer, or are baked, fried, or broiled.

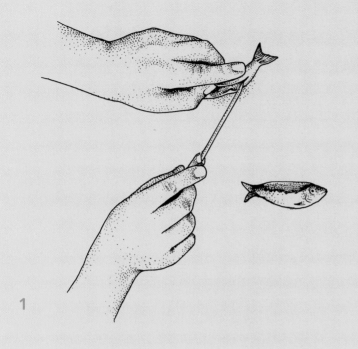

SARDINES

1. Use a knife to open the stomach, then remove the insides and cut off the head and tail and discard them.

2. With your fingers, grasp the bone at one end and pull it out.

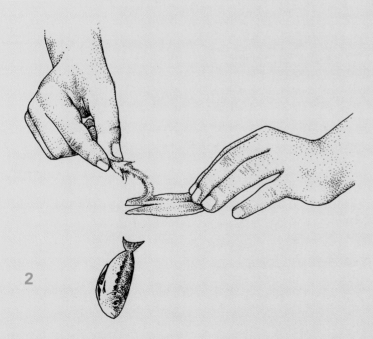

pasta alle sarde II
PASTA WITH FRESH SARDINES, SECOND VERSION

SERVES 6

3 ½ quarts cold water

Coarse-grained salt

¼ ounce dried wild fennel

2 ounces fresh green tops of fennel bulbs

1 medium-sized red onion, peeled

1 pound fresh sardines

4 anchovies in salt; or 8 anchovy fillets packed in oil, drained

¾ cup olive oil

3 tablespoons raisins

3 tablespoons pine nuts (*pignolis*)

Salt and freshly ground black pepper

Large pinch of ground saffron

1 pound dried *perciatelli* or *bucatini*, preferably imported Italian

This version of Pasta alle sarde *differs a bit from the first one in my* Classic Techniques of Italian Cooking. *Preserved anchovies are combined with the fresh sardines and an onion is added; the pignolis are more abundant and a little saffron is added; the wine vinegar is omitted, and the pasta is the substantial, thick* perciatelli *with the hole through it. Dried wild fennel is sufficiently available now outside of Sicily that no substitute is necessary. The dried herb looks like woody small stalks and yields intense flavor when cooked.*

In a large stockpot, bring the cold water to a boil, add coarse salt to taste, then add the dried fennel and the fennel tops and cook for 20 minutes. With a strainer-skimmer, transfer the herbs from the water onto a plate. Saving the water, discard the cooked dried fennel and save the fresh green tops.

Coarsely chop the onion with the cooked fennel tops on a board and set aside until needed. Clean the sardines, discarding the heads, tails, and bones (you should have ½ pound meat), and soak the fillets in a bowl of cold water with a little coarse salt. If using anchovies preserved in salt, clean them under cold running water, then remove the heads, bones, and excess salt. Set aside.

Place a medium-sized flameproof casserole with the oil over medium heat, and, when the oil is warm, add the chopped onion and fennel tops. Sauté for 5 minutes, then add the raisins, pine nuts, and anchovies, using a fork to mash the anchovies. Taste for salt and pepper, add the saffron, and cook over low heat for 10 minutes more.

Meanwhile, reheat the fennel water to a boil, taste for salt, add the pasta, and cook until al dente—9 to 12 minutes depending on the brand. Four minutes before the pasta is to finish cooking, add the sardines to the sauce; mix very well and cook over low heat until the pasta is ready. Drain the pasta, transfer it to a large, warmed platter, add the sauce, mix well using 2 forks, and serve immediately.

VARIATION

Sprinkle 3 tablespoons of toasted bread crumbs over the pasta when it is on the serving platter.

bavette sul pesce

BAVETTE WITH FISH SAUCE, LIVORNO STYLE

The two most famous sauces made from a puréed combination of saltwater fish come from Genoa and from Livorno. The Genoese Passato di pesce, *generally eaten with* spaghetti, *is very pure, with no broth or tomato added. This sauce is reduced for a long time, and the purity of the fish flavor is enhanced only by parsley, rosemary, and onion. Here, in the Livorno version, the fish is sautéed in olive oil before being puréed and reduced. The tomato and broth and celery are added and the rosemary is omitted. The preferred pasta is* bavette, *long and flat like* linguine *and available in dried form.*

Cut the fish into 2-inch pieces, leaving bones. Put the fish in a bowl of cold water with coarse salt to soak for 30 minutes. Soak the onions, celery, and parsley in another bowl of cold water for the same period.

Bring the 2 cups of cold water to a boil in a small saucepan over medium heat; add coarse salt to taste. Drain the vegetables and add the celery, parsley, and 1 onion. Simmer for 15 minutes. Drain the fish, rinse it under cold running water, and add it to the pan with the vegetables. Cover and cook for 10 more minutes. Set aside to rest, covered, for 15 minutes.

Remove and discard the bones from the fish, then pass the fish and the contents of the pan through a food mill, using the disc with the largest holes, into a small bowl. If the mixture does not pass through the mill easily, add up to 1 cup of hot water to thin it.

Finely chop the remaining onion on a board. Place a medium-sized saucepan with the oil over medium heat. When the oil is warm, add the onion and sauté until translucent, about 10 minutes. Dissolve the tomato paste in the broth. Add it to the pan. Simmer for 10 minutes, then add the fish mixture and simmer for 15 more minutes. Pass the contents of the saucepan through a food mill, using the disc with the smallest holes, into a bowl. Return the contents to the saucepan, taste for salt and pepper, and simmer over medium heat for 10 more minutes.

Bring a large pot of cold water to a boil, add coarse salt to taste, then add the pasta and cook for 7 to 10 minutes depending on the brand; that is, 2 minutes less than for normal al dente. Transfer the simmered mixture to a large skillet and place over high heat. Drain the pasta, add it to the skillet, and sauté for a minute or so. Mix the sauce with the pasta, using 2 forks. Transfer to a large, warmed serving dish, sprinkle with the parsley, and serve.

SERVES 4 TO 6

- 1 pound of several different kinds of saltwater fish
- Coarse-grained salt
- 2 large red onions, peeled and cut into large pieces
- 2 medium-sized stalks celery, cut into 2-inch pieces
- 10 large sprigs Italian parsley, leaves only
- 2 cups cold water
- ½ cup olive oil
- 4 tablespoons tomato paste
- ½ cup chicken or beef broth, preferably homemade
- Salt and freshly ground black pepper
- 1 pound dried *bavette* pasta, preferably imported Italian

TO COOK THE PASTA

Coarse-grained salt

TO SERVE

15 large sprigs Italian parsley, leaves only

pasta con pesce spada
PASTA WITH SWORDFISH

SERVES 4 TO 6

FOR THE SAUCE

15 large sprigs Italian parsley, leaves only

4 large cloves garlic, peeled

2 medium-sized carrots, scraped

3 large stalks celery

5 large basil leaves, fresh or preserved in salt

¼ cup olive oil

1 pound ripe, fresh tomatoes; or 1 pound canned tomatoes, preferably imported Italian, drained

4 tablespoons capers in wine vinegar, drained

15 large green olives in brine, drained, pitted, and cut into thirds

½ pound swordfish steak, in 1 piece

Salt and freshly ground black pepper

1 pound dried short tubular pasta, such as *rigatoni* or *penne*, preferably imported Italian

TO COOK THE PASTA

Coarse-grained salt

One would expect Sicily to have a fish sauce made with its favorite swordfish. Aromatic vegetables and herbs, basil, and parsley are chopped and sautéed, and the swordfish is cut into 1-inch squares without skin or bone. Tomatoes, olives, and capers are added to this tasty sauce, which is used to dress short tubular pasta, as in this recipe.

Finely chop the parsley, garlic, carrots, celery, and basil all together on a board. Place the oil in a medium-sized nonreactive flameproof casserole over medium heat, and when the oil is warm, add the chopped ingredients. Sauté for 5 minutes, stirring every so often with a wooden spoon. If using fresh tomatoes, cut them into pieces. Pass the fresh or canned tomatoes through a food mill, using the disc with the smallest holes, into a crockery or glass bowl. Add the tomatoes to the pot and simmer for 20 minutes; add the capers and olives and cook for 5 minutes more.

Remove the skin from the fish, cut the flesh into 1-inch cubes, and add them to the sauce. Simmer for 15 minutes, mixing every so often with a wooden spoon and mashing the fish pieces to incorporate them. Taste for salt and pepper.

Meanwhile, bring a large pot of cold water to a boil, add coarse salt to taste, then add the pasta and cook for 9 to 12 minutes depending on the brand. Drain the pasta, place it on a warmed serving platter, add the sauce, mix well, and serve.

VARIATIONS

1. Sprinkle leaves of 25 sprigs of Italian parsley over the dish before serving.
2. A large pinch of dried oregano can be added along with salt and pepper.

The pier in Viareggio, north of Pisa.

ravioli al sugo di filetti di sogliola

RAVIOLI WITH SAUCE OF SOLE FILLET

In the Marches on the Adriatic, we have a sauce made with sole fillets. Again, the aromatic vegetables and herbs are sautéed and tomatoes and white wine are added. Basil is omitted, and the abundant garlic of Sicilian fish sauce is reduced to a single clove. Interestingly, the sauce is used to dress a stuffed ravioli, filled simply with ricotta, egg yolks, Parmigiano, and parsley. This recipe is one of the rare exceptions to the avoidance of grated cheese in combination with fish; but here the cheese is a binder for the stuffing, and no grated cheese would be sprinkled on before serving.

Prepare the stuffing. Put the ricotta, egg yolks, and Parmigiano in a crockery or glass bowl; mix the ingredients with a wooden spoon. Finely chop the parsley on a board, then add it to bowl and season to taste with salt, pepper, and nutmeg. Mix well, cover the bowl, and refrigerate until needed.

Prepare the pasta with the ingredients and quantities listed, following the directions on page 12. Stretch layer to less than $\frac{1}{16}$ inch thick—on the pasta machine take it to the last setting. Prepare *ravioli* about 2 ½ inches square (see page 123). Use a heaping teaspoon of the stuffing for each square; let them sit on cotton towels until needed.

Prepare the sauce. Finely chop the carrot, celery, onion, garlic, and parsley all together on a board. Heat the olive oil in a medium-sized flameproof casserole, over low heat. Add the chopped ingredients and sauté for 10 minutes, stirring every so often with a wooden spoon.

If fresh tomatoes are used, cut them into pieces. Pass the fresh or canned tomatoes through a food mill, using the disc with the smallest holes, into a crockery or glass bowl. Pour the wine into the casserole, raise the heat to medium, and let the wine evaporate for 2 minutes. Add the tomatoes, season with salt and pepper, lower the heat, and simmer for 25 minutes. Add the whole sole fillets, sprinkle with a little salt and pepper, cover, and simmer for 15 minutes.

Meanwhile, bring a large pot of cold water to a boil, add coarse salt to taste, then gently drop in the *ravioli* one by one; cook them for 1 to 3 minutes, depending on dryness. Ladle one-fourth of the sauce and fish onto a large, warmed serving platter. Use a strainer-skimmer to transfer some of the cooked *ravioli* from the pot to the prepared platter. Repeat this procedure to make 3 more layers. Serve hot.

SERVES 6 TO 8

FOR THE STUFFING

15 ounces ricotta

3 extra-large egg yolks

½ cup freshly grated Parmigiano

20 large sprigs Italian parsley, leaves only

Salt and freshly ground black pepper

Freshly grated nutmeg

FOR THE PASTA

3 cups unbleached all-purpose flour

4 extra-large eggs

Pinch of salt

FOR THE SAUCE

1 medium-sized carrot, scraped

1 medium-sized stalk celery

1 medium-sized red onion, peeled

1 medium-sized clove garlic, peeled

15 large sprigs Italian parsley, leaves only

½ cup olive oil

1 ½ pounds ripe, fresh tomatoes; or 1 ½ pounds canned tomatoes, preferably imported Italian, drained

¾ cup dry white wine

Salt and freshly ground black pepper

1 pound sole fillets

Coarse-grained salt

pasta con bottarga
PASTA WITH PRESSED TUNA ROE

SERVES 4 TO 6

4 ounces *bottarga* (pressed salted tuna or mullet roe, imported from Italy), thinly sliced

20 large sprigs Italian parsley, leaves only

2 large cloves garlic, peeled

¾ cup olive oil

Freshly ground black pepper

1 pound dried *spaghetti*, preferably imported Italian

TO COOK THE PASTA

Coarse-grained salt

TO SERVE

10 large sprigs Italian parsley, leaves only

Freshly ground black pepper

Bottarga *is made by pressing salted tuna or mullet roe into a solid mass, which can be sliced and used for flavorings. It is a unique and wonderful flavor, especially popular in Sardinia and Sicily, where these fish are plentiful, but also used elsewhere in Italy. It also travels well.* Bottarga, *chopped with garlic and mixed with olive oil and black pepper, makes a simple, wonderfully lusty uncooked sauce for pasta.*

Fresh tuna roe or caviar is still popular in Sardinia and Sicily combined with pasta. The outer membrane is removed and the fresh eggs lightly sautéed in olive oil and butter. Older cookbooks show that the roe of a number of fish were prized for various dishes—sturgeon, then available in many Italian rivers, was among them. This Sicilian Pasta con bottarga *is an eloquent testimony to the tastes relished by earlier generations.*

Finely chop half the *bottarga* together with the parsley on a board, then transfer to a crockery or glass bowl. Finely chop the garlic on the board, then add the remaining *bottarga* and coarsely chop it with the garlic. Mix this into the bowl with the other ingredients, then start adding the oil, a little at a time, mixing continuously with a wooden spoon and seasoning with pepper. Cover and refrigerate this sauce until needed.

Bring a large pot of cold water to a boil, add coarse salt to taste, then add the pasta and cook until al dente—9 to 12 minutes depending on the brand. Meanwhile, coarsely chop the 10 sprigs of parsley. Drain the pasta, transfer to a large serving platter, add the sauce, toss very well, and serve with the chopped parsley and a twist of black pepper on top.

Tuna and mullet bottarga, the pressed roe.

spaghetti alla genovese
SPAGHETTI, GENOESE STYLE

When the Venetians speak of pasta al sugo, they are referring to "bigoli in sauce." The classic sauce is always an anchovy one. But the rival seaport of Genoa has its own classic anchovy sauce and the pasta is called alla genovese. The Venetian sauce is simpler; it combines white onions with the fish and the only flavoring is black pepper. The Genoese sauce has a more complex taste, including Genoa's favorites garlic and basil, and some oregano.

Bring a large stockpot of cold water to a boil, add coarse salt to taste, then add the pasta and cook until al dente—9 to 12 minutes depending on the brand.

Prepare the sauce. Finely chop the basil and garlic together on a cutting board, or using a food processor or a blender. If using anchovies preserved in salt, fillet them under cold water, discarding bones and washing away excess salt. Cut the anchovy fillets into ½-inch pieces. Heat the oil in a large skillet over low heat. When the oil is lukewarm, add the anchovies and mash them using a fork. The oil should be just lukewarm, not hot, otherwise the anchovies will become very salty and fishy. Add the basil mixture, mix well, then season with salt—very lightly because of the saltiness of the anchovies—and pepper. The sauce should be just lukewarm.

Drain the pasta, add to the skillet, season with oregano and mix very well, then transfer to a warmed serving platter. Sprinkle with the basil and serve.

WINE • Michele Chiarlo Gavi D.O.C.G.

SERVES 4 TO 6

Coarse-grained salt

1 pound dried *spaghetti*, preferably imported Italian

1 cup loosely packed basil leaves

2 medium-sized cloves garlic, peeled

4 anchovies in salt; or 8 anchovy fillets packed in oil, drained

½ cup extra-virgin olive oil

Salt and freshly ground black pepper

1 teaspoon fresh oregano leaves or a large pinch of dried oregano

TO SERVE

Fresh basil leaves

clams, mussels, shrimp, and calamari

The most common types of seafood sauces for pasta are those using a mixture such as clams, mussels, shrimp, and calamari, or those involving just clams. The most common ingredients are olive oil, parsley, garlic, and white wine. Tomatoes have come to be widely used in these sauces; but, particularly in northern areas, there are some who still object to the sweetness of tomatoes in combination with shellfish. They usually make their sauce with a *battuto* of parsley and garlic, and with white wine—a kind of green sauce sautéed in olive oil. But, as we can see from the following recipes, the tomato has all but conquered these sauces, even though the *bianco* version of pasta with clams remains popular.

The ink of the cuttlefish *(seppie)* or squid is used with *spaghetti* in Tuscany. (The Venetian version with rice is equally celebrated.) The ink is extracted and cooked into a sauce that exploits the spicy, peppery flavor of the ink itself. The color is really brownish, like sepia drawings of the old masters, which are made with this very ink (notice the derivation of *sepia* from *seppie*). It has become fashionably chic to make a black pasta by putting this ink or some substitute thereof directly into the dough. I find this questionable, as very little flavor is retained, and the color, though trendy, is not really attractive. Indeed, it is often so black that I wonder if the brownish ink is really the coloring agent in those instances.

pasta alla posillipo
PASTA WITH MIXED SEAFOOD

Pasta alla posillipo, *from the Naples area, combines shrimp, squid, mussels, and clams with other ingredients (tomatoes, of course, in Naples). The squid must be cooked a long time, by using some of the water from cooking the shrimp shells and then combining the shrimp with the squid. The clams and mussels are cooked separately, and then they are all combined.*

Place the shrimp, squid, mussels, and clams in 4 different bowls of cold water with a little coarse salt added to each, and soak for 30 minutes.

Drain the shrimp and rinse under cold running water, then shell them. Place the shrimp in a small bowl; put the shells in a small saucepan. Pour 2 cups cold water over the shells, place them over medium heat, and simmer for 30 minutes. Strain the broth (it will yield about 1 cup), discard the shells; set aside.

Coarsely chop the garlic on a board. Place a small saucepan with ¼ cup of oil over medium heat. When the oil is warm, add the garlic, sauté for 2 minutes, then add the tomatoes and simmer for 30 minutes, seasoning to taste with salt and pepper. Pass the mixture through a food mill, using the disc with the smallest holes, into a flame-proof casserole. Set casserole over low heat to reduce for 15 minutes.

Drain the squid and rinse under cold running water. Place another medium-sized saucepan with ¼ cup of oil over low heat. When the oil is warm, add the squid and sauté for 5 minutes. Pour in the wine. Let it evaporate for 5 minutes. Add ½ cup of broth from the shrimp shells, cover, and cook for 10 minutes. Season with salt and pepper, and keep adding the broth until the squid is tender, about 10 to 20 minutes.

Bring a large pot of cold water to a boil and add coarse salt to taste. Once the squid are cooked, add the pasta to the boiling water; cook for 8 to 11 minutes depending on the brand; that is, 1 minute less than for normal al dente. As the pasta cooks, drain the mussels and clams, scrub them under cold water, then place in a large skillet with the remaining ¼ cup of olive oil. Place over high heat, cover, and cook for 10 minutes, or until the shells open. (Discard any unopened shells.)

Add the shrimp to the squid pan and cook for 3 minutes. When the pasta is ready, drain it, transfer it to the skillet with the mussels and clams, add the tomato sauce with the shrimp and squid, then mix very well and let cook for 1 minute. Transfer to a warmed serving platter, sprinkle with the whole parsley leaves, and serve.

NOTE

See Note on page 144 regarding tomatoes.

SERVES 4 TO 6

- ½ pound small shrimp, unshelled
- 1 pound very small squid (*calamari*), cleaned and cut into ½-inch rings
- 1 pound mussels, unshelled
- 1 pound small clams (littlenecks), unshelled
- Coarse-grained salt
- 2 cups cold water
- 2 large cloves garlic, peeled
- ¾ cup olive oil
- 2 pounds canned tomatoes, preferably imported Italian, undrained
- Salt and freshly ground black pepper
- ½ cup dry white wine
- 1 pound dried *perciatelli*, preferably imported Italian
- 20 large sprigs Italian parsley, leaves only

TO COOK THE PASTA

- Coarse-grained salt

lasagne di gamberi e muscoli

LASAGNE WITH SHRIMP AND MUSSELS

SERVES 8 TO 10

FOR THE PASTA

4 cups unbleached all-purpose flour

2 extra-large eggs

¾ cup lukewarm water

Pinch of salt

TO COOK THE PASTA

Coarse-grained salt

2 tablespoons olive or vegetable oil

FOR THE STUFFING

2 ½ pounds medium-sized shrimp, unshelled

1 ½ pounds mussels, unshelled

Coarse-grained salt

1 large lemon, cut in half

7 tablespoons olive oil

1 medium-sized red onion, peeled

2 large cloves garlic, peeled

20 large sprigs Italian parsley, leaves only

4 tablespoons (2 ounces) sweet butter

1 cup dry white wine

Salt and freshly ground black pepper

Pinch of hot red pepper flakes

In Liguria, shrimp and mussels are used in combination with lasagne; the two shellfish are chopped to produce a pinkish stuffing. Typically northern is the addition of butter to the oil for sautéing and additional butter in the tomato sauce with basil flavoring, a Ligurian must.

Prepare the pasta with the ingredients and quantities listed, following the directions on page 12. Stretch the layer to ⅟₁₆ inch thick—on the pasta machine, take to the next to last setting. Cut the pasta sheet into *lasagne* squares, parboil for a few seconds in salted water, transfer to a bowl with the cold water and the oil, remove, and let rest on damp cotton dish towels until needed.

Place the shrimp and mussels in separate bowls of cold water with a little coarse salt added to each; let soak for 30 minutes.

Meanwhile, begin the tomato sauce. If fresh tomatoes are used, cut them into pieces. Put fresh or canned tomatoes in a medium-sized saucepan with the butter and basil, and cook over medium heat for 30 minutes.

Bring a large pot of cold water to a boil, add coarse salt and the lemon halves. Drain the shrimp, add to the boiling water, and simmer for 3 minutes. Drain the shrimp, rinse with cold water, then shell and devein them. Drain the mussels, put them in a large skillet with 3 tablespoons of the olive oil, cover, and place over high heat. Most of the mussels should open in about 10 minutes; discard any that do not. Shell the mussels and place the meat in a crockery or glass bowl.

Finely chop the onion, garlic, and parsley together on a board. Put the remaining 4 tablespoons of oil and the butter in a medium-sized heavy casserole; when the butter is melted, add the chopped ingredients and sauté for 5 minutes. Add the shrimp and mussels, mix well, and cook for 1 minute more. Pour in the wine, raise the heat to medium-high, and let evaporate for 5 minutes. Season the mixture with salt, pepper, and a large pinch of hot red pepper flakes. Remove the chopped ingredients and the seafood with a slotted spoon, and finely chop them on a board or in a food processor. Set aside the casserole with the reserved juices.

Finish the sauce. Pass the tomato mixture through a food mill, using the disc with the smallest holes, into a second saucepan. Season with salt and pepper. Reduce the sauce over medium heat for 15 more minutes. Add 1½ cups of the reduced tomato sauce to the shrimp-mussel mixture, then place everything back in the casserole with the leftover juices. Simmer for 2 minutes more, mixing with a wooden spoon. Transfer to a bowl and set aside until cool.

Preheat the oven to 375°F.

Oil a 13 ½-by-8 ¾-inch glass baking dish. Make a layer of pasta on the bottom of the pan, place some of the shellfish sauce over it, then put on more pasta and some of the tomato sauce. Keep alternating layers of pasta, shellfish sauce, pasta, and tomato sauce. The top layer of pasta should be covered with tomato sauce; reserve at least ½ cup of the tomato sauce for this layer. Bake for 30 minutes, remove from the oven, and let rest for 2 minutes before serving.

FOR THE TOMATO SAUCE

- **3 pounds ripe, fresh tomatoes; or 3 pounds canned tomatoes, preferably imported Italian, drained**
- **4 tablespoons (2 ounces) sweet butter**
- **4 large basil leaves, fresh or preserved in salt**
- **Salt or freshly ground black pepper**

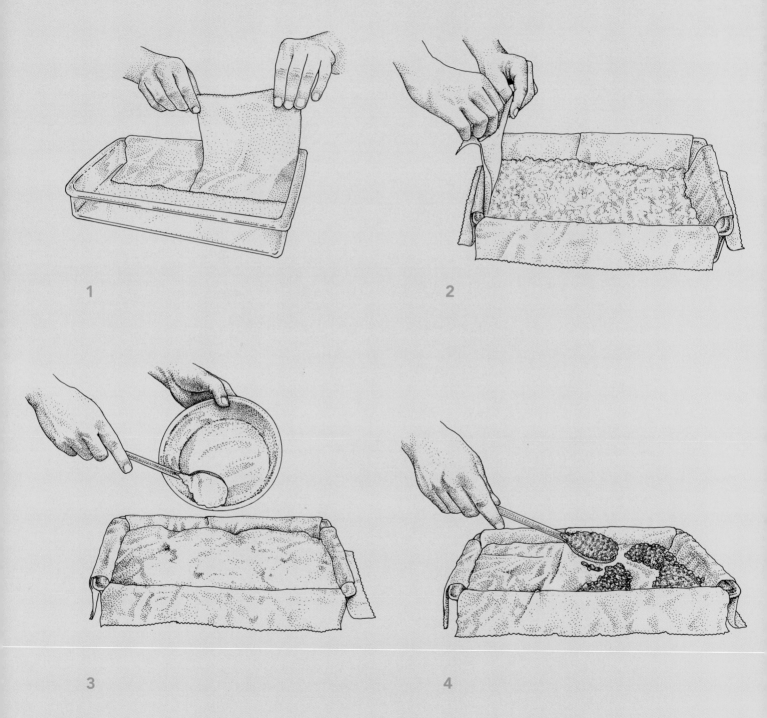

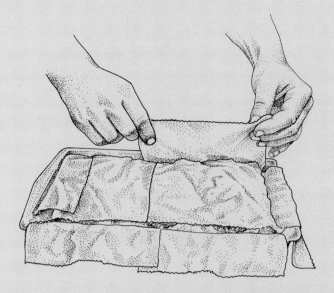

5

LASAGNE

1. Line the baking dish with the pasta squares and allow about 1 inch to hang out over the edges all around the dish.

2. Make a layer of stuffing, then add another layer of pasta, this time covering only the inside of the dish.

3. and 4. According to the individual recipe, keep alternating layers of stuffing (in some recipes there is more than one stuffing) with layers of pasta.

5. Fold the pasta ends over the top layer of pasta.

6. The assembled pasta goes directly into the oven or, depending on the recipe, another sauce is placed on top before baking the *lasagne*.

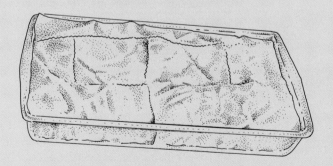

6

maccheroni alle vongole

PASTA WITH CLAMS

SERVES 4 TO 6

2 pounds very small clams, unshelled

Coarse-grained salt

2 large cloves garlic, peeled

20 large sprigs Italian parsley, leaves only

½ cup olive oil

2 pounds ripe, fresh tomatoes; or 2 pounds canned tomatoes, preferably imported Italian, drained

Salt and freshly ground black pepper

1 pound dried *perciatelli* or *vermicelli*, preferably imported Italian

TO COOK THE PASTA

Coarse-grained salt

Pasta with Clams exists in two classic versions, each marvelously simple. For in bianco, *the clams are simply added to a basic aglio-olio; for the "red" version, the clams are combined with a basic marinara. The white version is certainly older, and even suggests itself as the very first pasta-with-shellfish combination. As we see elsewhere in this book, "alla marinara" itself develops right out of aglio-olio, so only the addition of tomato is necessary to make the white version into the red one we have here.*

Scrub the clams very well; soak them in a bowl of cold water with a little coarse salt for 30 minutes.

To prepare the sauce and cook the pasta, follow the recipe for *Maccheroni alla marinara,* page 105. Add the clams to the simmering tomatoes when the pasta is added to the boiling water, and cook them at the same time as the pasta, for 9 to 12 minutes. Discard any clams that do not open. Serve the pasta and the clams in their shells.

For the "white" version, omit the tomatoes, add the clams to the oil with the garlic and cook for 10 minutes. Sprinkle with chopped parsley.

NOTE

Italians never add grated cheese to this dish.

vermicelli con calamari

VERMICELLI WITH SQUID

Pasta with squid alone is well documented, and we give here the Calabrian version, with lemon, basil, and just a little tomato. Squid must be cleaned well, removing the outer skin completely, and cooked for a long time to become really tender. Naturally, the smaller, more tender squid are preferable, though the baby ones should be reserved for frying.

Clean the *calamari* following the directions on page 142. Cut the bodies of the cleaned *calamari* into rings about ½ inch thick, and cut the tentacles into strips not longer than 3 inches. Place the *calamari* in a bowl of cold water, add 1 tablespoon of coarse salt, and soak for 30 minutes.

Place a medium-sized stockpot of cold water over high heat, and, when the water reaches a boil, add coarse salt and the lemon halves. Drain and rinse the *calamari* very well, add them to the boiling water, cover, lower the heat, and simmer for 25 minutes. By that time the *calamari* should be cooked but still a bit chewy. Let the *calamari* rest, covered, in the pot for 30 minutes, then drain.

Place a large, heavy skillet with the oil over medium heat, and when the oil is warm, add the tomato paste and sauté for 2 minutes. Add the drained *calamari* and the basil leaves, then add salt and pepper to taste. Cover and cook over low heat for 15 minutes.

Bring a large pot of cold water to a boil, add coarse salt, then add the pasta and cook for 8 to 11 minutes depending on the brand; that is, 1 minute less than for normal al dente. Drain the pasta, add it to the skillet, and mix well. Taste for salt and pepper, and sauté, continuously mixing with a wooden spoon until almost all the sauce is incorporated and the pasta is perfectly cooked. Transfer to a warmed serving dish and serve immediately.

SERVES 4 TO 6

3 pounds *calamari* (yields 2 pounds cleaned)

Coarse-grained salt

1 large lemon, cut in half

¾ cup olive oil

3 heaping tablespoons tomato paste, preferably imported Italian

10 large basil leaves, fresh or preserved in salt, torn into thirds

Salt and freshly ground black pepper

1 pound dried *vermicelli*, preferably imported Italian

TO COOK THE PASTA

Coarse-grained salt

Cuttlefish (seppie)*, left, are cleaned in the same way as squid* (calamari)*.*

SQUID AND CUTTLEFISH

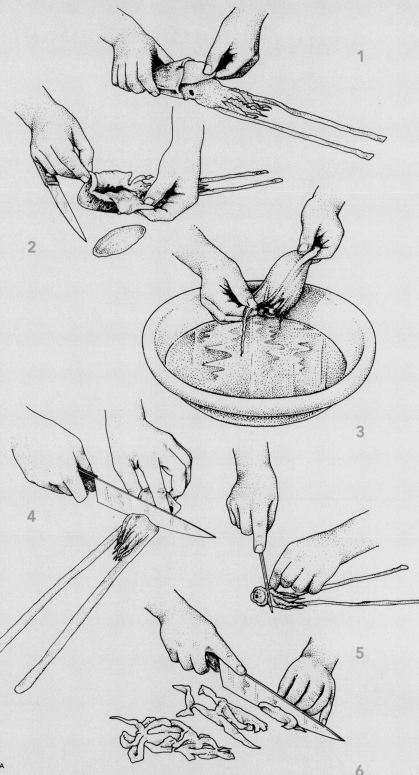

1. Pull out the large white bone in the stomach or casing of the cuttlefish, or the long translucent bone of the squid.

2. If using the ink sac of the cuttlefish, as in *Couscous nero*, page 372, use a knife to cut open the stomach or casing on the side where the bone was, being careful not to break the delicate sac. If using squid, do not cut open the stomach, but pull out the head from the stomach.

3. For both cuttlefish and squid, the tough dark outer skin of the stomach must be pulled off in cold water.

4. For both, cut the head off just below the eyes and discard, leaving the tentacles and arms attached to the lower part of the head.

5. Turn the lower part upside down. The tentacles and arms will now hang over the sides and the inside of the lower head will be pulled open to reveal a black spot which is the mouth. Cut it off.

6. Slice the stomach of the cuttlefish into strips, the squids into rings.

spaghetti alla marinara alla salernitana

SPAGHETTI, SAILORS' STYLE

Sauces including canned tuna form their own category apart from those using fresh tuna. Canned tuna is not simply a substitute for fresh, but a much-loved ingredient with its own unique characteristics and taste. The best is preserved in olive oil, and cut into large trance, *or slices, which look very appetizing. This tuna, when mixed with beans and onions, is frequently served as an appetizer even in refined restaurants, and, in large servings, as a main dish in* trattorie. *Imported brands can be found in specialty shops and are worth the extra cost. Canned tuna is used in pasta sauces* alla marinara, *such as this one, combined with anchovies, or the version from Trapani that is mixed with shrimp (page 146).*

Blanch the tomatoes in a pot of salted boiling water, then remove the skins and seeds and cut them into 1-inch squares. Lightly crush the garlic. Heat the oil in a large skillet over medium heat; when the oil is lukewarm, add the garlic and lightly sauté for 1 or 2 minutes or until very light gold in color. Add the tomatoes, mix very well with a wooden spoon, then add the olives and capers and cook for a few minutes more, shaking the skillet rather than mixing the contents, so the tomatoes remain in large pieces. Add the parsley and season lightly with salt and pepper.

Bring a large pot of cold water to a boil over medium heat, add coarse salt to taste, then add the pasta and cook until al dente—9 to 12 minutes depending on the brand.

As the pasta cooks, if using anchovies preserved in salt, fillet them under cold running water, discarding bones and washing away excess salt. Cut anchovy fillets into 1-inch pieces. Add the anchovies and tuna to the sauce and cook for 1 minute more without mixing. The tuna will remain in large pieces but the anchovies will break down.

Drain the pasta, transfer to a large bowl, then add the liquid from the sauce and mix very well. Transfer the pasta to a large warmed serving platter, arrange the remaining sauce over the top, and sprinkle with the basil. Serve hot.

SERVES 4 TO 6

- 1 ½ pounds fresh tomatoes, ripe but not overripe
- Coarse-grained salt
- 1 large clove garlic, peeled and left whole
- 4 tablespoons extra-virgin olive oil
- 4 ounces green olives, pitted and coarsely chopped
- 4 tablespoons capers in wine vinegar, drained
- 10 large sprigs Italian parsley, leaves only, coarsely chopped
- Salt and freshly ground black pepper
- 2 anchovies preserved in salt; or 4 anchovy fillets packed in oil, drained
- 4 ounces canned tuna packed in olive oil, drained
- 1 pound dried *spaghetti*, preferably imported Italian

TO COOK THE PASTA
Coarse-grained salt

TO SERVE
Large fresh basil leaves

minestra di pasta all'aragosta
LOBSTER SOUP WITH PASTA

SERVES 6 TO 8

2 medium-sized stalks celery

1 medium-sized red onion, peeled

2 medium-sized carrots, scraped

5 large sprigs Italian parsley, leaves only

1 lobster (about 1 ½ pounds), boiled

2 pounds canned tomatoes, preferably imported Italian, undrained

1 heaping teaspoon coarse-grained salt

2 quarts cold water

2 tablespoons extra-virgin olive oil

Salt and freshly ground black pepper

6 ounces dried *spaghetti*, preferably imported Italian, broken into thirds

TO SERVE

Sprigs of fresh basil leaves

This delicious Lobster Soup with Pasta is made with aromatic vegetables, including parsley, and with tomato. Water is added to make a soup rather than a sauce, and the spaghetti is broken into thirds. The rich flavor is obtained by simmering the lobster shells in the liquid for an hour and a half, then adding the lobster meat. The pasta is cooked in the broth.

Cut the celery, onion, and carrots into large pieces and put them, along with the parsley leaves, in a bowl of cold water to soak for 30 minutes. Remove all the meat from the lobster (you should have 6 ounces); cut the larger parts into 1-inch pieces, then put all the meat in a crockery or glass bowl and refrigerate, covered, until needed.

Place the lobster shells in a medium-sized flameproof casserole, drain the vegetables, and add them to the casserole. Add the tomatoes, the coarse salt, the cold water, and the oil. Place the casserole over medium heat, uncovered. Simmer for 1 ½ hours without stirring or mixing.

Remove and discard the lobster shells, then pass the remaining contents through a food mill, using the disc with the smallest holes, into another flameproof casserole. Place the casserole over medium heat, taste for salt and pepper, and, when the broth reaches a boil, add the *spaghetti* and reserved lobster meat. Stir very well and cook the pasta for 9 to 12 minutes depending on the brand. Transfer the soup to a warmed tureen and cover. Let the soup rest 2 minutes. Serve with sprig of fresh basil leaves.

NOTE

If the especially juicy fresh tomatoes grown for making sauce in Italy are available, they are best. Other types of fresh tomatoes, even very ripe, are not juicy enough.

pasta alla marinara alla trapanese

PASTA ALLA MARINARA, TRAPANI STYLE

SERVES 4 TO 6

1 pound small or medium-sized shrimp, unshelled

Coarse-grained salt

10 large sprigs Italian parsley, leaves only

2 medium-sized cloves garlic, peeled

12 ounces ripe, fresh tomatoes; or 12 ounces canned tomatoes, preferably imported Italian, drained

½ cup olive oil

1 (6 ½-ounce) can tuna packed in olive oil, drained

Salt and freshly ground black pepper

1 pound dried *vermicelli* or thick *spaghetti*, preferably imported Italian

TO COOK THE PASTA

Coarse-grained salt

TO SERVE

10 large sprigs Italian parsley, leaves only

Also from Sicily is this dish from Trapani that combines shrimp with canned tuna. It is a rather quick dish in which the shrimp are par-boiled and cooked for just a few minutes with the tuna in the tomatoes. As in the previous recipe, no wine is added. Both of these recent dishes are successful and delicious.

Soak the shrimp in a bowl of cold water for 30 minutes with 1 teaspoon of coarse salt. Bring a small saucepan of cold water to boil over medium heat; add coarse salt to taste. Drain and rinse the shrimp, then add them to the pan. Cover and cook until tender, about 2 to 3 minutes depending on the size of the shrimp. Drain, shell, and devein the cooked shrimp, leaving them whole.

Meanwhile, finely chop the parsley and garlic together on a board. If fresh tomatoes are used, cut them into 1-inch pieces. Pass fresh or canned tomatoes through a food mill, using the disc with the smallest holes, into a crockery or glass bowl. Bring a large pot of cold water to a boil.

Heat the oil in a large skillet over low heat; add the parsley and garlic, and sauté for 5 minutes. Add the puréed tomatoes to the garlic and parsley, and sauté for 5 more minutes. Add the shrimp and tuna, mix very well, and season with salt and pepper. Cook for 10 minutes, stirring every so often with a wooden spoon.

When the water in the pot reaches a boil, add coarse salt to taste, then add the pasta and cook until al dente—9 to 12 minutes depending on the brand. Drain the pasta and add it to the skillet, mix very well for 30 seconds, then transfer to a warmed serving dish and serve, sprinkled with parsley.

VARIATION

Boil 1 pound of mussels in salted water for 2 minutes. Drain, discard those that do not open, and remove the others from their shells. Add the mussels to the tomato sauce along with the shrimp and tuna.

mostaccioli del venerdi

MOSTACCIOLI WITH TUNA SAUCE

This recipe was described to me by a volunteer at Milwaukee's Festa Italiana, who said that Friday in the Abruzzese town of his childhood always meant they would have this pasta dish. It is made with fresh tuna that is cooked and then marinated overnight, so it can be prepared a day in advance. This leaves the family free to go to church and return home to an easily prepared pasta dressed with a fish sauce, which was essential for every Friday meal in a Catholic country. Mostaccioli are the southern Italian counterparts of the better known penne.

Place the tuna in a small bowl of cold water, add a little salt and the lemon halves, and soak for ½ hour. Drain the tuna and pat it dry with paper towels.

Heat the oil in a medium-sized skillet over medium heat. When the oil is warm, add the fish and lightly sauté for 1 minute on each side, or until completely cooked—it will lose its pink color—but still very juicy. Season with salt and pepper. Transfer the fish to a crockery or glass bowl and cover the bowl.

Add the onion and the bay leaves to the skillet, mixing them with the juices from the tuna, and slowly sauté, mixing every so often with a wooden spoon, until the onion becomes very soft, about 20 minutes, adding a little cold water if the liquid evaporates. Finely chop the garlic and parsley together on a board, add the mixture to the skillet, mix very well with the wooden spoon, and cook for 2 minutes more. Add the vinegar and simmer, allowing the vinegar to evaporate, for 15 minutes, then add the water and simmer until only ¼ of the cooking liquid remains. Add the capers, mix very well, then pour the sauce over the tuna. Cover the bowl and let rest until cool, about 1 hour, then refrigerate overnight.

The next day, bring a large pot of cold water to a boil, add coarse salt to taste, then add the pasta and cook until al dente—9 to 12 minutes depending on the brand. Chop the garlic very finely and chop the parsley coarsely, then mix them together. Drain the pasta and transfer to a large bowl. Add the cold, marinated fish with all of the sauce to the bowl and mix very well. Transfer everything to a large, warmed serving platter and sprinkle the garlic mixture over the top. Serve immediately at room temperature.

SERVES 4 TO 6

- 1 small fresh tuna steak, about 6 ounces
- Coarse-grained salt
- 1 lemon, cut in half
- 4 tablespoons extra-virgin olive oil
- Salt and freshly ground black pepper
- 1 large red onion, cleaned and thinly sliced
- 2 bay leaves
- 1 large clove garlic, peeled
- 10 large sprigs Italian parsley, leaves only
- ½ cup red wine vinegar
- 1 cup cold water
- 2 tablespoons capers in wine vinegar, drained
- 1 pound dried *mostaccioli* or *penne*, preferably imported Italian

TO COOK THE PASTA

Coarse-grained salt

TO SERVE

- 1 large clove garlic, peeled
- 10 large sprigs Italian parsley, leaves only

vermicelli ai granchi
PASTA WITH CRABMEAT

SERVES 4 TO 6

4 large cloves garlic, peeled

½ cup olive oil

2 ½ pounds very ripe, fresh tomatoes; or 2 ½ pounds canned tomatoes, preferably imported Italian, drained

Salt and freshly ground black pepper

1 teaspoon hot red pepper flakes

1 pound dried *vermicelli* or *spaghetti*, preferably imported Italian

½ pound lump crabmeat

TO COOK THE PASTA

Coarse-grained salt

TO SERVE

30 large sprigs Italian parsley, leaves only

Crabmeat is used with pasta in Adriatic localities, where the crabs are particularly good. Since crab is sweet, often the white wine is omitted and, as in this recipe from Apulia, a little hot pepper is used to spice it up. The whole crab is often simmered in the tomatoes rather than separately in water in order to maximize the flavor of the sauce before extracting the meat.

Coarsely chop the garlic on a board. Place the oil in a medium-sized heavy casserole over medium heat. Add the chopped garlic and sauté for 5 minutes. If fresh tomatoes are used, cut them into pieces. Pass the fresh or canned tomatoes through a food mill, using the disc with the smallest holes, into a bowl. Add the tomatoes to the casserole; season to taste with salt and pepper, and add the red pepper flakes. Simmer for 25 minutes, stirring every so often with a wooden spoon.

Meanwhile, bring a large pot of cold water to a boil. Add coarse salt to taste, then add the pasta and cook until al dente—9 to 12 minutes depending on the brand. When the tomato sauce is ready, add the crabmeat and simmer for 5 minutes more. Coarsely chop the parsley. Drain the pasta and transfer to a large, warmed serving platter; pour the sauce over the top and toss very well. Sprinkle with the parsley, toss again, and serve immediately.

Viareggio's famous fish market.

spaghetti e gamberi
SPAGHETTI WITH SHRIMP

Pasta with shrimp alone does not have a long tradition in Italy. One can only ponder why this combination was avoided for such a long time; the few recipes that do exist now are from the last fifty years. Why did they use shrimp in combination with other seafood, but not alone? Food for thought! The Spaghetti with Shrimp from Marsala in Sicily here emphasizes the sweetness of Sicilian cooking by the addition of onion and, of course, since it is a recent recipe, tomatoes. The shrimp are shelled raw and cooked briefly at the end before the sauce is mixed with the pasta.

Soak the shrimp in a bowl of cold water with coarse salt for 30 minutes. Finely chop the onion and garlic together on a board. Heat the oil in a large nonreactive skillet over medium heat, and, when the oil is warm, add the chopped onion and garlic; sauté for 5 minutes. Meanwhile, if fresh tomatoes are used, cut them into pieces. Pass the fresh or canned tomatoes through a food mill, using the disc with the smallest holes, into a small bowl. Add the tomatoes to the skillet, season with salt and pepper, and simmer for 15 minutes.

Drain the shrimp, rinse very well under cold running water, and shell and devein them. Bring a large pot of cold water to a boil, add coarse salt to taste, then add the pasta and cook for 8 to 11 minutes depending on the brand; that is, 1 minute less than for normal al dente. Meanwhile, add the shelled shrimp to the tomato sauce, cover the skillet, and cook for 2 more minutes. Taste for salt and pepper. Finely chop the parsley on a board and add it to the skillet. By that time, the shrimp should be almost cooked.

Drain the pasta, add it to the skillet, and sauté for 2 minutes, mixing very well with a wooden spoon. Transfer to a large, warmed serving dish and serve immediately.

SERVES 6 TO 8

- **1 pound medium-sized shrimp, unshelled**
- **Coarse-grained salt**
- **1 medium-sized red onion, peeled**
- **1 large clove garlic, peeled**
- **½ cup olive oil**
- **1 ½ pounds ripe, fresh tomatoes; or 1 ½ pounds canned tomatoes, preferably imported Italian, drained**
- **Salt and freshly ground black pepper**
- **1 pound dried *spaghetti*, preferably imported Italian**
- **15 large sprigs Italian parsley, leaves only**

TO COOK THE PASTA

Coarse-grained salt

spaghetti agli scampi
SPAGHETTI WITH SCAMPI

SERVES 6

8 scampi or large shrimp, unpeeled

Coarse-grained salt

1 lemon, cut in half

4 tablespoons extra-virgin olive oil

3 medium cloves garlic, peeled and finely chopped

Salt and freshly ground black pepper

¼ cup completely defatted chicken broth, preferably homemade

10 sprigs Italian parsley, leaves only, finely chopped

1 pound dried *spaghetti*, preferably imported Italian

TO COOK THE PASTA

Coarse-grained salt

TO SERVE

Sprigs of fresh Italian parsley

"Scampi" is a particular type of shrimp, not a method of preparation. They are sweeter than shrimp, which are smaller, and their meat is quite light in color. Therefore the term "Shrimp Scampi" as we often see it used on menus would be nonsensical to a diner from Italy. In Italy, scampi are cooked in as many ways as other kinds of shrimp. In fact, they are often preferred in dishes that call for a combination of shrimp and pasta.

Soak the scampi in a bowl of cold water with a pinch of coarse salt and the lemon halves for ½ hour. Drain the scampi and rinse them under cold running water.

Heat the oil in a large skillet over medium heat; when the oil is warm, add the garlic and sauté for 1 minute or less—it should be still very light in color. Add the scampi, season with salt and pepper, cover the skillet, and cook for 4 minutes. Add the broth and the parsley, cover again, and cook for 2 minutes more. Remove two of the scampi and extract the meat from the shells. Cut the meat into small pieces, add it to the skillet; cover, and remove the skillet from the heat.

In the meantime, bring a large pot of cold water to a boil, add coarse salt to taste, then add the pasta and cook for 8 to 11 minutes depending on the brand; that is, 1 minute less than for normal al dente. Drain the pasta. Remove the whole scampi from the skillet, and set them aside. Transfer the pasta to the skillet and sauté for 1 minute, mixing very well and tasting for salt and pepper. Transfer the pasta to a large serving platter, arrange the whole scampi over the top, and serve hot with sprigs of Italian parsley.

PROSCIUTTO
SAN DANIELE
L.60.000 KG
INTERO L.27.000 KG

pasta with m

eat and game

meat sauces

Each region and city has its classic meat sauces. Among the most famous are those from Bologna, Naples, Florence, Lucca, Abruzzi, Apulia, and Sicily. We include all these examples.

The famous Bolognese *ragù* is one of several meat sauces of its area and is the most popular one. Its distinctive features are the sautéing of the meat together with the aromatic chopped vegetables, the omission of garlic among those vegetables, the combination of snipped, chopped, or ground beef and pork for the meat, the frequent use of white rather than red wine, and, especially, the inclusion of heavy cream. We choose this one of the several Bolognese versions of meat sauce and would like to point out as well that the ones from Bologna differ slightly from those made in neighboring Romagna. (I should like to remind readers once again that pasta with meat sauce is not automatically *alla bolognese*. Only those pastas specifically using a Bolognese meat sauce are such; the many employing such sauces from other regions would never be considered *alla bolognese*.)

This Bolognese *ragù* is employed to dress the paprika pasta on page 314 as well as the *Tagliatelle al ragù alla bolognese*. The pasta used in Bologna is generally rolled thicker than my Tuscan-derived basic recipe, it uses a greater proportion of eggs to pasta, and because it omits the touch of olive oil it is generally less soft and is therefore more appropriate to this richer sauce.

Previous pages: A selection of Prosciutto di Parma.

It is the celebrated *ragù alla napoletana* that has created the legend of the sauce that cooks slowly for hours and hours. One hears stories about Neapolitan grandmothers who cooked the sauce over the lowest of flames for innumerable hours, even twenty-four. And lost in the mists of this legend is the fact that we are dealing here with a meat sauce, and particularly with a cut of meat—rump—that requires and benefits from a long cooking time. I have heard the legend of the long cooking time incorrectly applied to tomato sauces, a practice that produces rather dubious results. The recipe that follows takes a longish period but remains under three hours. In that time, the rump meat emerges succulent and tender, and the sauce is rich with the meat essence. The meat itself, tied like a salami, is served as a second dish at the same meal or, more often, at another meal; it is served hot, dressed with its *ragù*, or sliced cold and served with some other piquant sauce.

The simple Tuscan meat sauce so popular in central Italy uses only snipped (or chopped or ground) beef for the meat and includes the aromatic vegetables (carrot, onion, celery, garlic, parsley, lemon peel, but no leek), red wine, and a small amount of dried *porcini*, and the tomato is reinforced with a little tomato paste.

The meat sauce from Lucca in Tuscany, *tocco di carne*, is almost identical with the sauce just described, except that it is lightly flavored with clove and has nutmeg in the sauce itself. It also employs a higher percentage of tomatoes. *Tocco di*—"touch of"—is a term used in the name of a sauce that is also made in nearby Liguria. The pasta served with this dressing in Lucca is usually fresh rather than dried.

Pasta alla boscaiola, its name invoking the woods, clearly stresses wild mushrooms. It is a sauce with just a little lean meat, sometimes veal rather than beef, and a few chicken livers. But it is the mushrooms, added in larger quantity than in other meat sauces, that give greatest impact to the sauce. Some black Greek-type olives underline the flavors of the mushrooms and the chicken livers. In Italy, where wild mushrooms are part of everyone's diet, this sauce has an important place all over the country.

The *sugo di manzo* used with *tagliatelle* in Livorno and with boiled *lasagne* in Genoa extracts the essence of the beef by cooking it slowly for five hours. The meat is then removed and the sauce is passed through a mill and reduced to a rich denseness. With no garlic among the aromatic vegetables, the sauce is flavored with *pancetta* and cloves. The veal sauce from Livorno is used for their version of *Penne strascicate*. Dried *porcini, pancetta*, and clove flavor the veal shoulder and chicken drumstick cooked in wine, tomato paste, and broth. The technique is clearly related to that of the *sugo di manzo*, since the meats are simmered, again for five hours, passed through a mill, and reduced.

The remarkable pork of the Siena area is the basis for the meat sauce of nearby Montalcino, served with their unique *pinci*. Three kinds of pork—ground fresh, sausages, and *pancetta*—are combined with a little chicken breast and cooked in tomatoes and the incomparable Brunello wine, then sprinkled with the Sienese sheep's milk cheese, *pecorino*.

tagliatelle al ragù alla bolognese
TAGLIATELLE WITH BOLOGNESE RAGÙ MEAT SAUCE

Prepare sauce according to directions on page 314.

Make the pasta with the ingredients and quantities listed and following instructions on page 12. Stretch layer to 1/16 inch thick—on the pasta machine take it to the next to the last setting. Cut into *tagliatelle* (see page 34).

Bring a large pot of cold water to a boil. When the water reaches a boil, add coarse salt, then add the pasta and cook for 1 to 3 minutes depending on the dryness. Meanwhile, place the butter in a large, warmed serving platter and put over the boiling water to melt the butter.

When ready, drain the pasta, transfer to the prepared platter, mix very well with the melted butter, then pour the sauce all over. Mix and serve immediately. Pass cheese at the table.

SERVES 6 TO 8

FOR THE SAUCE
ragù alla bolognese (page 314)

FOR THE PASTA
4 cups unbleached all-purpose flour

5 extra-large eggs

Pinch of salt

TO COOK THE PASTA
Coarse-grained salt

TO SERVE
4 tablespoons (2 ounces) sweet butter

½ cup freshly grated Parmigiano

maccheroni spianati al tocco di carne

FLAT MACCHERONI WITH LUCCHESE MEAT SAUCE

SERVES 6 TO 8

FOR THE SAUCE

1 pound boneless beef sirloin, in 1 piece

2 Italian sweet sausages without fennel seeds; or 6 ounces ground pork

4 ounces *prosciutto*, in 1 piece

1 large carrot, scraped

1 medium-sized red onion, peeled

1 medium-sized leek (or 1 additional medium-sized red onion), cleaned

1 large clove garlic, peeled

10 large sprigs Italian parsley, leaves only

1 large stalk celery

1 small piece lemon rind

¼ cup olive oil

6 tablespoons (3 ounces) sweet butter

1 cup dry red wine

1 whole clove

1 ½ pounds ripe, fresh tomatoes; or 1 ½ pounds canned tomatoes, preferably imported Italian, drained

Salt and freshly ground black pepper

Pinch of freshly grated nutmeg

Prepare the sauce. Use a pair of scissors to snip the beef into tiny pieces. Remove the skins from the sausages and cut the *prosciutto* into very small pieces. Finely chop the carrot, onion, leek, garlic, parsley, celery, and lemon rind all together on a board.

Place the oil and butter in a heavy medium-sized saucepan over medium heat. When the butter is completely melted, add the *prosciutto* and sauté for 2 minutes. Put in the chopped vegetables and sauté for 15 minutes, stirring occasionally with a wooden spoon. Add the beef and sausages, and sauté for 10 minutes more. Pour in the wine, add the clove, and let the wine evaporate, cooking for 15 minutes.

Meanwhile, if fresh tomatoes are used, cut them into pieces. Pass fresh or canned tomatoes through a food mill, using the disc with smallest holes, into a crockery or glass bowl. Remove the clove from the sauce and discard. Add the tomatoes; season to taste with salt, pepper, and nutmeg; and simmer, covered, for 2 hours, adding the broth as needed, but keeping the sauce thick, not soupy.

As the sauce cooks, prepare the pasta with the ingredients and quantities listed, following the directions on page 12. Stretch layer to a little less than ¹⁄₁₆ inch thick—on the pasta machine take it to the last setting. Use a scalloped pastry wheel to cut the sheet of pasta into 2½-inch squares, and let squares rest on cotton dish towels until needed.

When the sauce is ready, bring a large quantity of cold water to a boil, add coarse salt to taste, then add the pasta; cook the pasta for 1 to 3 minutes depending on dryness. Drain the pasta, transfer to a warmed serving dish with the butter, and mix well. Start adding the sauce, a ladle-ful at a time, while tossing the pasta gently but thoroughly. Serve hot, sprinkling the cheese over each serving.

The famous "Cinta" pigs from Tuscany, source of the region's best prosciutto.

2 cups hot chicken or beef broth, preferably home-made

FOR THE PASTA

3 cups unbleached all-purpose flour

4 extra-large eggs

Pinch of salt

TO COOK THE PASTA

Coarse-grained salt

TO SERVE

2 tablespoons (1 ounce) sweet butter

8 tablespoons freshly grated Parmigiano

pasta al sugo con ricotta
PASTA WITH MEAT SAUCE AND FRESH RICOTTA

FOR THE MEAT SAUCE

4 ounces boneless beef sirloin, in 1 piece

2 carrots, scraped

2 stalks celery

1 medium-sized red onion, cleaned

5 sprigs Italian parsley, leaves only

4 leaves fresh basil

1 ½ pounds ripe, fresh tomatoes; or 1 ½ pounds canned tomatoes, preferably imported Italian, drained

2 tablespoons (1 ounce) sweet butter

2 tablespoons extra-virgin olive oil

Salt and freshly ground black pepper

FOR THE PASTA

1 pound dried short tubular pasta, such as small *rigatoni* or *penne*, preferably imported Italian

TO COOK THE PASTA

Coarse-grained salt

TO SERVE

4 ounces whole-milk ricotta

Freshly grated Parmigiano or pecorino romano cheese

The preferred ricotta in Italy is made with sheep's milk, molded in a special basket, and allowed to become dry enough to slice. The rich, assertive flavor makes it a favorite. Ricotta sauces for pasta may be as simple as ricotta alone with black pepper or ricotta with sautéed vegetables, such as zucchini or asparagus. There also are quite rich versions, such as this ricotta and meat sauce.

Prepare the sauce. Cut the meat into 1-inch pieces. Coarsely chop the carrots, celery, onion, parsley, and basil all together on a board. Use a meat grinder with the discs with the smallest holes to finely grind the meat, and the chopped vegetables and aromatic herbs directly into a crockery or glass bowl. Meanwhile, if fresh tomatoes are used, cut them into pieces. Pass the fresh or canned tomatoes through a food mill, using the disc with smallest holes, into a crockery or glass bowl. Place a nonreactive casserole with the butter and oil over medium heat and, when the butter is melted, add the ground ingredients and sauté for 15 minutes. Season with salt and pepper. Add the tomatoes to the casserole, cover, and let simmer for 30 minutes, stirring every so often with a wooden spoon to be sure none of the ingredients stick to the bottom of the casserole.

In the meantime, bring a large pot of cold water to a boil, add coarse salt to taste, then add the pasta and cook until al dente—9 to 12 minutes depending on the brand. Drain the pasta. Transfer to a warmed serving bowl, pour the sauce over, and mix very well. You can either add the ricotta at this point, tossing gently with a wooden serving spoon, or transfer the pasta to a large platter, then top each serving with some of the ricotta and abundant grated cheese.

vermicelli con ragù alla napoletana

PASTA WITH NEAPOLITAN MEAT SAUCE

Roll and tie the meat as you would a salami (see page 175). Cut into small pieces, then finely chop the *pancetta* with the parsley together on a board; transfer mixture to a plate, season with pepper, and mix very well. Lard the meat on all sides with the chopped ingredients and set aside.

To make the sauce, finely chop or grind the *pancetta* or *prosciutto,* onions, and garlic all together, and place in a heavy medium-sized casserole; add the lard or oil, and place the casserole over low heat. When the lard is melted or the oil is hot, put in the meat and then sauté for 20 minutes, turning the meat over twice. Add the wine and let it evaporate for 30 minutes. Add the tomato paste and 2 cups of lukewarm water, cover, and simmer for 1 hour. Season with salt and pepper, add 2 more cups of luke-warm water, and simmer for 1 hour more. The meat should be completely cooked and tender. Transfer the meat to a platter. Continue to simmer the sauce, uncovered, for 1 ½ hours more, stirring every so often with a wooden spoon and tasting for salt and pepper; it should reduce to about 2 cups.

Cook the pasta in a large quantity of salted water until al dente—9 to 12 minutes depending on the brand. Dress the pasta with the sauce—about 2 cups sauce to 1 pound of pasta.

NOTE

The meat can be eaten hot as a main dish at the same meal or can be reserved for another meal, sliced and served with some of the same sauce. It is particularly good eaten cold, sliced thin and accompanied by some piquant sauce.

In Naples, and Campania in general, pasta is eaten very al dente, cooked as much as 2 minutes less than for normal al dente.

SERVES 4 TO 6

FOR THE MEAT

2 pounds boneless beef rump roast

4 ounces *pancetta* or *prosciutto*

10 large sprigs Italian parsley, leaves only

Freshly ground black pepper

FOR THE SAUCE

4 ounces *pancetta* or *prosciutto*

2 medium-sized red onions, peeled

1 large clove garlic, peeled

8 tablespoons lard or olive oil

1 ½ cups dry red wine

6 ounces tomato paste, preferably imported Italian

4 cups lukewarm water

Salt and freshly ground black pepper

FOR THE PASTA

1 pound *spaghetti* or *vermicelli*, preferably imported Italian

TO COOK THE PASTA

Coarse-grained salt

pasta alla boscaiola

PASTA WITH MUSHROOM-MEAT SAUCE

SERVES 4 TO 6

2 ounces dried *porcini* mushrooms

2 medium-sized carrots, scraped

2 small cloves garlic, peeled

2 medium-sized stalks celery, scraped

15 large sprigs Italian parsley, leaves only

1 medium-sized red onion, peeled

4 tablespoons olive oil

2 tablespoons (1 ounce) sweet butter

4 ounces boneless veal shoulder or lean beef, in 1 piece

1 cup dry red wine

Salt and freshly ground black pepper

1 pound ripe, fresh tomatoes; or 1 pound canned tomatoes, preferably imported Italian, drained

1 cup meat or chicken broth, preferably homemade

5 chicken livers

4 ounces black Greek olives

1 pound dried *penne rigate* or *rigatoni,* preferably imported Italian

TO COOK THE PASTA

Coarse-grained salt

Soak the mushrooms in a bowl of lukewarm water for 30 minutes. Finely chop the carrots, garlic, celery, parsley, and onion all together on a board. Place the oil and butter in a medium-sized flameproof casserole over medium heat. When the butter is melted, add the chopped ingredients and sauté for 10 minutes, stirring every so often with a wooden spoon.

Use a pair of scissors to snip the meat into tiny pieces, add it to the casserole, and cook for 10 minutes. Clean the mushrooms, making sure no sand remains attached to the stems, and add them to the casserole; sauté for 10 more minutes. Add the wine and let it evaporate for 15 minutes. Season with salt and pepper, stir very well, and reduce the heat to low.

If using fresh tomatoes, cut them into pieces. Pass fresh or canned tomatoes through a food mill, using the disc with the smallest holes, into a bowl; add to the casserole and simmer for 30 minutes, stirring every so often with a wooden spoon. Put in ½ cup of the broth, cover the casserole, and cook for 15 minutes more. Add the remaining broth and cook for another 15 minutes. Taste for salt and pepper, and reduce the sauce for 10 minutes more, uncovered.

Bring a large pot of cold water to a boil. Add coarse salt to taste, then add the pasta and cook until al dente—9 to 12 minutes depending on the brand. Meanwhile, cut the chicken livers into fourths, add them to the sauce, and, 3 minutes later, put in the whole olives, cooking for 5 more minutes, stirring and tasting for salt and pepper. Drain the pasta, transfer to a warmed bowl, pour the sauce over the top, mix very well, and serve immediately.

orecchiette o lasagnette alla macellara

PASTA WITH A SAUCE OF MIXED MEATS

The wonderful sauce in this recipe, of pork, beef, veal, and lamb, is used throughout the southern Adriatic coast of Italy, Abruzzi and Apulia. Only onions among the aromatic vegetables and herbs are used; the sauce is also flavored with cloves and hot red pepper flakes, as popular in Abruzzi as in Calabria. The meat is cooked in olive oil, tomatoes, and red wine—and no broth. This meatiest of sauces requires a sturdy pasta; and indeed, in this fresh pasta dough, coarse semolina is used with the all-purpose flour. The complex flavors in this sauce should not be obscured by adding grated cheese when serving.

Use a meat grinder to coarsely grind all the meats together, or use scissors to cut the meat into tiny pieces. Finely chop the onions on a board. Heat the oil in a large heavy casserole over low heat; add the onions and sauté for 10 minutes. Put in the ground meat, raise heat to medium, and sauté for 15 minutes, stirring every so often with a wooden spoon. Add 1 cup of the wine, mix well, and simmer for 15 more minutes. If using fresh tomatoes, cut them into 1-inch cubes. Pass fresh or canned tomatoes through a food mill, using the disc with smallest holes, into a crockery or glass bowl. Season with salt and pepper to taste and add the red pepper flakes. Add the tomatoes to the sauce. Cook, covered, for 30 minutes.

If using fresh pasta, prepare it with the ingredients listed, following the directions on page 12 and shape into *orecchiette* (see page 27), or for *lasagnette*; stretch layer to ⅟₁₆ inch—on the pasta machine take it to the next to the last setting. See *trenette* (page 255), but cut both sides with a scalloped pastry wheel into 2-inch-wide strips. Set aside.

Add the remaining wine to the saucepan, taste for salt and pepper, and add the cloves. Cover and cook for 30 minutes, stirring every so often with a wooden spoon. Remove the lid and let the sauce reduce over medium heat for 15 minutes.

Meanwhile, bring a large quantity of cold water to a boil, add coarse salt, then add the pasta. If using dried pasta, cook for 9 to 12 minutes depending on the brand; if fresh, cook for 4 to 9 minutes depending on dryness. Drain the pasta. Transfer it to a large bowl, pour the sauce over the top, then mix very well. Transfer to a large, warmed serving dish and serve immediately.

SERVES 8 TO 12

FOR THE MEAT SAUCE

½ pound boneless pork, in 1 piece

½ pound boneless beef, in 1 piece

½ pound boneless veal, in 1 piece

½ pound boneless lamb, in 1 piece

2 large red onions, peeled

½ cup olive oil

2 cups dry red wine

1½ pounds ripe, fresh tomatoes; or 1½ pounds canned tomatoes, preferably imported Italian, drained

Salt and freshly ground black pepper

½ teaspoon hot red pepper flakes

2 whole cloves

FOR THE PASTA

2 pounds dried *orecchiette* or *lasagnette*, preferably imported Italian

or

2 cups semolina flour

4 cups unbleached all-purpose flour

Water

Large pinch of salt

TO COOK THE PASTA

Coarse-grained salt

penne strascicate alla lucchese

SAUTÉED PENNE, LUCCA STYLE

This meat sauce from Lucca departs from the ones previously presented, since it relies completely upon sausage. The pork in the Lucca and Siena area is sensationally good. The sausages are cooked, flavored with sage and rosemary, and only garlic is combined with them in the oil and butter. Tomatoes are added, as is heavy cream. Pork and cream are a favored combination in nearby Emilia, with whom Lucca shares this tradition and Liguria with its central Tuscan heritage. The cream in this recipe is used in place of the more usual Tuscan wine.

Remove the skins from the sausages and cut the links into 1-inch pieces. Finely chop the sage, rosemary, and garlic on a board. Place the oil and butter in a deep, medium-sized saucepan over medium heat; when the butter is melted, add the chopped ingredients along with the sausage pieces. Sauté for 10 minutes, mixing every so often with a wooden spoon. If using fresh tomatoes, cut them into pieces. Pass fresh or canned tomatoes through a food mill, using the disc with the smallest holes, into a bowl. Add the tomatoes to the saucepan and simmer for 30 minutes, stirring every so often. Taste for salt and pepper.

Bring a large stockpot of cold water to a boil, add coarse salt to taste, then add the pasta and cook for 8 to 11 minutes depending on the brand; that is, 1 minute less than for normal al dente. The pasta will continue cooking with the sauce, and so should be quite firm. Drain the pasta and add it to the saucepan, letting the pasta sauté directly in the sauce while continuously stirring with a wooden spoon and adding the cream ¼ cup at a time. Sauté until the liquid is completely absorbed by the pasta, about 4 minutes. Remove pan from the stove, transfer pasta onto a warmed platter, and serve hot.

WINE • Tenuta di Nozzole Chianti Classico Riserva "La Forra"

gramigna al sugo di salsicce

GRAMIGNA WITH SAUSAGE-FLAVORED SAUCE

In contrast to the version from Lucca, this sauce of sausages from Emilia-Romagna uses white wine and no cream; it contains a lot of butter, but no oil. Emilia-Romagna has almost no olive oil, so it is understandable if the natives overvalue the little there is. But the bottom line is that dishes from this area simply do not call for it. (In contrast, Lucca produces a soft and mild olive oil that is among the best that exist, especially if you can obtain it from a small local olive grove.) This wonderful butter-wine tomato sauce, served with gramigna *pasta, is sweetly flavored with onion and bay leaf.*

Prepare the sauce. Finely chop the onion on a board. Place the butter in a heavy saucepan over medium heat. When the butter is completely melted, add the chopped onion and sauté for 10 minutes, stirring every so often with a wooden spoon. Meanwhile, remove the skins from the sausages and break the meat into pieces; add the sausages or pork to the pan and sauté for 10 minutes more. Pour in the wine, salt and pepper to taste, and the bay leaf, and let the wine evapo-rate for 10 minutes. If using fresh toma-toes, cut them into pieces. Pass fresh or canned tomatoes through a food mill, using the disc with the smallest holes, into a small bowl, then add to the meat mixture and simmer, covered, for 20 minutes, stirring every so often.

Bring a large pot of cold water to a boil, add coarse salt to taste, then add the pasta. If dried, cook it for 9 to 12 minutes depend-ing on the brand; if fresh, cook it for 1 to 3 minutes depending on dryness. Reheat the sauce. When ready, drain the pasta and trans-fer it to a large, warmed serving dish. Pour the sauce over the top, toss very well, and serve. Sprinkle a heaping tablespoon of Parmigiano over each portion.

NOTE

To prepare fresh *gramigna*, prepare *spaghetti* using ingredients and quantities listed, following instructions on page 12. Stretch pasta to about ⅛ inch thick—on the pasta machine take it to several notches before the last setting—then cut into *spaghetti* (see page 59). Finally, cut *spaghetti* into 3-inch pieces.

SERVES 4 TO 6

FOR THE SAUCE

1 medium-sized red onion, peeled

8 tablespoons (4 ounces) sweet butter

4 Italian sweet sausages without fennel seeds; or 12 ounces coarsely ground pork

1 cup dry white wine

Salt and freshly ground black pepper

1 bay leaf

1 pound very ripe, fresh tomatoes; or 1 pound canned tomatoes, preferably imported Italian, drained

FOR THE PASTA

1 pound dried *gramigna* or fresh *gramigna* (made with 3 cups unbleached all-purpose flour, 4 extra-large eggs, and a pinch of salt; see Note)

TO COOK THE PASTA

Coarse-grained salt

TO SERVE

4 to 6 heaping table-spoons freshly grated Parmigiano

anellini al forno

BAKED PASTA RINGS, SICILIAN STYLE

SERVES 8 TO 10

FOR THE MEAT SAUCE

1 medium-sized red onion, peeled

2 large cloves garlic, peeled

2 ounces *pancetta*, sliced thick, then cut into tiny pieces

¼ cup olive oil

4 ounces ground pork

4 ounces ground beef

½ cup dry red wine

2 tablespoons tomato paste

2 pounds ripe, fresh tomatoes; or 2 pounds canned tomatoes, preferably imported Italian, drained

Salt and freshly ground black pepper

4 large basil leaves, fresh or preserved in salt

10 large sprigs Italian parsley, leaves only

1 bay leaf

2 cups lukewarm chicken or beef broth; preferably homemade

FOR THE PEAS

1 small red onion, peeled

10 large sprigs Italian parsley, leaves only

1 small clove garlic, peeled

¼ cup olive oil

This Sicilian meat sauce employs a mixture of pork and beef, plus pancetta *for flavoring. For aromatic vegetables, there are only onions and garlic, but there is also an array of herbs— basil, parsley, and bay leaves, even this last is generally available fresh on the island. A little wine and tomato paste are combined with lots of tomatoes. A favorite use of this sauce is in the baked pasta dish Anellini al forno: little pasta rings baked with the meat sauce and fresh peas cooked in olive oil, garlic, onion, and parsley with only enough broth to cook them (no water). Another flavor is added with the lusty* caciocavallo *cheese. These baked pasta dishes, sometimes layered, were once very popular, indeed. They are made less now, with the tendency toward shorter cooking times and the search for increased lightness in cooking. Some, such as this almost signature Sicilian dish, are so good, however, that they continue to be cherished.*

Prepare the sauce. Finely chop the onion, garlic, and *pancetta* all together on a board. Heat the oil in a medium-sized saucepan or heavy pot over medium heat. When the oil is warm, add the chopped ingredients and sauté for 5 minutes. Add the pork and beef, mix well, and cook for 5 minutes more. Add the wine and tomato paste, and let the wine evaporate for 10 more minutes. If using fresh tomatoes, cut them into pieces. Pass the fresh or canned tomatoes through a food mill, using the disc with the smallest holes, into a crockery or glass bowl. Add the tomatoes to the saucepan, season with salt and pepper, and simmer for another 15 minutes. Finely chop the basil and parsley together on a board and add to the saucepan along with the whole bay leaf and broth. Cover and simmer for 40 minutes, then discard the bay leaf.

Meanwhile, prepare the peas. Finely chop the onion and set aside. Then chop the parsley together with the garlic. Place a medium-sized skillet with the oil over low heat, and, when the oil is warm, add the chopped onion. Sauté for 2 minutes, then add the peas and sauté for another 2 minutes. Add the chopped parsley and garlic and 1 cup of the broth. Season with salt and pepper, cover, and cook for 10 to 20 minutes, depending on the tenderness of the peas, adding more broth as needed. Let the peas cool, about 30 minutes.

Bring a large pot of cold water to a boil, add coarse salt to taste, then add the pasta and cook until al dente—9 to 12 minutes depending on the brand. Drain the pasta and place it in a large bowl with half the sauce (about 4 cups). Mix well and let rest until the sauce is absorbed by the pasta and has cooled, about 1 hour. Meanwhile, reduce the remaining sauce over medium heat until it measures about 2 cups.

Preheat the oven to 375°F. Coarsely grate the *caciocavallo* cheese, then with 2 tablespoons of butter, heavily coat a 3-quart deep glass or other baking dish and coat it with bread crumbs. With one-fourth of the pasta, make a layer in the prepared dish. Arrange one-third of the peas over this, using a slotted spoon to avoid adding any liquid. Then use one-fourth of the remaining meat sauce, finally sprinkling one-third of the cheese over it. Repeat this procedure with 2 more layers of pasta. Add the fourth pasta layer and top with the remaining meat sauce only. Arrange the bits of butter on top and bake for 35 minutes. Remove from oven, let rest for a few minutes, then serve.

NOTE

Other than during the spring, when small, fresh peas are in season, a cook has two options in making this and other recipes based on peas:

1. Use the large fresh peas available out of season, but first shell and boil them with a clove or two of garlic, peeled but left whole, and a pinch of coarse salt for about 13 minutes. Then they can be sautéed for the same cooking time as the smaller ones.

2. Use the excellent *petit pois,* or "tiny tender" peas, sold frozen in 10-ounce packages. Do not defrost or precook them. Sauté them for the same cooking time as small fresh ones. (This is one of the very few frozen products I sometimes use, because the result is totally without compromise.)

3 ½ pounds fresh tiny peas, shelled; or 2 ½ pounds fresh large peas (see Note)

1 ½ cups lukewarm chicken or beef broth, preferably homemade

Salt and freshly ground black pepper

FOR THE PASTA

1 pound dried *anellini,* preferably imported Italian

TO COOK THE PASTA

Coarse-grained salt

TO BAKE

4 ounces *caciocavallo* cheese

4 tablespoons (2 ounces) sweet butter, half cut into small bits

6 tablespoons unseasoned bread crumbs

maccheroni all'abruzzese
MACCHERONI, ABRUZZI STYLE

SERVES 4 TO 6

FOR THE MEAT SAUCE

4 ounces pork, preferably pork loin, in one piece, fat removed

2 ounces *pancetta* or *prosciutto*, cut into 1-inch pieces

1 medium-sized red onion, cleaned

2 cloves garlic, peeled

2 stalks celery

2 carrots, scraped

5 sprigs Italian parsley, leaves only

1 sweet red pepper, cleaned, stemmed, and seeded

Salt and freshly ground black pepper

6 tablespoons extra-virgin olive oil

Pinch of hot red pepper flakes (optional)

2 tablespoons tomato paste, preferably imported Italian

1 cup dry white wine

FOR THE PASTA

Coarse salt

1 pound dried *maccheroni "alla chitarra"* or another thick long pasta, such as *spaghettoni* or *ciriole*, preferably imported Italian

TO SERVE

Freshly grated pecorino romano or Parmigiano cheese (optional)

Sprigs of fresh basil leaves

The preparation of the sauce for this dish is unique in that the meats, vegetables, and herbs are seasoned and ground together. This produces an unusually full-bodied sauce, which perfectly complements the robustness of the maccheroni "cut with a guitar" (see illustration on page 289).

Prepare the sauce. Cut the pork into about 1-inch pieces, then place in a crockery or glass bowl with the *pancetta*. Coarsely chop the onion, garlic, celery, carrots, parsley, and red pepper together on a board. Add to the bowl, season with salt and pepper, mix very well with a wooden spoon, and refrigerate, covered, for ½ hour. Use a meat grinder with the disc with the smallest holes to finely grind the chilled mixture directly into a second crockery or glass bowl.

Heat 4 tablespoons of the oil in a medium-sized casserole over medium heat.

When the oil is warm, add the ground mixture and sauté for 15 minutes, stirring every so often with a wooden spoon. If hot pepper is used, add it to taste to the casserole and mix well; add the tomato paste and mix again. Cook for 2 more minutes. Add the wine and simmer for 20 more minutes, stirring every so often with a wooden spoon. By that time, the wine should be almost evaporated and the sauce should be rather thick. Add the remaining 2 tablespoons of the oil, taste for salt and pepper, and mix very well.

Bring a large pot of cold water to a boil, add coarse salt to taste, then add the pasta and cook until al dente—9 to 12 minutes depending on the brand. Drain the pasta. Transfer it to a large bowl, pour the sauce over the top, then mix very well. Transfer to a large, warmed serving dish and serve immediately with sprigs of fresh basil. Pass the cheese at the table.

bucatini alla matriciana *or* all'amatriciana

PASTA, AMATRICE STYLE

SERVES 4 TO 6

1 medium-sized red onion, peeled

8 ounces *pancetta* or *prosciutto*, in 1 piece

3 tablespoons olive oil

1 ½ pounds very ripe, fresh tomatoes; or 1 ½ pounds canned tomatoes, preferably imported Italian, drained

½ teaspoon hot red pepper flakes

Salt and freshly ground black pepper

1 pound dried *bucatini*, *vermicelli*, or *spaghetti*, preferably imported Italian

TO COOK THE PASTA

Coarse-grained salt

TO SERVE

½ cup freshly grated pecorino romano or Parmigiano cheese

The famous all'amatriciana *treatment, which originates in Amatrice, near Rome, uses abundant* pancetta *or* prosciutto. *It is a simple and highly spiced preparation with black pepper and hot red pepper flakes. The dish is related to* pasta alla carbonara, *except that tomatoes replace the eggs; and, as in that treatment,* all'amatriciana *employs grated cheese, though not as abundantly as the other. This is certainly among the most popular recipes for its simplicity and excellence, so don't complicate it by adding extraneous ingredients or by trying to be original. Its classic simplicity is its strength. The substantial* bucatini, *with the hole down the middle, is the preferred pasta where this dish originates.*

Coarsely chop the onion. Cut the *pancetta* into cubes less than ½ inch thick. Place the oil and *pancetta* in a medium-sized saucepan over low heat and sauté for 15 minutes, or until all the fat has been rendered and the meat is very crisp. If fresh tomatoes are used, cut them into pieces. Pass the canned or fresh tomatoes through a food mill, using the disc with the smallest holes, into a crockery or glass bowl. Use a slotted spoon to transfer the meat to a plate and set it aside until needed. Add the onion to the saucepan and sauté for 5 minutes, then add the tomatoes along with the red pepper flakes and salt and black pepper to taste. Simmer for 20 minutes, stirring every so often with a wooden spoon.

Bring a large pot of cold water to a boil, add coarse salt to taste, then add the pasta and cook until al dente—9 to 12 minutes depending on the brand. Transfer the sauce to a large skillet set over low heat. Drain the pasta, and add it to the skillet. Raise the heat, and add the reserved meat; sauté for 30 seconds. Remove the skillet from the heat, add the cheese, mix very well, and transfer the pasta to a warmed serving platter. Serve immediately.

NOTE

In Italy, the cured meat used for this dish is pork cheek *(guanciale),* not easily available elsewhere, rather than *pancetta* or *prosciutto.* The dish is a rare example of the combination of cheese and hot red pepper.

meat fillings

Three recipes follow in which meat is assigned principally to a stuffing. In the interesting *Tortelli*, Prato Style, the stuffing is potatoes flavored with ground beef, eggs, and Parmigiano. They are dressed simply with butter and more cheese.

The large Stuffed Pasta Roll from Calabria is filled with beef, sausages, and salami as well as hard-boiled eggs. Sausages with fennel seeds, to be avoided in northern and central Italian recipes, are in order for a dish from this region. The poached pasta roll is dressed only with the juices left from sautéing the stuffing, and it is sprinkled with pecorino or Parmigiano cheese.

Prosciutto, beef, and chicken breast are in the stuffing for the *Cannelloni di carne ai funghi* from Lucca, along with *porcini* mushrooms. The mushroom sauce itself contains a fourth meat—sausage.

In additional recipes, the *tortelli* from Casentino are stuffed primarily with sausage. *Prosciutto* is used as the primary meat in several recipes: the stuffing for Bolognese *tortellini* contains *prosciutto, mortadella,** and veal marrow. And two Parma recipes naturally celebrate the local *prosciutto* in their sauces: *Tagliatelle* with Creamed *Prosciutto* Sauce and *Anolini* with *Prosciutto* Sauce with veal brains and prosciutto in the stuffing. As is usual with such meat combinations, the dressing is simple—butter, sage, and grated Parmigiano.

* The famous big sausage, sometimes called simply "bologna," which became "baloney" in the United States.

tortelli o mezzelune alla pratese

TORTELLI, OR HALF-MOON TORTELLI, PRATO STYLE

Prepare the stuffing. Place cold water in a medium-sized saucepan with the unpeeled potatoes and coarse salt to taste. Set the saucepan over medium heat and cook potatoes until soft, 30 to 40 minutes depending on size. Remove the potatoes, immediately peel them, then pass them through a potato ricer into a crockery or glass bowl. Let stand until cool, about 30 minutes.

Put a small saucepan with the oil over medium heat. When the oil is warm, add the bay leaf and ground beef. Sauté for about 5 minutes, then taste for salt and pepper. Discard the bay leaf, and put the meat and juices in the bowl with the potatoes. Let rest until cool, about 5 minutes.

Finely chop the garlic and coarsely chop the parsley on a board. When the meat is cool, add the egg, Parmigiano, chopped garlic, and parsley. Taste for salt and pepper and add the nutmeg. Mix well with a wooden spoon, cover the bowl, and refrigerate until needed.

Prepare pasta, using the ingredients and quantities listed, according to the directions on page 12. Stretch to less than ¹⁄₁₆ inch; on the pasta machine take it to the last setting. Make 1½-inch-square *tortelli* (see page 123), using ½ tablespoon of filling for each *tortello*. Let the *tortelli* rest on cotton towels until needed. If using the half-moon shape, follow directions on page 174, using a 3-inch-diameter scalloped cookie cutter.

Bring a large pot of cold water to a boil, and put a large serving dish with the butter on it over the pot so that the butter melts as the water heats. When the water reaches a boil and the butter is melted, remove the serving dish. Add coarse salt to the water, then add the *tortelli,* quickly but gently. Cook for 30 seconds to 2 minutes depending on the dryness of the pasta. When cooked, remove with a strainer-skimmer and arrange half in a layer on the prepared serving dish. Sprinkle it with half the Parmigiano and some black pepper. Use the remaining *tortelli* to make a second layer and sprinkle with the remaining Parmigiano and more black pepper. Serve immediately.

SERVES 8

FOR THE STUFFING

12 ounces potatoes (not new potatoes)

Coarse-grained salt

5 tablespoons olive oil

1 bay leaf

¼ pound lean ground beef

Salt and freshly ground black pepper

1 medium-sized clove garlic, peeled

10 large sprigs Italian parsley, leaves only

1 extra-large egg

½ cup freshly grated Parmigiano

Pinch of freshly grated nutmeg

FOR THE PASTA

4 cups unbleached all-purpose flour

4 extra-large eggs

4 teaspoons olive or vegetable oil

Pinch of salt

FOR THE SAUCE

16 tablespoons (8 ounces) sweet butter

1 cup grated Parmigiano

Freshly ground black pepper

TO COOK THE PASTA

Coarse-grained salt

MEZZELUNE

1. Place a line of dots of filling down the center of the pasta layer, then fold the sheet lengthwise in half. Press down around the dots of filling.

2. Prepare *mezzelune* by placing only half of a round *ravioli* cutter over the area containing the filling. For *mezzelune*, as for all types of *tortelli*, press the edges all around between two fingers to be sure they are completely sealed.

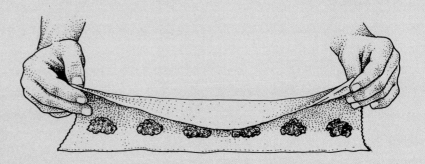

1

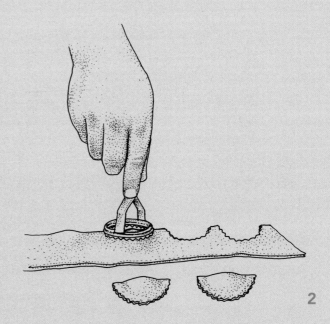

2

HOW TO TIE "LIKE A SALAMI"

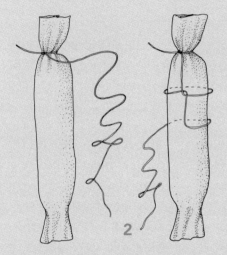

1. Use a string 6 times the length of the "salami." Knot the string at one end, leaving only a short length of string on one side.

2. Bring the long end of the string down about 2 inches and hold the string in place with your finger. With the other hand, pull the string under and around again to the point where the string has been held by your finger. Pass the end of the string over, then under. Remove your finger, hold the short end of the string with one hand and pull the other end tight with the other hand.

3. Repeat this procedure until you reach the other end.

4. & 5. Reverse the "salami" and, as the end of the string intersects with each ring of string wrapped around the "salami," pull under and over, fastening in the same way as was done on the other side.

6. After the last intersection, tie a knot using the two ends of the string.

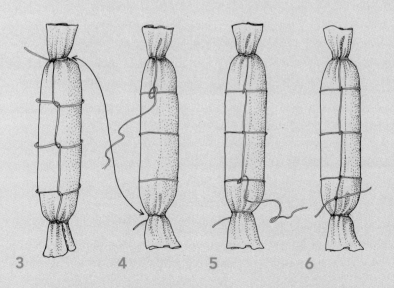

schiaffettoni alla calabrese

STUFFED PASTA ROLL, CALABRIAN STYLE

SERVES 8 TO 10

TO COOK THE PASTA

Coarse-grained salt

2 tablespoons vegetable or
   olive oil

FOR THE PASTA

2 cups unbleached all-
   purpose flour

3 extra-large eggs

Pinch of salt

FOR THE STUFFING

2 ½ pounds ground beef

4 Italian sweet sausages
   with fennel seeds (about
   1 pound), skinned

8 ounces Genoa salami, in
   1 slice

¼ cup olive oil

6 tablespoons tomato paste,
   preferably imported
   Italian

Salt and freshly ground
   black pepper

4 cups lukewarm chicken or
   beef broth, preferably
   homemade

4 extra-large eggs, hard-
   boiled

Bring a large pot of cold water to a boil, then add coarse salt to taste. Put a bowl of cold water with the oil next to the boiling water and dampen 4 cotton dish towels with cold water.

Prepare the pasta with the ingredients and quantities listed, following directions on page 12. Divide the dough into 2 pieces. Using a rolling pin, roll out the pieces of dough into 2 rectangular sheets of pasta, ⅟₁₆ inch thick, following directions on page 14.

When the sheets of pasta are ready, cook them one at a time in the boiling water for 1 minute each, then carefully—to avoid making holes—use a large strainer-skimmer to transfer the pasta to the bowl of cold water. When the pasta is cool, spread it on a damp towel and let it stand until needed, covered with another damp towel.

Prepare the stuffing. Place the ground beef in a bowl, then the skinned sausages. Finely chop the salami on a board and add it to the other meats; mix well with a wooden spoon. Heat the oil in a saucepan over medium heat, and, when the oil is warm, add the meat. Sauté for 4 minutes, continuously mixing with a wooden spoon, then add the tomato paste and season with salt and pepper. Pour in ½ cup of the broth. Cook for 5 minutes, then add the remaining broth. Taste again for salt and pepper and cook 5 more minutes. Remove the pan from the heat and, using a slotted spoon, remove the solids to a crockery or glass bowl, leaving the juices in the pan. Let the cooked meat cool, covered, for 30 minutes, then coarsely chop the hard-boiled eggs and add them to the meat. Mix gently but thoroughly, and taste for salt and pepper, keeping in mind that some of the saltiness will dissipate when the stuffed pasta is poached in boiling water.

Prepare the poaching broth. Place a large fish poacher filled with cold water over medium heat. Cut the vegetables into large pieces. When the water reaches a boil, add coarse salt to taste, the vegetables, and the parsley. Simmer for 30 minutes.

Remove the top towel from the pasta, and with a spatula, spread the stuffing over both sheets, leaving only a 1-inch edge all around. Roll up the *schiaffettoni* by taking one of the short sides in both hands and folding it over about 1 inch of the filling. Then pick up the edge of the towel on which it is resting with both hands. As you lift the edge of the towel a little higher, the pasta sheet will continue to roll up like a jelly roll. Repeat the procedure with the other pasta sheet. Move each roll onto a dry dish towel and wrap the towel all around, then tie like a salami (see page 175). Bring the poaching broth to a boil. Place the pasta rolls in the broth and simmer, covered, for 30 minutes.

While the rolls are cooking, place the juices left from the stuffing in the pan over medium heat and reduce until the pasta is ready; you should have about 2 cups of sauce. Remove the pasta rolls from the water, unwrap them on a board, and cut into 1-inch slices. Arrange the slices on a large serving platter, pour the sauce over the top, and sprinkle with the cheese. Serve immediately.

FOR THE POACHING BROTH

1 medium-sized red onion, peeled

1 large stalk celery

1 medium-sized carrot, scraped

1 large clove garlic, peeled

Coarse-grained salt

5 large sprigs Italian parsley

TO SERVE

½ cup freshly grated pecorino sardo or Parmigiano

cannelloni di carne ai funghi

CANNELLONI WITH WILD MUSHROOM STUFFING
AND SAUCE

MAKES ABOUT 12

FOR THE PASTA

2 cups unbleached all-purpose
flour

2 extra-large eggs

2 teaspoons olive or vegetable oil

Pinch of salt

TO COOK THE PASTA

Coarse-grained salt

2 tablespoons olive or
vegetable oil

FOR THE STUFFING

½ ounce dried *porcini*
mushrooms

4 cups lukewarm milk

4 ounces *prosciutto*, in 1
piece

8 ounces lean beef, in 1 piece

1 whole chicken breast,
skinned and boned

1 small red onion, peeled

1 medium-sized stalk celery

1 large carrot, scraped

1 large clove garlic, peeled

10 large sprigs Italian parsley,
leaves only

10 tablespoons (5 ounces)
sweet butter

¼ cup olive oil

1 cup dry red wine

3 tablespoons tomato paste

1 cup beef broth, preferably
homemade

Prepare the pasta with the ingredients and quantities listed, according to the directions on page 12. Stretch sheet to less than ⅟₁₆ inch thick; on the pasta machine, take it to the last setting and cut into squares (see page 180). Preboil the squares in a large amount of salted boiling water for 2 seconds. Transfer the pasta to a large bowl of cold water to which the oil has been added. Cool the pasta in the water, then let the precooked squares rest between dampened cotton dish towels until needed.

Prepare the stuffing. Soak the *porcini* in the lukewarm milk for 30 minutes. Using a meat grinder, coarsely grind the prosciutto, beef, and chicken together. Finely chop the onion, celery, carrot, garlic, and parsley on a board. Melt 2 tablespoons of the butter with the olive oil in a deep saucepan over medium heat, and when the butter is completely melted, add the chopped vegetables and sauté for 5 minutes. Add the ground meats and sauté for 5 minutes more. Drain the mushrooms, saving the soaking milk. (Be sure that no sand remains attached to the mushrooms.) Add mushrooms to the saucepan, pour in the wine, and let wine evaporate for 15 min-

utes. Meanwhile, pass the mushroom soaking milk through several layers of paper towels to remove all sand and set aside.

Add the tomato paste to the saucepan and gradually start adding the broth, ¼ cup at a time, until all the broth is incorporated and the stuffing is cooked and quite thick. Set aside.

Prepare a *balsamella,* to be incorporated later into the stuffing, using the remaining 8 tablespoons of butter, the ½ cup flour, and the strained mushroom milk. Follow the basic recipe on page 97 and add enough water to the mushroom milk to make 4 cups of liquid. Season with salt and pepper. Transfer this *balsamella* to a crockery or glass bowl, press a piece of buttered waxed paper over the surface, and let stand until cool.

Prepare a second *balsamella* for the topping, using the ingredients and quantities listed. Transfer it to a second crockery or glass bowl, press a piece of buttered waxed paper over the surface, and let stand until cool.

Prepare the mushroom sauce. Soak the mushrooms in the lukewarm water for 30 minutes. Remove the skins from the sausages and finely chop the meat with the onion, garlic, and parsley on a board. Heat the oil and 3 tablespoons of the butter in a saucepan over low heat. When the butter is melted, add the chopped ingredients and sauté for 15 minutes. Then add the tomato paste and ½ cup of the broth; cook for 15 minutes. Meanwhile, drain the mushrooms, saving the soaking water. (Be sure that no sand remains attached to the stems.) Pass the mushroom water through several layers of paper towels to strain out the sand. Add the mushrooms to the pan along with the remaining broth. Taste for salt and pepper, lower the heat, and cook for 1 hour, adding the strained mushroom water near the end. Using a fork, incorporate the remaining tablespoon of butter with the flour on a small plate and add it by bits to the sauce. Stir very well and cook for 10 more minutes.

Preheat the oven to 375°F. Butter 2 glass or other ovenproof 13½-by-8¾-inch baking dishes. Combine the first *balsamella* (made with the mushroom milk) and the stuffing together in a large bowl; mix very well with a wooden spoon.

If using the black truffle, chop it very fine and add it to the stuffing at this point.

To stuff the *cannelloni,* place a square of pasta on a wooden board and spread about 4 heaping tablespoons of the stuffing along one of the jagged edges. Then roll it up, starting at the same edge and ending with the other jagged edge on top. Repeat until all the *cannelloni* are rolled. Then place them seam side up in the baking dishes. Pour the second *balsamella* over the top and bake for 25 minutes. Meanwhile, reheat the mushroom sauce. When the *cannelloni* are ready, serve at once, spooning some of the mushroom sauce over each portion.

WINE • *Michele Chiarlo*
Barbara d'Asti

½ cup unbleached all-purpose flour

Salt and freshly ground black pepper

FOR THE BALSAMELLA

4 tablespoons (2 ounces) sweet butter

¼ cup unbleached all-purpose flour

2½ cups milk

Salt and freshly ground black pepper

Freshly grated nutmeg

FOR THE SAUCE

4 ounces dried *porcini* mushrooms

3 cups lukewarm water

3 Italian sweet sausages without fennel seeds; or 12 ounces ground pork

1 small red onion, peeled

1 large clove garlic, peeled

20 large sprigs Italian parsley, leaves only

¼ cup olive oil

4 tablespoons (2 ounces) sweet butter

3 tablespoons tomato paste

1 cup lukewarm chicken or beef broth, preferably homemade

Salt and freshly ground black pepper

1 tablespoon unbleached all-purpose flour

1 black truffle (about 2 ounces), fresh or canned (optional)

CANNELLONI

1. With a pastry cutter, cut the layer of pasta into pieces about 6 inches long. Let the pieces dry for a few minutes.

2. Once the pasta has been precooked in salted boiling water, then cooled in cold water with oil and transferred onto wet towels, spread stuffing along one of the jagged edges.

3. Then roll, starting at the edge containing the stuffing and

4. ending with the other jagged edge on top. *Cannelloni* are baked, seam side up.

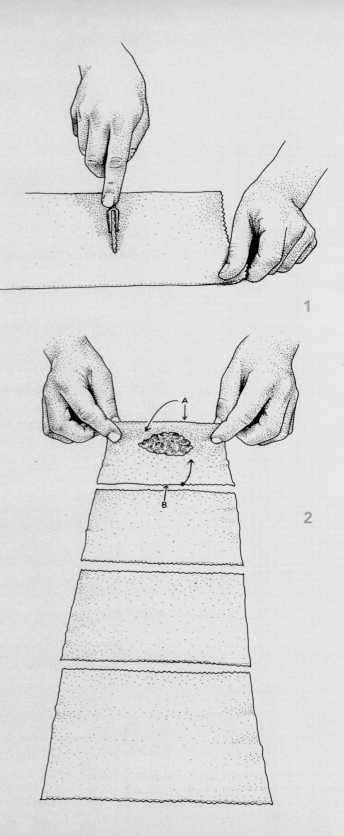

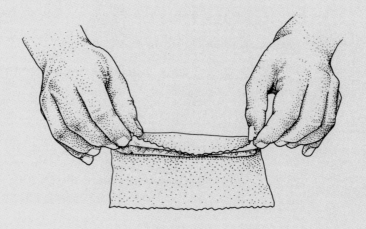

3

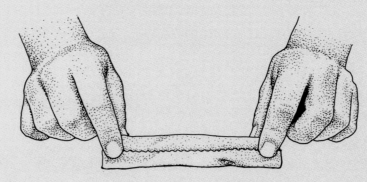

4

pasticcio di pasta alla trentina

STUFFED PASTA, TRENTO STYLE

SERVES 8

FOR THE MUSHROOM SAUCE

½ ounce dried *porcini* mushrooms

3 cups lukewarm water

3 tablespoons (1½ ounces) sweet butter

Salt and freshly ground black pepper

FOR THE MEAT SAUCE

1½ pounds ground sirloin

3 ounces *pancetta*, sliced

1 medium-sized carrot, scraped

1 medium-sized stalk celery

1 small red onion, cleaned

4 tablespoons (2 ounces) sweet butter at room temperature

2 tablespoons extra-virgin olive oil

Salt and freshly ground black pepper

2 tablespoons tomato paste, preferably imported Italian

3 cups completely defatted chicken or meat broth, preferably homemade

PLUS

2 extra-large egg yolks

1 cup freshly grated Parmigiano or *Grana Padano* cheese

The cooking of Trento, in the extreme north of Italy, is usually simple and straightforward, but this complex dish, designed for important occasions, is the great exception.

Although the pasta layering is quite simple, just top and bottom layers, this very special pasticcio requires several complex sauces. The mushroom sauce is based on precious porcini. The meat sauce calls for many ingredients, including ground sirloin, chopped vegetables, both butter and olive oil, broth, tomato paste, egg yolks, and grated cheese. Prosciutto strips are arranged before the top layer of pasta is added, and the dish is topped with balsamella (béchamel) sauce.

Soak the mushrooms in the water for 1 hour, then drain and clean them, carefully removing all the attached sand. Pass the soaking water repeatedly through paper towels or a coffee filter several times.

Prepare the mushroom sauce. Melt the butter in a medium-sized saucepan over low heat. Add the mushrooms and sauté for 3 minutes. Season with salt and pepper, then add the mushroom water ½ cup at a time; do not add the next ½ cup until the previous portion is reduced by half. When all the water has been added, the sauce should be quite thin. Use a strainer-skimmer to remove the mushrooms and coarsley chop them on a board. Return the mushrooms to the saucepan, remove from the heat, and let rest until cool, about 1 hour.

Meanwhile, prepare the meat sauce. Mix the sirloin and *pancetta* with the carrot, celery, and onion, then finely grind the mixture in an electric meat grinder.

Put the butter and oil in a casserole over medium heat. When the butter is melted, add the ground ingredients and sauté for 10 minutes, stirring every so often with a wooden spoon. Add the cooled mushroom sauce and simmer for 15 minutes, stirring constantly. Season with salt and pepper.

Dissolve the tomato paste in the broth and pour 1 cup into the casserole. Simmer, reducing, for 20 minutes. Then add 1 more cup and reduce for 20 minutes more. When the third cup of broth has been added and reduced, the sauce will have cooked for an hour total and should be rather thick. Transfer the sauce to a crockery or glass bowl and let rest until cool, about 1 hour.

Prepare the *balsamella* with the ingredients and quantities listed, following the instructions on page 97. Cool it in a crockery or glass bowl, covered with a piece of buttered waxed paper to prevent a skin from forming.

In the meantime, prepare the pasta using the ingredients and quantities listed, following the instructions on page 12. Stretch the layer of pasta to a thickness of a little less than 1/16 inch—on a hand pasta machine take it to the last setting. Cut the pasta into 6-inch squares. Precook the pasta squares in salted boiling water for a few seconds, then let them rest on wet cotton kitchen towels until needed.

Add the egg yolks to the meat sauce along with 1/2 cup of the cheese and mix very well.

Preheat the oven to 375°F. Heavily butter the bottom and sides of a jelly roll pan then line it with the pasta, allowing the squares to hang 2 inches over the sides all around. Pour the stuffing into the pan, level it, then sprinkle the remaining 1/2 cup of cheese over the top. Cut the *prosciutto* slices into thin strips, then arrange them over the cheese. Cover with the remaining pasta squares. Fold the overlapping pieces of pasta inward and spread the *balsamella* evenly over all. Bake for 25 minutes. Remove from the oven and let rest for 10 minutes before serving.

WINE • Zonin:Berengaio

2 ounces sliced *prosciutto*

FOR THE BALSAMELLA (BÉCHAMEL)

3 tablespoons (1 ½ ounces) sweet butter

1 ½ tablespoons unbleached all-purpose flour

2 cups whole milk

Salt and freshly ground black pepper

FOR THE PASTA

2 cups unbleached all-purpose flour

4 extra-large egg yolks

2 tablespoons vegetable or olive oil

3 tablespoons cold water

Pinch of salt

TO COOK THE PASTA

Coarse-grained salt

2 tablespoons vegetable or olive oil

TO BAKE

2 tablespoons (1 ounce) sweet butter

TO SERVE

Freshly grated *Grana Padano* cheese; or slivers of fresh white truffles

lasagne for carnival

The well-known and very popular *Lasagne imbottite*, using the long *lasagne* strips alternating layers of pasta with manifold ingredients, such as Neapolitan *ragù*, tiny meatballs, sausage pieces, slices of mozzarella and hard-boiled egg, ricotta, and grated Parmigiano, is Naples's version of the elaborate baked pasta made for the festivities of Carnival time. Such festival dishes once had a special meaning and were really made just at one time of year. Not only Carnival but each holiday season and even each saint's day had special dishes that were for just such occasions, and they varied among the different regions and towns. But now one finds *Lasagne imbottite* on menus all over and at most times of year, since the special meaning of such dishes has faded.

The *Lasagne imbottite* from neighboring Calabria is different. The fresh pasta is made with rougher semolina flour, whereas the Neapolitan is made with normal all-purpose flour; the little meatballs are made with pork rather than beef; the grated cheese is more likely to be *pecorino*; there is a simpler tomato sauce rather than Neapolitan *ragù;* and along with the mozzarella, ricotta, and hard-boiled eggs is a special vegetable stuffing including dried *porcini*, artichokes, peas, and aromatic vegetables flavored with bay leaf. A grand dish indeed to celebrate Carnival, it is called in dialect form by the name *Sagne chine*. Unfortunately, there are nonauthentic versions of the dish circulating that must be avoided. Inexplicably, one recent recipe for this dish calls for ginger, which is unknown in post-Renaissance Italian cooking and would be particularly out of place in Calabria, where hot spices are preferred over sweet ones. A little thought solves the mystery. Medieval Italian cooking, related to that of ancient Rome, used many Oriental spices brought in by the Venetian and Genoese traders, but these spices disappeared with the Renaissance. If one looks up *zenzero* in the Italian dictionary, it will say "ginger" because the strict Italian language academy keeps the classical meanings of words even more rigorously than the French academy. But *zenzero* in modern times has come to mean hot red pepper (though *peperoncino* is the "correct" word for hot red pepper), which came to Europe from the New World about the time ginger stopped being used there.

Our third type of *Lasagne imbottite* is a fascinating Abruzzese transformation of the dish in which *crespelle* (crêpes) are used instead of pasta for the layering. The result is a *timballo* of *crespelle* with manifold ingredients more related to the Neapolitan and Calabrian versions. The little meatballs are made of pork with Parmigiano and egg; there is a sauce of chicken gizzards cooked in white wine and bay leaf; a chicken breast is cut into small cubes; unsmoked *scamorza* cheese is used instead of mozzarella; and a simple tomato sauce is flavored with butter.

lasagne di carnevale (lasagne imbottite)

NEAPOLITAN "STUFFED" LASAGNE FOR CARNIVAL

SERVES 8 TO 10

2 cups *Ragù alla napoletana* (page 161)

FOR THE PASTA

3 cups unbleached all-purpose flour

3 extra-large eggs

¼ cup lukewarm water

Pinch of salt

TO COOK THE PASTA

Coarse-grained salt

2 tablespoons olive or vegetable oil

FOR THE *POLPETTINE*

1 large clove garlic, peeled

10 large sprigs Italian parsley, leaves only

1 pound ground beef

¼ cup freshly grated Parmigiano

2 extra-large eggs

Salt and freshly ground black pepper

1 quart vegetable oil (see Note)

¼ cup olive oil (see Note)

1 cup unbleached all-purpose flour

The sauce can be prepared several days in advance. Prepare the pasta with the ingredients and quantities listed, according to the directions on page 12. Stretch layer to less than $\frac{1}{16}$ inch—on the pasta machine take it to the last setting. Cut the pasta into Neapolitan "long" *lasagne* —not into squares, but into strips 12 inches long and 3 inches wide. Preboil the strips in a large amount of salted boiling water for 2 seconds. Transfer the pasta to a large bowl of cold water to which the oil has been added. Cool the pasta in the water, then let it rest on dampened cotton dish towels until needed.

Prepare the *polpettine,* the little meat balls for the stuffing. Finely chop the garlic and parsley together on a board. Place the ground beef in a crockery or glass bowl, add the chopped ingredients, Parmigiano, eggs, and salt and pepper to taste; mix all the ingredients, then shape by ½ tablespoons into *polpettine* the size of a hazelnut. Heat the vegetable and olive oils in a deep-fat fryer until hot (375°F). Lightly flour the meat balls and fry until golden all over, about 1 minute. Transfer to a platter lined with paper towels to drain excess fat; let stand until needed.

Cut the sausages into 1-inch pieces and sauté in a skillet with the lard or olive oil over medium heat for 5 minutes. Transfer them, without their juices, to a platter. Cut the mozzarella and hard-boiled eggs into thin slices.

Butter a 13½-by-8¾-inch glass baking dish and preheat the oven to 375°F. Make a layer of pasta on the bottom of the baking dish and cover with some of the meatballs, sausage, and mozzarella and egg slices. Crumble some ricotta over all, then sprinkle with Parmigiano, and spread some sauce over the top. Repeat with more layers of pasta and the other ingredients. The top layer should be sauce and Parmigiano only. Bake for 25 minutes. Remove from oven, let stand for a few minutes, then serve.

NOTE

In Naples and Campania, lard, rather than olive oil, would traditionally be used to sauté the sausages and fry the *polpettine.*

In Italy, ricotta, particularly the popular sheep's milk ricotta, is classically shaped in a mold.

TO BAKE

6 Italian sweet sausages
  (about 1 ½ pounds)

4 tablespoons lard or olive
  oil (see Note)

8 ounces mozzarella
  cheese

4 extra-large eggs, hard-
  boiled

15 ounces ricotta,
  preferably homemade

¾ cup freshly grated
  Parmigiano

sagne chine o lasagne imbottite
CALABRIAN "STUFFED" LASAGNE FOR CARNIVAL

SERVES 8 TO 10

FOR THE PASTA

4 cups semolina flour

1 ¾ cups cold water

Pinch of salt

TO COOK THE PASTA

Coarse-grained salt

2 tablespoons olive or vegetable oil

FOR THE VEGETABLE STUFFING:

1 ounce dried *porcini* mushrooms

2 cups lukewarm water

4 medium-sized artichokes

Juice of 1 lemon

1 medium-sized stalk celery

1 medium-sized red onion, peeled

1 medium-sized carrot, scraped

½ cup olive oil

1 pound shelled peas

1 bay leaf

Salt and freshly ground black pepper

1 cup lukewarm chicken or beef broth, preferably homemade, as needed

If using fresh pasta, prepare the dough first, using the ingredients and quantities listed, and according to the directions on page 12. Stretch to less than ¹⁄₁₆ inch—on the pasta machine take it to the last setting. Cut into squares for *lasagne*. Preboil the squares in a large amount of salted boiling water for 2 seconds. Transfer the pasta to a large bowl of cold water to which the oil has been added. Cool the pasta in the water, then let them rest on dampened cotton dish towels until needed.

Soak the *porcini* in the lukewarm water for 30 minutes. Clean the artichokes (see page 70), cut them into eighths, and set them aside in a bowl of cold water with the lemon juice.

Finely chop the celery, onion, and carrot on a board. Put the oil in a medium-sized flameproof casserole and set it over medium heat; when the oil is warm, add the chopped ingredients and sauté until the onion is translucent and soft but not browned, about 5 minutes. Drain the artichokes and add them to the casserole along with the peas and bay leaf. Season with salt and pepper, and sauté for 2 minutes. Drain the mushrooms, making sure that no sand remains attached to the stems; reserve the mushroom water. Add the mushrooms to the casserole and mix well. Strain the mushroom water by passing it through several layers of paper towels. Add ¼ cup of this water to the casserole, cover, and cook, adding more mushroom water or lukewarm broth as needed until the vegetables are cooked,

Dried porcini add an intense flavor to the lasagna.

about 30 to 45 minutes depending on their size and tenderness. (Do not add excess liquid to the vegetables—just enough to braise gently.) Transfer the vegetables to a crockery or glass bowl, discarding the bay leaf, and let cool for 30 minutes.

Prepare the meatballs. Place the ground pork in a crockery or glass bowl, add the cheese, salt and pepper to taste, and eggs. Mix well with a wooden spoon, then form into small balls, using ¼ tablespoon of the mixture for each. Heat the vegetable and olive oils in a deep-fat fryer over medium heat. When the oil is hot (about 375°F), lightly flour the meatballs and fry them until lightly golden all over, about 30 seconds. Transfer them, using a strainer-skimmer or slotted spoon, onto a platter lined with paper towels to absorb excess fat; let stand until needed.

Prepare the tomato sauce. If fresh tomatoes are used, cut them into small pieces. Put fresh or canned tomatoes in a medium-sized flameproof nonreactive casserole with the oil and basil, and place over medium heat. Cook for 25 minutes, then season with salt and pepper. Pass the sauce through a food mill,

using the disc with the smallest holes, into a second pot. Reduce the sauce over low heat for 10 minutes more.

Assemble the *lasagne.* Preheat the oven to 375°F. Shell the hard-boiled eggs and cut them into eighths. Cut the ricotta (in Italy, ricotta is quite solid and may be sliced) or mozzarella into small pieces (if the ricotta is too moist, separate it into small pieces). Oil a 13½-by-8¾-inch glass baking dish and make a layer of the pasta on the bottom of the dish, then layer each of the different preparations on top: vegetables, meatballs, tomato sauce, ricotta or mozzarella, and grated sardo cheese in that order. Continue alternating layers of pasta and stuffing. The top layer should have abundant tomato sauce and some grated cheese only. Bake for 30 minutes, then remove from the oven, let cool for a few minutes, and serve.

WINE • Tenuta del Terriccio-Lupicaia

FOR THE MEATBALLS

1 pound ground pork

¼ cup grated pecorino sardo or pecorino romano cheese

Salt and freshly ground black pepper

2 extra-large eggs

2 cups vegetable oil

¼ cup olive oil

1 cup unbleached all-purpose flour

FOR THE TOMATO SAUCE

3 pounds ripe, fresh tomatoes; or 3 pounds canned tomatoes, preferably imported Italian, drained

4 tablespoons olive oil

4 large basil leaves, fresh or preserved in salt

Salt and freshly ground black pepper to taste

TO BAKE

4 extra-large eggs, hard-boiled

12 ounces ricotta or mozzarella cheese

1 cup freshly grated pecorino sardo or pecorino romano cheese

scripelle all'abruzzese (crespelle all'abruzzese)

TIMBALE OF STUFFED CRÊPES FOR CARNIVAL

SERVES 8 TO 10

FOR THE *CRESPELLE*

1 cup unbleached all-purpose flour

4 extra-large eggs

1 ¼ cups cold milk

Pinch of salt

3 tablespoons (1 ½ ounces) sweet butter or olive oil

FOR THE PORK BALLS

8 ounces ground pork

1 cup freshly grated Parmigiano

1 extra-large egg

Salt and freshly ground black pepper

Freshly grated nutmeg

2 cups vegetable oil

¼ cup olive oil

FOR THE GIZZARD SAUCE

6 ounces chicken gizzards

4 tablespoons (2 ounces) sweet butter

¼ cup olive oil

1 bay leaf

1 cup dry white wine

Salt and freshly ground black pepper

1 cup lukewarm chicken or beef broth, preferably homemade

Prepare the *crespelle,* or *scripelle,* first. Sift the flour, then put it in a crockery or glass bowl and make a well in it. Place the eggs in the well and start incorporating some of the flour from the edges of the well into the eggs. When all the flour is incorporated and a thick batter is formed, start adding the cold milk, continuously stirring with a wooden spoon. When all the milk is incorporated, add salt, mix again, then cover the bowl and put it in a cool place to rest for at least 1 hour, to allow the gluten in the flour to relax.

When ready, use 3 ½ tablespoons of the batter to prepare each *crespella*, in an 8-inch crêpe pan (see page 192). Grease the pan each time with oil or melted butter, and cook on both sides until lightly golden. This amount of batter will yield 15 *crespelle*. Stack one on top of the other on a dish, cover, and let stand until needed.

Prepare the meat stuffings. For the pork balls, mix the ground pork with the Parmigiano in a crockery or glass bowl. Add the egg, salt, pepper, and nutmeg to taste. Stir well, then form into small meatballs, using ½ tablespoon of the mixture for each. Let all the meatballs rest on a board while you heat the vegetable

and olive oils in a deep-fat fryer over medium heat. When the oil is hot (375°F), add the balls a few at a time, and fry until lightly golden all over, about 30 seconds, then transfer to a dish until needed.

Clean the chicken gizzards very well under cold running water, removing any fat still attached. Place a medium-sized flameproof casserole with the butter and olive oil over medium heat. When the butter is melted, add the gizzards along with the bay leaf, and sauté for 10 minutes. Add the wine and let it evaporate for 15 minutes. Season to taste with salt and pepper, then add the broth, cover, and cook for 20 minutes. Discard the bay leaf. Drain and finely chop the gizzards on a board, then put them back into the casserole to cook, uncovered, over low heat for 20 minutes, stirring every so often with a wooden spoon. Transfer to a crockery or glass bowl to rest for 1 hour or until cool.

Cut the chicken breast in half. Place a medium-sized skillet with the oil over medium heat. When the oil is warm, add the chicken to pan and sauté for 3 minutes on each side, season to taste with salt and pepper; the breast should remain somewhat undercooked. Transfer chicken to a board, discarding the juices from the pan. Cut the chicken into pieces half the size of the meatballs, and set aside.

Prepare the tomato sauce. If using fresh tomatoes, cut them into pieces. Put fresh or canned tomatoes in a nonreactive saucepan with the butter over medium heat and cook for 35 minutes; stirring every so often with a wooden spoon, and season to taste with salt and pepper. Pass the tomatoes through a food mill, using the disc with the smallest holes, into a second nonreactive saucepan, then reduce over low heat for 15 minutes more. Transfer the sauce to a crockery or glass bowl and let stand until cool (about 30 minutes).

Preheat the oven to 375°F. Assemble the dish. Use 1 tablespoon of the butter to heavily butter an 11-inch round cake pan or the bottom and sides of a springform pan with the butter. Lay out 1 *crespella* in the pan and place on it modest amounts of pork balls, chicken breast, gizzard sauce, tomato sauce, Parmigiano, and *scamorza*. Gauge the amount carefully, remembering that the ingredients have to be divided evenly among 14 of the 15 *crespelle*. Top with some bits of the butter and continue to layer the rest of the preparations and *crespelle*, saving 1 tablespoon of butter for the top. Cover the pan with aluminum foil and bake for 35 minutes. (If using a springform pan, wrap the whole pan in aluminum foil so the juices do not leak out.) Remove the pan from the oven, let rest for 2 minutes before uncovering, then unmold onto a large serving platter. Serve, slicing the

FOR THE CHICKEN BREAST

1 whole chicken breast, skin removed

¼ cup olive oil

Salt and freshly ground black pepper

FOR THE TOMATO SAUCE

2 pounds ripe, fresh tomatoes; or 2 pounds canned tomatoes, preferably imported Italian, drained

2 tablespoons (1 ounce) sweet butter

Salt and freshly ground black pepper

TO BAKE

4 tablespoons (2 ½ ounces) sweet butter, cut into small bits

1 cup freshly grated Parmigiano cheese

4 ounces unsmoked *scamorza* cheese, thinly sliced; or 4 ounces additional freshly grated Parmigiano

CRESPELLE (CRÊPES)

1. Quickly swirl the batter around until the bottom of the pan is covered.

2. Once the batter sets, shake the pan vigorously to detach the *crespella* from the pan.

3. Shake the *crespella* onto the edge of the pan so you can either

4. flip it, by giving the pan a short abrupt movement forward then up, when the *crespella* should turn in the air,

5. or, leaving pan on the stove, hold the *crespella* and quickly turn it over.

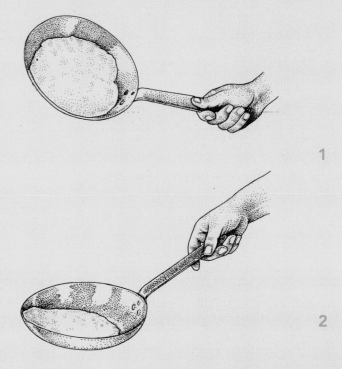

1

2

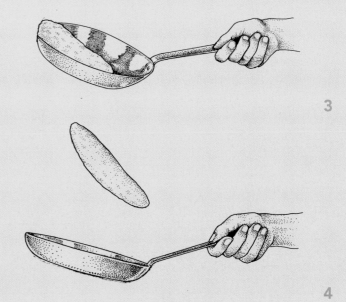

3

5

4

chicken and duck

Chicken is sometimes used to flavor a sauce, but there do not seem to be chicken sauces analogous to meat, duck, or rabbit sauces. Occasionally, one finds the combination of pasta and a chicken dish, such as a stew; or this striking recipe on the next page in which separately baked chicken pieces are added to a bell pepper sauce for the pasta. It is an unusual example of a *piatto unico,* or combination of first and second course.

There are two classic recipes in which duck meat is used in the sauce itself. One is from Arezzo, the other from Parma. They are really quite different, and, unfortunately, some recipes combine elements of both. In the Arezzo recipe, the duck liver is added at the end, a crucial difference; cold water rather than wine and broth is added to the tomatoes, and leeks are added to the aromatic vegetables. Two ingredients often mistakenly added are cloves, which is more typical of Bologna than Parma or Arezzo, and *Grano Padano* when Parmigiano would certainly be used in either place. The pasta in both places is made without oil and with an extra egg because of the richness of the sauce. Sage is used in Parma, not in Arezzo.

A third dish is the *Lasagne* with Duck, also from Arezzo. In this spectacular recipe, it is only the essence of the duck, cooked at length in the sauce and combined with the duck liver at the end, that ends up in the sauce. The meat is reserved for a later use at another meal.

pappardelle ai peperoni
PAPPARDELLE WITH CHICKEN IN SWEET PEPPER SAUCE

SERVES 6

1 chicken, about 3 ½ pounds

FOR THE MARINADE

3 large lemons

20 large sprigs Italian
parsley, leaves only

2 medium-sized cloves
garlic, peeled

½ cup olive oil

Salt and freshly ground
black pepper

FOR THE PASTA

3 cups unbleached all-
purpose flour

4 extra-large eggs

Pinch of salt

or

1 pound dried wide
egg pasta, such as
pappardelle, preferably
imported Italian

FOR THE SAUCE

3 red bell peppers

½ cup dry white wine

Salt and freshly ground
black pepper

TO COOK THE PASTA

Coarse-grained salt

TO SERVE

15 large sprigs Italian
parsley, leaves only,
coarsely chopped

Clean and wash the chicken well, and cut it into 12 pieces. Place the chicken in a crockery or glass bowl, squeeze the lemons, and add their juice to the bowl. Coarsely chop the parsley and finely chop the garlic; add them to the bowl along with the oil. Sprinkle with salt and pepper to taste. Mix all the ingredients with a wooden spoon, and let the chicken marinate for 1 hour, turning the pieces several times.

Prepare the fresh pasta with the ingredients and quantities listed, according to the directions on page 12. Stretch the pasta to ⅟₁₆ inch—on the pasta machine take it to the next to the last setting. To cut into *pappardelle,* follow directions for *trenette* (page 255), but cut both sides with the scalloped pastry wheel into 2-inch-wide strips.

Preheat the oven to 400°F. Prepare the sauce. Clean the peppers, removing stems, pulp, and seeds, then cut them into 1-inch strips. Place in a bowl of cold water for 30 minutes.

Use tongs to transfer the chicken pieces, with parsley and garlic clinging to them, from the bowl to a 13½-by-8¾-inch glass baking dish. Reserve the marinade and bake the chicken for 35 minutes. While the chicken bakes, trans-fer the marinade to a large saucepan and place over medium heat. When it is hot, drain the peppers and add them to the pan. Sauté for 10 minutes, then cover and cook the sauce for 15 minutes. Add the wine and let it evaporate, uncovered, for 5 minutes. Pass the sauce, including peppers, through a food mill into a bowl, then return the purée to the pan; simmer, uncovered, for 3 minutes, then taste for salt and pepper.

Bring a large pot of cold water to a boil, then add coarse salt to taste. Remove the baking dish from the oven and transfer the chicken pieces to a large serving dish, forming a ring of pieces around the edge of the dish. Cover with foil to keep the chicken warm. Add the liquid from the baking dish to the puréed peppers and mix well with a wooden spoon.

If using fresh *pappardelle,* cook in the boiling salted water for 30 seconds to 1 minute depending on dryness. If using dried pasta, boil the *pappardelle* for 9 to 12 minutes depending on the brand. Drain and place the pasta in the pan with the sauce, tossing very well. Remove the foil from the serving dish and arrange the pasta in the center. Sprinkle the parsley over the top and serve immediately.

pappardelle sull'anitra

PAPPARDELLE WITH DUCK

Prepare the pasta with the ingredients and quantities listed, following directions on page 12. Stretch the sheets of pasta to a thickness of 1/16 inch—on the pasta machine, take it to the next to last setting. To cut into *pappardelle,* follow directions for *trenette* (see page 255), but cut both sides with the scalloped pastry wheel into 2-inch-wide strips. Let the pasta rest on cotton towels until needed.

Prepare the sauce. Clean and wash the duck very well in cold water. Set the liver aside. Discard all the excess fat in the cavity. Place the leeks, celery, carrots, and onion in a bowl of cold water; let them soak for 30 minutes, then drain the vegetables and finely chop all together on a board. Cut the *prosciutto* into cubes less than 1/4 inch thick. Place the oil in a large, heavy casserole over medium heat; when the oil is warm, add the duck and sauté on all sides for 5 minutes. Add the chopped vegetables and *prosciutto,* mix very well, and sauté for 5 more minutes.

Pass the tomatoes and juice through a food mill, using the disc with the smallest holes, into a bowl. Add to the casserole, mix very well with a wooden spoon, and cook for 5 minutes. Season with salt, pepper, and nutmeg. Add 2 cups of the cold water, and cover; simmer for 1 hour, turning the duck every so often. Add the remaining water and cook, uncovered, for at least 1 more hour.

Remove the casserole from the heat. Transfer the duck to a chopping board. Remove the meat from the duck, and debone and skin. Cut the larger pieces of meat into 1/2-inch pieces. Coarsely chop the liver. Return the meat and liver to the casserole, set over medium heat, and cook for 15 minutes to reduce liquid, stirring often. Taste for salt and pepper.

Meanwhile, bring a large pot of cold water to a boil. Preheat the oven to 375°F. When the water reaches a boil, add coarse salt to taste, then add the pasta. If using fresh pasta, cook for 1 to 3 minutes depending on dryness; if dried, cook for 9 to 12 minutes depending on the brand. As the pasta cooks, use 1 tablespoon of the butter to heavily coat a 13½-by-8¾-inch glass baking dish. Place the remaining 5 tablespoons of butter in a large bowl. Drain the pasta, add it to the bowl with the butter, mix very well, then add the sauce and the Parmigiano and mix again. Transfer to the baking dish and bake for 10 minutes. Remove from the oven, let rest for 1 minute, then serve. No extra cheese should be added.

WINE • Tenuta San Guido-Sassicaia

SERVES 8 TO 10

FOR THE PASTA

4 cups unbleached all-purpose flour

5 extra-large eggs

Pinch of salt

or

1 pound dried *pappardelle,* preferably imported Italian

FOR THE SAUCE:

1 Long Island–type duck, (about 5 pounds), with liver

3 medium-sized leeks, cleaned

3 medium-sized stalks celery

4 medium-sized carrots, scraped

1 large red onion, peeled

4 ounces *prosciutto* or *pancetta,* in 1 piece

½ cup olive oil

2 pounds canned tomatoes, preferably imported Italian, undrained

Salt and freshly ground black pepper

Pinch of freshly grated nutmeg

4 cups cold water

TO COOK THE PASTA

Coarse-grained salt

TO BAKE

6 tablespoons (3 ounces) sweet butter

½ cup freshly grated Parmigiano

pasticcio di pasta alla maremmana

DUCK LASAGNE, MAREMMA STYLE

1 Long Island–type, duck, cleaned

2 medium-sized red onions, cleaned

4 stalks celery

2 medium-sized carrots, scraped

10 sprigs Italian parsley, leaves only

3 large cloves garlic, peeled

1 flat tablespoon rosemary leaves, fresh or preserved in salt

10 large leaves sage, fresh or preserved in salt

4 ounces *pancetta* or *prosciutto*, in 1 piece

8 tablespoons extra-virgin olive oil

Salt and freshly ground black pepper

4 bay leaves

Pinch of hot red pepper flakes

½ cup red wine vinegar

1 ½ pounds ripe, fresh tomatoes; or 1 ½ pounds canned tomatoes, preferably imported Italian, drained

6 heaping tablespoons tomato paste, preferably imported Italian

4 cups completely defatted chicken broth, preferably homemade

The Etruscans are thought to have first settled in Maremma in the southern part of Tuscany, where many ruins remain. After the Roman system of irrigation broke down, the region became a malarial swamp until the early twentieth century. When the swamps were drained and the famous umbrella pine woods were planted, it was developed as fashionable sea resorts, such as Porto Santo Stefano and the Argentario. The interior has remained quite unspoiled, still full of wild boar and other game, including different types of wild ducks.

The cooking of this region has remained rich, based on local ingredients and a love of wine, wine vinegar, and hot pepper. The Maremma-style lasagne *recipe that follows is really a* pasticcio *of* cannelloni: *the rich stuffing is "wrapped" in rolls of pasta and the resultant* cannelloni *are stacked two deep. The dish is served by cutting through the layers of* cannelloni *to create rectangular servings, as you would with* lasagne.

Prepare the duck sauce/stuffing first. Wash the duck very well and pat it dry with paper towels. Finely chop the onions, celery, carrots, parsley, garlic, rosemary, and sage all together on a chopping board. Cut the *pancetta* into very small pieces.

Place a large casserole with the oil over medium heat and when the oil is warm, add the *pancetta* and sauté for 2 minutes. Add the duck, season with salt and pepper, and sauté until golden all over, about 15 minutes. Add the chopped onion, celery, carrot, parsley, garlic, rosemary, and sage to the casserole along with the bay leaves, season with salt and pepper, to taste, and add the hot red pepper, mixing well with a wooden spoon.

Cook for 15 minutes, mixing every so often to be sure none of the ingredients stick to the bottom of the casserole, and turning the duck over twice. Add the vinegar and let evaporate for 5 minutes. Meanwhile, if using fresh tomatoes, blanch them in a pot of salted boiling water, then remove the skins and seeds and cut into pieces. If using canned tomatoes, pass them through a food mill using the disc with the smallest holes, into a crockery or glass bowl. Add the tomatoes to the casserole and cook for 15 minutes.

Dissolve the tomato paste in the broth and add 1 cup of this mixture to the casserole. Cook, adding more broth, 1 cup at a time, until the duck is very soft and a rich sauce forms, about 1 ½ hours. Discard the bay leaves and transfer the duck to a chopping board. Bone the duck, coarsely chop the meat, and return it to the sauce. Cook the sauce for 10 more minutes.

Using a slotted spoon, transfer the solid parts of the sauce, which will become the stuffing, to a crockery or glass bowl. Let both the stuffing and the juices in the casserole, which will become the sauce, rest until cool, about 1 hour. When completely cool, add the nutmeg, eggs and 1½ cups of the Parmigiano to the duck mixture, mix very well, cover, and refrigerate until needed. Remove half of the fat from the top of the sauce in the casserole and transfer the sauce to a medium-sized saucepan.

While the duck is cooking, prepare the pasta with the ingredients and quantities listed, following the directions on page 12. Stretch the pasta to a thickness of a little less than ⅟₁₆ inch—on a pasta machine, take it to the last setting. Cut the pasta into 24 (6-inch) squares. Precook the pasta squares in salted boiling water for a few seconds, then transfer them to a bowl of cold water containing the oil. Remove the squares from the water and let them rest on dampened cotton towels until needed.

Prepare the *balsamella* with the ingredients and quantities listed, following the instructions on page 97, then transfer to a bowl and press a piece of buttered waxed paper over the surface to prevent a skin from forming. Let the *balsamella* rest until cool, about ½ hour.

Preheat the oven to 375°F. Coat two 13½-by-8¾-inch glass baking dishes with the 2 tablespoons of butter, then pour ⅓ of the *balsamella* into the bottom of the dishes. Place 2 heaping tablespoons of the stuffing on each pasta square and fold two sides over the stuffing, spreading it out as you would for *cannelloni*. Place 6 of the stuffed pasta squares in each of the baking dishes, then pour ⅓ of the *balsamella* over them and sprinkle with the remaining Parmigiano. Place a second layer of stuffed pasta rolls directly over the first layer in each baking dish. Top with the remaining *balsamella*.

Bake, covered, for 20 minutes. Remove from the oven and let rest for 5 minutes. With a sharp knife, cut lengthwise through the middle of each *lasagne*, from one end of the pan to the other. Each serving consists of two halves, one on top of the other, with some of the duck sauce poured over them, and additional Parmigiano and a sprig of rosemary on top.

Freshly grated nutmeg to taste

4 extra-large eggs

2 cups freshly grated Parmigiano

FOR THE PASTA

2¼ cups unbleached all-purpose flour

6 extra-large egg yolks

¼ cup cold water

Pinch of salt

2 tablespoons olive oil or vegetable oil

TO COOK THE PASTA

Coarse-grained salt

2 tablespoons olive oil or vegetable oil

FOR THE BALSAMELLA (BÉCHAMEL)

6 tablespoons (3 ounces) sweet butter

6 tablespoons unbleached all-purpose flour

4 cups whole milk

Salt and freshly ground black pepper

Freshly grated nutmeg

TO BAKE

2 tablespoons (1 ounce) sweet butter

TO SERVE

Freshly grated Parmigiano

Rosemary sprigs

pasta all'anitra alla parmigiana
PASTA WITH DUCK SAUCE, PARMA STYLE

SERVES 6 TO 8

FOR THE SAUCE

1 Long Island–type duck (about 5 pounds)

1 medium-sized red onion, peeled

4 ounces *prosciutto*, in 1 piece

6 tablespoons (3 ounces) sweet butter

2 tablespoons olive oil

3 medium-sized cloves garlic, peeled but left whole

5 large sage leaves, fresh or preserved in salt

1 cup dry white wine

½ pound ripe, fresh tomatoes; or ½ pound canned tomatoes, preferably imported Italian, drained

Salt and freshly ground black pepper

1 to 2 cups lukewarm chicken or beef broth, preferably homemade

FOR THE PASTA

4 cups unbleached all-purpose flour

5 extra-large eggs

Pinch of salt

TO COOK THE PASTA

Coarse-grained salt

TO SERVE

4 tablespoons (2 ounces) sweet butter

½ cup freshly grated Parmigiano

Make the sauce. Clean the duck very well, discarding the extra fat from the cavity and the liver. Pat the duck dry with paper towels and cut into 3-inch pieces. Poultry shears are good for this.

Finely chop the onion on a board and cut the *prosciutto* into cubes less than ½ inch thick. Put the butter and oil in a heavy casserole over medium heat. When the butter is melted, add the onion, *prosciutto*, garlic, and sage leaves, left whole. Lightly sauté for 15 minutes, stirring every so often with a wooden spoon, then remove and discard the garlic and sage. Add the duck pieces and sauté until lightly golden all over, about 15 minutes. Then add the wine and let it evaporate for 15 minutes. Meanwhile, if using fresh tomatoes, cut them into small pieces. Pass the fresh or canned tomatoes through a food mill, using the disc with the smallest holes, into a small bowl. Add the tomato purée to the saucepan and season to taste with salt and pepper. Cook for 45 minutes, turning the meat several times and adding the broth as needed. By that time, the duck should be soft and the sauce thick and homogeneous.

Prepare the pasta with the ingredients and quantities listed, following the directions on page 12. Stretch the sheet of pasta to about $\frac{1}{16}$ inch thick—on a hand pasta machine, take it to the next to the last setting. Use a scalloped pastry wheel to cut the sheet into 2-inch squares and place the squares on cotton towels until needed.

Bring a large pot of cold water to a boil, and place a large serving dish containing the butter over the boiling water to melt. When the sauce is ready, and the water is boiling, remove the serving dish. Add coarse salt to the water, then add the pasta and cook for 1 to 3 minutes depending on dryness. Drain the pasta, transfer to the dish with the melted butter, toss very well, add the duck sauce, mix well, and arrange the duck pieces all over. Sprinkle with the Parmigiano and serve immediately.

game stuffings and sauces

Squab meat is popular for stuffing pasta, as in *Tortelli* Stuffed with Squab as well as the wonderful little *tortellini* eaten in broth, a recipe for which follows. They may also be made with the *cappelletti* shape. Squab meat is used in the sauce itself in Squab with Macaroni in a Pastry Drum.

Three recipes for pasta with rabbit sauce follow, one from Umbria and two from Tuscany. They share ingredients: all use the rabbit liver, and after cooking the rabbit itself in the sauce to extract its essence, two call for it to be removed and used for another meal. The main difference in flavoring—and it is significant—is that the Tuscan version stresses rosemary and sage, and the Umbrian version stresses parsley and black olives.

The most characteristic of all Tuscan dishes, *Pappardelle sulla lepre*, is made with a sauce of hare, its dark meat imparting a rich game flavor to the sauce. Many game sauces originate in Tuscany but have spread to other places, where sauces are also made with wild boar, when available.

pappardelle sulla pecora
PAPPARDELLE WITH LAMB SAUCE

SERVES 6 TO 8

FOR THE SAUCE

1 red onion, peeled

1 large stalk celery

1 carrot, scraped

½ pound coarsely ground lamb

4 tablespoons olive oil

½ pound boneless lamb, cut into ½-inch cubes

1 sprig fresh thyme

1 medium-sized sprig fresh rosemary

1 cup dry white wine

1 ½ pounds ripe, fresh tomatoes; or 1 ½ pounds canned tomatoes, preferably imported Italian, drained

Salt and freshly ground black pepper

1 cup lukewarm chicken or beef broth, preferably homemade

FOR THE PASTA

3 cups unbleached all-purpose flour

4 extra-large eggs

Pinch of salt

TO COOK THE PASTA

Coarse-grained salt

TO SERVE

8 tablespoons (4 ounces) sweet butter, cut into bits

½ cup freshly grated Parmigiano

The lamb sauce of Abruzzi, used with fresh pasta cut with the "guitar," (see page 289) is made with true lamb, but the Tuscan dish—made not so much in Prato as in the area between that town and Florence, called Campi—uses meat from an animal a year old, called there not lamb but "sheep," or pecora. *(In Italy, lamb is not likely to be more than twelve weeks old.) But the long-cooked* pecora *is a specialty of Campi, and indeed it is one of the few places in Italy where it can still be found. In earlier times, lamb, sheep, and mutton* (montone*) all had their separate repertories, but both* pecora *and* montone *dishes are extremely rare now. The lamb usually available suits this dish rather well; it is much older than the twelve-week-old "baby" lamb, though younger than the* pecora *used in Campi. Campi, Prato, and Florence were all once the center of the Western European wool industry; indeed, Florence's original fortunes were made in that trade, and only later in banking.*

Prepare the sauce. Finely chop the onion, celery, and carrot all together on a board, then mix with the lamb in a bowl. Heat the oil in a deep saucepan over low heat; add the contents of the bowl and sauté for 5 minutes. Add the lamb cubes and the thyme and rosemary. Sauté for 5 more minutes, then pour in the wine; let it evaporate for 5 minutes. If using fresh tomatoes, cut them into small pieces. Pass fresh or canned tomatoes through a food mill, using the disc with the smallest holes, into a small bowl. Add the tomatoes to the saucepan and season with salt and pepper to taste. Cook for 15 minutes, then add the broth. Simmer the sauce for 1 hour over low heat, stirring every so often with a wooden spoon.

As the sauce cooks, prepare the pasta with the ingredients and quantities listed, following the directions on page 12. Stretch the pasta to about $\frac{1}{16}$ inch—on a hand pasta machine, take it to the next to the last setting. To cut into *pappardelle* follow the directions for *trenette* (see page 255) but cut both sides with the scalloped pastry wheel into 2-inch-wide strips and set on cotton towels until needed.

When the sauce is ready, discard the sprigs of thyme and rosemary and transfer the sauce to a large skillet over low heat. Place a large pot of cold water over medium heat; when the water reaches a boil, add coarse salt to taste, then add the pasta, and cook for 1 to 3 minutes depending on dryness. Drain the pasta, transfer it to a large bowl, dot with the butter, and toss. Transfer to the skillet, mix very well, then transfer to a warmed serving dish. Sprinkle with cheese and serve immediately.

tortellini o cappelletti di piccione

TORTELLINI OR CAPPELLETTI STUFFED WITH SQUAB

Clean and wash the squab very well. Place the cold water in a small, deep saucepan over medium heat, and when the water reaches a boil, add coarse salt to taste, the bay leaf, and the clove. When the water returns to a boil, add the squab and simmer for 45 minutes. Transfer the squab to a chopping board and bone it.

Discard the bones and the water; reserve the meat and skin. Finely chop the *prosciutto,* squab meat, and skin together on a board, then transfer to a crockery or glass bowl. Add the egg and Parmigiano, and season with salt, pepper, and nutmeg. Mix well with a wooden spoon and refrigerate, covered, until needed.

Prepare the pasta with the ingredients and quantities listed, following the directions on page 12. Stretch to less than 1/16 inch thick—on the pasta machine, take it to the last setting. Prepare the *tortellini* or *cappelletti* (see page 202 or 203) using 1/4 teaspoon of stuffing for each *tortellino* or *cappelletto*. Let the pasta rest on floured cotton dish towels until needed. When ready, heat the broth in a medium-sized pot over medium heat. When the broth reaches a boil, add the *tortellini* or *cappelletti* and cook for 1 to 3 minutes depending on dryness. Serve in warmed bowls, along with some broth, and sprinkle each serving with Parmigiano.

*WINE • Michele Chiarlo
Barbaresco, D.O.C.G.*

Shaping tortellini.

SERVES 8 TO 10

FOR THE STUFFING

1 squab (about 1/2 pound)

About 1 quart cold water

Coarse-grained salt

1 bay leaf

1 whole clove

3 ounces *prosciutto*, in 1 piece

1 extra-large egg

1/4 cup freshly grated Parmigiano

Salt and freshly ground black pepper

Large pinch of freshly grated nutmeg

FOR THE PASTA

3 cups unbleached all-purpose flour

4 extra-large eggs

Pinch of salt

TO SERVE

2 1/2 quarts defatted chicken or beef broth, preferably homemade

1/2 cup freshly grated Parmigiano

TORTELLINI

1. As the pasta is prepared, immediately cut it into discs using a cookie cutter with smooth edges, the diameter of which is appropriate to the size required for the individual recipe. Place an amount of filling appropriate to the recipe in the center.

2. Moisten the edges slightly with water or egg whites, then double over one side of the pasta disc, but not all the way to the other edge; leave a little border arc of the pasta untouched.

3. Wrap the half-moon around your index or little finger, depending on the size of the pasta, with the top of your finger reaching only to the top of the filled section.

4. With your thumb, connect the 2 edges of the half-moon.

5. Grasp the pasta overlapping your fingers and curl it outward.

6. The finished *tortellino*.

1

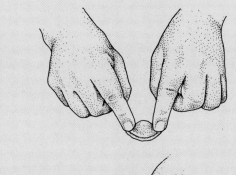

2

3

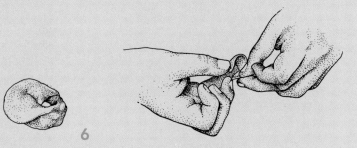

6

5

4

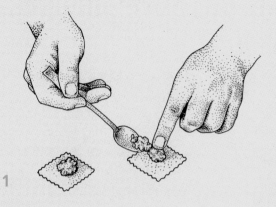

1

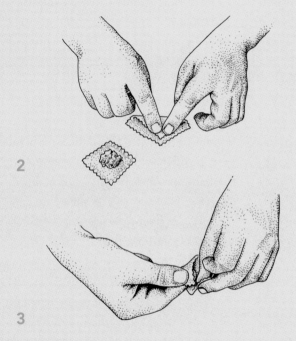

2

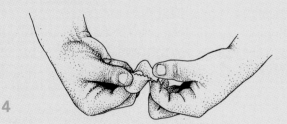

3

CAPPELLETTI

1. Using a pastry cutter with a scalloped or nonscalloped edge, cut the layer of pasta into squares of appropriate size for the individual recipe. Place the appropriate amount of filling in the center of each square.

2. Moisten the edges with water or egg whites. Pick up one corner and draw it to the opposite corner, but not all the way to the edge. Leave a border untouched.

3. Wrap the now triangular-shaped pasta around your index finger, the top of your finger reaching only to the top of the filled section.

4. With your thumb, connect the 2 edges of the pasta triangle and curl the overlap of pasta outward. The result should resemble the little hats that give *cappelletti* their name.

4

pappardelle sulla lepre alla maremmana

PAPPARDELLE WITH HARE OR RABBIT SAUCE, MAREMMA STYLE

SERVES 8

1 hare or rabbit, skinned and cleaned and liver reserved (or substitute 1 chicken liver, cleaned)

2 stalks celery

2 large carrots, scraped

1 large red onion, cleaned

1 large clove garlic, peeled

10 sprigs fresh Italian parsley, leaves only

3 fresh sage leaves

½ tablespoon fresh rosemary leaves

Large pinch of red hot pepper flakes

4 ounces *pancetta* or *prosciutto*, in 1 piece

6 tablespoons extra-virgin olive oil

3 bay leaves, fresh or preserved in salt

Salt and freshly ground black pepper

1 cup dry red wine or ¼ cup red wine vinegar

1½ pounds ripe, fresh tomatoes; or 1½ pounds canned tomatoes, preferably imported Italian, drained

A hare is not a rabbit, not even a wild rabbit: it is a game animal whose meat is quite dark, unlike a rabbit's white meat. Hare is available fresh in Italy only during the hunting season, mostly in the fall.

I have a personal interest in these animals, because they are my neighbors. At the end of August, when the wheat has been cut, leaving the ground covered with wheat grains, hares suddenly appear all around my house, which is in the Chianti area of Tuscany. After a few days they become quite friendly and it is not unusual in the morning to find three or four hares wandering in our garden. One even slept in the geranium bed. And so we feel the tragedy of their fate when the hunting season begins each year. Of course, it is difficult to blame the hunters, for the hare meat is so rare and prized and the pasta sauce made from it is one of the hallmarks of Italian gastronomy.

The substitution of rabbit when hare is not available is very good, but does not convey the complete experience.

Place the hare or rabbit in a skillet, covered, over medium heat for 3 minutes. Rinse the hare very well under cold running water then pat it dry with paper towels.

Coarsely chop the celery, carrots, onion, garlic, and parsley all together on a board; finely chop the sage, rosemary, and red pepper flakes all together on a board. Cut the *pancetta* into tiny pieces or grind it with a meat grinder, using the disc with medium-sized holes. Mix the coarsely chopped ingredients, finely chopped ingredients, and *pancetta* all together.

Place a large, flameproof casserole containg the oil over medium heat and, when the oil is warm, add the vegetable mixture. Sauté for 10 minutes, mixing every so often with a wooden spoon. Cut the hare into 3 pieces and add it to the casserole. Sauté for 15 minutes, turning the pieces several times. Season with salt and pepper. Add the wine and simmer, allowing it to evaporate for 5 minutes.

Meanwhile, if using fresh tomatoes, blanch them in a medium-sized pot of salted boiling water, then remove the skins and seeds, and cut them into 1-inch squares. If using canned tomatoes, pass them through a food mill, using the disc with the smallest holes, into a crockery or glass bowl. Add the tomatoes to the casserole, cover, and cook for 1 hour, mixing every so often with a wooden spoon and adding broth as needed. By that time the sauce should be rather thick and the hare completely cooked, but not dry or very soft. The cooking time will be at least 2 hours, but a rabbit will be ready in an hour or so.

Transfer the hare to a cutting board and bone it, cutting the meat into small pieces. Finely chop the liver and mix together with the meat. Return to the casserole and cook for 5 more minutes, adding more broth if needed. The sauce should be rather thick but with a smooth texture.

Meanwhile, bring a large pot of cold water to a boil over medium heat, add coarse salt to taste, then add the pasta and cook until al dente—9 to 12 minutes depending on the brand. Drain the pasta, transfer it to a warmed bowl, add the butter, and mix very well. Transfer the pasta to a serving platter, pour the sauce over the top, and sprinkle with the cheese. Serve hot with the rosemary or sage sprigs.

1 cup to 2 cups completely defatted beef or chicken broth, preferably home-made

1 pound dried *pappardelle*, preferably imported Italian

TO COOK THE PASTA
Coarse-grained salt

TO SERVE

2 tablespoons (1 ounce) sweet butter

4 heaping tablespoons freshly grated Parmigiano

Sage or rosemary sprigs

A true hare. Notice that the ears are longer than those of a rabbit.

tagliatelle alla frantoiana
TAGLIATELLE IN RABBIT SAUCE WITH OLIVES

SERVES 6 TO 8

FOR THE SAUCE

1 small rabbit (about 2 pounds), liver reserved

4 ounces *pancetta* or *prosciutto*, in 1 piece

2 tablespoons (1 ounce) sweet butter

½ cup olive oil

1 small red onion, peeled

3 medium-sized carrots, scraped

2 medium-sized stalks celery

10 large sprigs Italian parsley, leaves only

1 medium-sized clove garlic, peeled

1 cup dry red wine

Salt and freshly ground black pepper

4 tablespoons tomato paste, preferably imported Italian

2 ½ cups beef broth, preferably homemade

20 Greek black olives, packed in brine, pitted and finely chopped

Clean the rabbit very well and rinse it under cold running water. Place a large flameproof casserole over medium heat (with no oil or other fat), put in the rabbit, cover, and sauté for 3 minutes on each side to draw out the gamey white liquid. Remove the rabbit and rinse again in cold water.

Cut the *pancetta* into small pieces. Place the butter and oil in a medium-sized flameproof casserole over medium heat. When the butter is melted, add the *pancetta* and sauté until lightly golden, about 5 minutes.

Finely chop the onion, carrots, celery, parsley, and garlic all together on a board. When the *pancetta* is ready, add the chopped ingredients and sauté for 2 minutes. Put in the whole rabbit and cook for 15 minutes, stirring the vegetables constantly and turning the rabbit 3 or 4 times. Add the wine and let it evaporate for 5 minutes, then season with salt and pepper. Dissolve the tomato paste in the broth, and pour 1 cup of the mixture into the casserole. Cover and cook for 1 hour, adding the remaining broth ½ cup at a time, stirring the sauce each time. Turn the rabbit 4 or 5 more times while cooking.

Prepare the pasta using the ingredients and quantities listed, following the directions on page 12. Stretch the layer to $\frac{1}{16}$ inch thick—on the pasta machine take it to the next to the last setting. Cut into *tagliatelle* (see page 34). Set aside to rest on cotton towels until needed.

When the sauce is ready, taste again for salt and pepper and lift out the cooked rabbit, reserving it for a later use, at this or another meal. Finely chop the rabbit liver on a board.

When ready to serve, put a large pot of cold water over medium heat. When the water reaches a boil, place a large serving dish containing the butter over the pot to melt it. Reheat the sauce, and mix in the chopped liver and the chopped olives. Add coarse salt to the boiling water, then add the pasta and cook for 1 to 3 minutes depending on dryness. Drain the pasta, transfer it to the prepared serving platter, mix well, add all the sauce, mix again, sprinkle the parsley and whole olives over the top, and serve immediately.

An ancient farmhouse in Chianti Classico.

FOR THE PASTA

4 cups unbleached all-purpose flour

5 extra-large eggs

Pinch of salt

TO COOK THE PASTA

Coarse-grained salt

TO SERVE

4 tablespoons (2 ounces) sweet butter

10 large sprigs Italian parsley, leaves only, coarsely chopped

10 Greek black olives, pitted but left whole

pappardelle sul coniglio
PASTA WITH RABBIT SAUCE

SERVES 4 TO 6

FOR THE SAUCE

1 small rabbit with liver (about 2 pounds)

8 ounces *pancetta* or *prosciutto*, in 1 piece

2 medium-sized carrots, scraped

1 small red onion, peeled

3 medium-sized stalks celery

1 medium-sized clove garlic, peeled

1 tablespoon rosemary leaves, fresh or preserved in salt or dried and blanched

3 large sage leaves, fresh or preserved in salt

½ cup olive oil

1 cup dry red wine

2 tablespoons tomato paste, preferably imported Italian

2 cups lukewarm beef or chicken broth, preferably homemade

Salt and freshly ground black pepper

FOR THE PASTA

3 cups unbleached all-purpose flour

4 extra-large eggs

Pinch of salt

or

1 pound dried *pappardelle*, preferably imported Italian

TO COOK THE PASTA

Coarse-grained salt

Prepare the sauce. Wash the rabbit very well; set the liver aside until later. Cut the rabbit into 3 pieces and pat dry with paper towels. Place a large skillet over medium heat; when it is hot, add the rabbit pieces, without oil, cover and sauté for 4 minutes. Discard the juices that emerge, since their flavor is very gamey. Remove the skillet from the heat, wash the rabbit again, and pat dry with paper towels.

Mince the *pancetta*; finely chop the carrots, onion, celery, garlic, rosemary, and sage all together on a board. Heat the oil over medium heat in a large flame-proof casserole. When the oil is warm, add the rabbit and sauté for 5 minutes on each side. Pour in the wine and let it evaporate for 10 minutes. Add the chopped ingredients along with the *pancetta* and sauté for 15 minutes more. Dissolve the tomato paste in 1 cup of the broth and add it to the casserole; season to taste with salt and pepper, cover, and simmer for 25 minutes, stirring every so often with a wooden spoon. Add the second cup of broth and cook, uncovered, for 20 minutes more, or until the rabbit is very tender. Remove the rabbit and save it for another meal. Taste the sauce for salt and pepper. Finely chop the rabbit liver on a board, add it to the casserole, mix well, and cook for 5 minutes.

During the last stages of cooking the sauce, you will have time to prepare the pasta with the ingredients and quantities listed and following the directions on page 12. Stretch the pasta to 1/16 inch thick—on the pasta machine, take it to the next to the last setting. To cut the pasta into *pappardelle*, follow the directions for *trenette* (see page 255), but cut both sides with the scalloped pastry wheel into 2-inch-wide strips and let rest on cotton dish towels until needed.

Bring a large pot of cold water to a boil, add coarse salt to taste, then add the pasta. If fresh pasta is used, cook for 1 to 3 minutes depending on dryness; if dried, cook for 9 to 12 minutes depending on the brand. Drain the pasta and transfer it to a large, warmed serving platter; pour the sauce over the top, toss well, and serve.

WINE • Tenuta Di Nozzole Chianti Classico Riserva

pasta sul cervo

PASTA WITH VENISON SAUCE

Venison from a variety of deer is used in Italy, especially in the hilly and mountainous regions of the Apennines and Alps. In Friuli, a venison sauce is made from the meat marinated in wine, spices, and aromatic vegetables and mixed with broth, a little tomato, and the chopped vegetable marinade. This fragrant red wine sauce is usually served with a dried pasta and pieces of the meat itself.

Cut the onions into quarters and the celery and carrots into large pieces; place them with the wine, bay leaves, cloves, garlic, and venison steak in a large crockery or glass bowl. Cover and marinate in the refrigerator for 24 hours, turning the meat twice.

Remove the meat and vegetables. Discard the wine, bay leaves, and cloves. Lightly flour the steak on both sides. Place the oil in a heavy, medium-sized casserole and set over medium heat. When the oil is warm, add the meat and sauté for 5 minutes on each side. Meanwhile, finely chop the marinated vegetables on a board, then add them to the casserole and sauté for 15 minutes. Add 1 cup of the wine and cook again for 15 minutes, then add the second cup of wine and cook for 15 minutes. Add salt and pepper to taste. Dissolve the tomato paste in 1 cup of the broth, add it to the casserole, cover, and simmer for 3 hours, adding the remaining broth as needed, stirring every so often with a wooden spoon. The meat should become very tender and the sauce smooth and quite thick. Taste again for salt and pepper and cook for 2 more minutes, uncovered.

Bring a large pot of cold water to a boil, add coarse salt to taste, then add the pasta and cook until al dente—9 to 12 minutes depending on the brand. Meanwhile, place some of the liquid from the sauce on a large, warmed serving platter. Drain the pasta and transfer it to the warmed platter. Pour the remaining sauce and meat over the top, toss very well, and serve immediately. Pass the cheese, if desired, at the table.

WINE • Michele Chiarlo Barolo Riserva D.O.C.

SERVES 8 TO 10

FOR THE MARINADE:

2 medium-sized red onions, peeled

3 large stalks celery

3 medium-sized carrots, scraped

3 cups dry red wine

3 bay leaves

3 whole cloves

1 large clove garlic, peeled but left whole

2 pounds boneless venison steak

FOR THE SAUCE

¼ cup unbleached all-purpose flour

¼ cup olive oil

2 cups dry red wine

Salt and freshly ground black pepper

4 tablespoons tomato paste, preferably imported Italian

3 cups lukewarm chicken or beef broth, preferably homemade

FOR THE PASTA

1 ½ pounds dried *pappardelle*, preferably imported Italian

TO COOK THE PASTA

Coarse-grained salt

TO SERVE

8 to 10 tablespoons freshly grated aged *latteria* or Parmigiano cheese (optional)

fresh regi

onal pastas

Each region of Italy and many of its cities and towns have trademark pastas made only in that place and savored in their native habitat. I include here some of the most famous regional dishes. My choice necessarily must be limited and includes some notable ones that are not well known and some better known ones that I feel have not been presented authentically enough. We begin with Piedmont, with its various *agnolotti* and its bread-crumb pasta.

piedmont

Agnelotti, spelled in this older manner, appeared in an early 1798 Piedmont cookbook. It is interesting to see them in this early form, closer to their origins, to clarify the essentials behind today's many stuffings. At that time, dishes were divided between those without meat, called *di magro*, which were served on fasting days, and those with meat, called *di grasso*. (*Magro* and *grasso* also denote "thin" and "fat.")

The more common version, *di magro*, was usually made with spinach, butter, cream, cheese, eggs, and—to bind it together—"mollica," the crumb of the bread. On

Previous pages: A typical Tuscan farmhouse.

nonfasting days, breast of veal was boiled to make the broth in which the *agnelotti* were eaten, sprinkled with additional cheese. Since broth was generally made with some kind of meat, the *di magro* versions were eaten with butter and grated cheese.

One might speculate that the earliest versions of the butter-and-cheese dressing came about in just this manner, because the pasta, especially stuffed pasta, could not be eaten with a broth. On the other hand, in Boccaccio's fourteenth-century *Decameron,* the ladies are dressing pasta cooked in broth with butter and abundant cheese. Butter seems to have become popular in medieval times, so in Boccaccio's time it may still have been a new sensation. But this butter-and-cheese dressing would have remained necessary for fasting days, especially in areas like Piedmont, which produces no olive oil.

Under Classic *Agnolotti*, we discuss the general categories of ingredients used. Some vegetables remain in all versions as a reminder of the dishes' origins, but the varieties of meat have multiplied. Roasted meats, often mixed and left over from a feast of *arrosto misto*, are preferred, because the juices left over may be used as dressing. A combination of beef and pork is most often used, but both veal and chicken can also be used.

A unique adaptation is the large *tortelli* of *Agnolotti alla piemontese*, in which a little ring of rice and sauce contains an inner stuffing of meat and aromatic vegetables. The dressing is the usual butter and cheese.

agnolotti (agnelotti or agnollotti)
CLASSIC AGNOLOTTI

SERVES 6 TO 8

FOR THE STUFFING

1 ¾ pounds endive (about 3 bunches)

Coarse-grained salt

8 tablespoons (4 ounces) sweet butter

Salt and freshly ground black pepper

2 bay leaves

1 large clove garlic, peeled

6 ounces ground beef

6 ounces ground pork

3 extra-large eggs

½ cup freshly grated Parmigiano

Freshly grated nutmeg

FOR THE PASTA

3 cups unbleached all-purpose flour

4 extra-large eggs

Pinch of salt

TO COOK THE PASTA

Coarse-grained salt

FOR THE SAUCE

8 tablespoons (4 ounces) sweet butter

¾ cup freshly grated Parmigiano

Freshly ground black pepper

Many variations on the stuffing may be substituted, but keep in mind that there must be both vegetables and meat and that modern normal-sized agnolotti *are always sautéed in butter after they are boiled. See the variations listed below; any combination is possible.*

Prepare the stuffing. Bring a large pot of cold water to a boil over medium heat. Clean the endive, removing the large stems and washing the leaves well. When the water reaches a boil, add coarse salt to taste, then add the endive and cook for 25 minutes. Drain, cool under cold running water, and squeeze very well to remove as much water as possible. Finely chop the endive.

Place a large skillet with 4 tablespoons of the butter over medium heat; when the butter is melted, add the chopped endive, season with salt and pepper, and sauté, stirring with a wooden spoon, for 2 minutes. Transfer to a crockery or glass bowl and cool for 30 minutes.

Place a small saucepan with the remaining butter over medium heat. When the butter is melted, add the bay leaves and garlic, and sauté for 1 minute. Add the ground beef and pork, season with salt and pepper, and sauté for 5 minutes more, stirring every so often with a wooden spoon.

Discard the garlic and bay leaves, and transfer the meat with the juices to a crockery or glass bowl; let rest until cool, about 30 minutes. Combine the contents of the 2 bowls, add the eggs and Parmigiano, and mix well. Taste for salt and pepper and season to taste with nutmeg.

Prepare the pasta with the ingredients and quantities listed, following the directions on page 12. Stretch the sheet of pasta to less than 1⁄16 inch thick—on a pasta machine take it to the last setting. Prepare 2-inch-square *tortelli* (*agnolotti*), with 1 tablespoon of stuffing for each, following the directions on page 215. Let the *agnolotti* rest on floured cotton dish towels until needed.

Bring a large quantity of cold water to a boil, add coarse salt to taste, then add the *agnolotti* and cook for 6 to 9 minutes depending on dryness. Meanwhile, melt the butter for the sauce in a large skillet over low heat. As the *agnolotti* are cooked, transfer them to the skillet and sauté gently for 1 minute more. Arrange on a warmed serving platter and serve with cheese and abundant black pepper.

NOTE

The original *agnelotti* used pasta made with only the whites of eggs.

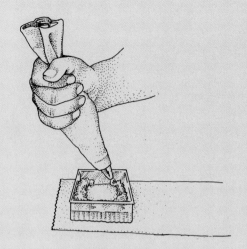

AGNOLOTTI

1. Using a pastry bag, make a narrow border of rice (see page 216) around the inside edge of a cookie cutter.

2. Fit the meat stuffing inside the rice border.

3. Fit a sheet of pasta of the same size over the prepared line of squares.

4. Cut all around the outside of the cookie cutter with a pastry wheel.

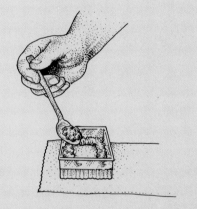

1

2

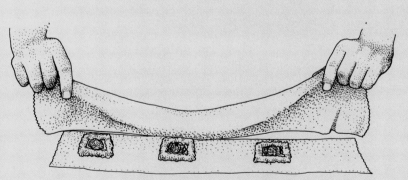

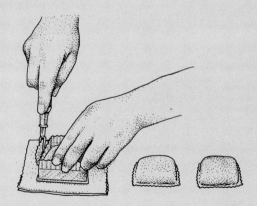

3

4

agnolotti alla piemontese
GIANT SQUARE AGNOLOTTI

SERVES 8

FOR THE MEAT STUFFING

4 ounces *prosciutto*, in 1 piece

6 tablespoons (3 ounces) sweet butter

2 tablespoons olive oil

1 medium-sized carrot, scraped

1 large white onion, peeled

1 large stalk celery

10 large sprigs Italian parsley, leaves only

1 pound boneless veal shoulder, in 1 piece

1 cup dry white wine

1 tablespoon tomato paste

Salt and freshly ground black pepper

Freshly grated nutmeg

1 cup beef broth, preferably homemade

FOR THE RICE STUFFING

1 medium-sized white onion, peeled

5 tablespoons (2½ ounces) sweet butter

1 tablespoon olive oil

1 cup rice, preferably Italian Arborio

3 cups beef broth, preferably homemade, heated to boiling

Cut the *prosciutto* into tiny pieces. Heat the butter and oil in a saucepan over medium heat; when the butter is completely melted, add the *prosciutto*, lower the heat, and cook for 5 minutes. Meanwhile, finely chop the carrot, onion, celery, and parsley together on a board. Add to the pan and sauté for 2 minutes more. Add the veal and sauté on all sides for 2 minutes. Pour in the wine and let it evaporate for 5 minutes. Then add the tomato paste; salt, pepper, and nutmeg to taste; and ½ cup of the broth. Keep adding broth, up to 1 cup total, while the veal cooks until tender, about 20 minutes. Remove the saucepan from the heat and, using a slotted spoon, transfer all the solid ingredients to a bowl. Reserve the cooking juices in the saucepan. With a meat grinder, coarsely grind everything back into the saucepan. Return the pan to medium heat, taste for salt and pepper, and cook until the mixture is quite thick, about 5 minutes longer. Transfer the stuffing to a crockery or glass bowl to cool for 1 hour.

Prepare the rice stuffing. Preheat the oven to 375° F. Finely chop the onion on a board, then heat the butter and oil in a medium-sized flameproof casserole over medium heat. When the butter is completely melted, add the onion and the rice and sauté for 4 minutes. Add the boiling broth to the rice, season with salt and pepper, and stir very well. Cover the casserole and bake in the oven for 20 minutes. Remove from the oven, transfer the rice to a crockery or glass bowl, and cool for 1 hour. When the meat and rice stuffings are both cool, incorporate one-third of the meat stuffing and all the Parmigiano into the rice stuffing, mixing thoroughly with a wooden spoon.

Prepare the pasta with the ingredients and quantities listed, following the directions on page 12. Stretch the pasta to less than ⅛ inch thick—on the pasta machine take it to the last setting. Place a 4-inch-square jagged-edged cookie cutter on the sheet of pasta. With a pastry bag, make a narrow border of rice stuffing all along the inside edge of the cookie cutter (see page 215). Fit a tablespoon of the meat stuffing inside the rice border. Carefully remove the cookie cutter. Repeat the procedure for the remaining *agnolotti*, then fit a similar size sheet of pasta over the prepared rice squares. Replace the cookie cutter, this time upside down (the top part is wider), and cut all around the cookie cutter with a pastry wheel. Seal the edges together well and let the squares rest on floured cotton dish towels until needed.

Bring a large pot of cold water to a boil. Meanwhile, melt the butter on a large serving platter and place it over the pot of water. When the water reaches a boil, remove the platter and add coarse salt to the pot. Put in the giant *agnolotti* one at a time, and cook each for 1 to 3 minutes depending on the dryness. With a slotted spoon, transfer the *agnolotti* to the warmed platter and spoon some of the butter over the top, then sprinkle with Parmigiano. When all the *agnolotti* are on the platter, serve immediately. If using the truffle, shave a few slices over each serving.

Salt and freshly ground black pepper

5 tablespoons freshly grated Parmigiano

FOR THE PASTA

4 cups unbleached all-purpose flour

5 extra-large eggs

Pinch of salt

TO COOK THE PASTA

Coarse-grained salt

TO SERVE

12 tablespoons (6 ounces) sweet butter

½ cup freshly grated Parmigiano

1 small white truffle (optional)

pisarei e faso

PASTA AND BEANS, MONFERRATO STYLE

SERVES 8

FOR THE BEANS

1 cup dried *borlotti* or cranberry beans

3 quarts cold water

2 tablespoons olive oil

2 ounces *pancetta* or *prosciutto*, in 1 piece

2 teaspoons coarse-grained salt

FOR THE SAUCE

1 medium-sized red onion, peeled

2 medium-sized stalks celery

1 medium-sized carrot, scraped

10 large sprigs Italian parsley, leaves only

1 small clove garlic, peeled

5 large basil leaves, fresh or preserved in salt

2 pounds ripe, fresh tomatoes; or 2 pounds canned tomatoes, preferably imported Italian, drained

4 ounces *pancetta* or *prosciutto*, in 1 piece

¼ cup olive oil

Salt and freshly ground black pepper

Pisarei e faso *is not a soup but is the combination of a special pasta made with bread crumbs and a sauce containing beans. The beans are first simmered with olive oil and* pancetta *and are then combined with the tomato sauce, which is made with aromatic vegetables and* pancetta. *The pasta combines finely ground bread crumbs with the flour and some water, and no eggs. This ancient preparation survives in the locale of Monferrato and, interestingly, in Piacenza, in the extreme north of Emilia-Romagna. It is curious that the dish survives in two places that are not very close together, and apparently nowhere else.*

Soak the beans overnight in a bowl of cold water. The next morning, drain the beans, rinse them under cold running water, and put them in a saucepan with the cold water, oil, *pancetta*, and coarse salt. Cover the pan and place over medium heat. Simmer until the beans are cooked but still firm, 1 to 2 hours depending on their dryness. Leave the beans in the pan, covered, until needed.

Meanwhile, prepare the sauce. Coarsely chop the onion, celery, carrot, parsley, garlic, and basil together on a board. If using fresh tomatoes, cut them into pieces. Pass fresh or canned tomatoes through a food mill, using the disc with the smallest holes, into a crockery or glass bowl. Cut the *pancetta* into less than ½-inch cubes. Place a medium-sized saucepan with the oil over medium heat, and, when the oil is warm, add the chopped ingredients, tomatoes, and *pancetta*. Cover and simmer for about 2 hours, stirring every so often with a wooden spoon. When the sauce is almost ready, taste for salt and pepper. Let the sauce stand, covered, until needed.

Prepare the *pisarei*. Soak the bread crumbs in a small bowl of lukewarm water for 15 minutes. Use a very fine strainer to drain the bread crumbs very well, and discard the water. Following the directions on page 12, prepare the pasta with the flour, ½ cup lukewarm water, the salt, and bread crumbs, placing the bread crumbs in the well with the water and salt. Knead the dough until it is very elastic. Cut into several pieces and use your hands to stretch each piece into a long cord less than ½ inch thick. Cut the cord into pieces of less than ½ inch, then use your thumb or a small knife to curl them up into tiny shells (see drawings on page 219). Let the *pisarei* stand on a lightly floured towel until needed.

Bring a large quantity of cold water to a boil, add coarse salt to taste, then add the pasta. Stir with a wooden spoon and cook for 1 to 3 minutes depending on dryness. Meanwhile, drain the beans, discarding the *pancetta*, and transfer along with the hot sauce to a large saucepan. Drain the *pisarei* and add to the saucepan. Place the saucepan over medium heat for 1 minute, mixing well to allow the pasta to absorb some sauce. If using grated Parmigiano, sprinkle a tablespoon of cheese over each portion, then serve.

NOTE

Pisarei are somewhere between pasta and *gnocchi*, and are therefore not as tender as pasta.

FOR THE PASTA

½ cup fine unseasoned bread crumbs, preferably homemade

3 ½ cups unbleached all-purpose flour

½ cup lukewarm water

Pinch of salt

TO COOK THE PASTA

Coarse-grained salt

TO SERVE

8 tablespoons freshly grated Parmigiano (optional)

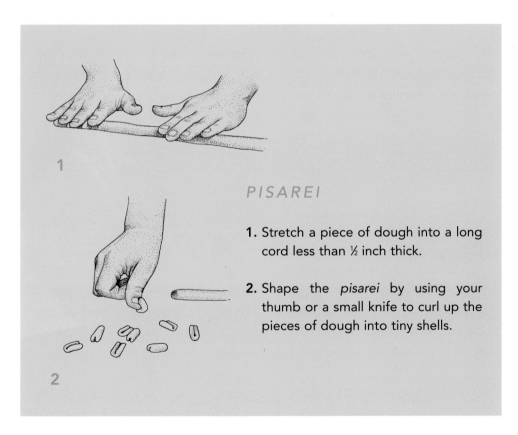

PISAREI

1. Stretch a piece of dough into a long cord less than ½ inch thick.

2. Shape the *pisarei* by using your thumb or a small knife to curl up the pieces of dough into tiny shells.

turteln alto adige

RYE FLOUR *TORTELLI*

SERVES 6 TO 8

FOR THE STUFFING

2 ½ pounds fresh spinach, large stems removed

Coarse-grained salt

Salt and freshly ground black pepper

1 tablespoon caraway seeds

FOR THE PASTA

3 cups rye flour

2 extra-large eggs

2 tablespoons (1 ounce) sweet butter, at room temperature

¼ cup cold milk

Salt

TO COOK THE PASTA

6 quarts chicken or beef broth, preferably homemade

FOR THE SAUCE

16 tablespoons (8 ounces) sweet butter

6 tablespoons unseasoned bread crumbs, preferably homemade

Salt and freshly ground black pepper

Turteln *uses a pasta made with rye flour—which, contrary to what many think, is even lighter than wheat flour—along with eggs and butter. The most popular stuffing is made of spinach flavored with ground caraway seeds. It is most important that the whole seeds be pulverized with a mortar and pestle, a tiring job because they are quite hard. Since part of the powdered caraway should be spread over one side of the layer of pasta, it would be quite unsuccessful to attempt this with whole seeds. And the flavor of the ground caraway is different—softer and more aromatic.*

I have chosen the version in which the turteln *are boiled in broth and served with bread crumbs browned in butter. In the fried version, they are cooked in lard, which makes them a bit heavier, though delicious. They are served completely without any dressing, not even the lemon juice commonly used with fried dishes. The boiled version is also known as* Krapfen, *a name once associated with* Bomboloni *pastries in other parts of Italy. Alto/Adige is a bilingual area, where German as well as Italian is spoken.*

*Other classic stuffings are sauerkraut sautéed in butter with onions (sauerkraut is preferred to plain cabbage), ricotta flavored with chives (*erba cipollina*), or ricotta with sautéed onions, marjoram, and parsley. Marjoram would not be used in a stuffing that employs caraway seeds, but is typical here.*

Prepare the stuffing. Soak the spinach in a bowl of cold water for 30 minutes. Bring a large pot of cold water to a boil, add coarse salt to taste, then drain the spinach, add it to the pot, and cook for 10 minutes. Drain and cool the spinach under cold running water, squeeze it very well, and finely chop it on a board. Place the spinach in a crockery or glass bowl, season with salt and pepper, mix well, and refrigerate, covered, until needed. Finely grind the caraway seeds in a marble mortar; this will take a little time.

Prepare the pasta with the ingredients and quantities listed, following the directions on page 12, placing the butter in the well of the flour together with the other ingredients. Stretch the sheet of pasta to less than 1/16 inch thick—on a pasta machine take it to the last setting. Cut the sheet into strips 12 inches long and about 6 inches wide.

Sprinkle half the strips with the powdered caraway. Place tablespoons of spinach 3 inches apart down the center of a pasta strip. Cover the strip with another strip, without caraway. Press down between mounds of filling. Use a pastry wheel with scalloped edges to cut into 3-inch *tortelli* squares. Press the edges together. Repeat with remaining pasta and filling. Let the *tortelli* rest on cotton dish towels until needed.

Bring the broth to a boil in a large pot over medium heat. Meanwhile, warm a large serving platter. Place the butter in a small saucepan over low heat. When the butter is melted, add the bread crumbs and sauté until golden, about 1 minute. Season with salt and abundant black pepper. When the broth reaches a boil, add the *tortelli* and cook for 1 to 3 minutes depending on dryness. With a strainer-skimmer, transfer some of the cooked *tortelli* to the warmed platter and spoon some of the melted butter and bread crumbs over the top. Continue to alternate layers of *tortelli* with butter and bread crumbs, making sure the top layer is butter and bread crumbs; top with some black pepper and serve immediately.

VARIATIONS

Below are some other stuffings for *turteln*.

1 medium-sized white onion, peeled and coarsely chopped

4 tablespoons (2 ounces) sweet butter

12 ounces sauerkraut

Salt and freshly ground black pepper

1 tablespoon caraway seeds

Sauté the onion in the butter. Coarsely chop the sauerkraut and add it to the sautéed onion. Season with salt, pepper, and caraway seeds.

1 ½ pounds whole-milk ricotta

20 chive leaves, coarsely chopped

Salt and freshly ground black pepper

1 tablespoon caraway seeds

Drain the ricotta, mix it with the chives, and season with salt, pepper, and caraway seeds.

1 medium-sized white onion, peeled and coarsely chopped

4 tablespoons (2 ounces) sweet butter

15 ounces whole-milk ricotta, drained

15 sprigs Italian parsley, leaves only, coarsely chopped

Salt and freshly ground black pepper

1 tablespoon fresh marjoram

Sauté the onion in the butter, let cool, and then mix with the ricotta and parsley. Season with salt, pepper, and marjoram.

lombardy

The two main pastas that employ buckwheat flour survive in Lombardy. Buckwheat is grown in the highlands and other areas, such as the hilly and mountainous parts of Friuli, where buckwheat once was used much more than now, and that usage even spilled over into neighboring Veneto. The special treatment of buckwheat flour, its liquid absorption, lack of gluten, and so forth, are discussed later on. We begin with *sciatt*, from the mountainous Valtellina region of northern Lombardy. *Sciatt* sometimes appears as a pasta, but is really most often found as batter enveloping bits of cheese and fried. In this form, it is really used as an appetizer rather than as a *primo piatto*.

Two versions of the batter follow. In one, a cup of cold water is added to the flours, along with an optional egg. In the other, sometimes called *chiscioi*, beer is the liquid, producing a crisp and luscious result. The beer batter is best when allowed to rest overnight before frying. Both of these employ a little baking soda and *grappa* (or aquavit or vodka as a substitute).

In the pasta version, additional flour is added to the water and egg to make the consistency of a dough rather than a batter—no more than 2 tablespoons of white flour should be added to the buckwheat and the dough requires truly expert handling to work it. Perhaps for this reason, the dough version has all but disappeared in favor of the batter. It is much easier to work this dough if additional white flour is added for its gluten, and this compromise has been adopted in recent years, using a mixture of one third white flour to two-thirds buckwheat. This is really no longer the original dish.

The layer of dough is used to make *ravioli* with any of the stuffings, which are then fried; lard is the authentic shortening. The cheese called for may be either a type of local fresh *formaggio di casera* or a *bitto,* which may be aged. Since these local cheeses are difficult to obtain, a good melting cheese from a nearby area may be substituted. *Fontina* is perhaps the closest and easiest to find.

Sciatt is often accompanied by a type of horseradish called *ramolaz neri*, which is grated and combined with olive oil to make a sauce or is eaten whole. Any grated horseradish may be substituted to produce a very similar result.

The dialect word *sciatt* means "frog," referring to the shape produced by the batter version, which is probably the original method. There is also a dough form of *chiscioi*, made with half white flour and half buckwheat, cut into pieces, and then shaped as discs. The discs are then generally boiled together with potatoes and salt and served with fresh cheese and grated Parmigiano. This is really a bridge between the pasta version of *sciatt* and Valtellina's other and more famous buckwheat pasta, *pizzoccheri*.

The famous philologist Giacomo Devoto traces the word from *pinzochero*, meaning "bigot," but possibly implying "provincial" or "rustic." Again, the original dish used very little white flour with the buckwheat, but in modern times, with reduced skill and patience in making pasta, the proportion has increased to one third. Because buckwheat is not a real cereal like wheat, its flour lacks the gluten to easily hold the dough together, and so it takes very great skill to make a sheet of pasta with it. The sheet will still emerge thicker than normal, from ⅟₁₆ to less than ⅛ of an inch, but anything thicker than that would make it more like a cookie than a pasta.

Buckwheat flour takes a little less liquid than ordinary flour. A cup of white flour absorbs an egg plus a little liquid, roughly ⅓ cup of liquid in all. A little more normal flour will be absorbed by water than egg, and still more buckwheat flour by the same amount. For the cup and a half of the mixed flours I use, a little more than half a cup of liquid should do—in this case, 1 egg plus 5 tablespoons (¼ cup plus 1 tablespoon) of milk. It would be good to keep these general measurements in mind when making pasta with eggs and pasta with water or other liquid.

This most classic version includes several vegetables, cooked one after the other in the same water, which is finally used to cook the pasta. I recommend *Asiago* cheese as a substitute for the *bitto* here, because there is general agreement in the sources that a leaner cheese should be used, leaving out *fontina*.

The *cappellacci* from Cremona feature the cooked unripe marinated fruit called *mostarda*, mixed together with the squash in the filling. No *Amaretti* would be used in this version, and the spiciness of the black pepper contrasts with the sweetness of the fruit, as preferred in these survivors of the Renaissance. Here, as in other such stuffings, it is not pumpkin that is used but squash, developed by the Italians from the New World originals of butternut and acorn.

The *casonsei* of Brescia differ from those of Bergamo in that they are stuffed a bit differently and aren't flavored with sage, but they retain the horseshoe shape generally. (See the discussion about the ones from Bergamo, which also explains the probable origin of the name from *cascio*, meaning cheese, with which they are most often dressed.) I retain the *mollica* in the stuffing rather than bread crumbs, as it is the older version as well as the more appropriate, since the dish is not particularly light.

Very special are the stuffed tiny squares, or *quadrucci*, served in broth. The stuffing of sweetbreads, ham, eggs, and cheese, held together by *mollica*, adds a rich touch to the broth. Dumplings in broth or dumplings covered with pasta in broth were once the most common type of first course, before pasta with sauce became so popular in the mid-nineteenth century.

Venetian *bigoli* spread to nearby Lombardy. The most common Venetian sauce, with salted sardines or anchovies, was transformed in Lombardy into one of fresh sardines. For this reason, the Sicilians sometimes add to their *Pasta alle sarde* the phrase *alla milanese*; that is, in the style of Milan.

Grana Padano is, like Parmigiano, a type of *Grana* cheese. In northern Italy, above Emilia-Romagna, it is used more often than Parmigiano, as it is produced there. If possible, use it in the recipes that follow.

sciatt

BUCKWHEAT "PASTA"

SERVES 6 TO 8

FOR THE BATTER

First version

1 cup buckwheat flour

2 tablespoons unbleached all-purpose flour

1 extra-large egg

1 cup cold water (and a little more if not using an egg)

Pinch of salt

1 tablespoon grappa (or vodka or aquavit)

6 ounces *bitto* or fontina cheese

1 quart vegetable oil

¼ teaspoon baking soda

Second version (*chiscioi*)

1 cup buckwheat flour

4 tablespoons unbleached all-purpose flour

1 ½ cups beer

Pinch of salt

1 tablespoon *grappa* (or vodka or aquavit)

6 ounces *bitto* or fontina cheese

1 quart vegetable oil

¼ teaspoon baking soda

Put the two flours in a crockery or glass bowl and with a wooden spoon mix them together very well. Make a well, and if using the egg, put it in and start incorporating some of the flour. Then add the water and salt and keep mixing until a homogeneous batter is formed. If making the second version, use the beer instead of the egg and water. Add the grappa. Mix well and let the batter rest, covered, in a cool place, the first batter for 2 hours, the beer batter overnight. When the batter is ready, cut the cheese into ½-inch cubes.

Heat the oil in a deep-fat fryer over medium heat. When the oil is hot (400° F), add the baking soda to the batter, mix well, put in the cheese cubes, and mix again. Place about 1½ tablespoons of the batter with one cheese cube in a small ladle and pour it into the hot oil. The batter should be surrounding and covering the cube of cheese and should puff up when it hits the hot oil. When the outside is uniformly crusty, transfer it with a strainer-skimmer to a serving dish that is lined with paper towels to absorb any excess fat. When all the *sciatt* are on the dish, remove the paper towels and serve hot, accompanied by a horseradish sauce made of grated horseradish (*ramolaz neri*) mixed with olive oil.

marubini

STUFFED PASTA FROM CREMONA

The really old traditional version of marubini, *Cremona's signature stuffed pasta, was made* di magro, *without real meat. The basis was* mollica, *the crumb of the bread, with beef* marrow. *Eggs, grated Parmigiano, and herbs and spices enriched the flavor. In modern times, there has been a tendency to lighten the dish by substituting bread crumbs for the* mollica.

There also exists a less classic meat version, much more recent, made with three kinds of braised meat and calves' brains, which is usually eaten without broth, in a dressing of butter and Parmigiano.

The older di magro may be eaten either with this dressing, as we have it, or in a wonderful, unique broth used primarily in the Cremona area and called tre brodi, *meaning "three broths." It is made from three different meats—veal, chicken, and beef or pork.*

Prepare the stuffing. Place the Parmigiano, bread crumbs, egg and egg yolks, and butter in a medium-sized crockery or glass bowl; mix well with a wooden spoon. Coarsely chop the parsley, add it to the bowl, and season to taste with salt, pepper, and nutmeg. Mix again until all the ingredients are well amalgamated. Cover bowl with aluminum foil and refrigerate until needed.

Prepare the pasta with the ingredients and quantities listed, following the directions on page 12. Stretch the sheet of pasta to less than ¹⁄₁₆ inch thick—on the pasta machine take it to the last setting. Prepare the *marubini* as you would *tortelli* (page 123), using a round, scalloped cutter not wider than 2 inches and placing a heaping teaspoon of the stuffing in each pasta circle. Let the *marubini* rest on cotton dish towels until needed.

Bring a large pot of cold water to a boil, add coarse salt to taste, then add the pasta and cook for 1 to 3 minutes depending on dryness. Meanwhile, melt the butter in a double boiler. Use a strainer-skimmer to transfer the *marubini* to a warmed platter. Pour some of the melted butter over the layer of *marubini*, then sprinkle on some cheese. Continue to make layers of *marubini* until all are on the platter. Top the last layer of pasta with the remaining butter and cheese. Serve immediately.

SERVES 6 TO 8

FOR THE STUFFING

1 cup freshly grated Parmigiano

Scant ½ cup unseasoned bread crumbs, preferably homemade

1 extra-large egg

2 extra-large egg yolks

4 tablespoons (2 ounces) sweet butter, at room temperature

15 large sprigs Italian parsley, leaves only

Salt and freshly ground black pepper

Freshly grated nutmeg

FOR THE PASTA

3 cups unbleached all-purpose flour

4 extra-large eggs

Pinch of salt

TO COOK THE PASTA

Coarse-grained salt

TO SERVE

8 tablespoons (4 ounces) sweet butter

½ cup freshly grated Parmigiano

pizzoccheri della valtellina

BUCKWHEAT PASTA FROM VALTELLINA

SERVES 6 TO 8

FOR THE VEGETABLES

1 pound savoy cabbage, cleaned and large stems removed

12 ounces string beans, cleaned

2 medium-sized potatoes (not new potatoes)

Coarse-grained salt

FOR THE PASTA

1 cup buckwheat flour

½ cup unbleached all-purpose flour

1 extra-large egg

5 tablespoons cold milk

Pinch of salt

or

½ pound dried *pizzoccheri*, preferably imported Italian

TO COOK THE PASTA

Coarse-grained salt

FOR THE SAUCE

12 tablespoons (6 ounces) sweet butter

15 large sage leaves, fresh or preserved in salt

4 large cloves garlic, peeled and left whole

Salt and freshly ground black pepper

¾ cup grated aged *bitto* cheese from Valtellina or aged Asiago cheese

Cut the cabbage into 1-inch strips and put in a bowl of cold water. Place the string beans in a second bowl of cold water. Cut the potatoes into 1-inch cubes and put them in a third bowl with cold water. Bring a large stockpot of cold water to a boil, add coarse salt to taste, then add the potatoes and cook for about 10 minutes; the potatoes should remain very firm, since they are to be cooked again. Use a strainer-skimmer to transfer the potatoes to a crockery bowl and cover with a wet towel. Drain the string beans and cook in the potato water for about 12 minutes or less, depending on their size, and also leaving them still very firm. Place the beans over the potatoes in the same bowl. Cook the cabbage in the same water for about 6 minutes, making sure that it does not become soft. With a strainer-skimmer, spoon the cabbage over the beans and cover again with the towel, letting the vegetables stand until needed.

Prepare the pasta. Make the dough using the ingredients and quantities listed, mixing the flours together and placing the egg, milk, and salt in the well of the flour at the same time following the directions on page 12. Knead the dough much longer than for a normal wheat dough, about 15 minutes. By hand or with a pasta machine, stretch the dough to a thickness of less than ⅛ inch with a hand pasta machine, take it to the next to the last setting. Cut the sheet of pasta into pieces about 2½ by ¾ inches, and let rest on cotton dish towels or paper towels for at least 1 hour before cooking. Buckwheat flour lacks the gluten of wheat flour, so it requires a longer kneading and resting time.

Bring a large pot of cold water to a boil. Warm a large serving dish by placing it over the water as it boils. Meanwhile, melt the butter in a small, heavy saucepan over low heat. When the butter melts, put in the sage leaves and garlic, and sauté for 1 minute, adding salt and abundant pepper.

When the water reaches a boil, add coarse salt to taste, then add the cooked vegetables. When the water returns to a boil, put in the pasta and cook until al dente—3 to 5 minutes for fresh pasta according to dryness, or 9 to 12 minutes for dried pasta depending on the brand.

Place some of the cheese and some of the melted butter in the warmed dish. Drain the pasta and vegetables, and arrange in a layer over the sauce. Repeat this procedure with butter-cheese layers and the pepper. Continue until all the ingredients are used up. Gently mix the pasta and vegetables with the butter and the melted cheese, and serve immediately with more freshly ground black pepper.

VARIATIONS FOR PASTA

1. The pasta can be prepared with equal amounts of buckwheat flour and unbleached all-purpose flour, with the egg omitted and the amount of cold or lukewarm milk increased by several tablespoons.

2. The pasta can be prepared with equal amounts of buckwheat flour and unbleached all-purpose flour, cold or lukewarm water instead of milk, and with or without egg.

VARIATIONS FOR COOKING

1. Cabbage and potatoes are present in all versions, but the string beans can be omitted and other vegetables added, such as sliced carrots and/or spinach and/or Swiss chard, cut into strips.

2. Cook the vegetables beginning with the ones requiring the longest cooking time and adding the others, timing it so that they all finish together. Meanwhile, cook the pasta so it is ready at the same time.

3. Fresh *bitto* cheese from the Valtellina can be used, but it should be thinly sliced instead of grated, placed over the different layers of pasta and vegetables, and the whole dish baked for a few minutes at the end.

4. Vegetables can be boiled first, then sautéed a little with butter. Once the pasta is cooked, the pasta and vegetables should be mixed together and dressed with a sauce prepared with onions, garlic, or both, sautéed in butter, and sprinkled with grated cheese.

cappellacci con la mostarda
CAPPELLACCI WITH MOSTARDA STUFFING

SERVES 4 TO 6

FOR THE STUFFING

1 medium-sized butternut squash

⅓ cup unseasoned bread crumbs, preferably homemade

1 extra-large egg yolk

Salt and freshly ground black pepper

6 ounces *mostarda di Cremona* (see Note), drained and finely chopped

FOR THE PASTA

2 cups unbleached all-purpose flour

3 extra-large eggs

Pinch of salt

TO COOK THE PASTA

Coarse-grained salt

TO SERVE

8 tablespoons (4 ounces) sweet butter

shavings of *Grana Padano* cheese

Preheat the oven to 375° F. Prepare the stuffing. Bake the squash on a jelly roll pan for 1 hour. Remove from the oven and cool for 30 minutes. Remove the peel, seeds, and filaments from the squash, then pass the pulp through a food mill, using the disc with medium-sized holes, into a crockery or glass bowl. Measure out 1 cup of the puréed pulp for the stuffing, put it in a crockery or glass bowl, and add the bread crumbs and egg yolk. Season to taste with salt and pepper, add the *mostarda di Cremona*, and mix well with a wooden spoon. Cover and place in the refrigerator until needed.

Prepare the pasta with the ingredients and quantities listed, following the directions on page 12. Stretch the sheet of pasta to less than ¹⁄₁₆ inch thick—on the pasta machine take it to the last setting. Make *cappellacci* shaped like *ravioli* (see page 123), 3 inches square, using 1 heaping teaspoon of the stuffing for each. Let them rest on cotton dish towels or paper towels for at least 15 minutes, turning them over at least once.

Bring a large pot of cold water to a boil, add coarse salt to taste, then add the *cappellacci* and cook for 1 to 3 minutes depending on dryness. Meanwhile, melt the butter in a double boiler and warm a large serving platter. Use a strainer-skimmer to transfer the pasta to the warmed platter. Make a layer of *cappellacci*, pour some of the melted butter over the top, and sprinkle on some of the cheese. Make another layer of the remaining pasta, butter, and cheese.

Mostarda di Cremona.

NOTE

Mostarda di Cremona is cooked unripe fruit that has been marinated in a syrup flavored with yellow mustard seeds. It is available commercially in jars, sometimes labeled "mustard fruits." It may also be made at home following the recipe in *Classic Techniques of Italian Cooking.*

casonsei di brescia
STUFFED PASTA FROM BRESCIA

Prepare the stuffing. Remove the skins from the sausages and put the meat or the ground pork into a crockery or glass bowl. Soak the bread in the milk for 10 minutes, then squeeze it dry and add to bowl with the meat. Put in the Parmigiano, season to taste with salt and pepper, and mix well, combining the meat thoroughly with the other ingredients. Cover the bowl and refrigerate until needed.

Prepare the pasta with the ingredients and quantities listed, following the directions on page 12. Stretch the sheet of pasta to less than 1/16 inch thick—on the pasta machine take it to the last setting.

Prepare *casonsei* (page 242) and let rest on cotton dish towels until needed.

Bring a large pot of cold water to a boil. Meanwhile, place the butter on a serving dish and melt it by placing the dish over the pot as a lid. When the water reaches a boil, remove the dish, add coarse salt to taste, then add the *casonsei* and cook for 1 to 3 minutes depending on dryness. Use a strainer-skimmer to transfer the *casonsei* to the serving dish and spoon some of the butter over each layer, also sprinkling each with some cheese. Serve hot.

SERVES 6 TO 8

FOR THE STUFFING

5 Italian sweet sausages, without fennel seeds; or 1 ¼ pounds ground pork

4 slices white bread, crusts removed

1 cup cold milk

½ cup freshly grated Parmigiano

Salt and freshly ground black pepper

FOR THE PASTA

4 cups unbleached all-purpose flour

5 extra-large eggs

Pinch of salt

TO COOK THE PASTA

Coarse-grained salt

TO SERVE

12 tablespoons (6 ounces) sweet butter

1 cup freshly grated *Grana Padano* cheese

quadrucci ripieni
STUFFED TINY PASTA SQUARES

SERVES 6 TO 8

FOR THE STUFFING

2 slices white bread, crusts
    removed

1 cup cold milk

Coarse-grained salt

4 ounces veal sweetbreads

2 ounces boiled ham

½ cup freshly grated
    Parmigiano

1 to 2 extra-large eggs

2 extra-large egg yolks

Salt and freshly ground
    black pepper

Large pinch of freshly
    grated nutmeg

FOR THE PASTA

3 cups unbleached
    all-purpose flour

4 extra-large eggs

Pinch of salt

TO COOK THE PASTA

2 quarts chicken or beef
    broth, preferably
    homemade

TO SERVE

Freshly grated Parmigiano

Prepare the stuffing. Soak the bread in the milk for 30 minutes. Place a medium-sized saucepan with cold water over medium heat, and when the water reaches a boil, add coarse salt, then add the sweetbreads and simmer for 5 minutes. Drain the sweetbreads and cool under cold running water. Remove and discard all the membrane around the sweetbreads. Finely chop the sweetbreads together with the boiled ham on a board and place in a crockery or glass bowl. Add the cheese. Squeeze the milk out of the bread and add to the bowl. Put in 1 egg and the egg yolks; season to taste with salt, pepper, and nutmeg; and mix everything with a wooden spoon. If the stuffing is too dense, add an additional egg. Cover the bowl and refrigerate until needed.

Prepare the pasta with the ingredients and quantities listed, following the directions on page 12. Stretch the sheet of pasta to less than $\frac{1}{16}$ inch thick—on the pasta machine take it to the last setting. Use a metal spatula to evenly spread out a very thin layer of stuffing over half the pasta layer, like one page of an open book. Cut in half and fit the other half layer over the stuffing. Gently press all over to attach the two layers together. With a scalloped pastry wheel, cut the stuffed pasta into 1-inch squares, then transfer these *quadrucci* onto floured cotton dish towels and let them rest until needed.

Place the broth over medium heat, and when it reaches a boil, add the *quadrucci* and cook for 1 to 3 minutes depending on dryness. Drain and serve with a sprinkling of Parmigiano.

bigoli con sardelle

PASTA WITH FRESH SARDINES

Clean the sardines following the instructions on page 127; you should have about ½ pound. Place the sardines in a bowl of cold water with ½ tablespoon coarse salt; let stand until needed.

Bring a large pot of cold water to a boil. Meanwhile, place a medium-sized saucepan with the oil over medium heat; when the oil is warm, add the garlic and sauté until golden brown all over, about 5 minutes. Discard the garlic and remove the pan from heat.

Drain and rinse the sardines under cold running water. Add the sardines to the pan with the oil. Using a fork, mash the sardines into the oil as they cook.

Season with salt and pepper, and place the pan over low heat for 2 minutes.

When the water reaches a boil, add coarse salt to taste, then add the pasta and cook until al dente—9 to 12 minutes depending on the brand. Coarsely chop the parsley on a board. Drain the pasta and transfer to a large, warmed serving platter; pour the sauce over the top, sprinkle on the parsley, toss very well, and serve immediately.

VARIATIONS

1. Mash 4 ounces of drained tuna packed in olive oil into the oil with the sardines.
2. Omit the parsley.

SERVES 4 TO 6

- 1 pound fresh sardines
- Coarse-grained salt
- ¾ cup olive oil
- 1 large clove garlic, peeled but left whole
- Salt and freshly ground black pepper
- 1 pound dried white *bigoli* or *spaghetti*, preferably imported Italian

TO SERVE

- 15 large sprigs Italian parsley, leaves only

Fresh sardines.

veneto

Bigoli is the sole traditional pasta of the Veneto. Other pastas used there are borrowed from other regions. Until recently, every Venetian home had a hand-operated *torchio* machine called *bigolo* permanently attached to the kitchen table, and the making of good *bigoli* was a test of domestic art. This pasta is still made to be longer than other long pasta nowadays, but we must remember that until dried pastas began being sold primarily in boxes, *spaghetti* and other forms were longer than they usually are now; *bigoli* have simply retained the older tradition. Passed through a *bigolo*, the pasta has a very thin hole through its length, like southern Italian *bucatini* or *perciatelli*. But commercially dried *bigoli* are made like *spaghetti* now, and this form has even been adopted by some for the fresh pasta if the *bigolo* is not available.

Originally, dark *bigoli* were probably made using buckwheat flour, since that grain was once plentiful in the Tre Veneti. (Today, part of that region is more commonly known as Friuli-Venezia Giulia.) But earlier in this century, the Italian government began to require that certified commercial pasta be made only from durum wheat flour, and soon, even in the home, whole-wheat flour came to replace the buckwheat.

Bigoli were made with eggs, butter, and milk added to the flour. When the Venetians said *bigoli* "in sauce," they referred to their most popular, classic dressing, using anchovies or sardines preserved in salt with olive oil and onion. Venice had to keep a store of preserved foods on hand in the event its islands were cut off from the mainland during a siege. Naturally, most of its fresh food came from the mainland territories it ruled, extending almost from Milan all the way down to Dalmatia on what is now the Balkan coast. Sardines preserved in salt are no longer as available as anchovies. As mentioned elsewhere, when the neighboring mainland Milanese adapted the dish, they employed fresh sardines.

As mentioned, the recipe for *Bigoli scuri in salsa* employs the whole-wheat flour now typically used, but also included is the old version, *Bigoli scuri con grano saraceno*, using buckwheat flour. Since this flour usually comes from Friuli, this version is still made there, but not often.

Another classic version is *Bigoli all'anitra* (*Bigoli* Cooked in Duck Broth) and dressed with the liver and giblets sautéed with rosemary and sage in olive oil. The broth may be defatted and saved, if you wish, but since the Venetians preferred the flavor imparted by the fat, they usually discarded the broth after the cooking. Naturally, the duck itself may be used at another time.

As traditionally Venetian as possible is *Bigoli con sugo di oca conservato* (not included here), the dish that combines *bigoli* with another standby, the *confit* of preserved goose, which was once traditional in the cucina of the "queen of the Adriatic." Venice once so dominated that region that it is far more likely that the *confit* went from Venice to Toulouse than the other way around. The Venetians, however, deboned the meat before preserving it.

A unique dish, *Tagliatelle* with Sauce of Preserved Goose, uses the old Venetian boneless *confit* of goose (goose with the goose fat in which it has been preserved) to dress the pasta. The flavor of the goose, seasoned for three to six months, is unlike anything else and should be tried at least once in everyone's life—though, when tried, once is not enough.

The large red crab of the Adriatic is one of the most delicious types of crab and is used in many dishes, among them a combination with *bigoli* called *Bigoli con granzeola*. Crabmeat is so popular now that the dish may be made even with *spaghetti* if *bigoli* are unavailable.

The two versions of *casonsei* from Bergamo, like the one from Brescia, have meat stuffings. There is a version with vegetable stuffing from Cortina d'Ampezzo.

The first Bergamo version of *casonsei* uses beef in the stuffing, cold water instead of the extra egg in the pasta, and simply butter, Parmigiano, and sage in the dressing. The second version, like the Brescia version, is stuffed with pork, usually sausage, has the egg-rich pasta as in the Brescia version, but adds abundant *pancetta* to the butter, sage, and cheese of the dressing. In both versions, I have opted for the lighter, more modern bread crumbs instead of *mollica*.

Pierrot, who is the Bergamo mask of the *commedia dell'arte*, could not have retained his sad face had he eaten one of these versions. And the moonlight-crazy Pierrot of Schoenberg's *Pierrot Lunaire* would certainly have been calmed by them.

bigoli scuri in salsa

WHOLE-WHEAT BIGOLI, VENETIAN STYLE

Prepare the pasta with the ingredients and quantities listed, following the directions on page 12, placing the butter in the well of flour with the other ingredients. Stretch the sheet to about ⅛ inch thick—on the pasta machine take it to several notches before the last setting. Prepare *spaghetti* (see page 59), but cut them about 15 to 16 inches long; this length is characteristic of the pasta. Let rest on cotton towels until needed.

Prepare the sauce. Cut the onion into paper-thin slices. Place a very small saucepan with the oil over medium heat. When the oil is lukewarm, add the onion slices—the olive oil should be barely covering the onion. Season with pepper and sauté, without raising the heat, for at least 45 minutes, stirring every so often with a wooden spoon. By that time, the onion should be almost dissolved. (The slow sautéing of onions and other vegetables into the perfect *soffritto* is a special Venetian art.) Remove the saucepan from the heat and set aside, covered.

Meanwhile, bring a large pot of cold water to a boil, adding very little or no coarse salt (the anchovies will add their salt to the sauce). Add the pasta and cook 1 to 3 minutes for fresh pasta depending on dryness; cook dried pasta for 9 to 12 minutes depending on the brand. While the pasta cooks, if you are using whole anchovies, clean them under cold running water, removing bones and excess salt. Add the cleaned whole anchovies or the drained fillets to the sautéed onion. The onion should still be very hot; use a fork to dissolve the fillets and incorporate them into the other ingredients. Drain the pasta, transfer to a large, warmed serving platter, pour the sauce over the top, toss very well, and serve.

VARIATIONS

1. Sometimes, 10 sprigs of Italian parsley leaves, coarsely chopped, are added to the sauce before pouring it over the pasta.
2. A half cup of dry white wine can be added to the onion when it is half cooked, along with a pinch of ground cinnamon.
3. Onion and anchovies are finely chopped together and sautéed in the oil for the same length of time, with or without wine and with or without parsley.
4. Two cloves of garlic can be substituted for the onion; they should be peeled and coarsely chopped.
5. With any of the above variations or the original recipe, 2 tablespoons of white wine vinegar can be added at the end and allowed to evaporate for 2 minutes.

SERVES 6 TO 8

FOR THE PASTA

3 cups whole-wheat flour

3 extra-large eggs

2 tablespoons (1 ounce) sweet butter, at room temperature

2 tablespoons cold milk

Pinch of salt

or

1½ pounds dried *bigoli scuri*, preferably imported Italian

FOR THE SAUCE

1 large white or red onion, peeled

Scant cup olive oil

Freshly ground black pepper

8 anchovies preserved in salt; or 16 anchovy fillets packed in olive oil (not in vegetable oil or brine), drained

TO COOK THE PASTA

Coarse-grained salt

bigoli scuri con grano saraceno
BIGOLI WITH BUCKWHEAT FLOUR

SERVES 4 TO 6

FOR THE PASTA

1 ½ cups unbleached all-purpose flour

1 ½ cups buckwheat flour

3 extra-large eggs

2 tablespoons (1 ounce) sweet butter, at room temperature

6 tablespoons cold milk

Pinch of salt

TO COOK THE PASTA

Coarse-grained salt

FOR THE SAUCE

¾ cup olive oil

5 anchovies preserved in salt; or 10 anchovy fillets packed in olive oil (not in vegetable oil or brine), drained

Freshly ground black pepper

Prepare the pasta. Mix the flours, then prepare the pasta with the ingredients and quantities listed, following the directions on page 12, placing the butter and milk in the well of flour with the other ingredients. Stretch the sheet to about ⅛ inch thick—on the pasta machine take it to several notches before the last setting. Cut into *spaghetti* (see page 59), but make them about 15 to 16 inches long. Let rest on cotton towels until needed.

Bring a large pot of cold water to a boil, add coarse salt to taste, then add the pasta and cook for 1 to 3 minutes depending on dryness.

If using whole anchovies, clean them under cold running water, removing bones and excess salt. As the pasta cooks, place a small saucepan with the oil over medium heat; when the oil is hot, remove the pan from the heat and add the anchovy fillets. Using a fork, mash them into the oil. Season with black pepper.

Drain the pasta, transfer to a large, warmed serving platter, pour the sauce over the top, toss very well, and serve immediately.

VARIATIONS

1. Twenty sprigs Italian parsley, leaves only, coarsely chopped, can be sprinkled over the pasta before serving.
2. One large clove of garlic, peeled and left whole, can be sautéed with the oil, then discarded before adding the anchovies.

bigoli all'anitra

BIGOLI COOKED IN DUCK BROTH

Clean and wash the duck very well, saving the liver and all the giblets for later use and discarding the extra fat from the cavity. Place a large stockpot with the duck, the cold water, and the vegetables over medium heat. When the water reaches a boil, add coarse salt to taste. Simmer, uncovered, until the duck is completely cooked, about 1½ hours.

Prepare the pasta with the ingredients and quantities listed, following the directions on page 12, placing the butter and milk in the well of flour with the other ingredients. Stretch the sheet to about ⅛ inch thick; on the pasta machine, take it to several notches before the last setting. Cut into *spaghetti* (see page 59), but make them about 15 to 16 inches long. Let the *bigoli* rest on cotton towels until needed.

When the duck is cooked, transfer it to a chopping board. Remove the meat from the bones; discard the carcass and skin. (The boiled duck meat is very good and may be served as a second course following the pasta, perhaps accompanied with a green sauce, but it is not part of the pasta course. It would be more typical to serve the duck at a different dinner.)

Use a coarse strainer to strain the duck broth, but do not remove any of the fat. Place the strained broth back in the stockpot and put the pot over medium heat. Meanwhile, prepare the sauce. Finely chop the reserved liver and giblets with the rosemary and sage all together on a board. Place a medium-sized saucepan with the chopped ingredients and the ¾ cup of olive oil over medium heat, and sauté for 10 minutes. Season with salt and pepper, then add a cup of the duck broth and simmer for 30 minutes.

When the broth in the stockpot reaches a boil, add the pasta and cook fresh pasta for 1 to 3 minutes depending on dryness; cook dried pasta for 9 to 12 minutes depending on the brand. Drain the pasta; transfer to a large, warmed serving platter, pour the sauce over the top, toss very well, and serve immediately. No cheese should be added.

WINE • Tenuta dell'Ornellaia Poggio alle Gazze

SERVES 6 TO 8

FOR THE BROTH

- 1 Long Island-type duck (about 5 pounds), with liver and giblets
- 4 quarts cold water
- 2 medium-sized stalks celery, cleaned and cut into large pieces
- 1 large red onion, peeled and cut into large pieces
- 2 medium-sized carrots, scraped and cut into large pieces
- Coarse-grained salt

FOR THE PASTA

- 3 cups unbleached all-purpose flour
- 3 extra-large eggs
- 2 tablespoons (1 ounce) sweet butter, at room temperature
- 2 tablespoons cold milk
- Pinch of salt

or

- 1½ pounds dried *bigoli bianchi* or *spaghetti*, preferably imported Italian

FOR THE SAUCE

- 2 tablespoons fresh rosemary leaves
- 15 large fresh sage leaves
- ¾ cup olive oil
- Salt and freshly ground black pepper

bigoli con granzeola
SPAGHETTI WITH CRABMEAT

SERVES 6 TO 8

FOR THE PASTA

3 cups unbleached
    all-purpose flour

3 extra-large eggs

2 tablespoons (1 ounce)
    sweet butter, at room
    temperature

2 tablespoons cold milk

Pinch of salt

or

1 ½ pounds dried *bigoli
    bianchi* or *spaghetti*,
    preferably imported
    Italian

FOR THE CRAB SAUCE

2 quarts cold water

Coarse-grained salt

¾ pound boiled crabmeat

4 tablespoons olive oil

Salt and freshly ground
    black pepper

TO COOK THE PASTA

Coarse-grained salt

**FOR THE PARSLEY
    SAUCE**

30 large sprigs Italian
    parsley, leaves only

4 medium-sized cloves
    garlic, peeled

8 tablespoons olive oil

Salt and freshly ground
    black pepper

Prepare the pasta with the ingredients and quantities listed, following the directions on page 12, placing the butter and milk in the well of flour with the other ingredients. Stretch the sheet to about ⅛ inch thick—on the pasta machine take it to several notches before the last setting. Cut into *spaghetti*, (see page 59), but make them about 15 to 16 inches long. Let the *bigoli* rest on cotton towels until needed.

Prepare the crab sauce. Place a large pot with the cold water over medium heat. When the water reaches a boil, add coarse salt to taste, then place the crabmeat in a small strainer and submerge the strainer in the boiling water for 4 minutes. Remove the strainer, transfer the crabmeat to a bowl, and reserve the boiling water. Add the oil and salt and pepper to taste to the crabmeat; set aside until needed.

Add enough additional cold water to the crab-boiling water to cook the pasta. When the water reaches a boil, add more coarse salt to taste, then add the pasta. Cook fresh pasta for 1 to 3 minutes depending on dryness; cook dried pasta for 9 to 12 minutes depending on the brand. Meanwhile, coarsely chop the parsley and garlic together on a board. Place a small saucepan with the oil over medium heat. When the oil is warm, add the chopped ingredients and sauté for 2 minutes. Season with salt and pepper. When the pasta is ready, drain and transfer it to a large, warmed serving platter. Add the crabmeat with its juices and the sautéed parsley with the oil, toss very well, and serve immediately.

casonsei alla bergamasca I

STUFFED PASTA, BERGAMO STYLE, FIRST VERSION

Prepare the stuffing. Combine the beef and butter in a crockery or glass bowl, mix very well, and season to taste with salt and pepper. Transfer to a skillet and place over medium heat. Sauté for 5 minutes, mixing constantly with a wooden spoon, then transfer the sautéed meat to a clean crockery or glass bowl and let rest until cool, 30 minutes. Coarsely chop the parsley and finely chop the garlic on a board, then add them to the bowl along with the bread crumbs and Parmigiano. Taste for salt and pepper. Mix all the ingredients well. Cover the bowl and refrigerate until needed.

Prepare the pasta with the ingredients and quantities listed, following the directions on page 12. Stretch the sheet to a thickness of less than $\frac{1}{16}$ inch—on a hand pasta machine take it to the last setting. Roll the dough into sheets.

Sometimes *casonsei* are shaped like round *tortelli*, but the classic shape is obtained by cutting the pasta into 3-by-2-inch rectangles (see drawing on page 242). Use 1 tablespoon of stuffing for each. Arrange the stuffing lengthwise along the 3-inch side; fold in half, covering the stuffing; and seal the 3 open sides by pressing them firmly together. Finally, twist the stuffed pasta into a horseshoe shape. Let the *casonsei* rest on floured cotton dish towels for 30 minutes before using.

Prepare the sauce. Melt the butter in a double boiler, then add the sage leaves; remove from heat and let rest, covered, for 30 minutes before using.

Bring a large stockpot of cold water to a boil. Add coarse salt to taste, then add the *casonsei* and cook for 30 seconds to 2 minutes depending on dryness. Use a strainer-skimmer to transfer them to a warmed platter, arranging the pasta in layers. Pour some of the sage butter and sprinkle some Parmigiano over each layer. Serve immediately with 2 or 3 twists of black pepper on each serving.

SERVES

FOR THE STUFFING

- 1 pound ground beef
- 4 tablespoons (2 ounces) sweet butter, at room temperature
- Salt and freshly ground black pepper
- 20 large sprigs Italian parsley, leaves only
- 2 medium-sized cloves garlic, peeled
- ¼ cup unseasoned bread crumbs, preferably homemade
- ¼ cup freshly grated Parmigiano

FOR THE PASTA

- 4 cups unbleached all-purpose flour
- 4 extra-large eggs
- 4 teaspoons cold water
- Pinch of salt

FOR THE SAUCE

- 12 tablespoons (6 ounces) sweet butter
- 20 large sage leaves, fresh or preserved in salt
- 1 cup freshly grated Parmigiano
- Freshly ground black pepper

TO COOK THE PASTA

- Coarse-grained salt

CASONSEI

1. Stuff and fold the rectangles of pasta.

2. Press the stuffed rectangles firmly together.

3. Shape the stuffed rectangles into horseshoes.

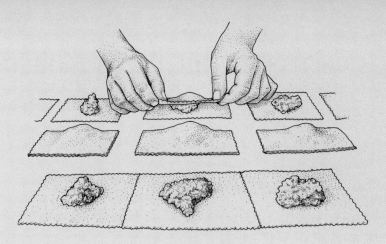

1

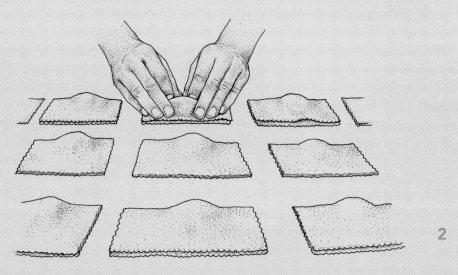

2

3

casonsei alla bergamasca II

STUFFED PASTA, BERGAMO STYLE, SECOND VERSION

Prepare the stuffing. Combine the sausage or pork and butter in a crockery or glass bowl, and mix very well. Transfer to a skillet and place over medium heat. Sauté for 5 minutes, mixing constantly with a wooden spoon, then transfer the sautéed meat to a clean crockery or glass bowl and let rest until cool, 30 minutes. Add the Parmigiano, eggs, nutmeg, and bread crumbs. Taste for salt and pepper. Mix all the ingredients well. Cover the bowl and refrigerate until needed.

Prepare the pasta with the ingredients and quantities listed, following the directions on page 12. Roll the pasta to a thickness of less than 1⁄16 inch, on a hand pasta machine take to the last setting, and roll the dough into sheets.

Sometimes, *casonsei* are shaped like round *tortelli*, but the classic shape is obtained by cutting the pasta into 3-by-2-inch rectangles (see drawing at left). To form, use 1 tablespoon of stuffing for each.

Arrange the stuffing lengthwise along the 3-inch side; fold in half, covering the stuffing; and seal the 3 open sides by pressing them firmly together. Finally, twist the stuffed pasta into a horseshoe shape. Let the *casonsei* rest on floured cotton dish towels for 30 minutes before using.

Prepare the sauce. Melt the butter in a double boiler, add the *pancetta* and lightly sauté it, then add the sage leaves and sauté for 1 more minute. Cover the pan and let rest for 30 minutes before using.

Bring a large stockpot of cold water to a boil. Add coarse salt to taste, then add the *casonsei* and cook for 30 seconds to 2 minutes depending on dryness. Use a strainer-skimmer to transfer them to a warmed platter, arranging the pasta in layers. Pour some of the sage butter and sprinkle some Parmigiano over each layer. Serve immediately with 2 or 3 twists of black pepper on each serving.

SERVES 8

FOR THE STUFFING

3 Italian sweet sausages without fennel seeds, skinned; or ½ pound coarsely ground pork

4 tablespoons (2 ounces) sweet butter, at room temperature

1 cup freshly grated Parmigiano

2 extra-large eggs

Pinch of freshly grated nutmeg

2 tablespoons unseasoned bread crumbs, preferably homemade

Salt and freshly ground black pepper

FOR THE PASTA

4 cups unbleached all-purpose flour

5 extra-large eggs

Pinch of salt

FOR THE SAUCE

8 tablespoons (4 ounces) sweet butter

6 ounces *pancetta* or *prosciutto*, in one piece, then cut into less than ½-inch cubes

20 sage leaves, fresh or preserved in salt

TO COOK THE PASTA

Coarse-grained salt

TO SERVE

1 cup freshly grated Parmigiano

friuli–venezia giulia

The Friuli-Venezia Giulia province has several pasta dishes not found elsewhere. *Ofelle* is pasta made with potatoes mixed with flour. After potatoes arrived in Europe from the New World, they were adapted for many uses. Potato starch is a lighter thickener than wheat flour; potatoes also ferment very slowly and make a slow-rising dough, used for some flat breads and pizzas. In Trieste, as in areas beyond the Alps, they are used in the pasta for various types of *ravioli*. *Ofelle* incorporate egg and baking soda to help with the rising. Stuffed with spinach, beef, and pork, they make a wonderful pasta dish dressed with the simple butter and *Grana* of northern Italy.

The plum-filled *gnocchi* also use a potato dough, incorporating a little semolina and all-purpose flour. The fruit filling may be fresh or dried plums, with a little sugar. The butter dressing is made with bread crumbs, cinnamon, and sugar. In Friuli, this dish is thought of as a typical first course.

The large half-moon pasta of Friuli, *cialzons*, is somewhat related to *casoncelli*, but is distinguished by the variety of fresh herbs in the stuffing with the meat. Here we combine sage, parsley, basil, marjoram, and mint. Dressed with butter and Parmigiano, they are cooked first in broth rather than water.

The unique very, very fine pasta used for the *lasagne* with poppy seeds is made primarily with egg yolks and one whole egg; thus it may be rolled out extremely thin. The pasta squares are served with the poppy-seed-and-butter dressing. In Trieste, this is not considered dessert but a first course.

ofelle alla triestina
STUFFED POTATO PASTA

SERVES 8

FOR THE PASTA

5 quarts cold water

2 pounds potatoes (not new potatoes)

Coarse-grained salt

2 cups plus ½ cup unbleached all-purpose flour

1 extra-large egg

2 teaspoons salt

1 teaspoon baking soda

FOR THE STUFFING

Coarse-grained salt

1 pound fresh spinach, stems removed, rinsed several times

1 medium-sized red onion, peeled

4 tablespoons (2 ounces) sweet butter

1 tablespoon olive oil

2 Italian sweet sausages without fennel seeds; or 6 ounces ground pork

2 ounces ground beef

Salt and freshly ground black pepper

TO COOK THE PASTA

Coarse-grained salt

Prepare the pasta. Place a large pot with the cold water over medium heat. Meanwhile, peel the potatoes and cut them into 2-inch cubes. When the water reaches a boil, add coarse salt to taste, then place a large colander with the potatoes over the boiling water. Be sure that the water is not touching the potatoes. Cover the colander with a large piece of aluminum foil so the steam does not escape, and let the potatoes steam for 30 minutes. Then pass the cooked potatoes through a potato ricer into a crockery or glass bowl, and let stand until cool, about 30 minutes.

Make the stuffing. Place a large pot of cold water over medium heat, and when the water reaches a boil, add coarse salt, then the spinach, and boil for 10 minutes. Drain the spinach, cool it under cold running water, and squeeze very well. Finely chop the onion on a board. Place the butter and oil in a small saucepan over medium heat, and when the butter is completely melted, add the onion and sauté for 5 minutes, stirring with a wooden spoon every so often. Remove the skins from the sausages. Add the ground beef and the sausages or ground pork to the onion. Sauté for 3 minutes more, stirring with a wooden spoon to amalgamate the ingredients. Add the spinach, taste for salt and pepper, and cook, until all the juices are incorporated, about 10 minutes longer, stirring constantly with a wooden spoon. Transfer the stuffing to a crockery bowl and let rest until cool, about 30 minutes.

Place the cooled potatoes in a mound on a board and make a well. Arrange the 2 cups of flour all around the potatoes, then put the egg, salt, and baking soda in the well. Use a fork to mix the ingredients in the well. Start incorporating the potatoes, then add the flour; use your hands to finish incorporating the flour. Knead the ball of dough for 2 minutes, then wrap in a cotton dish towel and let rest for 10 minutes in a cool place.

Spread the remaining flour all over the board and, using a rolling pin, roll out the ball of dough to a thickness of ⅟₁₆ inch, about 6 inches wide. Starting 1 inch from the top and side edges, begin a horizontal row of 1-tablespoon portions of stuffing, each 3 inches from its neighbor (see drawing). Carefully lift the bottom end of the sheet of dough and fold it over the row of filling. (The width of the doubled sheet should be about 3 inches.) Quickly press down around each filling. Using a scallop-edged pastry wheel, cut through the dough every 3 inches to form squares. Pinch the edges together with 2 fingers all around. Repeat the procedure until all the dough and filling is used. Transfer the *ofelle* onto a floured cotton dish towel and let stand until needed.

Place a large stockpot of cold water over medium heat. Put a large, deep serving dish containing the butter over it as a lid. When the water reaches a boil, add coarse salt to taste, then, one by one, add the *ofelle*. Cook for 10 to 12 minutes. Use a strainer-skimmer to transfer the pasta to the serving dish with the melted butter. Sprinkle the Parmigiano over the top and serve immediately with a twist of pepper on each serving.

TO SERVE

16 tablespoons (8 ounces) sweet butter

1½ cups freshly grated Parmigiano

Freshly ground black pepper

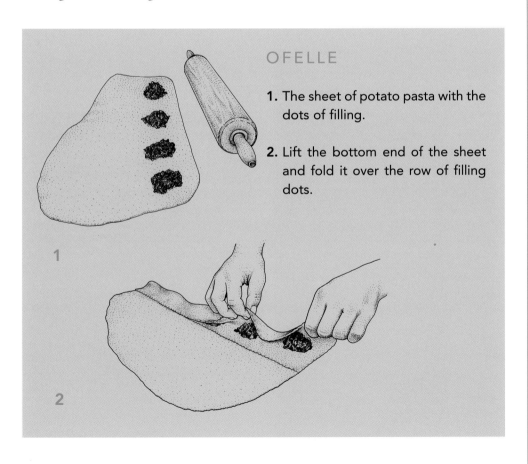

OFELLE

1. The sheet of potato pasta with the dots of filling.

2. Lift the bottom end of the sheet and fold it over the row of filling dots.

lasagne finissime con semi di papavero

FINE LASAGNE WITH POPPY SEEDS

SERVES 4 TO 6

FOR THE PASTA

1 ¾ cups unbleached all-purpose flour

5 extra-large egg yolks

1 extra-large egg

Pinch of salt

TO COOK THE PASTA

Coarse-grained salt

FOR THE SAUCE

8 tablespoons (4 ounces) sweet butter

1 heaping tablespoon granulated sugar

1 heaping tablespoon poppy seeds

Prepare the pasta with the ingredients and quantities listed, following the directions on page 12. When the ball of dough is formed, wrap it in a cotton dish towel dampened with cold water and let it rest in a cool place or on the bottom shelf of the refrigerator for 24 hours. Save the unincorporated flour—you will need it when stretching the dough.

Spread the unused flour on a board, unwrap the dough, and knead until very elastic and smooth, about 1 minute. Stretch the sheet of pasta less than 1⁄16 inch thick—on the pasta machine take it to the last setting, and cut into 5-inch squares using a pastry cutter. Let the squares rest on cotton dish towels for at least 30 minutes before cooking.

Bring a large pot of cold water to a boil and add coarse salt—a little more than usual because of the sweetness of the sauce. Put the butter, sugar, and poppy seeds in a small saucepan and place the pan over low heat. When the water returns to a boil, add the pasta and cook for 2 to 5 minutes depending on dryness. Use a strainer-skimmer to transfer the cooked pasta squares to a warmed serving platter, adding 2 tablespoons of the melted butter and poppy seeds every 3 or 4 pasta squares. Serve very hot.

NOTE

In Friuli, this is eaten as a first course (*primo piatto*). It may be used as a dessert, in which case ½ cup of warmed honey is added to the butter-sugar mixture with the poppy seeds.

gnocchi di susine

PLUM-FILLED GNOCCHI

Boil the potatoes in a medium-sized saucepan with salted water until very soft, about 45 minutes, depending on size. Peel the potatoes and pass them through a potato ricer, using the disc with the smallest holes, onto a board. Arrange the potatoes in a mound, make a well, and let rest until cool, about 20 minutes.

Prepare the plums. If using fresh plums, pit them by cutting them open on one side and pulling out the pits. If using prunes, poke them open. Put ⅛ teaspoon of sugar in the hole left by the pit, close again, and let stand until needed.

Put the eggs, salt, butter, and semolina flour in the potato well and use a fork to mix the ingredients. Then use your hands to knead the dough, incorporating about ½ cup of the all-purpose flour. Cut the dough into 4 pieces and, using your fingers and a little flour, roll each piece into a cord about 1 inch thick. Cut each cord into 8 pieces and, with your fingers, press each piece into a disc less than ½ inch thick. Place a plum in the center of each disc and wrap it up with the dough. When all the plums are ready, bring a very wide pot full of cold water to a boil. Add coarse salt to taste, then add the *gnocchi* and simmer for 2 minutes. Meanwhile, put the butter in a large skillet over medium heat, and when the butter is completely melted, add the bread crumbs, cinnamon, and sugar. Transfer the *gnocchi* to the skillet and sauté for 30 seconds, until they are coated with the butter mixture. Serve from the skillet, pouring some

---

SERVES 6 TO 8

FOR THE GNOCCHI

1 pound potatoes (not new potatoes)

Coarse-grained salt

32 fresh Italian prune plums or pitted dried prunes

4 teaspoons granulated sugar

2 extra-large eggs

Pinch of salt

1 tablespoon (½ ounce) sweet butter, at room temperature

1 tablespoon semolina flour

¾ cup to 1 cup unbleached all-purpose flour

TO COOK THE GNOCCHI

Coarse-grained salt

FOR THE SAUCE

12 tablespoons (6 ounces) sweet butter

4 tablespoons unseasoned bread crumbs

2 large pinches ground cinnamon

1 ½ tablespoons granulated sugar

cialzons

LARGE HALF-MOON PASTA STUFFED WITH MEAT AND MANY HERBS

SERVES 6 TO 8

FOR THE STUFFING

2 slices white bread, crusts removed

1 cup lukewarm chicken or beef broth, preferably homemade

6 tablespoons (3 ounces) sweet butter

1 pound ground beef

5 large sage leaves, fresh or preserved in salt

10 large sprigs Italian parsley, leaves only

6 large basil leaves, fresh or preserved in salt

1 tablespoon fresh marjoram leaves

1 heaping tablespoon fresh mint leaves

Salt and freshly ground black pepper

Pinch of freshly grated nutmeg

2 extra-large eggs

½ cup freshly grated Parmigiano

FOR THE PASTA

1½ cups unbleached all-purpose flour

½ cup very fine semolina flour

4 extra-large eggs

Pinch of salt

Prepare the stuffing. Soak the bread in the broth for 30 minutes. Place the butter in a heavy, medium-sized saucepan over low heat; when the butter is completely melted, add the meat and sauté for 2 minutes, stirring several times with a wooden spoon. Meanwhile, finely chop the sage, parsley, basil, marjoram, and mint all together on a board. Add the herbs to the pan, mix very well, and cook for 10 minutes more, seasoning with salt and pepper. Transfer the meat mixture to a crockery or glass bowl. Squeeze the broth from the bread, then add the bread to the bowl and incorporate it into the meat. Let rest until cool—about 30 minutes. When cool, season with nutmeg, then add the eggs and Parmigiano, mix well, and refrigerate, covered, until needed.

Prepare the pasta with the ingredients and quantities listed, following the directions on page 12. Let the ball of dough rest for 30 minutes, wrapped in a cotton dish towel and tightly covered by a bowl.

Stretch the layer of pasta to less than $\frac{1}{16}$ inch thick—on the pasta machine take it to the last setting. Use a 4-inch round cookie or biscuit cutter with a scalloped edge to cut the pasta into discs. Place a scant tablespoon of stuffing on one side of each disc, leaving a little border of pasta, then fold the other half over it. Seal the edges very well and transfer the prepared *cialzons* onto floured cotton dish towels to rest until needed.

Place a large pot with the broth over medium heat, and put a large serving platter with the butter over the pot as a lid. When the broth reaches a boil and the butter is melted, remove the platter, add the pasta to the pot, and cook for 3 to 6 minutes depending on dryness. Use a strainer-skimmer to transfer the cooked *cialzons* onto the platter, spooning some of the butter over each layer. Sprinkle some Parmigiano and grind some black pepper over each layer. The last layer should be topped with butter, Parmigiano, and pepper. Serve hot.

Using a mezzaluna (half-moon) to chop herbs.

5 quarts chicken or beef
   broth, preferably homemade

FOR THE SAUCE

8 tablespoons (4 ounces)
   sweet butter, cut in pieces

¾ cup freshly grated
   Parmigiano

Freshly ground black pepper

liguria

Liguria, with its chief city, Genoa, has a variety of pastas that are its own. *Trenette*, the pasta made without eggs and the classic recipient of the pesto sauce, are also traditionally paired with the famous artichoke sauce. *Trenette* are made with a combination of whole-wheat and white flours, but here a single egg is usually added. Since the Genoese are legendary for their frugality, it gives rise to comment in other parts of Italy when they hear that the recipe uses only one egg. But here we can be sure that the single egg is appropriate for gastronomic rather than economic reasons. *Trenette avvantaggiate con fagiolini* combines string beans, preferably the small young ones used in Italy, with the pasta and another, slightly different but still Ligurian, version of pesto.

Troffiette, also generally eaten with pesto, are twisted into a corkscrew shape. They may be made with white or whole-wheat flour, or even with a little chestnut flour mixed with the white flour.

Corzetti stampati, named after old Genoese money, are stamped on both sides, like coins. The old wooden stamps, made of two pieces of beechwood, have a cutter at the end of one piece and contain the two images to be impressed on the pasta. Traditionally, the stamps were highly personal, using a family coat of arms on one side and perhaps a ship or some other image of Genoa's maritime glory on the other. The old families often have them as heirlooms, but, unfortunately, few continue to make this pasta. I have made a real attempt to revive this great traditional dish and have had some stamps hand-carved by an old Ligurian who remembers how they were once hand carved. (One locale in Emilia-Romagna, Bedonia, also makes this shape as *crosetti*.)

Corzetti stampati may be made with white, whole-wheat, or chestnut flour and dressed with a simple sauce of fresh marjoram and pine nuts in good Ligurian olive oil or with a traditional veal sauce. It is also fun and authentic to serve a combination of *corzetti* made with three different flours, so you have three different colors or shades of pasta and, of course, three somewhat different tastes.

Also called *corzetti* are the figure-eight shapes made by pushing the little ball of pasta down with both thumbs simultaneously. These are traditionally served with a *Genoese* mushroom sauce. The older version is made with a fine semolina flour, the more modern but still authentic second version is made with all-purpose flour.

The *Genoese* often use *lasagne* simply boiled and dressed with an intense sauce. They use a more normal dough for the *lasagne* squares. The special eggless pasta using white wine for the liquid instead of water is a special feature of the *Fazzoletti di seta*, or "silk handkerchiefs" (also called *Mandilli de sêa*). They are so called because after being boiled, these delicate pasta squares are dropped on the plate like a handkerchief rather than flattened out and sauced; the silky texture of the pasta also accounts for the name.

Ravioli stuffed with fish have become a standard feature of "nuova cucina" and "nouvelle cuisine," but there is a perfectly traditional version from Liguria that uses a stuffing containing both fish and cooked greens. The greens used are escarole and watercress, not often encountered in stuffings. Tomatoes, butter, garlic, and marjoram form the basis of the sauce for these wonderful *Zembi d'arzillo*.

The most characteristic Ligurian stuffed pasta, however, is the *ravioli*-like *pansoti*. The fresh local cheese called *prescinséua* that binds the filling can be approximated using ricotta, and the unique mixture of wild field greens called *pregoggión* using Swiss chard and watercress. These are not unauthentic substitutions, and in any case these greens in their wild form are present in *pregoggión*. Undoubtedly, the stuffing cannot be reproduced exactly outside the specific localities, which are Rapallo, Camogli, and others rather than Genoa itself. The grated cheese, marjoram, and nutmeg are always used. The dressing is a version of the celebrated and ancient Ligurian sauce that combines walnuts with garlic, cream, butter, oil, and marjoram thickened with *mollica*. Traditionally, of course, this sauce, like the more familiar pesto made with basil, was pounded to a paste in a mortar and pestle.

NOTE

Troffiette and *troffie* could be spelled with one or two fs. *Troffiette* are not small *troffie* but, rather, Ligurian *gnocchi*.

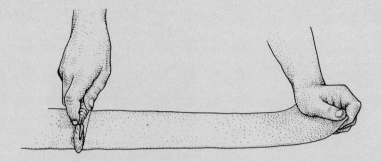

1

TRENETTE

1. Cut the layer of pasta with a pastry cutter into pieces about 15 inches long.

2. Use the pastry cutter to cut into ½-inch-wide scalloped strips on one side, and

3. on the other, use a knife to cut a straight edge.

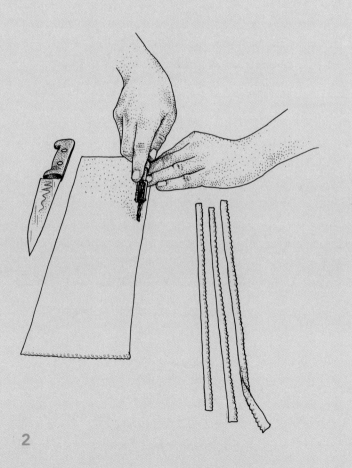

2

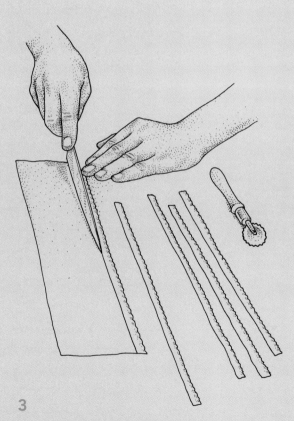

3

trenette avvantaggiate con fagiolini
WHOLE-WHEAT TRENETTE WITH STRING BEANS

SERVES 6 TO 8

FOR THE PASTA

2 ¼ cups unbleached all-purpose flour

2 ¼ cups whole-wheat flour

1 extra-large egg (see Note)

1 cup cold water

Pinch of salt

PLUS

1 pound string beans, cleaned and left whole

Coarse-grained salt

FOR THE PESTO

15 large sprigs Italian parsley, leaves only

25 large fresh basil leaves

5 tablespoons pine nuts (*pignolis*)

2 large cloves garlic, peeled

¾ cup freshly grated Parmigiano; or ½ cup freshly grated Parmigiano and ¼ cup freshly grated pecorino sardo cheese

4 tablespoons (2 ounces) sweet butter, at room temperature

Salt and freshly ground black pepper

½ cup olive oil

TO COOK THE PASTA

Coarse-grained salt

PLUS

Fresh basil leaves

Mix the 2 flours together and prepare the pasta according to the directions on page 12. Stretch the sheet to a thickness of ⅟₁₆ inch—on the pasta machine, take it to the next to the last setting. Cut it into *trenette* (see page 255). Let the pasta rest on cotton towels until needed.

Place the beans in a bowl of cold water to soak for 30 minutes. Meanwhile, prepare the pesto. If using a mortar and pestle, place the parsley, basil, pine nuts, and garlic in the mortar and grind until very smooth. Transfer to a crockery or glass bowl; add the cheese, butter, salt, and pepper, and mix with a wooden spoon until all the ingredients are well incorporated. Add the olive oil a few drops at a time, continuously mixing in a rotating motion until all the oil is incorporated. Taste for salt and pepper. If using a food processor, put in all the ingredients except the olive oil and, using the metal blade, grind until the texture is very creamy. With the blade still rotating, add the olive oil through the funnel, a very small amount at a time, until all the oil is amalgamated. Add salt and pepper to taste, and transfer the pesto to a crockery or glass bowl; refrigerate, covered, until needed.

Bring a large pot of cold water to a boil, and add coarse-grained salt to taste. Drain the beans and add to the pot.

The cooking time of the beans will vary greatly, depending on their thickness and freshness, from 5 to 10 minutes. They should retain their shape but be tender enough to match the tenderness of the fresh pasta; crisp, half-cooked beans rarely work in combination with other ingredients in Italian cooking, and this is particularly true in this dish.

Add the pasta to the beans so that both finish cooking at the same time. The cooking time of fresh *trenette* also varies, from 1 to 3 minutes depending on dryness.

As the pasta cooks, measure ¼ cup of the boiling pasta water and mix it into the pesto. Spread out half the sauce on a large, warmed serving plate. Drain the pasta and beans, and place them over the sauce. Pour the remaining sauce over the top, toss gently but very well, top with fresh basil leaves, and serve immediately. No extra cheese should be added to the individual servings.

NOTE

When trenette, usually eggless, are made with whole-wheat flour, one egg is added.

troffiette
GENOESE CORKSCREW PASTA

SERVES 4 TO 6

FOR THE PASTA

2 cups unbleached all-purpose flour

¾ cup boiling water

Pinch of salt

FOR THE PESTO SAUCE

1 ½ cups olive oil

12 whole walnuts, shelled

2 tablespoons pine nuts (*pignolis*)

4 cups loosely packed fresh basil leaves

3 heaping tablespoons boiled and chopped spinach

3 medium-sized cloves garlic, peeled

4 ounces freshly grated Parmigiano

4 ounces freshly grated sardo or romano cheese; or additional freshly grated Parmigiano

Salt and freshly ground black pepper to taste

TO COOK THE PASTA

Coarse-grained salt

TO SERVE

Freshly grated Parmigiano

Prepare the pasta with the ingredients and quantities listed, following the directions on page 12, and kneading the dough for 15 minutes, incorporating the flour a little at a time. Detach pieces of dough the size of a chick-pea, roll them to finger-length cords between your palms, then flatten the cord a little with your fingertips. Let dry for 30 seconds, then, holding onto both ends, make several twists in the cords (see drawing on page 259). Let pasta rest on floured cotton dish towels until needed.

Prepare pesto sauce with the ingredients and quantities listed, using a blender or food processor, following directions on page 256, but adding ½ cup of the oil at the beginning.

Bring a large quantity of cold water to a boil, add coarse salt to taste, then add the pasta and cook for 9 to 12 minutes depending on dryness (like dried rather than fresh pasta). Add 2 tablespoons of the boiling water from the pasta pot to the pesto sauce, and mix well. Drain the pasta, add the sauce, mix well, and serve, sprinkled with Parmigiano.

VARIATIONS

1. Whole-wheat flour can be used instead of all-purpose flour in the pasta.
2. The pasta can be made with 2 cups less 3 tablespoons all-purpose flour and 3 tablespoons of chestnut flour as a substitute.
3. Green pasta can be used, made with 2 ½ cups unbleached all-purpose flour; 1 tablespoon boiled, chopped spinach; ¾ cup boiling water; and a pinch of salt.

Italian "umbrella" pine trees, the source of pignolis.

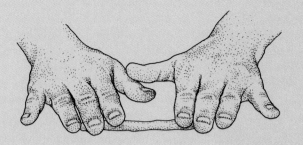

TROFFIETTE

1. Flatten finger-length cords with your fingertips.

2. Hold onto both ends and make several twists.

3. *Troffiette.*

corzetti stampati alla maggiorana
STAMPED LIGURIAN PASTA

SERVES 6 TO 8

FOR THE PASTA

3 ½ cups unbleached
   all-purpose flour

1 cup cold water

1 extra-large egg

Pinch of salt

TO COOK THE PASTA

Coarse-grained salt

FOR THE SAUCE

12 tablespoons (6 ounces)
   sweet butter

3 teaspoons dried marjoram

6 tablespoons pine nuts
   (*pignolis*)

Salt and freshly ground
   black pepper

VARIATIONS

Whole-wheat *corzetti*

2 ½ cups unbleached
   all-purpose flour

1 cup whole-wheat flour

1 cup cold water

1 extra-large egg

Pinch of salt

Chestnut-flour *corzetti*

3 cups unbleached
   all-purpose flour

1 cup fresh chestnut flour
   (imported from Italy or
   France)

1 cup cold water

1 extra-large egg

Pinch of salt

Prepare the pasta with the ingredients and quantities listed, following the directions on page 12. Stretch the sheet a little thicker than usual, ¹⁄₁₆ inch—on the pasta machine take it to the next to the last setting. *Corzetti* stamps are in 2 pieces. The bottom piece serves two functions. Its bottom side is like a cookie cutter, the top side is carved to produce an image. The top piece has a handle and its bottom produces a second image. Cut the pasta layer into discs using the cutter of the stamp and let them rest for several minutes on cotton towels. Discard pasta remnants.

Place a disc of pasta between the 2 carved images and press, producing a disc with different images on each side. Continue until all discs are stamped, lightly flouring the 2 carved sides each time. Let the *corzetti* rest on cotton towels at least 1 hour before using, otherwise the printed design will disappear in the boiling water.

Bring a large pot of cold water to a boil, add coarse salt to taste, then add the pasta and cook for 3 to 5 minutes depending on dryness. Don't overcook. This type of pasta is different from other fresh pastas, since once it is cooked it retains some kind of "bite" and is not completely soft and tender.

As the pasta cooks, place the butter, marjoram, and pine nuts in a small saucepan over medium heat and sauté for 3 minutes, stirring very often with a wooden spoon. Season to taste with salt and pepper.

Drain the pasta, transfer to a warmed serving dish, pour on the sauce and more freshly ground black pepper, toss gently but very well, and serve immediately.

NOTE

It is traditional to prepare all 3 types of *corzetti* together, cook them in the same stockpot, and serve them with the marjoram sauce.

corzetti stampati con sugo di vitella

STAMPED CORZETTI WITH VEAL SAUCE

Prepare the pasta, following the directions on page 260.

Prepare the sauce. Soak the mushrooms in a bowl of lukewarm water for 1 hour. Meanwhile, cut the onion into quarters and the carrots into 2-inch pieces; place in a bowl of cold water to soak for 30 minutes. Drain.

Place the olive oil, butter, veal, and onion and carrots in a medium-sized heavy saucepan over medium heat. Sauté for 15 minutes without mixing or stirring. Sprinkle the flour over the top, mix very well with a wooden spoon, and cook for 1 minute more. Add the wine, raise the heat to high, and let it evaporate for 5 minutes. Season to taste with salt and pepper. If using fresh tomatoes, cut them into 1-inch pieces. Add fresh or canned tomatoes to the saucepan, mix, and cook for 5 minutes more. Drain the mushrooms and clean them very well, removing any sand attached to the stems. Add the mushroom pieces to the saucepan along with the broth. Cover and simmer for 1½ hours, stirring every so often with a wooden spoon.

Remove the veal and undissolved bits of meat and reserve for another use; pass the contents of the saucepan through a food mill, using the disc with the smallest holes, into a second pan. Place the sauce over medium heat, taste for salt and pepper, and reduce for 10 more minutes; at that time the sauce will be ready to be used immediately. If you wish to use it later, let it cool completely, then transfer to a crockery or glass bowl, cover, and refrigerate until needed.

Bring a large pot of cold water to a boil, add coarse salt to taste, then add the pasta. Cook the *corzetti* for 3 to 5 minutes depending on dryness. Drain the pasta, transfer to a warmed serving dish, pour the sauce over the top, toss gently, and serve immediately.

VARIATION

A similar sauce can be prepared by substituting the same amount of beef (chuck) for the veal.

SERVES 6 TO 8

FOR THE PASTA

3 ½ cups unbleached all-purpose flour

1 cup cold water

1 extra-large egg

Pinch of salt

FOR THE SAUCE

2 ounces dried *porcini* mushrooms

1 large red onion, peeled

4 medium-sized carrots, scraped

1 tablespoon olive oil

6 tablespoons (3 ounces) sweet butter

1 pound boneless veal, any cut, untrimmed, in 1 piece

2 tablespoons unbleached all-purpose flour

1 cup dry white wine

Salt and freshly ground black pepper

1 pound very ripe, fresh tomatoes; or 1 pound canned tomatoes, preferably imported Italian, drained

1 quart lukewarm chicken or beef broth, preferably homemade

TO COOK THE PASTA

Coarse-grained salt

corzetti alla polceverasca con tocco di funghi

FIGURE-EIGHT CORZETTI (TWO VERSIONS) WITH GENOESE MUSHROOM SAUCE

SERVES 6 TO 8

FOR THE ORIGINAL, AUTHENTIC PASTA

2 ½ cups fine semolina flour

1 extra-large egg

3 extra-large egg yolks

¼ cup lukewarm water

Pinch of salt

FOR A MODERN, LIGHTER PASTA

3 cups unbleached all-purpose flour

4 extra-large eggs

Pinch of salt

FOR THE SAUCE

1 ounce dried *porcini* mushrooms

2 cups lukewarm water

1 medium-sized red onion, peeled

1 large clove garlic, peeled

15 large sprigs Italian parsley, leaves only

4 tablespoons (2 ounces) sweet butter

4 tablespoons olive oil

1 pound ripe, fresh tomatoes; or 1 pound canned tomatoes, preferably imported Italian, drained

1 tablespoon tomato paste

Salt and freshly ground black pepper

TO COOK THE PASTA

Coarse-grained salt

Prepare either pasta dough with the set of ingredients listed for it, following the directions on page 12. If you are making the semolina version, wrap the dough in a cotton dish towel and let it rest for 1 hour, covered with a bowl. If using all-purpose flour, make the figure-eights immediately, without letting the pasta rest.

Prepare the *corzetti*. Detach pieces of dough the size of chick-peas. Form solid figure-eights by pressing the "chick-pea" down with both thumbs, then stretching the middle a little by pulling the thumbs in opposite directions. Let the prepared *corzetti* rest on floured dish towels until needed.

Meanwhile, prepare the sauce. Soak the mushrooms in the lukewarm water for 30 minutes. Drain, saving the soaking water, and clean the mushrooms very well, being sure that no sand remains attached to the stems. Pass the mushroom water through several layers of paper towels to strain out remaining sand. Finely chop the mushrooms, onion, gar-

lic, and parsley all together on a board. Place the butter and oil in a medium-sized skillet over medium heat, and when the butter is completely melted, add the chopped ingredients and sauté for 15 minutes. If using fresh tomatoes, cut them into pieces. Pass fresh or canned tomatoes through a food mill, using the disc with the smallest holes, into a second bowl. Add the tomatoes and tomato paste to the skillet, season to taste with salt and pepper, and cook for 25 minutes. Add the strained mushroom water, cover, and simmer for 1 hour, stirring every so often with a wooden spoon.

Bring a large pot of cold water to a boil, add coarse salt to taste, then add the pasta. Cook the *corzetti* made with semolina for 9 to 12 minutes depending on dryness; the others take 5 to 8 minutes. Drain the pasta, put it in the skillet with the sauce, sauté for 30 seconds, then transfer to a large, warmed serving platter and serve.

fazzoletti di seta

PASTA SQUARES WITH PESTO SAUCE ("SILK HANDKERCHIEFS")

Prepare the pasta with the ingredients and quantities listed, following the directions on page 12, placing the wine with the salt in the well of the flour. Stretch the sheet to less than ¹⁄₁₆ inch—on the pasta machine take it to the last setting and cut it into squares, as for *lasagne*. Let the pasta rest on cotton dish towels until needed, turning the squares once or twice to avoid sticking.

Prepare the pesto with a mortar and pestle or food processor. Grind the basil and garlic finely, then place them in a crockery or glass bowl. Add the butter, oil, and cheese, and mix the ingredients with a wooden spoon. Season to taste with salt and pepper, cover the bowl with alu-minum foil, and refrigerate until needed.

Bring a large pot of cold water to a boil, add coarse salt to taste, then add the pasta a few squares at a time. Cook for 1 to 3 minutes depending on dryness, then use a strainer-skimmer to transfer the squares from the pot to individual dishes, dropping the squares on the plate so they assume the form of dropped handkerchiefs (see below). While the pasta is cooking, remove the pesto from the refrigerator and add ¼ cup of the boiling pasta water, mixing very well with a wooden spoon. Each portion consists of 4 or 5 pasta squares, with 2 or 3 tablespoons of the pesto and 1 tablespoon of cheese sprinkled on top. Serve with fresh basil leaves.

SERVES 6 TO 8

FOR THE PASTA

3 ½ cups unbleached all-purpose flour

1 cup dry white wine

Pinch of salt

FOR THE PESTO

3 cups fresh basil leaves (about 2 ounces)

5 medium-sized cloves garlic, peeled

8 tablespoons (4 ounces) sweet butter

½ cup olive oil

3 ounces freshly grated pecorino romano or Parmigiano cheese

Salt and freshly ground black pepper

TO COOK THE PASTA

Coarse-grained salt

TO SERVE

6 to 8 tablespoons freshly grated pecorino romano or Parmigiano

Fresh basil leaves

pansoti o pansooti alle noci
STUFFED GENOESE PASTA

SERVES 6 TO 8

FOR THE STUFFING

1 pound Swiss chard, cleaned, large stems removed

4 ounces watercress, large stems removed

Coarse-grained salt

8 ounces whole-milk ricotta

¾ cups freshly grated Parmigiano

2 extra-large eggs

20 fresh marjoram leaves, or 1 teaspoon dried

Salt and freshly ground black pepper

Pinch of freshly grated nutmeg

FOR THE PASTA

4 cups unbleached all-purpose flour

1 extra-large egg

¼ cup dry white wine

¾ cup cold water

Pinch of salt

FOR THE SAUCE

3 slices white bread, crusts removed

1 cup cold milk

8 ounces walnuts, shelled

1 large clove garlic, peeled

Put the Swiss chard and watercress in a bowl of cold water and let them soak for 30 minutes. Meanwhile, bring a large pot of cold water to a boil, then add coarse salt to taste. Drain the greens, add them to the boiling water, and cook for 10 minutes. Drain and cool the greens under cold running water; squeeze them very well. Finely chop the greens on a board and transfer to a large crockery or glass bowl. Add the ricotta, Parmigiano, eggs, and marjoram. Season with salt, pepper, and nutmeg. Mix all the ingredients together with a wooden spoon, cover the bowl, and refrigerate until needed.

Prepare the pasta with the ingredients and quantities listed, following the directions on page 12. Stretch the sheet to less than ¹⁄₁₆ inch thick—on the pasta machine take it to the last setting. Cut the layer into 5- or 6-inch squares, and divide the strips diagonally into triangles (see drawing). Put a scant tablespoon of stuffing in the center of each triangle, fold the triangle in half, and seal on the 2 open sides. (Sometimes, 2 of the ends are then brought together and attached.) Let the *pansoti* rest on cotton dish towels for at least 30 minutes before cooking them.

Prepare the sauce. Soak the bread in a small bowl with the milk for 10 minutes. Use a mortar and pestle or food processor to finely grind the walnuts, garlic, and marjoram all together, then place them in a crockery or glass bowl. Squeeze the milk from the bread and add the bread to the bowl along with the Parmigiano. Mix all the ingredients together well. Season with salt and pepper, then start adding the cream, butter, and olive oil, constantly mixing with a wooden spoon until all the ingredients are well amalgamated and the sauce is smooth. Cover the bowl and refrigerate until needed.

Bring a large pot of cold water to a boil, add coarse salt to taste, then add the *pansoti* and cook for 1 to 3 minutes depending on dryness. Remove the sauce from refrigerator, add 2 tablespoons of the boiling pasta water, and mix very well. Use a strainer-skimmer to transfer the *pansoti* to a warmed serving dish. Make a layer of pasta, pour some of the sauce over the top, then add more layers of pasta and sauce. Serve very hot.

PANSOTI

1. Cut the strips of pasta divided into triangles.

2. Place a scant tablespoon of stuffing in the center of each triangle.

3. Fold the triangle in half and seal the 2 open sides.

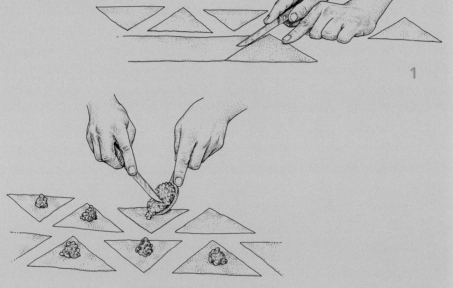

1

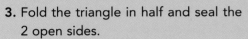

2

3

20 fresh marjoram leaves, or 1 teaspoon dried

½ cup freshly grated Parmigiano

Salt and freshly ground black pepper

1 cup heavy cream

2 tablespoons (1 ounce) sweet butter

4 tablespoons olive oil

TO COOK THE PASTA

Coarse-grained salt

zembi d'arzillo (ravioli di pesce)

RAVIOLI STUFFED WITH FISH

SERVES 6 TO 8

FOR THE VEGETABLE STUFFING

¾ pound escarole, dark outer leaves removed

4 ounces watercress, large stems removed

Coarse-grained salt

10 large sprigs Italian parsley, leaves only

1 medium-sized clove garlic, peeled

½ tablespoon fresh marjoram leaves, or 1 teaspoon dried

FOR THE FISH STUFFING

¾ pound fish fillets, a mixture of 2 or 3 of the following: sea bass, porgy, grouper, red snapper

Coarse-grained salt

1 large lemon

1 ½ quarts cold water

½ cup dry white wine

2 tablespoons olive oil

2 tablespoons (1 ounce) sweet butter

Salt and freshly ground black pepper

½ cup freshly grated Parmigiano

1 extra-large egg

2 extra-large egg yolks

Prepare the vegetable stuffing. Soak the escarole and watercress in a bowl of cold water for 30 minutes. Bring a large pot of cold water to a boil, and add coarse salt to taste. Drain the greens, add them to the pot, and cook for 10 minutes. Drain again and cool under cold running water; squeeze them very well. Finely chop the cooked greens together with the parsley, garlic, and marjoram on a board; let stand until needed.

Prepare the fish stuffing. Put fish in a bowl of cold water with a little salt and the lemon, cut in half and squeezed, for 30 minutes. Bring the cold water and the wine to a boil in a saucepan. Drain the fish, wash it under cold running water, and add it to the pan. Lower heat, and simmer for 5 minutes. Remove the fish and bone it; on a board, finely chop the fish.

Place a medium-sized skillet with the olive oil and butter over medium heat; when the butter is completely melted, add the vegetable stuffing and the fish. Sauté, stirring constantly, for 2 minutes. Season to taste with salt and pepper. Transfer to a crockery or glass bowl and let stand for 30 minutes, until cool. Add the Parmigiano, egg and egg yolks, and salt and pepper to taste, cover, and refrigerate until needed.

Prepare the pasta with the ingredients and quantities listed, following the directions on page 12. Stretch the sheet to less than 1/16 inch thick—on the pasta machine, take it to the last setting. Prepare 2-inch-square *tortelli* and put ½ tablespoon of stuffing on each (see page 123). Let pasta rest on cotton dish towels until needed.

Prepare the sauce. Place a medium-sized nonreactive saucepan with the tomatoes (if using fresh, cut them into pieces) and the garlic over medium heat. Cook for 20 minutes, then pass through a food mill, using the disc with the smallest holes, into a bowl. Melt the butter in a medium-sized nonreactive saucepan over low heat, add the tomatoes, taste for salt and pepper, and simmer for 10 minutes more.

Meanwhile, bring a large pot of cold water to a boil, add coarse salt to taste, then add the *tortelli* and cook for 1 to 3 minutes depending on dryness. When ready, add the marjoram to the tomato sauce and ladle some of the sauce onto a large, warmed serving platter. Use a strainer-skimmer to transfer the *tortelli* from the boiling water to the prepared platter. Ladle more tomato sauce over each layer of pasta. Serve hot.

Cleaning fish for a customer at the Viareggio fish market.

FOR THE PASTA

4 cups unbleached
    all-purpose flour

2 extra-large eggs

1 cup lukewarm water

Pinch of salt

FOR THE SAUCE

3 pounds ripe, fresh
    tomatoes; or 3 pounds
    canned tomatoes,
    preferably imported
    Italian, drained

2 medium-sized cloves
    garlic, peeled

8 tablespoons (4 ounces)
    sweet butter

Salt and freshly ground
    black pepper

4 tablespoons fresh
    marjoram leaves, or 2
    teaspoons dried

TO COOK THE PASTA

Coarse-grained salt

emilia–romagna, tuscany

Many of the egg pastas that originated in central Italian Tuscany and Emilia-Romagna—such as *lasagne alla ferrarese*, *tagliatelle*, *tortellini*, and *tortelli*—have spread throughout Italy and are no longer considered specifically regional. Early cookbook manuscripts suggest, surprisingly, that these pastas moved from Tuscany to Emilia-Romagna and not the other way around. But these areas do retain certain regional specialties, such as *Pinci di Montalcino* and *Tortelli di zucca* and the ones that follow.

The most celebrated *tortelli* with a tail, *Turtei cu la cua*, come from Piacenza and are stuffed not with meat but with *mascarpone* cheese combined with ricotta and spinach, and are bound with Parmigiano, egg yolks, and whole egg. The twisting of the two ends of overlapping pasta to make the "tails" is reminiscent of the way some hard candies are wrapped (see page 272). They are dressed with either a butter–basil or tomato–basil sauce.

The *cappellacci* from Ferrara are stuffed with squash, like the *Tortelli di zucca* from nearby Modena. These stuffings are often approximated abroad with the use of pumpkin (sweet potato is an inappropriate substitution here). The squash used in Mantua and Ferrara is a large version of either butternut or acorn squash, widely available, so there really is no need for a substitution. All these squashes originated in the New World and were taken to Italy, probably in the sixteenth century.

The most typical fresh *garganelli* are made with grated cheese in the pasta itself. This ridged, twisted short pasta works well with two characteristic dressings, one a sweetish sauce made with boiled ham, *prosciutto cotto* (rather than the more common *prosciutto crudo*), butter, cream, and nutmeg; the other with the baconlike smoked *pancetta* in place of the more usual unsmoked version. The lightly smoked meat is combined with tomatoes, butter, and oil. Both sauces are from Emilia-Romagna, as is this regional pasta.

The form of *cappelli* in the shape of a three-cornered hat, very popular in Tuscany a generation or two ago, has all but disappeared there, though it is said to still be used in parts of certain other northern regions. The way my family used to make them is described below, and I would be most grateful if the dish were revived. The stuffing with pork is flavored with bay leaf and clove, *mollica*, eggs, and cheese. The Tuscan sauce we used was tomato flavored with sage, garlic, and olive oil. The pasta used was the basic Tuscan egg pasta with some oil in it. When we made it with a vegetable stuffing, artichokes formed the base, as can be seen in the variation included here.

turtei cu la cua
TORTELLI WITH A TAIL

SERVES 8

FOR THE STUFFING

2 pounds fresh spinach, large stems removed

Coarse-grained salt

¼ pound ricotta

½ pound *mascarpone* cheese; or ¼ pound ricotta blended with 1 cup heavy cream

½ cup freshly grated Parmigiano

1 extra-large egg

3 extra-large egg yolks

Salt and freshly ground black pepper

Pinch of freshly grated nutmeg

FOR THE PASTA

3 cups unbleached all-purpose flour

4 extra-large eggs

Pinch of salt

FOR THE SAUCE

8 ounces (16 tablespoons) sweet butter

1 cup freshly grated Parmigiano

10 large fresh basil leaves

Prepare the stuffing. Clean the spinach well, then soak in a bowl of cold water for 30 minutes. Bring a large pot of cold water to a boil. Add the coarse salt, then add the spinach and boil for 10 minutes. Drain the spinach and cool it under cold running water. When cool, squeeze spinach dry, finely chop on a board, and transfer to a glass or crockery bowl. Add the ricotta, mascarpone, Parmigiano, and egg and egg yolks to the bowl; mix all the ingredients with a wooden spoon. Season with salt, pepper, and nutmeg, and mix again to blend all the ingredients very well. Cover the bowl and refrigerate until needed.

Prepare the pasta with the ingredients and quantities listed, following the directions on page 12. Stretch the sheet to 5 ½ inches wide and less than ¹⁄₁₆ inch thick—on the pasta machine take it to the last setting. Cut into 4 ½-by-5 ½-inch rectangles, using a scalloped pastry wheel. Place 1 heaping tablespoon of the stuffing in the middle of each rectangle, fold the left third of the longer side over, then the right third. Holding the top and bottom of the pasta, twist one end to the left and the other to the right to make a shape resembling a wrapped candy (see page 272). Let *turtei* rest on a floured wooden surface or cotton towel, being sure that they do not touch and stick together. If prepared in advance, turn them over once or twice.

Bring a large pot of cold water to a boil over medium heat. Place a large serving dish with the butter for the sauce on the pot as a lid. When the water reaches a boil, add coarse salt to taste, then add 5 to 10 *turtei* (depending on the size of the pot) and cook for 1 to 2 minutes depending on dryness. Use a strainer-skimmer to transfer the cooked pasta to the serving dish with the butter. Sprinkle some cheese over this first layer. Repeat the same procedure until all the *turtei* are

Fresh mascarpone.

cooked. On top of the last layer of pasta and Parmigiano, sprinkle the basil leaves and serve immediately.

If using the tomato sauce, heat the oil in a small saucepan over medium heat. When warm, add the garlic and sauté for 3 minutes. Discard the garlic, then add the tomatoes, cover, and cook for 20 minutes. Pass the contents of the saucepan through a food mill, using the disc with the smallest holes, into a different pan. Add salt and pepper to taste, and reduce over medium heat for 15 minutes more. Melt the butter and cook the pasta as for the main recipe, pouring the sauce on the top layer of pasta, then sprinkling with Parmigiano and basil leaves.

TO COOK THE PASTA
Coarse-grained salt

**VARIATION: TURTEI
WITH TOMATO SAUCE**

3 tablespoons olive oil

**1 medium-sized clove garlic,
peeled and left whole**

**2 pounds ripe, fresh
tomatoes, cut in pieces;
or 2 pounds canned
tomatoes, preferably
imported Italian, drained**

**Salt and freshly ground black
pepper**

**4 ounces (8 tablespoons)
sweet butter**

**1 cup freshly grated
Parmigiano**

10 large fresh basil leaves

TURTEI CU LA CUA

1. Twist the ends of the stuffed pasta. Turn one end toward you, and

2. the other end away from you. Be careful not to press the 2 layers of pasta too tightly together.

3. The final shape.

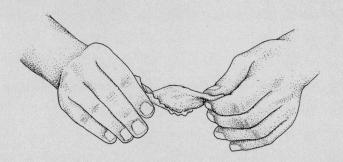

1

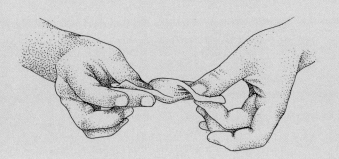

2

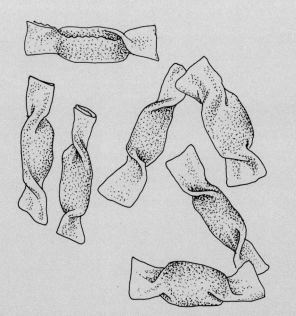

3

garganelli al prosciutto
GARGANELLI IN HAM SAUCE

Sift the Parmigiano to be sure there are no lumps. Prepare the pasta with the ingredients and quantities listed, following the directions on page 12. Place the Parmigiano in the well with the other ingredients. When the ball of dough is formed, wrap it in a cotton dish towel and let it rest for 30 minutes in a cool place, covered with a bowl. When ready, stretch the pasta to a very thin sheet, less than $\frac{1}{16}$ inch thick, by hand or machine. Cut the sheet of pasta into 1½-inch squares, and prepare *garganelli* (see page 274).

Prepare the sauce. Cut the ham into pieces smaller than ½ inch. Place the butter in a large skillet over low heat; when the butter is melted, add the ham and sauté for 5 minutes, stirring every so often with a wooden spoon. Keep warm.

Bring a large pot of cold water to a boil, add coarse salt to taste, then add the pasta and cook for 1 to 3 minutes depending on dryness. Drain the pasta, add it to the skillet with the ham, and start adding the cream, a very small quantity at a time, constantly mixing with a wooden spoon. Season to taste with salt, pepper, and nutmeg, and when all the cream is incorporated (about 1 minute), sprinkle the cheese over the top, mix, and transfer immediately to a warmed platter and serve.

VARIATIONS

1. A pinch of grated nutmeg can be added to the dough along with the grated cheese.
2. Though the classic *garganelli* are made with Parmigiano in the dough, the pasta also exists in a form without cheese. Mix 2½ cups unbleached all-purpose flour, 3 extra-large eggs, 2 teaspoons cold water, and a pinch of salt.

SERVES 6

FOR THE PASTA

½ cup freshly grated Parmigiano

2 cups unbleached all-purpose flour

3 extra-large eggs

Pinch of salt

FOR THE SAUCE

4 ounces boiled ham, in 1 piece

6 tablespoons (3 ounces) sweet butter

1 cup heavy cream

Salt and freshly ground black pepper

Freshly grated nutmeg

1 cup freshly grated Parmigiano

TO COOK THE PASTA

Coarse-grained salt

GARGANELLI

1. Place the pasta squares on the *pet-tine*, the traditional "comb," and, starting from one corner, wrap them around a stick.

2. Roll up the square until it is closed along the *pettine* to create a ridged pattern.

3. Slip the finished *garganelli* off the stick.

1

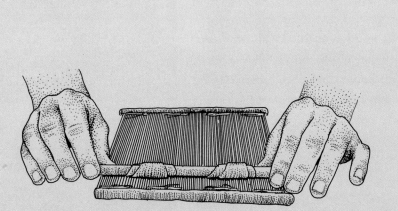

3

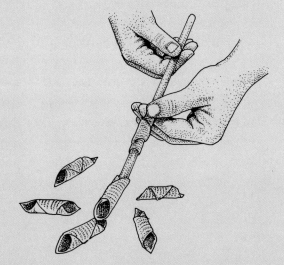

2

garganelli con pancetta affumicata

GARGANELLI WITH SMOKED PANCETTA

Cut the smoked *pancetta* or bacon into ½-inch pieces. Place a medium-sized skillet with the oil and butter over low heat. When the butter is completely melted, add the *pancetta* or bacon and sauté for 15 minutes, stirring every so often with a wooden spoon. Meanwhile, bring a large pot of cold water to a boil.

If using fresh tomatoes, cut them into pieces. Pass fresh or canned tomatoes through a food mill, using the disc with the smallest holes, into a crockery or glass bowl. Add the tomatoes to the skillet with salt and pepper to taste, and simmer for 15 minutes more.

When the water reaches a boil, add the pasta and cook for 8 to 11 minutes depending on the brand; that is, 1 minute less than for normal al dente. Drain the pasta, add it to the skillet, raise the heat, and sauté for 1 minute. Transfer to a warmed platter and serve immediately. If fresh pasta is used, cook it for 30 seconds to 2½ minutes depending on the dryness, then follow recipe as for dried pasta.

VARIATION

Half a pound of fresh peas, shelled and parboiled in water, can be added to the tomatoes 5 minutes before they finish simmering.

NOTE

Smoked *pancetta* is not widely available outside Italy, but bacon is just about the same thing and substitutes well.

SERVES 4 TO 6

- ½ pound smoked *pancetta*; or ½ pound bacon (not too smoky; see Note), sliced

- 3 tablespoons olive oil

- 4 tablespoons (2 ounces) sweet butter

- 1 pound ripe, fresh tomatoes; or 1 pound canned tomatoes, preferably imported Italian, drained

- Salt and freshly ground black pepper

- 1 pound dried *garganelli*, preferably imported from Italy or fresh *garganelli* (use the ingredients and quantities on page 273)

TO COOK THE PASTA

Coarse-grained salt

cappellacci di zucca
CAPPELLACCI WITH SQUASH STUFFING

Preheat the oven to 375° F. Prepare the stuffing. Bake the squash on a jelly roll pan for 1 hour. Remove from the oven and cool for 30 minutes. Remove the peel, seeds, and filaments from the squash, then pass the pulp through a food mill, using the disc with medium-sized holes, into a crockery or glass bowl. Measure out 1 cup of the puréed pulp for the stuffing, put it in a crockery or glass bowl, and add the bread crumbs, egg and egg yolk, and *Grana Padano*. Season to taste with salt, pepper, and nutmeg, and mix well using a wooden spoon. Cover and place in the refrigerator until needed.

Prepare the pasta with the ingredients and quantities listed, following the directions on page 12. Stretch the sheet to less than 1/16 inch thick—on the pasta machine take it to the last setting. Make *cappellacci* shaped like *ravioli* (see page 123), 3 inches square, using 1 heaping teaspoon of the stuffing for each. Let them rest on cotton dish towels or paper towels for at least 15 minutes, turning them over at least once.

Bring a large pot of cold water to a boil, add coarse salt to taste, then add the *cappellacci* and cook for 1 to 3 minutes depending on dryness. Meanwhile, melt the butter in a double boiler and warm a large serving platter. Use a strainer-skimmer to transfer the pasta to the warmed platter. Make a layer of *cappellacci*, pour some of the melted butter over the top, and sprinkle on some of the cheese. Make another layer of the remaining pasta, butter, and cheese. Serve with a twist of black pepper.

VARIATION

Cappellacci di zucca can also be served on top of a halved squash (see picture at right).

cappelli del prete (nicchi)
"THREE-CORNERED HATS"

FOR THE STUFFING

4 tablespoons (2 ounces) sweet butter

1 pound ground pork

2 bay leaves

2 whole cloves

Salt and freshly ground black pepper

3 extra-large eggs

2 slices white bread, crusts removed

Freshly grated nutmeg

¼ cup freshly grated Parmigiano

FOR THE SAUCE

2 pounds ripe, fresh tomatoes; or 2 pounds canned tomatoes, preferably imported Italian, drained

5 large sage leaves, fresh or preserved in salt

1 medium-sized clove garlic, peeled and left whole

¼ cup olive oil

Salt and freshly ground black pepper

FOR THE PASTA

3 cups unbleached all-purpose flour

3 extra-large eggs

3 tablespoons olive or vegetable oil

Pinch of salt

Begin the stuffing. Melt the butter in a small saucepan over low heat, then add the pork, bay leaves, and cloves. Sauté for 10 minutes, mixing with a wooden spoon; season to taste with salt and pepper. Remove from the stove, transfer to a crockery or glass bowl, and set aside until cool, about 30 minutes.

Break the eggs in a crockery or glass bowl and lightly beat them with a fork. Crumble the bread into the eggs to soak for 30 minutes.

Begin the sauce. If using fresh tomatoes, cut them into pieces. Put fresh or canned tomatoes in a medium-sized flameproof nonreactive casserole with the sage, garlic, and oil, and simmer over medium heat for 45 minutes.

Finish the stuffing. Discard the bay leaves and cloves, and transfer the meat and all the juices to the bowl with the eggs. Season with salt, pepper, and nutmeg to taste, add the Parmigiano, and thoroughly mix the ingredients with a wooden spoon. Cover the bowl and refrigerate until needed.

Prepare the pasta with the ingredients and quantities listed, following the directions on page 12. Stretch the sheet to less than $\frac{1}{16}$ inch thick—on a hand pasta machine take it to the last setting.

Cut the dough into 4 pieces and stretch one sheet of dough at a time, so the rest does not dry out while you are filling and shaping the *nicchi*. Cut each sheet of pasta into a 6-inch square, then use a knife to cut each diagonally into 2 triangles (see page 280). Place 1 heaping tablespoon of stuffing in the center of each triangle, then fold the longer side in half, pressing the edges together very well to seal them. Holding the top point between your right thumb and index finger, use your other hand to lift the point of the free side to meet the others 1 inch from the top. Seal both sides to close the triangle completely. The resultant shape resembles an old *tricorno*, or three-cornered hat, with the top end able to flop over like a feather. Let the *nicchi* rest on cotton towels until needed.

Finish the sauce. Pass the contents of the casserole through a food mill, using the disc with the smallest holes, into a crockery or glass bowl. Transfer back to the casserole, taste for salt and pepper, and reduce over medium heat for 15 minutes more.

Bring a large quantity of cold water to a boil, add coarse salt to taste, then add the *nicchi* carefully, one by one, and cook for 8 to 12 minutes depending on dryness.*Meanwhile, pour some of the sauce onto a warmed platter. When the pasta is ready, transfer it to the platter using a strainer-skimmer, being careful to let all the water drain off. Serve hot with the remaining sauce served on the side, with or without the Parmigiano.

For the artichoke stuffing, clean the artichokes according to the directions on page 70, and cut them into eighths. Place them in a bowl of cold water with the lemon halves, and let rest for 30 minutes. Heat the oil in a medium-sized flame-proof casserole over low heat; when the oil is warm, drain the artichokes and add to the casserole. Sauté for 5 minutes, then add some of the broth, cover, and cook for 15 minutes. Season with salt and pepper, and keep adding broth as needed until the artichokes are cooked. Use a strainer-skimmer to transfer the artichokes to a crockery or glass bowl and set aside until cool, about 30 minutes. Coarsely chop the artichokes on a board, transfer to a crockery or glass bowl, add the eggs and Parmigiano, then add salt and pepper to taste and mix very well. Use a heaping tablespoon of the stuffing for each of the *nicchi*.

*The long cooking time is necessary because of the thickness produced when several ends of pasta are pressed together in the corners.

TO COOK THE PASTA

Coarse-grained salt

TO SERVE

Freshly grated Parmigiano (optional)

VARIATION: ARTICHOKE STUFFING

3 large artichokes

1 large lemon, cut in half

4 tablespoons olive oil

1 cup lukewarm chicken or beef broth, preferably homemade

Salt and freshly ground black pepper

3 extra-large eggs

¼ cup freshly grated Parmigiano

NICCHI

1. Cut the pasta squares diagonally into triangles.

2. Place the stuffing in the center of the triangle.

3. The longer sides of the triangle are folded and pressed together.
The shorter side is lifted to meet the other 1 inch from the top.

4. Seal all the sides well.

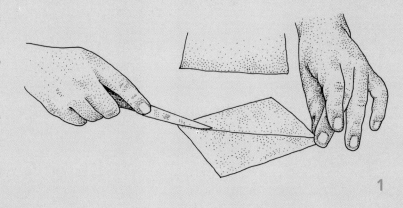

1

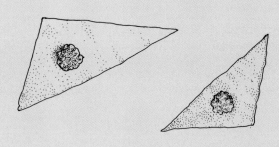

2

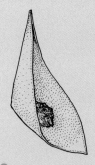

3

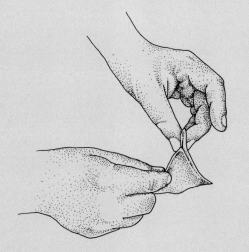

4

umbria

Hilly Umbria has maintained some of its traditional pastas more than some other less rustic regions. Long, thick *ciriole*, sometimes called *umbrici*, are made with semolina mixed with white flour and do not include eggs. (None of the following Umbrian specialties are made with eggs.) *Ciriole* are as thick as the *bucatini* of the south, but do not have holes through the center. Umbrians like a tomato sauce spiced with hot red pepper, which appears here in the version from Terni.

Umbrici may also be hand-rolled and are made by using the same technique as the *pinci* of Montalcino. In the version here made with a basil-flavored tomato sauce and ricotta, they are probably rolled a little thinner than those in the *ciriole* recipe. Even with this sauce, hot red pepper is an option.

Stringozzi are rolled thick before cutting, sometimes giving a square shape to the width of the stringlike pasta. They are typical of the Spoleto area, but share with other Umbrian specialties the spicy sauce and the combination with ricotta, usually homemade, in these areas. A special feature of this Spoleto recipe is the rosemary flavoring.

ciriole alla ternana
PASTA FROM TERNI

from Terni (Umbria)

SERVES 6

FOR THE PASTA

1¾ cups semolina flour

¾ cup unbleached
   all-purpose flour

1 cup lukewarm water

Pinch of salt

FOR THE SAUCE

2 large cloves garlic, peeled

¼ cup olive oil

1½ pounds ripe, fresh
   tomatoes; or 1½ pounds
   canned tomatoes,
   preferably imported
   Italian, drained

Salt and freshly ground
   black pepper

½ teaspoon hot red pepper
   flakes

TO COOK THE PASTA

Coarse-grained salt

Prepare the pasta. Mix the semolina flour with ½ cup of the all-purpose flour, then prepare the dough following the directions on page 12, kneading for at least 15 minutes. Wrap the dough in cheesecloth and let rest for 30 minutes, covered by a bowl. Spread out the remaining ¼ cup of flour on a board and, using a rolling pin, stretch the pasta dough into a sheet a little more than ⅛ inch thick and about 18 inches long. Let the sheet of pasta rest until a thin film forms, then cut into *taglierini*, using a cutter (see page 35) or by hand. The result should resemble thicker and longer *spaghetti*. These are *ciriole*. Let the pasta rest on cotton dish towels until needed.

Prepare the sauce. Cut the garlic into small pieces, then place the oil in a medium-sized nonreactive flameproof casserole over low heat. When the oil is warm, add the garlic and sauté until lightly golden, about 5 minutes. Meanwhile, if using fresh tomatoes, blanch them in salted boiling water, remove seeds, and cut flesh into fourths or eighths—i. e. *in filetto.* If using canned tomatoes, pass them through a food mill, using the disc with the smallest holes, into a crockery or glass bowl. Add the tomatoes to the casserole and season with salt, pepper, and the red pepper flakes. Simmer for 35 minutes, stirring every so often with a wooden spoon.

Bring a large pot of cold water to a boil, add coarse salt to taste, then add the pasta and cook for 1 to 3 minutes depending on dryness. Drain the pasta, transfer to a warmed serving dish, pour the sauce over the top, mix well, and serve immediately.

umbrici con pomodoro e ricotta

UMBRIAN PINCI WITH RICOTTA AND TOMATO SAUCE

Prepare the pasta with the ingredients and quantities listed, following the directions on page 12. Cut into *umbrici* (*pinci*) (see drawing), and let pasta rest on cotton dish towels until needed.

Prepare the sauce. Place a medium-sized nonreactive flameproof casserole over medium heat. Add the garlic, olive oil, tomatoes, and basil; simmer for 30 minutes, stirring every so often with a wooden spoon. Pass the contents of the casserole through a food mill, using the disc with the smallest holes, into a crockery or glass bowl. Return the sauce to the casserole and simmer over low heat for 15 minutes, seasoning to taste with salt and pepper. If using red pepper flakes, add them at this point.

Bring a large pot of cold water to a boil, add coarse salt to taste, then add the pasta and cook for 1 to 3 minutes depending on dryness; if dried pasta is used, cook it until al dente—9 to 12 minutes depending on the brand. As the pasta cooks, arrange the ricotta in a flat layer over the surface of a large serving platter. Drain the pasta, arrange it over the ricotta, then pour the tomato sauce over everything and mix well. Serve with several twists of black pepper.

SERVES 4 TO 6

FOR THE PASTA

3 cups unbleached all-purpose flour

1 cup cold water

1 tablespoon olive oil or vegetable oil

Pinch of salt

or

1 pound dried *spaghetti*, preferably imported Italian

FOR THE SAUCE

2 medium-sized cloves garlic, peeled and left whole

4 tablespoons olive oil

1½ pounds ripe, fresh tomatoes, cut into pieces; or 1½ pounds canned tomatoes, preferably imported Italian, drained

6 large basil leaves, fresh or preserved in salt

Salt and freshly ground black pepper

½ teaspoon hot red pepper flakes (optional)

TO COOK THE PASTA

Coarse-grained salt

TO SERVE

15 ounces ricotta, preferably homemade

Freshly ground black pepper

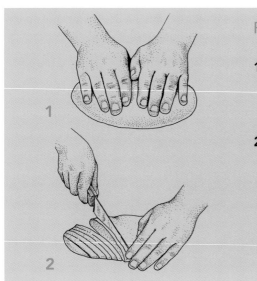

PINCI

1. Flatten the ball of dough with both hands to a thickness of less than ½ inch.

2. Cut the thick layer of dough into strips less than ½ inch wide.

(continued on next page)

PINCI (CONTINUED)

3. Cut across the pasta, making the strips into small cubes.

4. Take an individual cube and, holding it between the thumbs and first fingers of both hands, pinch the cube.

5. Pull the dough so that it extends sideways only, into a nonrounded strip about 3 inches long.

6. With the 4 fingers of both hands, lightly roll the strip of dough, moving both hands gradually apart from the center.

7. Keep repeating this motion until the strip is rounded and about 9 inches long.

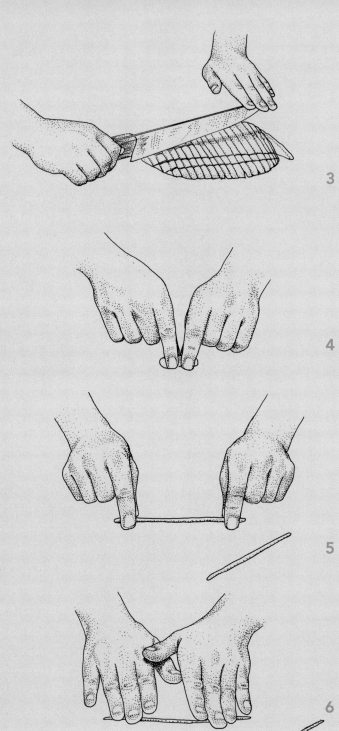

3

4

5

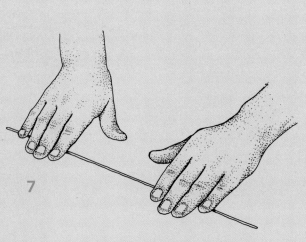

7

6

stringozzi al pomodoro
STRINGOZZI WITH SPICY TOMATO SAUCE

Prepare the pasta with the ingredients and quantities listed, following the instructions on page 12. Cut into *pinci* (see page 283), and let rest on cotton dish towels until needed.

Prepare the sauce. If using fresh tomatoes, cut them into large pieces. Place fresh or canned tomatoes in a medium-sized nonreactive saucepan. Finely chop garlic and rosemary together, add them to the pan along with the oil, and place the pan over medium heat for 30 minutes, stirring every so often with a wooden spoon. Pass the contents of the pan through a food mill, using the disc with the smallest holes, into a crockery or glass bowl. Return the tomatoes to the pan, add salt, pepper, and the red pepper flakes, and simmer for 15 minutes more.

Bring a large pot of cold water to a boil and reheat the sauce over low heat. Place the ricotta in a crockery or glass bowl, season with salt and pepper, then start adding the oil and *pecorino romano* little by little, constantly mixing with a wooden spoon, until all the oil and cheese are integrated.

When the water reaches a boil, add coarse-grained salt to taste, then the pasta, and cook it for 1 to 3 minutes depending on dryness. Combine the tomato sauce with the ricotta mixture. Drain the pasta, transfer it to a large serving dish, and add the sauce and mix very well, putting in a little of the pasta water if the sauce is too thick. Season with more freshly ground black pepper and serve.

SERVES 8

FOR THE PASTA

3 cups unbleached all-purpose flour

1 cup cold water

1 tablespoon olive oil or vegetable oil

Pinch of salt

FOR THE SAUCE

2 pounds ripe, fresh tomatoes; or 2 pounds canned tomatoes, preferably imported Italian, drained

2 large cloves garlic, peeled

1 heaping teaspoon rosemary leaves—fresh, preserved in salt, or dried and blanched

¼ cup olive oil

Salt and freshly ground black pepper

½ teaspoon hot red pepper flakes

TO COOK THE PASTA

Coarse-grained salt

TO SERVE

15 ounces ricotta

Salt and freshly ground black pepper

¼ cup olive oil

¼ cup freshly grated pecorino romano cheese

abruzzi

Throughout Abruzzi, the pasta is cut with a "guitar." To make the sauce for the *maccheroni alla chitarra*, the lamb is cut into sizable cubes, and red wine, onion, rosemary, and *pancetta* are used. The hot red pepper, so typical of the region, is also used in the sauce. (See page 289 for the technique of making the *maccheroni* and cutting it with the "guitar.")

The *scripelle* or *crespelle* used for the stuffed *lasagne* made during Carnival time in the Abruzzi version is also used simply, rolled up with a Parmigiano stuffing and eaten in a rich broth. More Parmigiano may be sprinkled over all.

maccheroni alla chitarra sull'agnello

MACCHERONI CUT WITH THE "GUITAR," WITH LAMB CUBES AND PANCETTA SAUCE

SERVES 6 TO 8

FOR THE SAUCE

1 ½ pounds boneless lamb shoulder

1 medium-sized red onion, peeled

1 teaspoon rosemary leaves, fresh, preserved in salt, or dried and blanched

4 ounces *pancetta* or *prosciutto*, in 1 piece

¼ cup olive oil

½ cup dry red wine

2 tablespoons tomato paste

2 cups lukewarm chicken or beef broth, preferably homemade

Salt and freshly ground black pepper

½ teaspoon hot red pepper flakes

FOR THE PASTA

4 cups unbleached all-purpose flour

5 extra-large eggs

Pinch of salt

TO COOK THE PASTA

Coarse-grained salt

TO SERVE

¾ cup freshly grated pecorino or Parmigiano

Cut the lamb into 1-inch cubes. Finely chop the onion and rosemary together on a board. Cut the *pancetta* into ½-inch cubes. Place a heavy, medium-sized flame-proof casserole, preferably of terra cotta or enamel, with the olive oil over low heat. When the oil is warm, add the onion and rosemary and the *pancetta*. Sauté for 10 minutes, then add the lamb, mix well, and cook for 5 minutes more. Pour in the wine and let it evaporate for 5 minutes. Dissolve the tomato paste in 1 cup of the broth and add to the casserole. Season to taste with salt, pepper, and the red pepper flakes; simmer, covered, for 1 hour, stirring every so often with a wooden spoon. Add the remaining cup of broth, and simmer, still covered, for 1 hour more. Remove the lid, taste for salt and pepper, raise the heat, and cook for 5 minutes more.

As the sauce is simmering, prepare the pasta with the ingredients and quantities listed, following the directions on page 12. Stretch sheet to ⅛ inch thick—on the pasta machine take it to several notches before the last setting. Prepare the *maccheroni* cut with the "guitar" (see drawing), cutting the layer into pieces 2 inches shorter than the length of the guitar. Let the pasta rest on cotton dish towels until needed.

When the sauce is almost ready, bring a large quantity of cold water to a boil, add coarse salt to taste, then add the pasta and cook for 1 to 3 minutes depending on dryness. Meanwhile, warm a large serving platter and ladle half the sauce onto the platter. Drain the pasta, arrange it over the sauce, pour the remaining sauce over the top, and sprinkle with the Parmigiano. Mix well and serve.

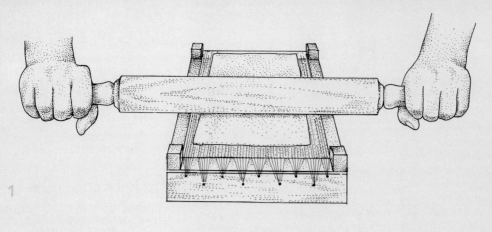

1

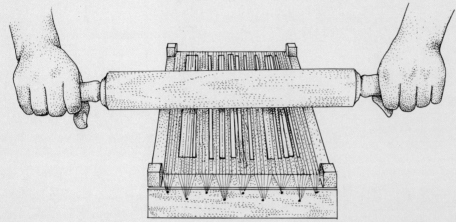

2

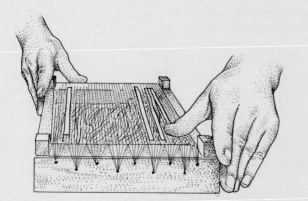

3

MACCHERONI ALLA CHITARRA

1. Place a piece of pasta, about 12 inches long, on the "guitar", leaving about 2 inches free on each end of the guitar.

2. Roll back and forth with a rolling pin.

3. "Play" the guitar, drawing your thumb across the string, until all the loosened strips fall through onto the tray below.

scripelle 'mbusse (crespelle in brodo)
CRÊPES IN BROTH

SERVES 6 TO 8

FOR THE BATTER

½ cup unbleached
  all-purpose flour

2 extra-large eggs

½ cup plus 2 tablespoons
  cold milk

Pinch of salt

10 large sprigs Italian
  parsley, leaves only,
  finely chopped

**TO COOK/STUFF THE
CRESPELLE**

2 tablespoons (1 ounce)
  sweet butter or olive oil

16 tablespoons freshly
  grated Parmigiano

TO SERVE

2 quarts defatted chicken or
  beef broth, preferably
  homemade

Freshly grated Parmigiano

Fresh Italian parsley

Prepare the *crespelle* batter. Use the ingredients listed, and follow the directions on page 192. Add the parsley to the batter.

Use a 4-inch crêpe pan and less than 2 tablespoons of batter to form each *crespella*, adding butter or olive oil to the pan as necessary. As each is cooked, sprinkle it with 1 teaspoon of Parmigiano, then roll it up and put it on a large serving dish. When all the *crespelle* are prepared, bring the broth to a boil over medium heat. Place 2 or 3 rolled-up *crespelle* in each soup bowl and pour 1 cup of broth over each portion. Serve with Italian parsley.

VARIATIONS

1. The Parmigiano used for the stuffing can be incorporated directly into the batter instead of sprinkling it over the already cooked *crespelle*; in that case increase milk to 1 cup.

2. A local, very soft, fresh pecorino cheese is sometimes used instead of grated Parmigiano in Abruzzi. It is spread over the *crespelle* before rolling. No grated cheese is then used at all.

NOTE

Black pepper is absolutely never used in any authentic version of this batter.

sardinia

The pasta for Sardinian *ravioli*, *culingionis*, contains both semolina and white flours. The one with the ricotta-mint stuffing uses equal amounts of each, while the recipe with the eggplant stuffing uses only a tiny bit of semolina, though there is some in the stuffing itself. Saffron is added to both pastas, as is a little water, cold in one case, lukewarm in the other. The first pasta uses mostly egg whites and only one whole egg. The other uses only yolks. We see there is infinite variety in the way pasta is traditionally made, and it is enlightening to ponder why the pasta varies for each particular stuffing.

Fresh mint is important for both Sardinian stuffings and it is used abundantly. The use of saffron in both pastas and, in some cases, in the stuffing itself is very special. A light tomato sauce is favored for these pastas, with basil, a good combination with the flavor of mint.

Malloreddus, the Sardinian short pasta, is ridged with a little opening in the center. The technique for making it follows. Dried *malloreddus* are now widely exported and easily available outside of Sardinia. As usual, saffron may be included in the dough itself and most of the flour is semolina with a little white flour added.

The favored tomato sauce for *malloreddus* combines onion, garlic, and abundant basil. An alternative sausage dressing combines bay leaves, garlic, basil, and some saffron in the sauce. Sausage made with fennel seeds is appropriate for this recipe.

The Sardinian version of the large wheels of *pecorino romano* cheese, called *sardo* for short, is the right cheese for these dishes and is widely available.

culingionis *or* culurzones *or* culurjones

SARDINIAN RAVIOLI

Prepare the stuffing. Place the ricotta in a cheesecloth square, and let it hang, draining very well to remove all excess water. Place the ricotta in a crockery or glass bowl, add the egg yolks, mint leaves, salt and pepper to taste, and a generous pinch of saffron. Mix all the ingredients, then cover the bowl with aluminum foil and refrigerate until needed.

Prepare the pasta with the ingredients and quantities listed, following the directions on page 12. Wrap the dough in a cotton dish towel and let rest for 30 minutes in a cool place under a bowl or on the bottom shelf of the refrigerator.

Prepare the sauce. Blanch the tomatoes in salted boiling water, slip off the skins, then cut them into fourths and seed them. Coarsely chop the parsley, celery, and basil on a board. Place the oil in a medium-sized, nonreactive saucepan over medium heat, and when the oil is warm, add the chopped ingredients and sauté for 10 minutes. Put in the tomatoes and salt and pepper to taste, cover, and cook for

15 minutes, stirring every so often with a wooden spoon. Let the sauce stand, covered, until needed.

Use about ¼ cup of all-purpose flour to roll out the pasta until very thin, less than ¹⁄₁₆ inch thick—on the pasta machine take it to the last setting. Prepare 2-inch *ravioli*, and fill each with 1 heaping teaspoon of stuffing (see page 123). Let the *ravioli* rest on cotton dish towels until needed, turning them several times while drying to keep them from sticking.

Bring a large pot of cold water to a boil, add coarse salt to taste, then add the *ravioli* a few at a time, and cook for 1 to 3 minutes depending on dryness. Meanwhile, reheat the sauce and warm a serving dish. When the pasta is ready, use a strainer-skimmer to transfer it to the warmed dish. Make a layer of the *ravioli*, spoon some of the sauce over the top, and sprinkle with cheese. Keep making layers of pasta with sauce and cheese until all the ingredients are on the dish. Serve immediately.

SERVES 6 TO 8

FOR THE STUFFING

15 ounces ricotta

4 extra-large egg yolks

30 large fresh mint leaves, torn into thirds

Salt and freshly ground black pepper

Ground saffron

FOR THE PASTA

1½ cups fine semolina flour

1½ cups unbleached all-purpose flour

4 extra-large egg whites

1 extra-large egg

⅛ teaspoon ground saffron

¼ cup cold water

Pinch of salt

All-purpose flour

FOR THE SAUCE

2 pounds ripe, fresh tomatoes

Coarse-grained salt

10 large sprigs Italian parsley, leaves only

2 large stalks celery

5 large basil leaves, fresh or preserved in salt

½ cup olive oil

Salt and freshly ground black pepper

TO COOK THE PASTA

Coarse-grained salt

TO SERVE

1 cup freshly grated pecorino sardo cheese

culingionis di melanzane
RAVIOLI STUFFED WITH EGGPLANT

SERVES 6 TO 8

FOR THE STUFFING

4 medium-sized eggplants (2 pounds), cleaned and peeled

Coarse-grained salt

3 cups vegetable oil

¼ cup olive oil

2 tablespoons very fine semolina flour

2 extra-large eggs

2 extra-large egg yolks

1 cup grated pecorino romano or pecorino romano sardo cheese

40 large fresh mint leaves, torn into thirds

Freshly ground black pepper

FOR THE SAUCE

3 pounds ripe, fresh tomatoes; or 3 pounds canned tomatoes, preferably imported Italian, drained

10 large basil leaves, fresh or preserved in salt

½ cup olive oil

Salt and freshly ground black pepper

Begin the stuffing. Peel the eggplants, cut them into 1-inch cubes, place them on a large serving platter, and sprinkle with 2 tablespoons of coarse salt. Place a second platter on the eggplant as a weight and let rest for 30 minutes. Rinse the eggplant under cold running water to remove all the salt, and dry with paper towels. Place the vegetable and olive oils in a deep-fat fryer over medium heat. When the oil is hot (375° F), add the eggplant and fry until lightly golden all over, about 4 minutes. Transfer to a large serving platter lined with paper towels to drain excess oil; let rest until cool, about 30 minutes.

Begin the sauce. If using fresh tomatoes, cut them into pieces. Place a heavy, medium-sized casserole over medium heat. Add the fresh or canned tomatoes, basil, and olive oil and simmer for 30 minutes.

Finish the stuffing. Transfer the eggplant to a crockery or glass bowl; add the semolina flour, eggs and egg yolks, cheese, and mint leaves. Mix very well and season with pepper only, since the cheese is salty. Cover the bowl and refrigerate until needed.

Prepare the pasta with the ingredients and quantities listed, following the directions on page 12, but placing the semolina flour in the flour well along with the egg yolks, the saffron dissolved in the water, and salt. Let the dough rest, wrapped in a cotton dish towel and tightly covered by a bowl, for 30 minutes.

Finish the sauce. Pass the tomato mixture through a food mill, using the disc with smallest holes, into a second flameproof casserole and reduce over low heat for 5 minutes more, seasoning to taste with salt and pepper. Set aside.

Stretch the sheet of pasta to very thin, less than $\frac{1}{16}$ inch thick—on a pasta machine take it to the last setting. Cut into *culingionis* (round *tortelli* or *ravioli*, page 123) that have a 2-inch diameter. Use a heaping teaspoon of stuffing for each, placed in the center of the disc of pasta, and then fold the pasta over the stuffing. Let *culingionis* rest on floured cotton dish towels until needed.

Bring a large pot of cold water to a boil, add coarse salt to taste, then add the *culingionis* and cook for 6 to 9 minutes depending on dryness (semolina requires a long cooking time). As the pasta cooks, reheat the sauce and then spoon some onto a large, warmed serving platter. Add some of the cooked *culingionis* and repeat the layers of sauce and pasta until all the *culingionis* are on the platter. Add a final layer of tomato sauce and serve hot, with just a teaspoon of cheese sprinkled over each serving.

NOTE

Ravioli and *tortelli* can be either round or square.

Wild (top) and cultivated arugula.

FOR THE PASTA

3 cups unbleached all-purpose flour

¼ cup very fine semolina flour

3 extra-large egg yolks

Pinch of ground saffron, or threads of saffron ground with a marble mortar and pestle, dissolved in 1 cup lukewarm water

Pinch of salt

TO COOK THE PASTA

Coarse-grained salt

TO SERVE

6 to 8 tablespoons freshly grated pecorino romano or pecorino romano sardo cheese

homemade malloreddus

SERVES 6

2 ½ cups very fine semolina
    flour

½ cup unbleached
    all-purpose flour

Pinch of salt

Pinch of ground saffron or
    threads of saffron ground
    with a marble mortar and
    pestle dissolved in 1 cup
    lukewarm water

1 cup lukewarm water

Place the semolina flour in a mound on a pasta board, make a well in it, then place the all-purpose flour in the well. Dissolve the salt and saffron in the lukewarm water, then pour the water into the well of the flour. Prepare a ball of dough and knead it for 15 minutes, following the directions on page 12. Divide the dough into several pieces and use your hands to roll out long cords about ½ inch in diameter. Cut the cords into pieces the size of chick-peas. Use the special straw screen, the *cuilini* (see drawing), to shape the individual *malloreddus*, using the same technique as for making *gnocchi* (see page 352). Let the *malloreddus* rest on floured cotton dish towels until needed.

VARIATION

The saffron can be omitted. Also, 1 tablespoon of tomato paste or boiled, finely chopped spinach can be substituted.

NOTE

If you do not have a *cuilini*, you can shape the *malloreddus* with a fork or cheese grater (see *gnocchi*, page 353).

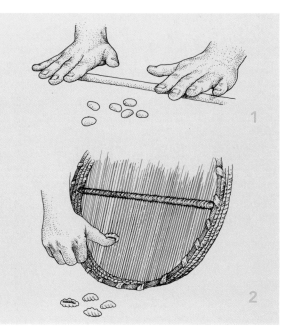

MALLOREDDUS

1. Roll out the dough in a cord about a half inch in diameter. Cut into pieces the size of chick-peas.

2. Use the traditional straw screen to shape the individual *malloreddus* using the thumb with the same cursive motion as for shaping *gnocchi*.

malloreddus con sugo di pomodoro

MALLOREDDUS WITH SARDINIAN TOMATO SAUCE

Prepare the sauce. Finely chop the onion and garlic together on a board. Place the oil in a medium-sized nonreactive saucepan over low heat; when the oil is warm, add the chopped ingredients and sauté for 10 minutes. If using fresh tomatoes, cut them into pieces. Pass fresh or canned tomatoes through a food mill, using the disc with the smallest holes, into a crockery or glass bowl. Add the tomatoes and salt and pepper to taste, and simmer for 25 minutes, stirring every so often with a wooden spoon.

Bring a large pot of cold water to a boil, add coarse salt to taste, then add the pasta and cook dried pasta for 10 minutes, or 6 to 10 minutes for homemade pasta, depending on dryness. Drain the pasta, transfer to the saucepan with the sauce, add the basil leaves torn into thirds, and let the malloreddus absorb the sauce, simmering them over low heat for 1 minute more, stirring constantly. Serve with cheese.

VARIATION

Onion can be omitted, and 25 sprigs of Italian parsley leaves chopped together with the garlic can be added.

SERVES 6

FOR THE SAUCE

1 medium-sized white or red onion, peeled

1 medium-sized clove garlic, peeled

½ cup olive oil

1 ½ pounds ripe, fresh tomatoes; or 1 ½ pounds canned tomatoes, preferably imported Italian, drained

Salt and freshly ground black pepper

20 large basil leaves, fresh or preserved in salt, torn into thirds

FOR THE PASTA

1 pound dried *malloreddus* or homemade *malloreddus* (page 296)

TO COOK THE PASTA

Coarse-grained salt

TO SERVE

Freshly grated pecorino romano sardo or pecorino romano cheese

NOTE
If dried *malloreddus* are not available, *cavatelli* from Apuglia are a good substitute.

malloreddus alla campidanese
SARDINIAN PASTA WITH SAUSAGES

SERVES 6 TO 8

FOR THE SAUCE

1 ½ pounds ripe, fresh tomatoes; or 1 ½ pounds canned tomatoes, preferably imported Italian, drained

Coarse-grained salt

4 sweet Italian sausages with fennel seeds or without (about 1 pound)

½ cup olive oil

2 large cloves garlic, peeled but left whole

2 bay leaves

5 basil leaves, fresh or preserved in salt

Pinch of ground saffron

Salt and freshly ground black pepper

FOR THE PASTA

1 pound dried *malloreddus* (containing some *malloreddus* prepared with saffron), preferably imported Italian

TO COOK THE PASTA

Coarse-grained salt

TO SERVE

¾ cup freshly grated pecorino sardo cheese

Fresh basil leaves

Blanch the tomatoes in boiling salted water, slip off the skins, then cut them into quarters and seed them. Cut the sausages into thirds. Place the oil in a heavy saucepan over low heat; when the oil is warm, add the sausages and sauté until completely cooked, about 10 minutes. Use a slotted spoon to transfer the sausages to a bowl; cover with aluminum foil. Add the garlic to the pan and sauté for 4 minutes. Remove and discard the garlic, then add the tomatoes along with the bay leaves, basil, and saffron. Cook for 15 minutes, stirring every so often with a wooden spoon. Taste for salt and pepper.

Meanwhile, bring a large pot of cold water to a boil, add coarse salt to taste, then add the *malloreddus* and cook until al dente—about 15 minutes depending on the brand. Drain the *malloreddus* and add to the saucepan, mixing very well and letting them incorporate all the sauce over low heat. Add the reserved sausages, mix well, and simmer for 2 or 3 minutes. Each portion consists of some *malloreddus*, sausage pieces, and a generous tablespoon of the cheese. Serve with fresh basil leaves.

apulia

Cavatelli (*cavatieddi* in dialect), along with *orecchiette*, the little "ear-shaped" pasta, are regional contributions of Apulia made with a combination of semolina and white flours. The little dough pieces are shaped with the thumb for *orecchiette*, while *cavatieddi* are formed with a cursive movement, like *gnocchi* or *malloreddus*.

A very popular dish is the *cavatieddi* combined with cooked arugula and dressed with a tomato sauce. A number of greens eaten only in salad in most places are also cooked in Italy. Lettuce is a good example, forming the basis for a delicious soup. The cooked arugula is excellent; its peppery bitterness combines well with the substantial semolina pasta, and generations of Apulians have verified its good flavor.

Stracnar, attractive pasta rectangles, patterned in herringbone from a textured antique board called a *cavarola*, are another contribution from Apulia. Some semolina is mixed in with the white flour, but the pasta is rich with egg. This is another of those great old pastas that must be made manually and is disappearing, but let us revive it. The Apulian name is actually *stracenate*, while I have used the better-known name from Lucania, where it is also made. The sauce is made with halved cherry tomatoes (another Apulian speciality), anchovy, and croutons, which may represent the *midolla* or "marrow," of the name.

cavatieddi con la rucola
CAVATELLI WITH ARUGULA

Begin the pasta. Mix the flours, arrange in a mound, and make a well. Add the lukewarm water and salt, and prepare a ball of dough following the directions on page 12. Keep kneading the dough for 10 minutes, then wrap it in a cotton dish towel and let it rest, covered with a bowl, for 30 minutes.

Prepare the sauce. Finely chop the onion and garlic together on a board. Put the olive oil in a medium-sized nonreactive saucepan over medium heat. When the oil is warm, add the chopped ingredients and sauté for 10 minutes, stirring every so often with a wooden spoon. If using fresh tomatoes, cut them into pieces. Pass fresh or canned tomatoes through a food mill, using the disc with smallest holes, into a crockery or glass bowl and add them to the pan. Season with salt and pepper, and cook over medium heat for 20 minutes more, stirring every so often.

Finish the pasta. Break off a small piece of dough and use your hands to roll out a cord not more than ½ inch thick; cut it into pieces the size of chick-peas.

Use a butter knife with a round tip to shape the individual *cavatelli*, making the same curling *c* motion as when preparing *gnocchi* (see page 353), but doing it against a board instead of a grater. Let the *cavatelli* rest on a floured cotton dish towel until needed.

Place the arugula in cold water to soak until needed. Bring a large pot of cold water to a boil, add coarse salt to taste, then add the pasta and cook for 9 to 12 minutes depending on dryness. After the pasta has been cooking for 5 minutes, drain the arugula, add it to the pot, and mix well. When the pasta is ready, drain the pasta and arugula; transfer to a large, warmed serving platter, add the sauce, toss well, and serve, with or without cheese.

VARIATIONS

1. The garlic can be left whole, sautéed with the chopped onion, and discarded when the sauce is ready.
2. A large pinch of hot red pepper flakes can be added to the sauce together with the salt and pepper.

SERVES 4 TO 6

FOR THE PASTA

1½ cups unbleached all-purpose flour

1 cup very fine semolina flour

1 cup lukewarm water

Pinch of salt

FOR THE SAUCE

1 large red onion, peeled

1 large clove garlic, peeled

½ cup olive oil

2 pounds ripe, fresh tomatoes; or 2 pounds canned tomatoes, preferably imported Italian, drained

Salt and freshly ground black pepper

FOR THE ARUGULA

1½ pounds arugula (rocket), large stems removed and leaves washed

TO COOK THE PASTA

Coarse-grained salt

TO SERVE

¾ cup freshly grated pecorino romano or pecorino romano sardo cheese (optional)

CAVATELLI

1. Cut the cord of dough into pieces about the size of chick-peas.

2. Shape the *cavatelli* using a knife in the same cursive *c* motion used for shaping *gnocchi*.

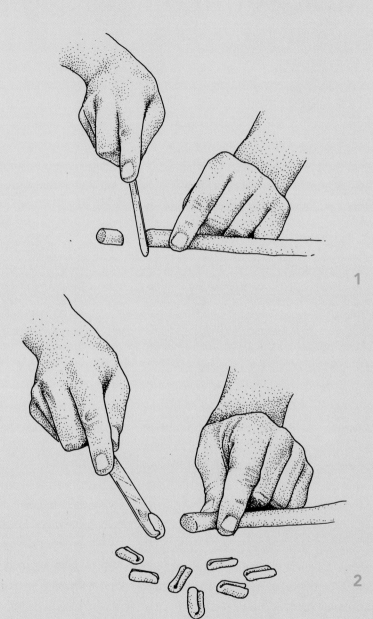

stracnar con la midolla

PATTERNED PASTA WITH CHERRY TOMATOES AND CROUTONS

Prepare the pasta with the ingredients and quantities listed, following the directions on page 12. Stretch the sheet of pasta to ¹⁄₁₆ inch—on the pasta machine, take it to the next to the last setting. Cut the pasta into pieces ¾ inch wide and 2¼ inches long. If possible, place the pasta pieces on the traditional little ridged pasta board called a *cavarola* to make the herringbone pattern, pressing the pasta down with your fingers to get the impression. In the absence of the *cavarola*, approximate the pattern by making the ridges with a fork in a herringbone arrangement. Let the pasta pieces rest on cotton dish towels until needed.

Prepare the sauce. Finely chop the onion and celery together on a board.

Heat the oil in a large skillet, and when the oil is warm, add the chopped ingredients and sauté for 5 minutes. Meanwhile, if using whole anchovies, clean them, removing bones and rinsing away excess salt under cold water. Remove the skillet from the heat, add the anchovy fillets, and, using a fork, mash them into the sautéed vegetables. Let the skillet rest off the heat for 10 minutes.

Bring a large pot of cold water to a boil, add coarse salt to taste, then add the pasta and cook for 1 to 3 minutes depending on dryness. As the pasta cooks, place the skillet over high heat and add the tomato halves. Season with salt and pepper, and set aside.

Prepare the croutons. Place a small saucepan with the oil over high heat. When the oil is warm, add the bread pieces and sauté until golden, about 3 minutes. Use a strainer-skimmer to transfer the sautéed bread to a dish lined with paper towels to drain excess oil.

When the pasta is ready, place the skillet with the sauce over medium heat, drain the pasta, add it to the skillet, mix very well, then transfer to a warmed serving dish. Sprinkle the bread pieces over the pasta and serve immediately.

Anchovies preserved in salt.

SERVES 6 TO 8

FOR THE PASTA

2 cups unbleached all-purpose flour

1 cup semolina flour

5 extra-large eggs

Pinch of salt

FOR THE SAUCE

1 medium-sized red onion, peeled

1 large stalk celery

½ cup olive oil

3 anchovies in salt; or 6 anchovy fillets packed in oil, drained

1 ½ pounds cherry tomatoes, cut into halves

Salt and freshly ground black pepper

TO COOK THE PASTA

Coarse-grained salt

FOR THE CROUTONS

½ cup olive oil

1 slice white bread, crust removed, cut into very small pieces

sicily

Among the native Sicilian fresh pastas are *crusetti*, or *rosette*. They are *cannelloni* that are closed at both ends, a highly unusual feature. The pasta is rich with egg yolk to which only a little water is added. The pasta squares are precooked and filled with a meat–zucchini–tomato stuffing. The *crusetti* are baked without *balsamella*, just half of the tomato sauce poured on top. They are typical of splendorous Monreale, a city graced with incredible Byzantine mosaics.

Pasta with a hole through the middle appears in the dried form of *bucatini* and *perciatelli*. But they may also be homemade with fresh dough, and Sicily is probably the chief locus of this version. Shorter than the dried versions, these *maccheroni inferrettati* were once made with a special square implement, but for several generations now it has been more common to make them with knitting needles. The pasta, rolled into a thin rope, is cut into small pieces, then wrapped around the needle and pushed off. The tomato sauce is flavored with oregano.

crusetti o rosette alla siciliana

SICILIAN CLOSED CANNELLONI

Prepare the sauce/stuffing. Finely chop the onion, celery, and parsley all together on a board. Place the oil in a medium-sized nonreactive saucepan over medium heat. When the oil is warm, add the chopped ingredients and sauté for 10 minutes. If using fresh tomatoes, cut them into pieces. Pass fresh or canned tomatoes through a food mill, using the disc with smallest holes, into a crockery or glass bowl. Add the beef to the saucepan and sauté for 5 minutes on each side, then add the tomatoes and salt and pepper to taste. Simmer, covered, until the beef is fork-tender, about 20 minutes.

Transfer the cooked meat to a board and finely chop it. Reduce the sauce for 5 more minutes. Place the chopped meat in a crockery or glass bowl, add ½ cup of the sauce, mix well, cover the bowl, and set the stuffing aside until needed.

Clean the zucchini and cut into thin slices—less than ½ inch thick. Heat the oils in a large skillet and when it is hot (about 375° F), put in the zucchini. Fry until golden on both sides, about 5 minutes, then use a strainer-skimmer to transfer the zucchini to the bowl of stuffing. Cover the bowl again and set aside. Preheat the oven to 375° F.

Prepare the pasta with the ingredients and quantities listed, following the directions on page 12. Stretch the sheet to less than 1/16 inch thick—on the pasta machine, take it to the last setting—and cut into squares using a pastry wheel. Preboil the squares in a large amount of salted boiling water for two seconds. Transfer the pasta to a large bowl of cold water to which 2 tablespoons of the oil have been added. Cool the pasta, then place between wet cotton dish towels. When all the pasta squares are on the wet towels, add the cheese to the stuffing and gently mix all the ingredients. Use the remaining olive oil to heavily grease a 13½-by-8¾-inch glass baking pan. Place a heaping tablespoon of the stuffing in the center of a pasta square, fold over the 2 scalloped sides, and gently press the ends closed. Put the prepared *crusetto* in the baking dish. Repeat procedure with more pasta squares until the bottom of the pan is completely covered. Pour half the reserved tomato sauce over the *crusetti*, then finish stuffing the remaining pasta squares. Make 1 or more additional layers and pour the remaining sauce over the top. Cover the baking dish with aluminum foil and bake for 35 minutes. Remove from the oven, let rest for a few minutes, then remove the foil and serve.

SERVES 6 TO 8

FOR THE SAUCE/STUFFING

1 large red onion, peeled

3 medium-sized stalks celery

20 large sprigs Italian parsley, leaves only

½ cup olive oil

2 pounds ripe, fresh tomatoes; or 2 pounds canned tomatoes, preferably imported Italian, drained

1 pound boneless beef roast, such as top round or sirloin, in 1 piece

Salt and freshly ground black pepper

2 pounds small zucchini (not miniature)

1 quart vegetable oil

¼ cup olive oil

3 tablespoons freshly grated *pecorino romano* or *pecorino sardo* cheese

FOR THE PASTA

2 cups unbleached all-purpose flour

4 extra-large egg yolks

⅓ cup cold water

Pinch of salt

TO COOK THE PASTA

Coarse-grained salt

2 tablespoons vegetable or olive oil

flavore

d pastas

It is difficult to say when the idea first occurred to flavor or color pasta by adding ingredients—usually a vegetable or herb—to the dough itself; but several traditional colored or flavored pastas have been around for quite a while. The most popular, of course, is the green pasta created by adding chopped spinach to the dough. This classic method produces a beautifully flecked, irregular color, unlike the uniform green resulting from the commercial method in which green coloring is sometimes used. Made into *tagliatelle*, *taglierini*, and other long types, and combined with regular fresh pasta, this method produces the popular dish *Paglia e fieno*, or Straw and Hay.

Red pasta colored with beets is more common in the north. Red pasta is sometimes combined with yellow and green pasta to approximate the three colors of the Italian flag; and the mixture is, in fact, referred to as *tricolore*, or sometimes *arlecchino*, after Harlequin, the commedia dell'arte character who wears a costume of such colors. Red pasta is also often colored with tomato paste. An example follows in the Red Pasta with Onion-Flavored Pesto, in which the sauce is a Sicilian basil pesto to which uncooked onion and fresh hot green pepper are added. *Tagliatelle alla pizzaiola* is an interesting example from the Veneto, in which the full *pizzaiola* sauce is put into the well of the dough with the eggs. The lightly tomato-flavored pasta is then dressed with a simpler tomato sauce, melted butter, and fresh basil.

Adding saffron to the pasta dough gives it not only a bright yellow color but also a different flavor and texture. Saffron *tagliatelle* may be dressed with an *ossobuco* sauce; it also appears here in the more elaborate and fancy Pasta Timbale with Braised Veal.

A unique recipe, *Lasagne* with Paprika Pasta, from a border area of Emilia-Romagna, gives food for speculation. Uniquely associated with Hungary, paprika was developed from chilies brought from the New World; trade in the powder continued with shippers from the Italian maritime cities. One wonders at which point paprika became the cheaper substitute for saffron in this small area. It is also possible that paprika entered through the Hapsburg influence from adjoining Tuscan border areas, which were ruled by a Hapsburg dynasty after the Medici. Tuscany itself does not have this paprika pasta so it is likely it entered with the Venetians or the Genoese merchants during an earlier period. The pasta itself is remarkably good in its classic combination with the rich Bolognese *ragù*.

pasta rossa con pesto alla ragusana

RED PASTA WITH ONION-FLAVORED PESTO

SERVES 6 TO 8

FOR THE PASTA

3 ½ cups unbleached all-purpose flour

3 extra-large eggs

3 tablespoons tomato paste

Pinch of salt

4 twists black pepper

FOR THE SAUCE

1 small red onion, peeled

½ to 1 small, fresh green hot pepper (jalapeño may be used), seeds and membranes removed

3 cups fresh basil leaves, loosely packed

¾ cup olive oil

Salt and freshly ground black pepper

TO COOK THE PASTA

Coarse-grained salt

Prepare the pasta with the ingredients and quantities listed, following the directions on page 12, placing the tomato paste in the well with the other ingredients. Cut the pasta into fresh *spaghetti* as directed on page 59, and let rest on cotton dish towels until needed.

Prepare the sauce. Grind with mortar and pestle or finely chop the onion, hot pepper, and basil all together on a board. Transfer to a crockery or glass bowl and begin adding the oil, constantly stirring with a wooden spoon until the oil is completely incorporated. Season with salt and pepper, cover the bowl, and refrigerate until needed. (If using a blender or food processor, finely grind the onion and pepper first, then add the basil and oil, and grind again.)

Bring a large pot of cold water to a boil, add coarse salt to taste, then add the pasta and cook for 1 to 3 minutes depending on dryness. Drain the pasta; transfer to a large, warmed serving platter, add the sauce, mix well, and serve (without cheese).

NOTE

The sauce can be prepared as much as a week in advance and kept in the refrigerator.

Tropea onions, the basic red onions from southern Italy.

pasta in forma

PASTA TIMBALE WITH BRAISED VEAL

SERVES 8 TO 10

FOR THE SAFFRON PASTA

3 cups unbleached all-purpose flour

4 extra-large eggs

½ teaspoon ground saffron

Pinch of salt

TO COOK THE PASTA

Coarse-grained salt

2 tablespoons olive oil or vegetable oil

FOR THE VEAL SPEZ-ZATINO STUFFING

1 medium-sized carrot, scraped

1 medium-sized red onion, peeled

1 large stalk celery

4 ounces *prosciutto* or *pancetta*

¼ cup olive oil

2 tablespoons (1 ounce) sweet butter

2 pounds boneless veal shoulder, cut into 1-inch cubes

½ cup dry white wine

Salt and freshly ground black pepper

Prepare the pasta with the ingredients and quantities listed, placing the saffron in the flour well along with the eggs and salt, following the directions on page 12. Stretch the pasta dough to ¹⁄₁₆ inch thick—on the pasta machine, take it to the notch before the last setting —and cut into *tagliatelle* (see page 34). Then let rest on floured cotton dish towels for 30 minutes before cooking.

Bring a large pot of cold water to a boil, add coarse salt to taste, then add the pasta and partially cook it for 30 seconds to 1 minute depending on dryness. Undercook the pasta slightly—it will cook more while baking. Drain the pasta and place it in a bowl of cold water with the oil and let cool. Drain the pasta again and lay it out between dampened cotton dish towels to rest until needed.

Prepare the veal *spezzatino*. Finely chop the carrot, onion, celery, and *prosciutto* all together on a board. Place the oil and butter in a heavy, medium-sized flameproof casserole over medium heat, and when the butter is melted, add the chopped ingredients and sauté for 5 minutes. Put in the veal, stir well, and sauté for 5 minutes more. Add the wine and let it evaporate for 5 minutes. Season with salt and pepper, then add the tomato paste and 1 cup of the broth. Simmer, covered, for 45 minutes, stirring every so often with a wooden spoon and adding more broth if needed.

As the *spezzatino* cooks, prepare the sauce. Melt the butter in a heavy, medium-sized saucepan over low heat. Coarsely chop the truffle on a board and add it to the melted butter. Add the flour, mix very well until it is all incorporated, then slowly add 1 cup of the heavy cream, continuously stirring with a wooden spoon. Simmer for 5 minutes, then season with salt and pepper, and transfer the sauce to a crockery or glass bowl. Butter a piece of waxed paper, press it down over the sauce, and let rest until cool, about 30 minutes.

Preheat the oven to 375°F. Mix the cooled sauce with the egg yolks and Parmigiano, and taste for salt and pepper. Transfer to a large mixing bowl, add the pasta and the remaining cup of cream, and mix gently but thoroughly. With half the butter and all the bread crumbs, butter and dust a 3-quart ring mold. Prepare a large baking dish as a water bath (*bagnomaria*) by placing several layers of paper towels in the pan along with a wedge of lemon. Half-fill the pan with hot water. Fill the mold with pasta and sauce, dotting with bits of the remaining butter throughout. Place mold in the prepared water bath and bake for 30 minutes. Remove the mold from the oven and let rest for 2 minutes.

Meanwhile, reheat the veal *spezzatino*. Unmold the pasta onto a large, round serving platter. Spoon the veal pieces into the center of the ring and pour the cooking liquid into a sauceboat. Serve each portion of pasta with several pieces of veal and a little sauce on the side.

2 tablespoons tomato paste

1 to 2 cups lukewarm chicken or beef broth, preferably homemade

FOR THE SAUCE

6 tablespoons (3 ounces) sweet butter

½ ounce fresh or canned black truffle

2 tablespoons unbleached all-purpose flour

2 cups heavy cream

Salt and freshly ground black pepper

4 extra-large egg yolks

½ cup freshly grated Parmigiano

TO BAKE

4 tablespoons (2 ounces) sweet butter

4 tablespoons unseasoned bread crumbs, preferably homemade

1 wedge of lemon

lasagne con paprika
LASAGNE WITH PAPRIKA PASTA

SERVES 8

FOR THE SAUCE (RAGÙ ALLA BOLOGNESE)

1 medium-sized red onion, peeled

1 medium-sized carrot, scraped

1 large stalk celery

3 ounces *pancetta* or *prosciutto*, in 1 piece, then cut into cubes

6 ounces lean boneless beef, in cubes

6 ounces boneless pork, in cubes

4 tablespoons (2 ounces) sweet butter

2 tablespoons olive oil

1 pound ripe, fresh tomatoes; or 1 pound canned tomatoes, preferably imported Italian, drained

½ cup dry white wine

Salt and freshly ground black pepper

Pinch of freshly grated nutmeg

¾ cup lukewarm beef broth, preferably homemade

¾ cup heavy cream

Prepare the sauce. Finely chop the onion, carrot, and celery on a board. Coarsely grind the *pancetta*, beef, and pork all together in a meat grinder or mince with a knife. Heat the butter and oil in a heavy, flameproof casserole of terra cotta, lined copper, or enameled iron over medium heat. When the oil mixture is warm, add the chopped vegetables and the ground meats, and sauté for 10 minutes, stirring every so often with a wooden spoon.

If using fresh tomatoes, cut into pieces. Press fresh or canned tomatoes through a food mill, using the disc with smallest holes, into a crockery or glass bowl. Add the wine to the casserole and let it evaporate for 5 minutes. Add the strained tomatoes and simmer for 20 minutes. Season to taste with salt, pepper, and nutmeg, then add the broth, cover the casserole, and simmer for 45 minutes, stirring every so often with a wooden spoon. Add the cream, mix very well, lower the heat, and reduce for 20 minutes; for the last 5 minutes, remove the lid from the casserole. Remove the sauce from the heat and let rest until cool, about 1 hour.

Prepare the pasta with the ingredients and quantities listed, placing the paprika in the flour well with the eggs and salt, following the directions on page 12. Stretch the pasta dough to about 1/16 inch thick—on the pasta machine, take it to the next to the last setting. Cut the sheet into squares and place on cotton dish towels.

Precook the pasta squares in salted boiling water for 10 seconds after the water returns to a boil, then transfer to a large bowl of cold water with the oil added. When all the squares have been precooked, place them in a single layer on dampened cotton dish towels. Preheat the oven to 375°F.

To assemble the dish, use 1 tablespoon of the butter to heavily coat a 13½-by-8¾-inch glass baking dish. Fit in enough pasta squares to cover the bottom of the dish, but not the sides. Lightly cover this layer with about

5 tablespoons of the sauce, and sprinkle some of the grated cheese over the sauce. Keep alternating layers of pasta with sauce and cheese. The top layer should be sauce and cheese; cut the remaining 3 tablespoons of butter into pats and spread out all over the top. Bake for 35 minutes. Remove the dish from the oven and let rest for 5 minutes before serving.

FOR THE PASTA

4 cups unbleached all-purpose flour

5 extra-large eggs

2 teaspoons sweet paprika

Pinch of salt

TO COOK THE PASTA

Coarse-grained salt

2 tablespoons vegetable or olive oil

TO BAKE

4 tablespoons (2 ounces) sweet butter

¾ cup freshly grated Parmigiano

From left to right: vegetables cut into pieces, coarsley chopped, and minced.

tagliatelle alla pizzaiola
PIZZAIOLA TAGLIATELLE WITH TOMATO SAUCE

SERVES 8

FOR THE PASTA FLAVORING

2 large cloves garlic, peeled

4 tablespoons olive oil

½ pound ripe, fresh tomatos; or ½ pound canned tomatoes, preferably imported Italian, drained

1 teaspoon salt

½ teaspoon freshly ground black pepper

1 teaspoon dried oregano

FOR THE SAUCE

1 ½ pounds ripe, fresh tomatoes; or 1 ½ pounds canned tomatoes, preferably imported Italian, drained

Salt and freshly ground black pepper

FOR THE PASTA

3 ½ cups unbleached all-purpose flour

2 extra-large eggs

TO COOK THE PASTA

Coarse-grained salt

PLUS

8 tablespoons (4 ounces) sweet butter

10 large fresh basil leaves, torn into thirds

Begin the pasta. Make the *pizzaiola* flavoring by coarsely chopping the garlic on a board. Place the oil in a small nonreactive saucepan over medium heat, and when the oil is warm, add the garlic and gently sauté for 3 minutes. Add the tomatoes, salt, black pepper, and oregano to the pan, mix, and simmer for 15 minutes.

Begin the sauce. Place the tomatoes in a large, nonreactive saucepan over medium heat and simmer for 30 minutes, stirring every so often.

When the *pizzaiola* flavoring for the pasta is cooked, pass it through a food mill, using the disc with the smallest holes, into a second small saucepan. Return the pan to medium heat and reduce for 10 minutes, then transfer to a crockery or glass bowl and set aside until cool, about 30 minutes. By that time the mixture should be very thick.

Finish the sauce. Pass the cooked tomatoes through a food mill, using the disc with the smallest holes, into a second saucepan and return the pan to medium heat. Season with salt and pepper and reduce for 15 minutes, stirring every so often.

Prepare the pasta with the ingredients and quantities listed, placing the thick flavoring and eggs in the well of the flour mound and following the directions on page 12. Cut into *tagliatelle* (see page 34).

Bring a large pot of cold water to a boil over medium heat. Place the butter in a large serving dish and put it over the pot as a lid. Reheat the tomato sauce. When the water reaches a boil, add coarse salt, then add the *tagliatelle* and cook for 30 to 45 seconds. depending on dryness. Ladle half the sauce onto the serving dish. Drain the pasta and add it to the dish. Pour the remaining tomato sauce over the top, sprinkle with the basil, toss gently but thoroughly and serve immediately.

puréed vegetable–flavored

Certain puréed vegetables can be successfully added to pasta dough for both flavor and color. Those that work best are bell peppers, artichokes, and green tomatoes all producing various shades of green pasta. Red peppers produce their own color.

Green pepper pasta served with a sauce made from red bell peppers is a combination made in heaven, and included here are two recipes using that combination. In the first and simpler version, the pasta is cut into *spaghetti*, which adds a thickness suitable for this texture. Garlic is puréed into the dough along with the peppers, and its flavor is repeated in the sauce. The red of the peppers is reinforced with some tomato in the sauce, and parsley is added. Black pepper flavors both the pasta and the sauce.

The more elaborate dish is the *lasagne* employing the same pasta and sauce, but layered also with *balsamella* and baked. The *spaghetti* is served without grated cheese—only with additional fresh parsley—while the *lasagne* incorporates Parmigiano into its layers.

From the Veneto we have pasta in which a thick artichoke purée is incorporated into the dough; it is served with a simple sauce of melted butter and sage, and finished with grated Parmigiano.

A great deal of experimentation is going on adding ingredients to flavor pasta dough. Many times these creations are not always very well thought out, and are not based on an understanding of basic principles. If we are lucky, some new ideas will emerge that are really valid. Ponder why the successful flavors do work; use that understanding to choose new possibilities.

lasagne di peperoni

GREEN AND RED PEPPER LASAGNE

FOR THE PASTA

2 medium-sized green bell peppers

2 medium-sized cloves garlic, peeled

5 ¼ cups unbleached all-purpose flour

3 extra-large eggs

1 tablespoon olive or vegetable oil

Pinch of salt

4 or 5 twists black pepper

TO COOK THE PASTA

Coarse-grained salt

2 tablespoons olive or vegetable oil

FOR THE PEPPER-TOMATO SAUCE

2 medium-sized red bell peppers

15 large sprigs Italian parsley, leaves only

¾ cup olive oil

2 medium-sized cloves garlic, peeled

2 pounds ripe, fresh tomatoes; or 2 pounds canned tomatoes, preferably imported Italian, drained

Salt and freshly ground black pepper

Prepare the pasta. Remove the stems, pulp, and seeds from the green peppers, then cut them into small pieces. Use a food processor or blender to finely grind the peppers and garlic together. Prepare the pasta with the ingredients and quantities listed, placing 5 ounces of the pepper-garlic mixture in the flour well together with the other ingredients, following the directions on page 12. Stretch the dough to a thickness of $\frac{1}{16}$ inch—on the pasta machine, take it to the next to last setting. (Do not try to use the thinnest setting because the pasta will break.) Cut the sheet into squares of about 6 inches and place on wet cotton dish towels.

Precook the pasta squares in salted boiling water for 10 seconds after the water returns to a boil, then transfer to a large bowl of cold water with the vegetable oil. Let these squares of pasta rest on wet cotton dish towels until needed.

Prepare the pepper-tomato sauce. Remove the stems, pulp, and seeds from the red peppers and cut them into small pieces. Coarsely chop the parsley. Place the oil in a heavy nonreactive saucepan over medium heat; when the oil is warm, add the peppers and garlic and sauté for 5 minutes. If using fresh tomatoes, cut them into quarters. Add fresh or canned tomatoes to the pan along with the chopped parsley. Cover and cook for 25 minutes, stirring every so often with a wooden spoon and tasting for salt and pepper. Pass the contents of the pan through a food mill, using the disc with the smallest holes, and return it to the saucepan to cook until the sauce is smooth, 15 minutes more. Taste again for salt and pepper, then transfer the sauce to a crockery bowl to cool for 1 hour.

Make the *balsamella*. Melt the butter in a heavy, medium-sized saucepan over low heat. When the butter bubbles, mix in the flour. Remove from the heat for 15 seconds, then return to low heat and add the milk all at once, stirring until smooth. Bring to a boil, then lower the heat and simmer for 10 minutes, stirring constantly. Season with salt and pepper, and transfer to a large bowl. Press a sheet of buttered waxed paper onto the surface of the sauce to prevent a skin from forming. Let cool to room temperature.

Preheat the oven to 375°F. To assemble the dish, butter a 13 ½-by-8 ¾-inch glass baking dish. Fit in enough squares of to allow about 1 inch to hang over the edge all around (see page 138). Cover this bottom layer with one-third of the *balsamella* and sprinkle one-third of the Parmigiano on top. Add another layer of pasta just to cover the *balsamella* and Parmigiano, not to hang over. Cover this pasta with about 6 tablespoons of the cooled pepper-tomato sauce. Alternate pasta layers and sauce in the same way 3 more times. Over the top layer of pasta, place another third of the *balsamella* and another third of the Parmigiano. Then make 4 more layers of pasta and sauce, using up all the remaining sauce. Over this last layer of pasta, spread the remaining *balsamella* and Parmigiano, covering these with a final layer of 3 squares of pasta. Pick up the ends of the bottom layer of pasta hanging over the edges of the baking dish and fold them in over the top layer of pasta squares. Bake for 25 minutes. The top layer should emerge lightly golden and crisp. Remove the dish from the oven and allow to cool for 5 minutes. Serve from the baking dish, slicing the *lasagne* with a knife and lifting out each portion with a spatula.

FOR THE BALSAMELLA

8 tablespoons (4 ounces) sweet butter

½ cup unbleached all-purpose flour

3 ½ cups milk

Salt and freshly ground black pepper

TO BAKE

1 cup freshly grated Parmigiano

spaghetti di peperoni

SWEET BELL PEPPER SPAGHETTI

SERVES 4 TO 6

FOR THE PASTA

1 medium-sized green
   bell pepper

1 medium-sized clove garlic,
   peeled

2 ¾ cups unbleached all-
   purpose flour

2 extra-large eggs

2 teaspoons olive or
   vegetable oil

Pinch of salt

5 twists black pepper

FOR THE SAUCE

1 large red bell pepper

5 large sprigs Italian parsley,
   leaves only

1 medium-sized clove garlic,
   peeled

1 ½ pounds ripe, fresh
   tomatoes; or 1 ½ pounds
   canned tomatoes,
   preferably imported
   Italian, drained

¼ cup olive oil

Salt and freshly ground
   black pepper

TO COOK THE PASTA

Coarse-grained salt

TO SERVE

15 large sprigs Italian
   parsley, leaves only,
   coarsely chopped

Remove the stem, pulp, and seeds from the green pepper, then cut it into small pieces. Place the garlic and pepper in a blender or food processor and finely purée. Weigh out 3 ounces of the mixture, discarding the rest.

Prepare the pasta with the ingredients and quantities listed, placing the pepper-garlic mixture in the flour well together with the eggs, oil, salt, and pepper, following the directions on page 12. Stretch the sheet to about ⅛ inch thick—on the pasta machine, take it to several notches before the last setting—then cut into *spaghetti* (see page 59), and let rest on cotton dish towels until needed.

Prepare the sauce. Remove the stem, pulp, and seeds from the red pepper and cut it into small pieces. Coarsely chop the parsley together with the garlic on a board. If using fresh tomatoes, cut them into pieces. Heat the oil in a small nonre-active saucepan over medium heat, and when it is warm, put in the pepper pieces and sauté for 5 minutes. Add the chopped ingredients along with the fresh or canned tomatoes. Cover the pan and cook for 30 minutes, stirring every so often with a wooden spoon. Taste for salt and pepper, then pass the contents of the pan through a food mill, using the disc with the smallest holes, and return the strained sauce to the pan. Cook for 15 minutes over medium heat, uncovered. By that time, the sauce should be smooth.

Bring a large pot of cold water to a boil, add coarse salt to taste, then add the pasta and cook for 1 to 3 minutes depending on dryness. Pour 1 ladleful of the sauce onto a warmed serving dish, drain the pasta, and arrange it over the sauce. Pour the remaining sauce over the pasta, toss well, and serve immediately, sprinkling the chopped parsley on top.

pasta di carciofi
ARTICHOKE PASTA

Prepare the artichoke base. Place the artichokes in a bowl of cold water, squeeze the lemon halves over the bowl and drop them in, and let soak for 30 minutes. Meanwhile, coarsely chop the parsley and garlic together on a board. Clean the artichokes following the instructions on page 70, and cut them into eighths. Place the artichokes back in the water with the lemon until needed.

Place the oil in a heavy medium-sized casserole, preferably of terra cotta or enamel, over medium heat; when the oil is warm, add the chopped ingredients and sauté for 2 minutes. Drain the artichokes, add them to the casserole, and sauté for 5 more minutes. Add the wine, raise the heat to high, and cook for 10 minutes. Season with salt and pepper, lower the heat, cover the casserole, and cook until the artichokes are very tender, about 15 more minutes, stirring every so often with a wooden spoon.

Pass the contents of the casserole through a food mill, using the disc with the smallest holes, into a second flameproof casserole. Place the puréed artichokes over low heat and cook for 2 or 3 minutes to let all the liquid evaporate, stirring constantly with a wooden spoon. Transfer the artichoke base to a crockery or glass bowl, and let rest until completely cold, about 1 hour.

Prepare the pasta with the ingredients and quantities listed, placing the artichoke purée in the well of the flour with the eggs and more salt and pepper to taste, following the directions on page 12. Make the sheet of pasta a little thicker than for usual *tagliatelle*, about $\frac{1}{16}$ inch thick—on the pasta machine, take it to the next to last setting. Cut into *tagliatelle* (see page 34), and let rest on cotton towels until needed.

Bring a large pot of cold water to a boil, add coarse salt to taste, then add the pasta and cook for 1 to 3 minutes depending on dryness. As the pasta cooks, place a small saucepan with the butter over medium heat, and when the butter is melted, put in the sage leaves and sauté for 1 minute. Season to taste with salt and pepper. Drain the pasta; transfer to a large, warmed, serving platter, pour the sauce over, and sprinkle with the Parmigiano, if used; toss very well and serve.

SERVES 8 TO 10

FOR THE ARTICHOKE BASE

- 3 large artichokes (yields almost 2 pounds cleaned)
- 1 large lemon, cut in half
- 15 large sprigs Italian parsley, leaves only
- 3 large cloves garlic, peeled
- ¼ cup olive oil
- 1 cup dry white wine
- Salt and freshly ground black pepper

FOR THE PASTA

- 5 ½ cups unbleached all-purpose flour
- 3 extra-large eggs
- Salt and freshly ground black pepper

TO COOK THE PASTA

- Coarse-grained salt

FOR THE SAUCE

- 12 tablespoons (6 ounces) sweet butter
- 15 large fresh sage leaves
- Salt and freshly ground black pepper

TO SERVE

- ¾ cup freshly grated Parmigiano (optional)

wild mushroom- and truffle-flavored

Dried wild mushrooms, specifically *porcini*, easily impart their remarkable fragrance to pasta when soaked, puréed with garlic and parsley, and added to the pasta dough. The resulting pasta should be cooked in water to which has been added some of the mushroom soaking water to reinforce the flavor. Only melted butter and the special wild mint called *nipitella*, or *mentuccia*, are used to flavor the dish, but if the herb is unavailable, a clove of garlic can be used instead. Common mint is not a reasonable substitute.

Black truffle paste added to pasta dough produces a pasta with little black flecks. The pasta is best enhanced by butter, cream, nutmeg, and, if you wish, some grated Parmigiano. These simple *tagliatelle* are, however, a most rare dish because of the prized truffle flavoring.

tagliatelle al tartufo

BLACK TRUFFLE TAGLIATELLE IN CREAM SAUCE

Make the pasta using the ingredients and quantities listed, following the directions on page 12, placing the truffle paste in the well of flour together with the other ingredients. Stretch the sheet of pasta to less than ⅟₁₆ inch thick—on the pasta machine, take it to the last setting. Cut into *tagliatelle* (see page 34). Let the pasta rest on cotton dish towels until needed.

Bring a large pot of cold water to a boil over medium heat. Place a flameproof casserole with the butter over the pot.

When the water reaches a boil, lift off the casserole, add coarse salt to the water, then add the pasta and cook it for a 5 to 30 seconds, depending on dryness. Meanwhile, place the casserole containing the butter over very low heat. Drain the pasta well and add it to the casserole, pour the cream over, toss very well, and season with salt, pepper, and nutmeg. When the cream is incorporated, transfer the pasta to a warmed serving platter and serve immediately. Sprinkle with cheese, if desired.

SERVES 6

FOR THE PASTA

3 cups unbleached all-purpose flour

3 extra-large eggs

3 teaspoons black truffle paste

3 teaspoons vegetable or olive oil

Pinch of salt

FOR THE SAUCE

12 tablespoons (6 ounces) sweet butter

1 cup heavy cream

Salt and freshly grated black pepper

Freshly grated nutmeg

6 tablespoons freshly grated Parmigiano (optional)

TO COOK THE PASTA

Coarse-grained salt

spaghetti ai funghi
WILD MUSHROOM SPAGHETTI

SERVES 6 TO 8

FOR THE MUSHROOM BASE

1 ounce dried *porcini* mushrooms

5 cups lukewarm water

2 large cloves garlic, peeled

15 large sprigs Italian parsley, leaves only

5 tablespoons olive oil

Salt and freshly ground black pepper

FOR THE PASTA

4 cups unbleached all-purpose flour

2 extra-large eggs

TO COOK THE PASTA

Coarse-grained salt

FOR THE SAUCE

12 tablespoons (6 ounces) sweet butter

1 heaping tablespoon *nipitella* or *mentuccia* (wild mint); or 1 large clove garlic, peeled

Salt and freshly ground black pepper

TO SERVE

15 large sprigs Italian parsley, leaves only

Freshly ground black pepper

Soak the mushrooms in a small crockery or glass bowl with the lukewarm water for 1 hour. Drain the mushrooms, saving the soaking water. Clean them very well, removing the sand attached to the stems. Clean the water by pouring it through a strainer lined with several layers of paper towels into a second bowl. Finely chop the mushrooms, garlic, and parsley on a board, transfer to a crockery or glass bowl, add the oil, and mix very well. (If using a food processor, grind all the ingredients together along with the oil.) Place a small saucepan with the mushroom mixture and 1 cup of the mushroom water over low heat. Season with abundant salt and pepper because none will be added later to the flour. Simmer for 30 minutes, stirring every so often with a wooden spoon. Remove the pan from the heat and let rest until completely cooled, about 1 hour.

Prepare the pasta with the ingredients and quantities listed, placing the mushroom base in the well of the flour with the other ingredients, following the directions on page 12. Stretch the sheet to about ⅛ inch thick—on the pasta machine, take it to several notches before the last setting. Prepare *spaghetti* following the instructions on page 59. Let the pasta rest on cotton towels until needed.

Coarsely chop the parsley on a board. Add the remaining mushroom water to a large pot of cold water and put it over medium heat. When the water reaches a boil, add coarse salt to taste, then add the pasta and cook for 1 to 3 minutes, depending on dryness. As the pasta cooks, melt the butter over low heat, add the *nipitella*, *mentuccia* (wild mint) or garlic and salt and pepper to taste; sauté until the pasta is ready. Drain the pasta and transfer to a large, warmed serving platter. If garlic has been used, discard it. Pour the sauce over the top and sprinkle on the parsley, toss very well, and serve. To each serving, add 1 or 2 twists of black pepper.

herb–flavored

The herbs preferred to flavor pasta are rosemary, as we see in the Chick-pea Pasta, and parsley or sage. In Sage Pasta, sage leaves are torn into tiny pieces and placed in the well with the eggs and black pepper. The cooked pasta is put on a bed of melted butter and grated Parmigiano, and the individual servings are sprinkled with additional Parmigiano and pepper. If the sage is fresh rather than dried or preserved in salt, a whole sage leaf is added to each serving.

Parsley Pasta, with whole leaves showing through sheets of dough and resembling a tapestry, is one of my proudest rediscoveries. My own enthusiasm for it, which began when I introduced it several years ago, has been met by that of many chefs, among them practitioners of "nouvelle cuisine," who love its striking visual appeal. (See my book *Giuliano Bugialli's Foods of Italy*.)

pasta di ceci al rosmarino
CHICK-PEA PASTA

FOR THE PASTA

2 tablespoons rosemary leaves, fresh or preserved in salt or dried and blanched

3 medium-sized cloves garlic, peeled

5 teaspoons olive oil

2 ¼ cups unbleached all-purpose flour

½ cup chick-pea flour (see Note)

3 extra-large eggs

1 teaspoon salt

10 twists black pepper

FOR THE SAUCE

6 ounces *pancetta* or *prosciutto*, in 1 piece

6 tablespoons olive oil

TO COOK THE PASTA

Coarse-grained salt

The Chick-pea Pasta is made from a combination of chick-pea flour and wheat flour. Dried chick-peas produce a fine flour, which of course needs the gluten of wheat to hold together in a pasta; but the chick-pea flavor dominates and mixes well with the flavors of rosemary and garlic, which are also chopped and placed in the well with the eggs. To keep the chick-pea and rosemary flavors, a simple sauce of oil with pancetta *or* prosciutto *is generally matched with this pasta.*

This pasta could be served even with a very light tomato sauce or just good uncooked olive oil.

Prepare the pasta. Finely chop the rosemary leaves and garlic together on a board. Transfer to a small crockery or glass bowl, add the oil, and mix very well. Make a mound of the all-purpose flour. Shape a well in the center and place the chopped mixture in the well along with the chick-pea flour, eggs, salt, and pepper. Combine the ingredients and knead well, following the directions on page 12. Immediately stretch the sheet to less than ¹⁄₁₆ inch thick—on the pasta machine, take it to the last setting. Cut into *tagliatelle* (see page 34).

Prepare the sauce. Cut the *pancetta* into cubes less than ½ inch thick. Place the oil and *pancetta* in a small saucepan over medium heat and sauté until the meat is crisp, about 15 minutes. Set aside.

Bring a large pot of cold water to a boil. When the water reaches a boil, add coarse salt to taste, then add the pasta. Stir and cook the pasta for 40 seconds to 1 minute depending on dryness. Drain; transfer the pasta to a large, warmed serving platter, pour the sauce over the top, mix gently but thoroughly, and serve immediately.

NOTE

Chick-pea flour is available at Italian (especially Sicilian) or Indian groceries; the Indian stores have both toasted and regular chick-pea flour, so be sure to get the regular.

pasta alla salvia
SAGE PASTA

Prepare the pasta with the ingredients and quantities listed, placing the sage pieces in the flour well along with the eggs, salt, and pepper, following the directions on page 12. Stretch the sheet to about ⅟₁₆ inch thick—on the pasta machine, take it to the next to the last setting. Cut into *tagliatelle* (see page 34) and let rest on a cotton dish towel until needed.

Bring a large pot of cold water to a boil over medium heat, and place a large serving dish with the butter over the pot in order to melt the butter. When the water reaches a boil and the butter is melted, remove the dish, add coarse salt to the water, then add the pasta and cook for 1 to 3 minutes depending on dryness. Drain the pasta, transfer it to the prepared dish, sprinkle with the Parmigiano, mix well, and serve immediately. Over each portion, grind some black pepper, add 1 tablespoon grated Parmigiano, and place a whole fresh sage leaf on top.

SERVES 4 TO 6

FOR THE PASTA

2 cups unbleached all-purpose flour

3 extra-large eggs

Pinch of salt

½ teaspoon freshly ground black pepper

25 large sage leaves, fresh or preserved in salt, stems removed and leaves torn into small pieces

FOR THE SAUCE

8 tablespoons (4 ounces) sweet butter

¼ cup freshly grated Parmigiano

TO COOK THE PASTA

Coarse-grained salt

TO SERVE

Freshly ground black pepper

4 to 6 tablespoons freshly grated Parmigiano

4 to 6 large fresh sage leaves

Fresh rosemary, a staple in Italy.

pepper–flavored

Black pepper has been prized as flavoring for many centuries, and indeed at one time was the basis for great trading activities across the seas. In the Middle Ages and Renaissance, pepper sometimes formed the principal seasoning for a dish; so much pepper was used that its particular flavor as well as its spiciness became central to many dishes. A few such dishes still survive in the Italian repertory, one of which is the fresh pasta that follows, made with abundant black pepper in the dough itself. A simple tomato sauce and fresh parsley are enough to dress it and allow the pepper to reign.

A regional pasta is made in Pistoia, in Tuscany, which incorporates hot red pepper, dried and ground with a mortar and pestle, into the dough itself. The dough is formed into *tagliatelle* and very simply dressed with olive oil and fresh parsley.

pasta con pepe nero

BLACK PEPPER PASTA

Prepare the pepper pasta using the ingredients and quantities listed, placing the ground pepper in the flour well together with the eggs and salt, following the directions on page 12. Stretch the sheet to about ⅟₁₆ inch thick—on the pasta machine, take it to the next to the last setting, and cut it into *tagliatelle* (see page 34). Let the *tagliatelle* rest on cotton towels until needed.

If using fresh tomatoes, cut them into pieces. Place fresh or canned tomatoes, garlic, and oil in a medium-sized nonreactive saucepan, and cook over medium heat for 15 minutes. Taste for salt and pepper. Pass the contents of the pan through a food mill, using the disc with the smallest holes, into a medium-sized crockery or glass bowl. Return the strained tomatoes to the saucepan and reduce the sauce over low heat for 5 minutes.

Bring a large pot of cold water to a boil, add coarse salt to taste, then add the pasta and cook for 1 to 3 minutes depending on dryness. When the pasta is ready, drain and transfer it to a warmed serving dish, pour the sauce over the top, and sprinkle with the parsley. Toss very well and serve immediately. No cheese should be served with this dish.

SERVES 4 TO 6

FOR THE PASTA

3 cups unbleached all-purpose flour

4 extra-large eggs

1 tablespoon coarsely ground black pepper

Pinch of salt

FOR THE SAUCE

1 pound ripe, fresh tomatoes; or 1 pound canned tomatoes, preferably imported Italian, drained

1 medium-sized clove garlic, peeled

½ cup olive oil

Salt and freshly ground black pepper

TO COOK THE PASTA

Coarse-grained salt

TO SERVE

25 large sprigs Italian parsley, leaves only

fiocchetti al pomodoro
"PINCHED" LEMON-FLAVORED PASTA

SERVES 4 TO 6

FOR THE PASTA

2 large lemons with thick skins

½ teaspoon freshly grated nutmeg

3 extra-large eggs

Pinch of salt

2 ¼ cups unbleached all-purpose flour

FOR THE SAUCE

1 ½ pounds ripe, fresh tomatoes; or 1 ½ pounds canned tomatoes, preferably imported Italian, drained

2 medium-sized cloves garlic, peeled

5 large basil leaves, fresh or preserved in salt

¼ cup olive oil

Salt and freshly ground black pepper

TO COOK THE PASTA

Coarse-grained salt

The use of grated lemon in pasta, the Umbrian fiocchetti, *works because the pasta is not cut into thin ribbons; it is thicker and cut into diamonds, pinched to almost resemble little bows. The lemon is combined with nutmeg in the pasta dough, and most important, the sauce of tomato or meat provides balancing flavor that does not allow any bitterness to emerge from the oil of the lemon.*

Grate the lemons to obtain 2 tablespoons grated peel, and put it in a small bowl. Add the nutmeg, eggs, and salt, and mix the ingredients with a fork. Prepare the pasta with the ingredients listed, placing the lemon mixture in the flour well, following the directions on page 12. Stretch the pasta dough to ¹⁄₁₆ inch—on the pasta machine, take it to the next to the last setting. Use a scalloped pastry wheel to cut the sheet into diamonds with 2-inch sides. Use your thumb and index finger to pinch each diamond into a bow, then transfer them onto a cotton dish towel to rest until needed.

Prepare the sauce. If using fresh tomatoes, cut them into pieces. Place fresh or canned tomatoes in a nonreactive saucepan with the garlic, basil, and oil, and put the pan over medium heat to simmer for 15 minutes. Pass the contents of the pan through a food mill, using the disc with the smallest holes, into a crockery bowl. Return the tomatoes to the pan and reduce over medium heat for 5 minutes; season with salt and pepper.

Bring a large pot of cold water to a boil, add coarse salt to taste, then add the pasta and cook for 1 to 3 minutes depending on dryness. Reheat the sauce and, when pasta is ready, drain it, transfer to a large skillet, add the sauce, and incorporate it over medium heat for a few seconds. Transfer to a warmed serving dish and serve.

VARIATION

Instead of the tomato sauce, a meat sauce can be used.

PECORINO TOSCANO
20

pasta an

d cheese

The combination of pasta and cheese is used frequently in Italy, but it is even more popular in Italian cooking abroad.

Italy has so many flavorful cheeses that little by little they have found their way into pasta dishes during the twentieth century. Many cheeses are used almost exclusively in dishes of their own region, but Lombard dishes with *Gorgonzola, Taleggio,* or *mascarpone* cheeses have spread over much of Italy.

Here, I give a selection of pasta-and-cheese recipes that have only recently become classics. This is, naturally, a small assortment of recipes, but they include pasta dishes based on a variety of good Italian cheeses: Parmigiano reggiano, *Grana Padano,* buffalo milk mozzarella, *pecorino Toscano,* and *fontina.*

Parmigiano reggiano needs no explanation. The most famous *grana* (any cheese of a hard grainy texture), *Grana Padano,* was also developed by the Etruscans millennia ago. It is produced over a much larger region in the Po River Valley, the area above Parma, the province of Parmigiano production. A well-aged hard-crusted cheese, like Parmigiano, it is a part-skim-milk cheese; however, it is used as a dessert cheese as well as for grating. In its region, *Grana Padano* completely replaces Parmigiano.

Production of buffalo milk mozzarella, made from the milk of domesticated water buffalo, is now centered in the Salerno area, south of Naples, where cooks often prefer the *fior di latte* (the flower of the milk) type of mozzarella, made with cows' milk. However, the taste and texture of the buffalo milk version is generally preferred by the *conoscenti*.

It bears repetition that ricotta is not a cheese but is the primary example of a different category made from the second curd after the cheese is made. Ricotta is used not so much for flavoring, but as a binder, and Italians never refer to it as "ricotta cheese."

Pecorino cheese, made from sheep's milk, is produced in many parts of Italy, but it is a specialty of Tuscany, where cows' milk cheeses are not produced. *Pecorino* cheeses are eaten both young and aged, ranging from soft and creamy to hard and suitable for grating, with a wide variety in the middle. Different types of *pecorino Toscano* cheeses are produced throughout the region under different names: the *crete* variety from Siena, the *Pienza* type, *Maremma* type, and so on. *Pecorino Toscano*, uncooked, combines especially well with fresh fava beans or pears and honey, but it is also used frequently in cooking, either grated or shaved.

pasta cacio e pepe

PASTA WITH GRATED CHEESE AND BLACK PEPPER

SERVES 4 TO 6

1 pound dried *spaghetti* or *vermicelli*, preferably imported Italian

1 tablespoon olive oil

6 tablespoons (3 ounces) sweet butter

Salt

¾ cup freshly grated Parmigiano

Freshly ground black pepper

TO COOK THE PASTA

Coarse-grained salt

In earlier chapters, we have discussed categories of pasta with oil and garlic or bread crumbs. The third simple category is pasta with oil (or, in this case, butter) and abundant grated cheese or ricotta. This category is always flavored with much black pepper—enough to be mentioned in the name of the dish and to serve as the main aromatic ingredient in place of the garlic. Butter can be substituted for oil in this category (though not in the other two) because of its relation to the cheese.

Bring a large pot of cold water to a boil over medium heat, and, when the water reaches a boil, add coarse salt to taste, then add the pasta and cook it for 9 to 12 minutes depending on the brand. As the pasta cooks, heat the oil in a small saucepan over low heat; when the oil is warm, add the butter and let it melt completely but do not let it brown. Season to taste with salt.

When the pasta is ready, drain it and place on a warmed serving platter. Pour the hot oil and butter over the pasta, sprinkle with Parmigiano, and toss very well. Grind abundant black pepper over the top, toss again, and serve immediately.

More black pepper and cheese can be served at the table.

VARIATIONS

1. Omit olive oil and increase butter to 7 tablespoons.
2. Use 7 tablespoons of warmed olive oil and omit the butter.
3. Mix 2 ounces of ricotta with 2 tablespoons of oil or butter and 2 tablespoons of ricotta salata. Omit the grated Parmigiano, although some may be served at table. (The selection of a very good ricotta is essential. In Italy, I use sheep's milk or buffalo milk ricotta. Since these types are not widely available outside Italy, the readily available ricotta salata, often made of sheep's milk, can flavor the more common cows' milk ricotta.)

NOTE

I use mostly butter in this recipe, since I prefer it in combination with cheese in this very exposed form, rather than oil. Of course, oil is a legitimate option.

pennette alla mozzarella e pomodoro

SMALL PENNE WITH MOZZARELLA AND TOMATOES

Blanch the tomatoes in a small pot of salted boiling water, then remove the skins and seeds and cut them into large pieces. Bring a large pot of cold water to a boil, add coarse salt to taste, then add the pasta and cook it for 8 to 11 minutes depending on the brand; that is, 1 minute less than for normal al dente.

In the meantime, cook the tomatoes. Heat the oil in a large nonreactive skillet over medium heat and, when the oil is warm, add the tomatoes, and lightly sauté for 2 or 3 minutes. Tomatoes should be barely cooked and still in large pieces. Season with salt and pepper, add the basil leaves, and mix. Drain the pasta, add it to the skillet, mix very well, and sauté for less than 1 minute more.

Transfer to a large, warmed serving platter and sprinkle the Parmigiano all over. Cut the mozzarella into 1-inch cubes, then arrange them over the pasta. Serve immediately with the additional basil leaves on each serving.

SERVES 4 TO 6

- **1½ pounds fresh tomatoes, ripe but not overripe**
- **1 pound dried small *penne—pennette* or *pennine*—preferably imported Italian**
- **6 tablespoons extra-virgin olive oil**
- **Salt and freshly ground black pepper**
- **½ cup loosely packed basil leaves, stems removed**
- **6 tablespoons freshly grated Parmigiano**
- **4 ounces fresh mozzarella or buffalo milk mozzarella cheese, preferably imported Italian**

TO COOK THE PASTA

Coarse-grained salt

TO SERVE

Fresh basil leaves

Mozzarella and bocconcini.

zitoni ripieni

STUFFED ZITONI OR SHELLS

MAKES ABOUT 24 STUFFED ZITONI OR SHELLS

FOR THE STUFFING

4 ounces *prosciutto*

4 ounces fresh mozzarella or buffalo milk mozzarella cheese, preferably imported Italian

10 large sprigs Italian parsley, leaves only

4 ounces whole-milk ricotta

2 extra-large egg yolks

4 heaping tablespoons freshly grated Parmigiano

Salt and freshly ground black pepper

FOR THE SAUCE

2 ½ pounds ripe but not overripe fresh tomatoes; or 2 ½ pounds canned tomatoes, preferably imported Italian, drained

5 tablespoons extra-virgin olive oil

2 large cloves garlic, peeled but left whole

15 large basil leaves, torn into several pieces

Salt and freshly ground black pepper

Zitoni is a large tubular pasta, popular in southern Italy, that is stuffed with a variety of fillings as well as served plain with sauce. If zitoni *are difficult to find, another shape suitable for stuffing, such as large shells, may be substituted.*

Stuffing dried pasta is one of the arts of southern Italian cooking, and there are many fine examples. Here, the stuffing, composed of chopped mozzarella and ground prosciutto, *ricotta, eggs, and Parmigiano, is quite typical of the south, as are the bread crumbs sprinkled over the top.*

Prepare the stuffing. Cut the *prosciutto* and mozzarella into small pieces. Put the *prosciutto*, mozzarella, parsley, and ricotta in a medium-sized crockery or glass bowl with the egg yolks and Parmigiano; mix with a wooden spoon. Season with salt and pepper, then mix again. Cover the bowl and refrigerate until needed.

Prepare the tomato sauce. If using fresh tomatoes, blanch them in a medium-sized pot of salted boiling water, then remove the skins and seeds, and cut them into 1-inch squares. If using canned tomatoes, pass them through a food mill, using the disc with the smallest holes, into a crockery or glass bowl.

Heat the oil in a nonreactive casserole over medium heat and, when the oil is warm, add the cloves of garlic and sauté for 2 minutes or until golden all over. Add the tomatoes and lightly sauté for 2 or 3 minutes. Tomatoes should be barely cooked and still in large pieces. Add the basil, season with salt and pepper, and cook for 1 minute more. Transfer the sauce to a crockery or glass bowl and let rest until needed.

Bring a large pot of cold water to a boil over medium heat, add coarse salt to taste, then add the pasta and cook it for 8 to 11 minutes; that is, 1 minute less than for normal al dente.

In the meantime, prepare a large bowl of cold water and add the oil. Transfer the pasta, using a slotted spoon, first to the bowl of water with the oil, then onto dampened cotton dish towels.

Preheat the oven to 375° F. Lightly oil a glass baking dish and lightly dust the bottom and the sides with the bread crumbs. If you are using *zitoni*, stuff them using a pastry bag. If you are using large shells, stuff them with a tablespoon, then close the shells back into their original shape. Place the *zitoni* or the shells in the baking dish, then pour the tomato sauce over the top. Cut the mozzarella into 1-inch cubes and sprinkle on top. Cover the baking dish with aluminum foil and bake for 20 minutes. Serve hot with the fresh basil leaves on top.

Fresh buffalo milk mozzarella.

fritto di ziti

FRIED STUFFED ZITI

SERVES 8

FOR THE PASTA

Coarse-grained salt

½ pound dried *ziti* or *rigatoni*, preferably imported Italian

2 tablespoons vegetable oil or olive oil

FOR THE STUFFING

4 ounces fresh mozzarella or buffalo milk mozzarella cheese, preferably imported Italian

4 ounces *prosciutto*, preferably imported Italian

4 ounces whole-milk ricotta

10 large sprigs Italian parsley, leaves only

2 extra-large egg yolks

4 heaping tablespoons freshly grated Parmigiano

Salt and freshly ground black pepper

PLUS

3 extra-large eggs

Pinch of salt

½ cup unbleached all-purpose flour

½ cup fine unseasoned bread crumbs, preferably homemade, lightly toasted

2 cups vegetable oil (1 cup sunflower oil plus 1 cup corn oil)

TO SERVE

Salt to taste

We should not be surprised that this pasta appetizer is from the area around Naples, where pasta is king. In Naples, many appetizers are coated with bread crumbs and then fried, as is the case with this recipe. The stuffing varies. Because you need pasta with a large enough opening to contain the stuffing, small rigatoni, which may be more readily available than ziti, may be substituted.

Bring a large pot of cold water to a boil, add coarse salt to taste, then add the pasta and cook for 8 to 11 minutes; that is, 1 minute less than for normal al dente. Transfer the pasta, using a slotted spoon, first to a bowl of cold water with the oil added, then onto dampened cotton dish towels. Let the pasta rest until needed.

Prepare the stuffing. Coarsely chop the mozzarella on a board. Coarsely chop the *prosciutto*. Drain the ricotta very well to remove all the excess water. Put the mozzarella, *prosciutto*, parsley, ricotta, egg yolks, and Parmigiano in a crockery or glass bowl; mix with a wooden spoon. Season with salt and pepper, then mix again. Use a pastry bag or a teaspoon to stuff the *ziti*.

Using a fork, lightly beat the eggs with a pinch of salt in a small bowl. Prepare two shallow dishes, one with the flour and the second with the bread crumbs. Heat the oil in a medium-sized skillet over medium heat and, when the oil is hot—about 400°F—lightly flour the *ziti*, dip them in the eggs, then lightly bread them; fry a few at time until they are golden all over, about 1 minute.

Transfer the fried pasta to a serving platter lined with paper towels to absorb excess fat. When all the *ziti* are cooked, remove the paper towels, sprinkle with a little salt, and serve hot.

timballo di melanzane
EGGPLANT TIMBALE

A timbale is a drum-shaped mold—timballo means "drum" in Italian—used for baking. The crust of the timbale is usually made of savory or sweet pastry or pasta. For this recipe, however, the "crust" is created from slices of eggplant. This crust is then filled with pasta combined or layered with other ingredients. The timbale can be further enriched by adding layers of a meat sauce or of tiny meatballs.

Perhaps the most famous timbale that features a pasta crust is a southern Italian dish called Pasta nell'Alveare: *cut* ziti *baked in a beehive made of pasta. In the south a timbale is sometimes known as* timpano, *which also means "drum."*

Prepare the tomato sauce. If using fresh tomatoes, blanch them in a medium-sized pot of salted boiling water, then remove the skins and seeds, and cut tomatoes into 1-inch squares. If using canned tomatoes, pass them through a food mill, using the disc with the smallest holes, into a glass or crockery bowl.

Place a medium-sized nonreactive flameproof casserole with the oil over medium heat; when the oil is lukewarm, add the onions and lightly sauté for 5 minutes, or until translucent, stirring every so often with a wooden spoon. Add the tomatoes, lower the heat, cover, and cook for 20 minutes or until the tomatoes are very soft but still in small pieces, stirring every so often with a wooden spoon. Season to taste with salt and pepper, add the parsley and basil, mix very well, and cook for 5 minutes more. Transfer the sauce to a crockery or glass bowl and let rest until cool, then cover the bowl and refrigerate until needed.

Meanwhile, peel the eggplants and cut them vertically into slices a little more than ¼ inch thick. Place the eggplant in a single layer on serving dishes or jelly roll pans lined with parchment paper, and sprinkle with coarse salt. Stack the serving dishes one on top of the other and let rest for 1 hour. In this way the bitter taste of the eggplant will come out in the form of a darkish liquid. Rinse the eggplant very well under cold running water and pat dry with paper towels.

Heat the vegetable oil in a large skillet over medium heat; when the oil is

SERVES 8 TO 10

FOR THE TOMATO SAUCE

Coarse-grained salt

2 ½ pounds ripe, fresh tomatoes; or 2 ½ pounds canned tomatoes, preferably imported Italian, drained

6 tablespoons extra-virgin olive oil

1 pound Tropea onions or red onions, cleaned and finely chopped

Salt and freshly ground pepper

15 large sprigs Italian parsley, leaves only, finely chopped

5 large fresh basil leaves, torn into thirds

FOR THE EGGPLANT

2 ½ pounds Italian eggplants

Coarse-grained salt

2 cups vegetable oil (1 cup sunflower oil plus 1 cup corn oil)

1 cup unbleached all-purpose flour

FOR THE PASTA

1 pound *mezzani* pasta or *penne* or any dried short tubular pasta, preferably imported Italian

TO COOK THE PASTA

Coarse-grained salt

8 heaping tablespoons freshly grated Parmigiano

8 ounces fresh mozzarella or buffalo milk mozzarella cheese, preferably imported Italian cut into less-than-½-inch-thick slices

10 large fresh basil leaves, torn into thirds

TO BAKE

2 tablespoons extra-virgin olive oil

¼ cup fine unseasoned bread crumbs, preferably homemade, lightly toasted

TO SERVE

Sprigs of fresh basil leaves

hot, about 400° F, lightly flour the eggplant and fry, a few slices at a time, until golden all over, about 30 seconds on each side. Transfer the cooked eggplant to a serving platter lined with paper towels to remove excess oil. Let the eggplant rest until needed.

Bring a large pot of cold water to a boil, add coarse salt to taste, then add the pasta and cook for 5 minutes. Drain the pasta and transfer it to a crockery or glass bowl. Add half of the tomato sauce to the pasta and mix very well, incorporating 4 tablespoons of the Parmigiano.

Lightly oil a 4-quart glass heatproof bowl and dust it with bread crumbs. Line the bottom and sides of the bowl with the fried eggplant, barely overlapping each slice. If you have extra slices of eggplant, add them toward the top of the bowl, which will become the bottom of the timbale, the weakest part, once you unmold it. Preheat the oven to 375° F.

Arrange half of the pasta on the bottom of the bowl, pour half of the remaining tomato sauce over the top, then sprinkle with half of the remaining Parmigiano. Add the mozzarella in a single layer over the Parmigiano, then add the remaining Parmigiano. Top with the remaining pasta and finally pour on the last of the tomato sauce. The stuffing should reach the top of the bowl.

Place a piece of parchment paper or aluminum foil over the bowl and a heatproof dish on top as a weight. Bake for 35 minutes. Remove from the oven and let the timbale rest for at least 10 minutes. If you let the timbale cool further, to room temperature, the servings will be easier to cut into attractive portions. Generally, when the timbale is served at room temperature, extra tomato sauce is prepared and poured hot over each portion. Serve each portion with a sprig of fresh basil.

spaghetti in bianco al pecorino toscano

SPAGHETTI WITH PECORINO-MEAT SAUCE

SERVES 6 TO 8

FOR THE SAUCE

8 ounces boneless top round or beef sirloin, in 1 piece

8 ounces boneless pork loin, in 1 piece

1 medium-sized red onion, cleaned

2 cloves garlic, peeled

15 sprigs Italian parsley, leaves only

10 large fresh basil leaves

8 tablespoons extra-virgin olive oil

Salt and freshly ground black pepper

1 ½ cups dry white wine

FOR THE PASTA

1 ½ pounds dried *spaghetti*, preferably imported Italian

Coarse-grained salt

TO SERVE

4 ounces aged pecorino cheese, preferably Tuscan, shaved into large pieces

Fresh basil leaves

Cut the meats into cubes and chop the onion into small pieces on a board. Use a meat grinder, food processor, or blender to coarsely grind the meat, onion, garlic, parsley, and basil all together. Heat the oil in a medium-sized flameproof casserole over medium heat and, when the oil is warm, add the ground ingredients and sauté slowly for 15 minutes, stirring every so often with a wooden spoon. Season with salt and pepper, then add ½ cup of the wine. Let the wine evaporate for 10 minutes, then add the remaining wine; lower the heat and simmer, covered, for 30 minutes. By that time, the sauce should have a very smooth consistency and rather thick texture.

Bring a large pot of cold water to a boil, add coarse salt to taste, then add the pasta and cook it until al dente—9 to 12 minutes depending on the brand.

Drain the pasta, transfer it to a warmed serving bowl, pour the sauce over the top, and mix very well. Transfer to a warmed serving platter, arrange the pecorino shavings on top, and serve with the fresh basil leaves.

The Tuscan hill towns where pecorino Toscano is produced, also abound with caper plants growing out of their ancient walls.

penne ai quattro formaggi
PENNE WITH FOUR CHEESES

Blanch the pistachio nuts in a small pot of salted boiling water, then remove the skins under cold running water and discard them. Remove the crust from the *Gorgonzola* and cut into 1-inch cubes on a board. Combine the cheese and the butter in a crockery or glass bowl, using a wooden spoon to mix very well; they should be thoroughly amalgamated and almost whipped.

Bring a large pot of cold water to a boil, add coarse salt to taste, then add the pasta and cook for 8 to 11 minutes; that is, 1 minute less than for normal al dente.

As the pasta cooks, cut the mozzarella and *fontina* into rough cubes, and place them in a heavy casserole over low heat; stir constantly, using a wooden spoon, until the two cheeses melt. Add the pistachio nuts to the casserole. Drain the pasta, then add it to the casserole, and mix very well. Season with salt and pepper.

When the pasta is completely coated with the cheese, remove the casserole from the heat, add the *Gorgonzola* mixture, and mix very well again. Transfer the pasta to a warmed serving platter and serve hot.

NOTE

In this classic Italian dish, butter is traditionally considered to be the fourth cheese.

SERVES 4 TO 6

FOR THE SAUCE

30 unsalted, undyed fresh pistachio nuts, shelled

Coarse-grained salt

4 ounces *Gorgonzola* cheese, preferably sweet

8 tablespoons (4 ounces) sweet butter, at room temperature

4 ounces fresh mozzarella or buffalo milk mozzarella cheese, preferably imported Italian

4 ounces Italian *fontina*, preferably from the Valle d'Aosta area of Italy

Salt and freshly ground black pepper

FOR THE PASTA

1 pound dried *penne*, preferably imported Italian

TO COOK THE PASTA

Coarse-grained salt

fagottini al mascarpone

LITTLE PASTA PACKAGES WITH MASCARPONE AND TRUFFLES

SERVES 8

FOR THE STUFFING

2 pounds fresh spinach, large stems removed

Coarse-grained salt

4 ounces whole-milk ricotta, drained very well

½ pound *mascarpone cheese*

½ cup freshly grated Grana Padano cheese

1 extra-large egg

3 extra-large egg yolks

Salt and freshly ground black pepper

Pinch of freshly grated nutmeg

FOR THE PASTA

2 ¼ cups unbleached all-purpose flour

4 extra-large egg yolks

¼ cup cold water

Pinch of salt

TO COOK THE PASTA

Coarse-grained salt

2 tablespoons olive oil or vegetable oil

Soak the spinach in a bowl of cold water for ½ hour. Place a large pot of cold water over medium heat and, when the water reaches a boil, add coarse salt to taste, then drain the spinach, add it to the pot, and boil for 5 minutes. Drain the spinach again and cool under cold running water. Squeeze the spinach to remove excess water, and finely chop it on a board.

Put the spinach, ricotta, *mascarpone*, *Grana Padano*, egg, and the egg yolks in a crockery or glass bowl and, using a wooden spoon, mix very well. Season with salt, pepper, and nutmeg, mix again, then refrigerate, covered, until needed.

Prepare the pasta using the ingredients and quantities listed, following the directions on page 12. Stretch the sheet to a little less than ⅟₁₆ inch thick—on the pasta machine take it to the last setting (do not try to stretch it thinner). Cut the sheet into 6-inch squares as for *lasagne*, precook for a few seconds in salted boiling water, transfer to a bowl of cold water with the oil, then remove and let rest on dampened cotton dish towels until needed.

Prepare the *balsamella* with the ingredients and quantities listed, following the directions on page 97, sautéing the garlic with the butter and adding the truffle paste, if desired, just before removing the *balsamella* from the heat. Transfer the sauce to a crockery or glass bowl and let it rest with a piece of buttered wax paper directly against its surface until cool, to prevent a skin from forming.

Preheat the oven to 375° F and butter a glass or other ovenproof 13½-by-8¾-inch glass baking dish. Place 2 heaping tablespoons of the stuffing in the center of each pasta square. Make a package of each by folding two sides over the filling, leaving the ends open. With the seams on top, gently transfer the stuffed *fagottini* to the prepared dish. Pour the *balsamella* over the top and bake for 25 minutes.

Arrange the *Grana Padano* cheese and, if using, the fresh white truffle shavings on top and serve hot.

Grana Padano and Fagottini al mascarpone.

FOR THE BALSAMELLA

1 medium-sized clove garlic, peeled

8 tablespoons (4 ounces) sweet butter

4 tablespoons unbleached all-purpose flour

4 cups milk

1 tube (about 1 ½ ounces) white truffle paste (optional)

Salt and freshly ground black pepper

PLUS

2 tablespoons (1 ounce) sweet butter

TO SERVE

Fresh white truffles, shaved into small pieces (optional)

Grana Padano cheese, shaved into large pieces

gnocchi, ravioli r

udi, and passatelli

origin of gnocchi

Gnocchi go back to the original *ravioli*, which were round dumplings with no pasta covering. Gradually, the variation, called "*ravioli* covered with pasta," displaced the original almost completely. However, during the Renaissance the most common first course was a spicy broth made with meat, fish, or fowl. The meat used was ground and made into *ravioli* without pasta and served in the broth. There was an enormous variety of these dumplings which were served with their own broths, and some were taken to neighboring Austria, Germany, Hungary, and other countries. The Italian ancestry of these dishes has been forgotten, since they have disappeared in their place of origin. The best-known Italian survivors from that early period are the *ravioli nudi* (the "naked" in the name is an appellation from my own family, not the traditional name). These are very much alive in Florence to the present day, although only in family cooking, not in restaurants.

While variations of *gnocchi* are made with semolina (in Rome) or with cornmeal, the overwhelming favorite in modern times is made with a potato base. These are popular, in slight variations, all over Italy—but the less flour used to hold them together, the lighter they are. When *gnocchi* are prepared with no flavoring in the dough itself, which is most of the time, eggs and cheese are omitted. The result is a very light texture.

Potato *gnocchi* can also be flavored, and many varieties are popular, especially in Tuscany. Recipes follow for two of the most interesting. The first is flavored with a dense tomato sauce; the *gnocchi* are then dressed only with butter and cheese. The second type is made with dried *porcini* mushrooms. The mushroom flavor is enhanced by boiling the *gnocchi* in the mushroom soaking water. They are dressed only with butter—cheese as an option is not popular with Italians, who generally do not put grated cheese on anything flavored with wild mushrooms. (See the note on the use of cheese on page 10.)

However, potato *gnocchi* are baked with cheese in Piedmont, a practice originating in Cuneo. When the hot cheese melts and boils, it suggests, to the Piedmontese, the frothing at the mouth of an animal, and so the dialect word *bava*, which means just that, is applied to this dish. There is often an earthy, not quite polite, but humorous touch to such Italian names, and this one is typical.

The Piedmontese version of Naked Ravioli is, as one might expect, more complex, richer, and heavier than the Tuscan version. Chard is mixed with the spinach; and most typically, *Gorgonzola* cheese is incorporated along with the grated Parmigiano. Sage is added to the butter sauce.

From old Mantua, in Lombardy, we have dumplings of meat served in the Renaissance manner. They are cooked in broth, but the broth is no longer eaten. These *Agnolotti ignudi* are then served with butter, cream, and *mascarpone* sauce and sprinkled with Parmigiano. Mantua retains its traditions from the time when, as we know from *Rigoletto* or from Shakespeare, it was an independent duchy. Another holdover from an earlier era is the inclusion of bread crumbs in the stuffing.

The Genoese *gnocchi*, or *troffie*, eaten with the traditional pesto, include *mollica* mixed with the potatoes. Of course, potatoes blend superbly with pesto.

gnocchi o topini di funghi
MUSHROOM GNOCCHI

SERVES 6

FOR THE MUSHROOM BASE

2 ounces dried *porcini* mushrooms

2 quarts lukewarm water

1 medium-sized clove garlic, peeled

15 large sprigs Italian parsley, leaves only

2 tablespoons (1 ounce) sweet butter

3 tablespoons olive oil

½ cup dry red wine

Salt and freshly ground black pepper

½ tablespoon tomato paste, preferably imported Italian

FOR THE GNOCCHI

Coarse-grained salt

1 pound all-purpose potatoes (not new potatoes)

1 ¾ cups unbleached, all-purpose flour

Salt and freshly ground black pepper

Freshly grated nutmeg

TO COOK THE GNOCCHI

Coarse-grained salt

Soak the mushrooms in the lukewarm water for 30 minutes. Drain the mushrooms into a strainer lined with several layers of paper towels, saving the soaking water. Make sure that no sand remains attached to the stems, then finely chop the mushrooms and set aside.

Finely chop the garlic and parsley on a board. Heat the butter and oil over medium heat in a heavy saucepan. When the butter is melted, add the chopped ingredients, sauté for 10 minutes, and then add the mushrooms. Sauté for 10 minutes longer, then add the wine and salt and pepper to taste. Let the wine evaporate over low heat for 10 minutes. Put in the tomato paste and cook for 15 minutes more, stirring every so often so that nothing sticks to the pan. Remove the pan from the heat and let rest for a few minutes. Use a food processor or blender to finely grind the contents, but do not completely purée. Transfer to a crockery or glass bowl and let cool completely.

Meanwhile, bring a large pot of cold water to a boil and add coarse salt to taste. Peel the potatoes and put them in a colander or large strainer. Insert the colander in the pot of boiling water, but be sure the water level is low enough so that water does not touch the bottom of the colander. Place aluminum foil over the potatoes in the colander and steam for 45 minutes or until tender but not mushy.

Place the flour on a pasta board in a mound. Pass the potatoes through a potato ricer onto the flour. Make a well in the potatoes and put in the ground mushroom mixture. Add salt, pepper, and nutmeg to taste. Start incorporating the flour into the potato-mushroom mixture little by little until the dough is homogeneous and only a little of the flour remains. Cut the dough into several pieces, and with your hands, roll each piece into a long roll about 1 inch in diameter. Cut the rolls into ¾-inch-long pieces.

To shape the *gnocchi*, use the concave part of a curved hand grater. Start by holding a piece of dough at the top of the grater with the index and middle fingers of one hand. Lightly draw the piece of dough around in a motion that makes the letter *C* and let it drop. Continue this procedure until all the *gnocchi* are prepared (see page 353).

Add 2 cups of cold water to the reserved mushroom-soaking water and bring to a boil in a large pot, then add coarse salt to taste. Meanwhile, melt the butter on the serving dish by placing the dish over a second pot of boiling water. Gently drop the *gnocchi* into the pot with the boiling mushroom water and stir gently with a wooden spoon to keep them from sticking. After a few seconds the *gnocchi* will rise to the surface of the water; cook for 1 minute more. Then, using a strainer-skimmer, transfer the *gnocchi* to the prepared serving dish. Sprinkle the parsley over the top and serve immediately. Pass the grated Parmigiano at the table if you choose.

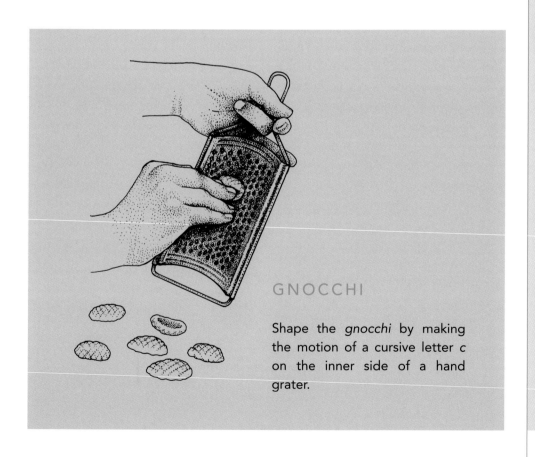

GNOCCHI

Shape the *gnocchi* by making the motion of a cursive letter *c* on the inner side of a hand grater.

gnocchi o topini rossi
RED GNOCCHI

SERVES 6

FOR THE TOMATO BASE

¼ cup olive oil

1 large clove garlic, peeled but left whole

5 large sprigs Italian parsley, leaves only

¼ cup tomato paste, preferably imported Italian

½ cup lukewarm chicken broth, preferably homemade

Salt and freshly ground black pepper

FOR THE GNOCCHI

Coarse-grained salt

1 pound all-purpose potatoes (not new potatoes)

2 ¼ cups unbleached all-purpose flour

Salt and freshly ground black pepper

Freshly grated nutmeg

TO COOK THE GNOCCHI

Coarse-grained salt

TO SERVE

6 tablespoons (3 ounces) sweet butter

6 tablespoons freshly grated Parmigiano

15 large sprigs Italian parsley, leaves only

Make a tomato base that is to be incorporated into the potatoes. Heat the oil in a small, heavy saucepan over medium heat. When the oil is warm, add the garlic and sauté until golden, about 2 minutes. Finely chop the parsley on a board, then discard the garlic and add the parsley, tomato paste, and broth to the saucepan. Stir well and simmer over low heat until the sauce is thick, about 15 minutes; taste for salt and pepper.

Bring a large pot of cold water to a boil and add coarse salt to taste. Peel the potatoes and put them in a colander or large strainer. Insert the colander in the pot of boiling water, but be sure the water level is low enough so that water does not touch the bottom of the colander. Place aluminum foil over the potatoes in the colander and steam for 45 minutes or until tender but not mushy.

Place the flour on a pasta board in a mound. Pass the potatoes through a potato ricer, using the disc with the smallest holes, onto the flour. Make a well in the potatoes and put in the tomato base. Add salt, pepper, and nutmeg to taste. Start incorporating the flour into the potato-tomato mixture little by little until the dough is homogeneous and only a little of the flour remains. Cut the dough into several pieces, and with your hands, roll each piece into a long roll about 1 inch in diameter. Cut the rolls into ¾-inch-long pieces.

To shape the *gnocchi*, use the concave part of a curved hand grater. Start by holding a piece of dough at the top of the grater with the index and middle fingers of one hand. Lightly draw the piece of dough around in a motion that makes the letter C and let it drop. Continue this procedure until all the *gnocchi* are prepared (see page 353).

Cook the *gnocchi* in boiling salted water and finish with butter, as with *Gnocchi di funghi* (page 353). Sprinkle with the cheese and parsley and serve.

gnocchi di patate alla "bava"
GNOCCHI BAKED WITH MELTING CHEESE

Bring a large pot of cold water to a boil and add coarse salt to taste. Peel the potatoes and put them in a colander or large strainer. Insert the colander in the pot of boiling water, but be sure the water level is low enough so that water does not touch the bottom of the colander. Place aluminum foil over the potatoes in the colander and steam for 45 minutes or until tender but not mushy.

Heavily butter a 13½-by-8¾-inch glass baking dish and preheat the oven to 400°F.

Place the flour on a pasta board in a mound. Pass the potatoes through a potato ricer, using the disc with smallest holes, onto the flour. Make a well in the potatoes and put in the egg. Add salt to taste. Start incorporating the flour into the potato-egg mixture little by little until the dough is homogeneous and only a little of the flour remains. Cut the dough into several pieces and, with your hands, roll each piece into a long roll about 1 inch in diameter. Cut the rolls into ¾-inch-long pieces.

To shape the *gnocchi*, use the concave part of a curved hand grater. Start by holding a piece of dough at the top of the grater with the index and middle fingers of one hand. Lightly draw the piece of dough around in a motion that makes the letter *c* and let it drop. Continue this procedure until all the *gnocchi* are prepared (see page 353).

Bring a large pot of cold water to a boil, add coarse salt to taste, then add the *gnocchi*. When they rise to the surface, cook for 30 seconds more. Using a strainer-skimmer, transfer the *gnocchi* to the prepared baking dish. When they are all in the dish, arrange the bits of butter all over, then make a layer of the cheese slices on top. Bake for 5 minutes—just enough time for the cheese to melt and "froth." Remove from the oven and serve hot.

SERVES 4 TO 6

FOR THE GNOCCHI
Coarse-grained salt

¾ pound all-purpose potatoes (not new potatoes)

Butter

1 cup unbleached all-purpose flour

1 extra-large egg

Salt

TO COOK THE GNOCCHI
Coarse-grained salt

TO BAKE

3 tablespoons (1½ ounces) butter, cut into small bits

3 ounces *fontina* cheese preferably from Valle d'Aosta, thinly sliced

gnocchi verdi alla calabrese in brodo

GREEN GNOCCHI, CALABRIAN STYLE

SERVES 6

FOR THE GNOCCHI

4 ounces whole-milk ricotta

2 ounces crustless white bread (½ cup)

½ cup whole milk

4 tablespoons freshly grated Parmigiano

10 large sprigs Italian parsley, leaves only, finely chopped

3 extra-large egg yolks

Salt and freshly ground black pepper

¼ cup unbleached all-purpose flour

TO COOK THE GNOCCHI

6 cups completely defatted chicken broth or vegetable broth, preferably homemade

Coarse-grained salt

About ½ cup unbleached all-purpose flour

TO SERVE

Sprigs of fresh basil leaves

Green gnocchi are made throughout Italy, most often employing spinach as the defining green element. They are held together by flour and eggs. While they are not as light as Florence's ravioli nudi *(naked ravioli), which avoid even flour in the dough, they generally are not as heavy as this Calabrian version. Calabrian gnocchi verdi get their green color from abundant parsley leaves rather than spinach and contain both flour and* mollica, *or the crumb of the bread. The resultant texture is more substantial, similar to Central and Eastern European dumplings, and works very well in broth.*

Prepare the stuffing. Drain the ricotta very well to remove all the excess water, then place in a large ceramic or glass bowl. Soak the bread in the milk in a shallow dish for 10 minutes, then squeeze the bread, discarding the milk, and add the bread to the bowl with the ricotta, along with the Parmigiano, parsley, and the egg yolks. Season with salt and pepper, then add the flour and mix very well.

Bring a large pot of cold water to a boil and a second pot with the broth to a simmer. When the water reaches a boil, add coarse salt to taste. Prepare the *gnocchi* by shaping two heaping tablespoons of the ricotta mixture into a small, tightly compressed ball, making sure there are no air pockets inside. Flour the ball lightly and drop it gently into the boiling water. Repeat until you have used up all of the ricotta mixture. As each *gnocco* rises to the surface of the water, transfer it to the pot of broth using a slotted spoon. Repeat until all the *gnocchi* are in the broth.

Float a sprig of fresh basil leaves in the broth with the hot *gnocchi* and serve.

ravioli nudi con gorgonzola

"NAKED" RAVIOLI WITH GORGONZOLA

SERVES 8 TO 10

FOR THE RAVIOLI

1 ½ pounds fresh spinach, large stems removed

1 ½ pounds fresh Swiss chard, large stems removed

Coarse-grained salt

½ pound ricotta, drained very well

½ pound *Gorgonzola* cheese, preferably sweet

5 extra-large egg yolks

3 cups freshly grated Parmigiano

Salt and freshly ground black pepper

½ teaspoon freshly grated nutmeg

2 cups unbleached all-purpose flour

TO COOK THE RAVIOLI

Coarse-grained salt

TO SERVE

12 tablespoons (6 ounces) sweet butter

10 large fresh sage leaves, torn into thirds

Put the spinach and chard in a large bowl of cold water. Bring a large pot of cold water to a boil, add coarse salt to taste, then drain and add the greens and cook for 10 minutes. Drain again, rinse under cold running water, squeeze very dry, and finely chop on a board. Place the chopped greens in a bowl along with the ricotta, *Gorgonzola*, egg yolks, 2 cups of the Parmigiano, salt and pepper to taste, and nutmeg. Use a wooden spoon to mix all the ingredients, then taste again for salt and pepper.

Bring a large stockpot of cold water to a boil over medium heat. Spread the flour on a pasta board. Take a heaping tablespoon of the mixture from the bowl and roll it on the floured board into a small ball. Be sure the ball is uniformly compact, with no air pockets inside; the outside should be uniformly floured. When the water reaches a boil, add coarse salt to taste, then gently drop the first ball in. When it rises to the top, let it cook for 30 seconds. Meanwhile, melt the butter by putting it on a large serving dish and placing the dish over a second pot of boiling water. Continue to form *ravioli*, rolling them on the flour, until the dough has been used up. Drop the *ravioli* into the salted boiling water, 5 or 6 at a time. The *ravioli* will rise to the surface; after an additional 30 seconds, use a strainer-skimmer to transfer them directly onto the serving dish containing the melted butter. They should be arranged in a single layer. When all the *ravioli* are on the dish, sprinkle with the remaining Parmigiano and the sage leaves. Serve immediately.

agnolotti o agnelotti ignudi al mascarpone

"NAKED" AGNOLOTTI IN MASCARPONE SAUCE

Cut the *prosciutto* and *pancetta* into small pieces and remove the casing from the sausages. Using a meat grinder or food processor, grind together the *prosciutto*, *pancetta*, and sausages or pork. Place the ground meat in a crockery or glass bowl, add the butter and eggs, and mix very well with a wooden spoon until the butter is completely incorporated. Add the bread crumbs and Parmigiano, and season with salt and pepper. Cover the bowl and refrigerate for at least 1 hour before using.

When ready, bring the broth to a boil in a large pot over medium heat. Meanwhile, place a large skillet with the butter over low heat. When the broth reaches a boil, start shaping the stuffing into tiny meatballs; a heaping tablespoon of stuffing will be enough to prepare several. Make sure the meatballs are solid with no air pockets inside. Drop the balls into the boiling broth a few at a time, and as they rise to the top, transfer them with a slotted spoon to the skillet containing the butter. When all the *agnolotti* are cooked and in the skillet, add the *mascarpone* and heavy cream. Mix very well and simmer for 1 or 2 minutes, or until the *mascarpone* is completely liquefied. Season with salt, pepper, and nutmeg. Mix very well, then transfer to a warmed serving platter. Serve immediately, with some Parmigiano on the side.

SERVES 8

FOR THE STUFFING

4 ounces *prosciutto*, in 1 piece

4 ounces *pancetta*, in 1 piece

2 Italian sweet sausages, without fennel seeds; or 6 ounces boneless pork

4 tablespoons (2 ounces) sweet butter

4 extra-large eggs

About ¾ cup unseasoned bread crumbs, preferably homemade

5 tablespoons freshly grated Parmigiano

Salt and freshly ground black pepper to taste

TO COOK THE AGNOLOTTI

4 quarts chicken broth, preferably homemade

FOR THE SAUCE

8 tablespoons (4 ounces) sweet butter

½ pound (8 ounces) *mascarpone* cheese

½ cup heavy cream

Salt and freshly ground black pepper to taste

Pinch of freshly grated nutmeg

TO SERVE

8 tablespoons freshly grated Parmigiano

troffie *or* trofie

GENOESE GNOCCHI

SERVES 4 TO 6

FOR THE TROFFIE

Coarse-grained salt

½ pound all-purpose pota-
  toes (not new potatoes)

2 slices good-quality white
  bread, crusts removed

1 cup cold milk

1 cup unbleached all-
  purpose flour

¼ cup freshly grated
  Parmigiano

1 extra-large egg

Salt

TO COOK THE TROFFIE

Coarse-grained salt

TO SERVE

Genoese Pesto Sauce
  (page 258)

Bring a large pot of cold water to a boil and add coarse salt to taste. Peel the potatoes and put them in a colander or large strainer. Insert the colander in the pot of boiling water, but be sure the water level is low enough so that water does not touch the bottom of the colander. Place aluminum foil over the potatoes in the colander and steam for 45 minutes or until tender but not mushy.

Soak the bread in the cold milk for 30 minutes.

Place the flour on a pasta board in a mound. Pass the potatoes through a potato ricer, using the disc with smallest holes, onto the flour. Make a well in the potatoes. Mix the Parmigiano with the egg in a small bowl and season with salt. Squeeze the milk out of the bread, crumble up the bread, and add to the well along with the egg-cheese mixture, using a wooden spoon to mix thoroughly. Start incorporating the flour into the mixture little by little until the dough is homogeneous and only a little of the flour remains. Cut the dough into several pieces, and using your hands, roll each piece into a long roll about 1 inch in diameter. Cut the rolls into ¾-inch-long pieces.

To shape the *gnocchi*, use the concave part of a curved hand grater. Start by holding a piece of dough at the top of the grater with the index and middle fingers of one hand. Lightly draw the piece of dough around in a motion that makes the letter *C* and let it drop. Continue this procedure until all the *gnocchi* are prepared (see page 353).

Cook the *gnocchi* in boiling salted water, then dress with the Genoese Pesto Sauce. Serve hot.

passatelli

Passatelli are made by passing a stuffing mixture through the holes of a *passatelli* maker or potato ricer directly into boiling broth. In the broth, the *passatelli* congeal into tender strips, which are then eaten with the broth. They are found throughout central Italy, with variations in the different regions. The basis is always bread crumbs, grated Parmigiano, and eggs. In Tuscany, a little spinach is added and grated lemon rind is used for flavor.

In Romagna, butter and a little flour are added to the *passatelli*, but not spinach. And in the Marches, they use finely ground veal, with spinach and butter. A little nutmeg rather than lemon peel flavors the mixture, and additional Parmigiano can be grated over each portion of broth.

Special *passatelli* makers are still available, but a potato ricer is usually used instead, with fine results. I do not recommend using a food mill, since the holes are too small to make really characteristic *passatelli*. There is nothing more soothing and warming than a delicious bowl of rice broth, made even more interesting by the *passatelli* floating in it.

passatelli alla toscana
PASSATELLI IN BROTH, TUSCAN STYLE

SERVES 6 TO 8

1 pound fresh spinach, large stems removed

Coarse-grained salt

4 ounces unseasoned bread crumbs, preferably homemade

6 ounces freshly grated Parmigiano

4 extra-large eggs, at room temperature

Grated zest of 1 large lemon with thick skin

Salt and freshly ground black pepper

3 quarts beef or chicken broth, preferably homemade

TO SERVE

Freshly grated Parmigiano (optional)

Clean the spinach and cook it in a large quantity of boiling water with coarse salt. Drain, rinse, and squeeze well to eliminate water. Finely chop the spinach, then weigh out exactly 3 ounces. If there is any extra, save it for another use.

Place the bread crumbs in a crockery or glass bowl along with the Parmigiano and eggs. Use a wooden spoon to mix ingredients very well. Add the lemon zest to the bowl. Taste for salt and pepper. Add the spinach to the bowl and mix very well.

Cover the bowl with aluminum foil and refrigerate until needed, at least 30 minutes.

When ready to make the *passatelli*, place the broth over medium heat. When it reaches a boil, use a *passatelli* maker or a potato ricer fitted with the disc with large holes, to pass the mixture directly into the boiling broth; the *passatelli* should not be more than 4 inches in length. Cook for 1 ½ minutes, then serve immediately with the broth. Serve with Parmigiano, if desired.

passatelli alla romagnola
PASSATELLI, ROMAGNA STYLE

Place the eggs in a crockery or glass bowl along with the butter, lemon zest, bread crumbs, and Parmigiano. Use a wooden spoon to mix ingredients well. Add the flour, season to taste with salt and pepper, mix again, cover the bowl with aluminum foil, and refrigerate until needed, at least 30 minutes.

When ready to make the *passatelli*, place the broth over medium heat. When it reaches a boil, use a *passatelli* maker or a potato ricer fitted with the disc with large holes, to pass the mixture directly into the boiling broth; the *passatelli* should not be more than 4 inches in length. Cook for 1½ minutes, then serve immediately with the broth. Serve with Parmigiano, if desired.

SERVES 4 TO 6

3 extra-large eggs

2 tablespoons (1 ounce) sweet butter, at room temperature

Grated zest of ½ large lemon with thick skin

8 tablespoons unseasoned bread crumbs, preferably homemade

8 tablespoons freshly grated Parmigiano

1 tablespoon unbleached all-purpose flour

Salt and freshly ground black pepper

2 quarts beef or chicken broth, preferably homemade

Freshly grated Parmigiano (optional)

couscous and

other grains

Coarsely milled grain, usually hard wheat, that is first rubbed with water, sometimes with oil, then steamed and eaten with a stew of meat or fish and vegetables, often including chick-peas, has become known in the English-speaking world as couscous. Assumed to be of North African Berber origin, couscous is also found in other Mediterranean places. It is further assumed that couscous reached Sicily and other parts through Arab invasions from North Africa.

Knowing of couscous dishes in Sicily, Sardinia, and Livorno in Tuscany, I began to search for other such dishes throughout Italy. In the course of my travels, I came to seriously doubt the accepted theory about the origin and spread of couscous. Throughout Italy, in places untouched by a medieval Arab presence, I found the use of a hard wheat more coarsely ground than the usual Italian semolina. And this wheat is prepared with the same method of rubbing water into the coarse grain as is used for couscous. It appears in preparations of the following dishes, among others: *manfregoli* (Tuscany), *manfrigoli* (Romagna), *fregoli* (Trentino), and *fregula* (Sardinia).

In Sardinian recipes for *fregula* (also spelled *firegoli*) the grains are parboiled, then spread out. The recipe for *fregula* included here incorporates water, egg yolks, and saffron into the grains, which enlarges them; they are then dried in the oven and finally boiled for the final preparation, like a pasta.

In Sardinian *Cascá*, a real couscous, the grain cooks—really steams—in a hermetically sealed terra-cotta pot.

I should like to suggest that all of these dishes are survivors of the ancient Roman

Previous pages: Fregola pasta and Sardinian saffron.

world. Egypt, North Africa, Sicily, and Tuscany were, at different times during the Roman epoch, the main sources of wheat. If couscous is of Berber origin, its use must have spread northward much earlier than during the Arab conquests. I suggest that the supposed Berber origin of couscous be subjected to further verification.

For instance, looking into the 2,000-year-old cookbook fragment by the Roman Apicius, we find in his chapter on *pulse* a number of dishes that sound suspiciously like couscous. In *Pultes Iulianae*, the coarse wheat grain is cooked with water and oil, and a meat stew flavored with herbs and wine is gradually mixed in. There are three similar dishes described, including one using bread crumbs instead of grain. Bread crumbs are still used instead of wheat in couscous dishes, not only in modern North Africa but also in Livorno, Italy. So there is no question here of Arabic influence. Coarsely ground barley as well as bread crumbs were used in *pulse* dishes, and its use also survives in Italy as well as North Africa.

Couscous is made by Italian Jews and is assumed to be Sephardic, having traveled with the Arab-influenced Spanish Jews when they were expelled. But not all Italian Jews are Sephardic; some communities survive from Roman times. In Leghorn, the Jewish couscous is paralleled by the one made with bread crumbs by the rest of the population.

Spain was a great part of the Roman world, producing some of its most important emperors. It would be interesting to try to verify surviving dishes in Spain and Portugal of a similar nature. In much later times, after the discovery of the Americas, we see

Spanish influences on North African couscous. Harissa, the spicy sauce used there, is made from peppers brought back by the Spanish from the New World. Several of the squashes, which are common vegetables in their stews, made a similar trip. Couldn't the traffic have been both ways, even in ancient times?

Sicily, as the meeting place of European and North African cultures, is a most fascinating place to examine for culinary survivors. Let us examine the differences between the North African and Sicilian pots used for cooking the grain. The Sicilian *cuscusera* is made of glazed or unglazed terra cotta. The top section has quite large holes in the bottom, so large that the grain probably fell through without a typically secret Sicilian device not shared with outsiders—that the pot must be lined with bay or basil leaves, which flavor the grains as well as contain them. The top section rests on what is simply a terra-cotta stockpot. Strikingly, however, the Sicilians have a special terra-cotta lid because, unlike the North Africans, they always use a lid while steaming couscous. One further folkloristic touch is that the area where the upper and lower pots meet is covered with a thick rope of dough made from a simple mixture of flour and water. This rope seals the escape route of steam, and sets the imagination reeling. It seems more ancient than the commonsense cloth method, and further suggests that in Sicily wheat was so plentiful it could be wasted, whereas in North Africa they had to be more frugal. Was this the original sealing method, and the cloth a later substitution? Did the steaming arrive in Sicily with the eleventh-century Arab occupiers, or was it already there in late Roman times, when the island had so much excess wheat that dried pasta was invented as a way of preserving it?

Farro, soft wheat berries.

cuscusu

COUSCOUS, SICILIAN STYLE

SERVES 6

FOR THE COUSCOUS

1 pound couscous (not instant)

1 tablespoon salt

9 cups cold water

FOR THE FISH SOUP

2 ½ pounds non-oily fish, 2 or 3 types, cut into slices, with bone

Coarse-grained salt

1 large red onion, peeled

½ cup olive oil

1 pound canned tomatoes, preferably imported Italian, drained

4 large cloves garlic, peeled

20 large sprigs Italian parsley, leaves only

5 large fresh basil leaves, torn into thirds

1 cup dry white wine

4 tablespoons white wine vinegar

1 tablespoon tomato paste

Salt and freshly ground black pepper

2 generous pinches hot red pepper flakes

FOR THE STEAMER

3 ½ cups unbleached all-purpose flour

1 cup cold water

15 large fresh or dried bay leaves; or large fresh basil leaves

There are a number of traditional couscous dishes that survive in Sicily. This is the most popular one. It uses as its stew the Ghiotta di pesce, *which also exists as an independent dish; some of the broth is added to the steaming water, and when reduced is reused as a sauce.*

Prepare the couscous. Spread out the grain on a large serving platter or cookie sheet. (In the Mediterranean there are special plates for this purpose; in Italy they are made of terra cotta.) Dissolve the salt in a small bowl with 1 cup of the water. Sprinkle 2 teaspoons of the salted water on the grain, then use the fingers of one hand to rub some grains against the palm itself, using a rotating motion to incorporate the water evenly into the grain. Keep repeating this with additional teaspoons of salted water and grains until you have used up ¼ cup of water and the couscous is evenly wet all over. Spread the grain evenly over a cotton dish towel and let rest for 1 hour.

Prepare the fish soup. Soak the fish in a bowl of cold water with coarse salt for 30 minutes. Finely chop the onion on a board. Place the oil in a heavy, nonreactive flame-proof casserole over medium heat; when

the oil is warm, add the onion, lower the heat, and sauté for 15 minutes, stirring every so often with a wooden spoon. Pass the tomatoes through a food mill, using the disc with the smallest holes. Finely chop the garlic and coarsely chop the parsley on a board. Add the tomatoes to the casserole, cover, and simmer for 25 minutes. Add the garlic, parsley, basil, wine, vinegar, tomato paste, salt and pepper to taste, and red pepper flakes. Stir very well, cover again, and simmer for 15 more minutes.

Drain the fish and rinse under cold running water. Add the fish to the soup, cover, and cook for 10 minutes. When the fish is cooked, remove the casserole from the heat and transfer two-thirds of the broth to the bottom part of a terra-cotta *cuscusera* or stockpot. Cover the casserole containing the fish and remaining broth and set aside until needed.

Add the remaining 8 cups cold water to the soup in the bottom part of the *cuscusera* or stockpot, then put the top part of the *cuscusera* or a strainer over it. Using the flour and the cup of cold water, prepare a thick dough to seal the area connecting the 2 halves of the steamer. Roll this dough into a thick rope long enough to fit around the perimeter of the pot. Using the rope of dough, cover the circle where the top and bottom parts of the steamer (whether *cuscusera* or stockpot with strainer) meet to seal it. Place the steamer over medium heat, and when the broth-water reaches a boil and the steam begins to rise through the holes of the strainer, cover the holes with the bay or basil leaves, and then add the couscous grain (see Note). Cover tightly with the lid of the *cuscusera* (in contrast to some other Mediterraneans, Italians do cover the pot) with a lid or aluminum foil and steam for 30 minutes.

Spoon out the couscous onto a large platter (be sure leaves are still covering the holes) and start rubbing the grains between the palms of your hands, incorporating the remaining ¾ cup of salted water, little by little, to separate any that have stuck together and to retain an even and uniform consistency of individual grains. Let the couscous cool for 15 minutes, then put the grain back into the leaf-lined steamer and cook for 20 more minutes. Reheat the fish, transfer the couscous onto a large warmed platter and discard the bay or basil leaves. Make a well in the grain and arrange the fish in the well. Pour the soup over the fish and serve, adding some of the now reduced broth from the steaming.

NOTE

It is also convenient to spread a cheesecloth over the herbs to facilitate removing the steamed grains.

For a flavorful fish broth, use a variety of fish.

couscus nero

BLACK COUSCOUS

SERVES 4 TO 6

FOR THE SAUCE

3 pounds cuttlefish (*seppie*), uncleaned and with ink sacs

Coarse-grained salt

1 medium-sized red onion, peeled

5 large cloves garlic, peeled

30 large sprigs Italian parsley, leaves only

½ cup olive oil

1 cup dry white wine

6 cups lukewarm water

2 tablespoons tomato paste

Salt and freshly ground black pepper

½ teaspoon hot red pepper flakes

FOR THE COUSCOUS

1 pound couscous (not instant)

1 tablespoon salt

1 cup cold water

8 cups fish broth (*fumetto*)

FOR THE STEAMER

3 ½ cups unbleached all-purpose flour

1 cup water

20 large bay leaves

Here is the couscous with the sauce made from cuttlefish and their ink. This so-called black couscous is a traditional specialty of the nuns of a convent near Trapani. The sauce is the same as that used in Tuscany with pasta and in Venice with rice.

Sardinian couscous is characterized by an olive oil flavor in the grain and by skinning the chick-peas before cooking. Removing the skins is not merely for aesthetic reasons; it produces a sweeter flavor. Though time consuming, it is worth trying at least once to taste the difference. The stew in Sardinia is always of chick-peas and vegetables only, and the meat is always an independently prepared dish, served together with the grain. Aside from the chicken used in this recipe, a number of Sardinian beef, lamb, and fish dishes are traditionally used.

Prepare the sauce. Clean the cuttlefish carefully, saving the sacs full of the ink and cutting the meat into strips about ¼ inch thick, following the directions on page 142. Place the strips in a bowl of cold water with a little coarse salt and let rest until needed.

Finely chop the onion with 3 cloves of the garlic and half of the parsley all together on a board. Place the oil in a heavy, flame-proof casserole over medium heat; when the oil is warm, add the chopped ingredients and sauté for 5 minutes. Finely chop the remaining 2 cloves of garlic and the remaining parsley leaves together on a board; set aside. Drain and rinse the cuttlefish under cold running water. Add the chopped ingredients and the cuttlefish to the casserole, raise the heat, and sauté for 5 minutes longer. Add the wine and let it evaporate for 10 minutes.

Put the ink sacs in a very fine strainer and submerge the strainer in a bowl with 2 cups of the lukewarm water. Rub the sacs against the strainer, using a wooden spoon, until all the ink is extracted from the membranes. Discard the membranes. Add the water with the ink to the casserole, together with the tomato paste, and simmer, covered, for 3½ hours, adding the remaining 4 cups of lukewarm water as needed; the mixture should be like a soup. Stir with a wooden spoon every so often; add salt and pepper to taste and the red pepper flakes when the cuttlefish is half cooked. (Cooking time here is for large cuttlefish. If they are smaller, they may become tender much sooner. Check every 30 minutes.)

Prepare the couscous. Spread out the grain on a large serving platter or cookie sheet. (In the Mediterranean, there are special plates for this purpose; in Italy, they are made of terra cotta.) Dissolve the salt in a small bowl with 1 cup of water. Sprinkle 2 teaspoons of the salted water on the grains, then use the fingers of one hand to rub the grains against the palm itself, using a rotating motion to incorporate the water evenly into the grains. Keep repeating this with additional teaspoons of the water until you have used ¼ cup and the couscous is evenly wet all over. Spread the grain evenly on a cotton dish towel and let rest for 1 hour.

Place the fish broth in the bottom part of a *cuscusera* or a stockpot, then put the top part of the *cuscusera* or a strainer over it. Use the flour and water to prepare a thick dough to seal the area connecting the 2 parts of the steamer (see page 370). Line the bottom of the colander with the bay leaves (see Note), then put in the couscous grains. Cover tightly with the lid of the *cuscusera* or with a piece of aluminum foil, and steam for 30 minutes.

Transfer the couscous to a large platter and rub the grains between the palms of your hands, incorporating the remaining ¾ cup of salted water, little by little, and separating grains that have stuck together. There should be a uniform consistency of individual grains. Let the couscous cool for 15 minutes, then put the grains back into the steamer, cover, and cook for 20 minutes more.

Transfer the couscous to a large, warmed platter; discard the bay leaves, then make a large well in the center and place the fish with its sauce in the well. Serve immediately.

NOTE

It is also convenient to spread a cheesecloth over the herbs to facilitate removing the steamed grains.

cuscus

COUSCOUS, LIVORNO STYLE

The Etruscans were once famous for the quality of their wheat, and perhaps this is connected with the survival of a variety of couscous-type dishes in Tuscany, especially among the Jewish communities, who tend to preserve their culinary traditions. More interesting than the well-known Pitigliano version is this one from Livorno. The delicate little meatballs are wrapped in lettuce leaves rather than cabbage, and the more recent tomato sauce is avoided in favor of a wine broth. Attesting to its antiquity is the addition of saffron to strongly season the grain.

Prepare the chick-peas. Soak them in a bowl of cold water overnight. The next morning, drain and then rinse the peas under cold running water. Put them in a heavy, medium-sized flameproof casserole with the whole onion and water. Place over medium heat and simmer until cooked and very soft, about 1 hour. Add coarse salt and pepper to taste, and simmer for 5 more minutes. Remove and discard the onion. Pass the contents of the casserole through a food mill, using the disc with smallest holes, into a small saucepan (see Note). Place the pan over medium heat, taste for salt and pepper, and simmer for 15 minutes, mixing every so often until a fairly thick sauce is formed. Cover the pan and set aside until needed.

Prepare the couscous. Spread out the grain on a large serving platter or cookie sheet. (In the Mediterranean there are special plates for this purpose; in Italy they are made of terra cotta.) Dissolve the salt in a small bowl with 1 cup of water. Sprinkle 2 teaspoons of the salted water on the grain, then use the fingers of one hand to rub some grains against the palm itself, using a rotating motion to incorporate the water evenly into the grain. Keep repeating this with additional teaspoons of the water until you have used up ¼ cup and the couscous is evenly wet all over. Spread the grain evenly over a cotton dish towel and let rest for 1 hour.

While the couscous is resting and, later, steaming, prepare the sauce and the *polpettine* (little wrapped meatballs). Begin with the sauce. Finely chop the onions and parsley together on a board. Heat the oil in a large skillet over medium heat, add the chopped ingredients, and sauté for 10 minutes; then add the wine and let it evaporate for 10 minutes more. Put in the broth, taste for salt and pepper, and simmer for 1 hour, uncovered. Cover the skillet and set aside until needed.

For the *polpettine*, soak the lettuce leaves in cold water for 30 minutes. Bring a large pot of cold water to a boil and add coarse salt to taste. Have a bowl of cold water next to the pot of boiling water; line a cookie sheet with paper towels. Blanch each lettuce leaf for 40 seconds. Use a slotted spoon to quickly transfer it to the bowl of cold water for 1 minute, then onto the prepared towels; gently spread out the leaf. Repeat until all the leaves are blanched.

Soak the bread in a small bowl of cold water for 5 minutes. Finely chop the garlic and parsley on a board. Place the ground veal and beef in a crockery bowl, then add the chopped ingredients, olive oil, and salt and pepper to taste. Squeeze the water out of the bread and add the bread to the bowl. Mix very well with a wooden spoon until everything is well combined. Place 2 tablespoons of stuffing on each lettuce leaf, then wrap it up, being sure that the leaf completely encloses the meat. Place the *polpettine*, leaf ends facing down, in the skillet with the sauce. Cover the skillet and put it over low heat to simmer for 15 minutes.

When the couscous is ready, reheat the chick-pea purée, then spread the grain over a large, warmed serving platter. Pour the chick-pea purée on top to cover it, then arrange the *polpettine* with their sauce over everything. Serve immediately.

NOTE

To pass easily through the holes, the chick-pea purée needs liquid, so keep pouring the liquid from the pan back into the food mill until all the mixture has passed through.

FOR THE POLPETTINE

24 large leaves Boston lettuce

Coarse-grained salt

3 slices white bread, crusts removed

1 medium-sized clove garlic, peeled

15 large sprigs Italian parsley, leaves only

1 pound ground veal shoulder

1 pound ground beef

2 tablespoons olive oil

Salt and freshly ground black pepper

cascá

COUSCOUS, SARDINIAN STYLE

SERVES 6

FOR THE CHICK-PEAS

2 cups dried chick-peas

2 medium-sized cloves garlic, peeled

3 tablespoons olive oil

2 tablespoons tomato paste

Salt and freshly ground black pepper

FOR THE COUSCOUS

1 pound couscous (not instant)

½ teaspoon salt

¾ cup cold water

FOR THE STEAMER

3 ½ cups unbleached all-purpose flour

1 cup cold water

FOR THE VEGETABLES

3 large artichokes

1 large lemon, cut in half

1 pound carrots, scraped and cut into quarters lengthwise

3 large bulbs fennel, cleaned and cut into quarters

3 medium-sized red onions, peeled and cut into halves

½ cup olive oil

Salt and freshly ground black pepper

Saffron was used centuries ago in the Mediterranean as an omnipresent condiment, like salt and pepper (pepper was then a luxury as saffron is today). Many surviving dishes in Italy were once made with saffron but are now usually prepared without it except in Sicily and Sardinia. (Sicilian pasta with fresh sardines is an example.) The pinches of saffron in this Sardinian chicken dish, as well as the large amount in the Livorno couscous, are survivors of an earlier era, as is Italian couscous itself.

Prepare the chick-peas. Soak them in a bowl with cold water overnight or until the skins are loosened. Drain and rinse under cold running water. Hold each chick-pea between the thumb and index finger, and pinch off the skin.

Finely chop the garlic on a board. Heat the oil in a heavy saucepan over medium heat and add the garlic and tomato paste. Sauté for 1 minute, then add the chick-peas, stir very well, and add enough cold water to cover completely. Simmer uncovered until the peas are cooked but still firm, about 45 minutes when skinned. Add salt and pepper to taste. Cover again and let the peas rest until needed.

Prepare the couscous. Spread out the grain on a large serving platter or cookie sheet. (In the Mediterranean, there are special plates for this purpose; in Italy, they are made of terra cotta.) Dissolve the salt in a small bowl with 1 cup of the water. Sprinkle 2 teaspoons of the salted water on the grain, then use the fingers of one hand to rub some grains against the palm itself, using a rotating motion to incorporate the water evenly into the grain. Keep repeating this with additional teaspoons of salted water and grains until you have used up ¼ cup of water and the couscous is evenly wet all over. Spread the grain evenly over a cotton dish towel and let rest for 1 hour.

While the couscous is resting and, later, steaming, prepare the vegetables. Clean the artichokes (page 70), cut them into quarters, then place them in a bowl with cold water with the lemon halves squeezed in. Place the other vegetables together in a second large bowl of cold water and soak for 30 minutes. When ready, heat the oil in a stockpot over medium heat. Drain all the vegetables and add them to the pot, first the carrots, then the artichokes, fennel, and onions. Sauté for 1 minute without stirring, then add enough water to completely cover the vegetables. Season with salt and pepper to taste, cover, and simmer without mixing until they are cooked but still firm; this will take about 30 minutes. Transfer the vegetables to a crockery bowl and cover the bowl with aluminum foil to keep them warm until needed. Reduce the vegetable poaching water by half.

Meanwhile, prepare the chicken. Heat the oil in a large nonreactive skillet over high heat, then add the chicken pieces in a single layer. Sauté for 10 minutes, until golden brown all over. Sprinkle the scallions over the top; season with salt, pepper, and saffron, then cover with a layer of tomatoes. Cover, lower the heat, and cook for 20 minutes.

Arrange the chicken on a serving dish. Reheat the chick-peas and the vegetable poaching water. Transfer the prepared couscous to a large serving platter and start adding the broth from the chick-peas, always mixing it thoroughly into the grain. When all the broth is absorbed, add the chick-peas and mix very well. Form a mound and make a well in it. Place the cooked vegetables in the well. Each serving should be arranged with the grain on the bottom of the plate, then the vegetables and chicken with its sauce on top. Some of the reduced vegetable poaching broth should then be added.

FOR THE CHICKEN

½ cup olive oil

1 chicken (about 3 ½ pounds), cleaned and cut into 12 pieces

10 medium-sized scallions including white and green parts, coarsely chopped

Salt and freshly ground black pepper

2 generous pinches ground saffron

2 pounds ripe, fresh tomatoes, cut into quarters and seeded; or 2 pounds canned tomatoes, preferably imported Italian, drained and seeded

Fresh fennel bulbs.

fregola o fregula
BOILED SARDINIAN COUSCOUS

SERVES 6 TO 8

FOR THE COUSCOUS

1 pound fregola couscous (not instant)

½ cup cold water

2 extra-large egg yolks

½ teaspoon salt

2 large pinches ground saffron

FOR THE FISH

½ pound squid (*calamari*), cleaned

½ pound octopus, cleaned

Coarse-grained salt

1 sea bass (about 2 ½ pounds), cleaned, with head and tail left on

1 whiting (about 1 ½ pounds), cleaned, with head and tail left on

FOR THE SAUCE

1 large red onion, peeled

1 medium-sized stalk celery

2 large cloves garlic, peeled

¾ cup olive oil

1 cup dry white wine

Salt and freshly ground black pepper

2 large pinches hot red pepper flakes (optional)

Fregola is another coarse grain with historical connections. It is interesting to speculate that Pasta grattugiata, *which is made by grating dough that has been allowed to dry, is a later way of approximating* fregula, *particularly since it swells up when boiled, as does the Sardinian couscous.*

The couscous can be prepared up to 3 days in advance. Preheat the oven to 375° F. Place the couscous on a large serving platter and spread it all over. Start adding the cold water drop by drop in the center, incorporating some of the grains surrounding it. Keep pouring in the water, incorporating more grains until all the grains have absorbed the water and all the water has been used. At that point, start rubbing the grains between your hands so the water is absorbed uniformly and the grains remain separated as they swell. Spread the grains out over the platter again. Mix the egg yolks, salt, and saffron in a small bowl and repeat the previous procedure, using the eggs instead of water. When all the egg is incorporated, the grains will have swelled to a much greater thickness.

Transfer the couscous to a cookie sheet and spread it out again. Place the cookie sheet on the middle rack of the oven and bake for 10 minutes. Turn off the oven but leave the couscous inside for 3 hours, with only the pilot left on.

NOTE

If using an electric oven or an oven without a pilot, bake the couscous for 10 minutes, remove the cookie sheet from the oven, reduce the heat to its lowest setting, and wait 20 minutes. Then repeat this procedure twice.

Remove the couscous from the oven and set aside to cool for about 2 hours. The couscous can be stored in a jar, tightly closed, until needed.

Prepare the fish (see page 142). Cut the squid into 1-inch rings and the octopus into 1-inch pieces, and put them in a small bowl with cold water and a little coarse salt. Cut off the heads and tails of the fish, then cut the bodies into 1½-inch slices. Place the heads and tails in a bowl with cold water and a little salt; soak the fish slices in a second bowl of salted water.

Start the sauce. Finely chop the onion, celery, and garlic together on a board. Heat the oil in a medium-sized flameproof casserole over low heat; when the oil is warm, add the chopped vegetables and sauté for 5 minutes. Drain the squid and octopus, rinse under cold running water, and add to the casserole. Cook for 20 minutes, stirring every so often with a wooden spoon.

Start the broth. Heat the water with the wine in a medium-sized saucepan and bring to a boil. Drain the fish heads and tails, rinse under cold running water, and add to the pan. Simmer for 20 minutes, adding salt and pepper to taste.

Finish the sauce. Add the wine to the squid and octopus in the casserole, and let the wine evaporate for 15 minutes. Add some lukewarm water if the fish is not soft and tender.

Finish the broth. Strain the broth and discard the heads and tails. Dissolve the tomato paste in the hot liquid. Combine the broth with the sauce, taste for salt and pepper, and put in the red pepper flakes if desired. Cover and cook for 30 minutes.

Bring a large stockpot of cold water to a boil. Warm a large serving platter. When the water in the stockpot reaches a boil, add coarse salt to taste, then add the *fregola* and boil for 10 minutes, stirring every so often with a wooden spoon. Meanwhile, drain the fish slices, rinse under cold running water, and add to the casserole. Cook, covered, for 5 to 6 minutes.

Drain the *fregola* into a colander lined with cheesecloth. Spread it out over a warmed platter. Pour the sauce over the top, and arrange the fish pieces in the center. Sprinkle with parsley and serve.

NOTE

Commercial *fregola* can be bought. It requires a longer cooking time, up to 25 minutes.

FOR THE BROTH

3 cups cold water

1 cup dry white wine

6 tablespoons tomato paste

Salt and freshly ground black pepper

TO COOK THE COUSCOUS

Coarse-grained salt

TO SERVE

25 large sprigs Italian parsley, leaves only

pasta grattugiata *or* pasta grattata *or* pasta rasa

GRATED PASTA IN BROTH

SERVES 6 TO 8

1 ½ cups unbleached all-purpose flour

¼ cup very fine semolina flour

¼ cup freshly grated Parmigiano, grated very fine with no lumps

3 extra-large eggs

Salt to taste

Large pinch of freshly grated nutmeg

2 quarts defatted chicken or beef broth, preferably homemade

TO SERVE

Freshly grated Parmigiano

Pasta grattugiata *exists in different parts of Italy under a variety of names. While this kind of pasta is homemade, it has even been adapted to commercial dried pasta under the name of* grandinine *or* pastine*, and in modern times is used mostly in broth.*

Arrange 1 cup of the flour in a mound on a board. Make a well in the flour, then place the semolina in the well. Mix the Parmigiano and eggs in a small bowl and season with salt and nutmeg. Pour the mixture into the well, then use a fork to start incorporating the egg mixture into the flours. Keep mixing until a homogeneous ball of dough is formed.

Begin kneading, incorporating more flour, until the ball of dough is very hard, about 15 minutes. Wrap the dough in plastic and freeze for 45 minutes; this replaces several hours of drying.

Place a 4-sided hand cheese grater on a well-floured surface. Use the large-hole side to coarsely grate the hard ball of dough, letting the pieces fall onto the flour so they do not stick together. When all is grated, bring the broth to a boil in a large pot over medium heat. While the broth is heating, place the *pasta grattugiata* and the remaining flour in a colander and shake very well, both to coat the pasta and to remove the excess flour. Add the pasta to the broth and cook for 1 to 3 minutes depending on dryness. Serve with some Parmigiano sprinkled over each portion of broth and pasta.

VARIATIONS

1. Nutmeg can be omitted from the dough.
2. Black pepper can be added to the dough, with or without nutmeg.

NOTE

This pasta can be prepared 3 or 4 days in advance.

gran farro *or* minestra di farro
TUSCAN BEAN SOUP WITH WHEAT BERRIES

Farro, *an ancient form of wheat called spelt in English, is still treasured in certain Italian dishes. Whole grains of soft wheat are used, cooked in a way that suggests the coarsely milled harder wheat of couscous. In the mythic Neapolitan dessert served to celebrate the coming of spring and Easter,* Pastiera, *soft spring wheat grains are used. They must have originated in ancient times with* farro. *The dish that most strongly survives is* Gran farro *in Tuscany, a thick* minestrone *incorporating the whole grains of* farro, *which probably date back to the days of the Etruscans.*

Farro has increased in popularity in recent years. It is now dried in a variety of ways; some types need to be soaked before cooking, others do not; the cooking time also varies. Cooking times are approximate: the best approach is to follow the instructions on the package you are using. You can tell that farro *is completely cooked when the grains open.*

In Tuscany and Sicily, farro *is usually cooked whole. In Abruzzi, they are also used, mainly for soups, already broken up. This broken* farro *is sold in packages labeled "farretto."*

Soak the beans in cold water overnight. The next morning, coarsely chop the carrots, onion, celery, and garlic together on a board. Cut the *pancetta* into small pieces. Drain and rinse the beans; put them in a medium-sized stockpot, preferably of terra cotta, along with the chopped ingredients, *pancetta*, and the broth. Place the pot over medium heat (if using terra cotta, place a flame tamer between the burner and the pot) and heat, uncovered, until the broth reaches a boil. Cover the pot; simmer for 1½ hours (the beans should be very soft). Pass the contents of the pot through a food mill, using the disc with the smallest holes, into a second pot over medium heat. Taste for salt and pepper. After the broth reaches a boil, simmer for 5 minutes.

Rinse the *farro* under cold running water, then add it to the broth, stir very well with a wooden spoon, and cook for 25 minutes, stirring every so often; the *farro* is thoroughly cooked when the grains open. Remove the soup from the heat and let it rest, covered, for 10 minutes before serving. Place a teaspoon of oil and a twist of black pepper on each serving. Serve at room temperature after a few hours, or reheat, adding an additional cup or so of lukewarm broth.

NOTE

Farro is is available in Italian groceries or natural food stores.

SERVES 8 TO 10

- 1 cup dried *cannellini* (white kidney beans)
- 2 medium-sized carrots, scraped
- 1 medium-sized red onion, peeled
- 1 large stalk celery
- 1 medium-sized clove garlic, peeled
- 4 ounces *pancetta* or *prosciutto*, in 1 piece
- 3 quarts cold chicken broth, preferably homemade, or water
- Salt and freshly ground black pepper
- 1 cup *farro*
- 8 to 10 teaspoons olive oil

passato di fagioli con farro
FARRO IN BEAN BROTH

SERVES 6 TO 8

1 cup dried *cannellini* (white kidney beans)

3 quarts cold water

2 tablespoons extra-virgin olive oil plus ¼ cup

4 medium-sized cloves garlic, peeled, but left whole

4 large fresh sage leaves

2 heaping teaspoons fresh rosemary leaves

4 ounces *pancetta*, in 1 piece

Coarse-grained salt

6 ounces *farro* or 1 scant cup

1 large stalk celery

2 medium-sized carrots, scraped

5 sprigs large Italian parsley, leaves only

3 large basil leaves

1 small red onion, cleaned

1 ripe, fresh tomato, about 6 ounces; or 6 ounces canned tomatoes, preferably imported, Italian, drained

Salt and freshly ground black pepper

TO SERVE

4 to 6 teaspoons extra-virgin olive oil

Freshly ground black pepper

Soak the beans in cold water overnight. The next morning, put the cold water in a medium-sized stockpot over medium heat and bring to a boil. Drain the beans, and add them to the pot along with the 2 tablespoons of the olive oil, 2 cloves of the garlic, 2 of the sage leaves, 1 heaping teaspoon of rosemary leaves, the *pancetta*, and coarse salt to taste; cover and simmer for 1 hour or until the beans are very soft.

Meanwhile, soak the *farro* in a bowl of cold water for 45 minutes, or according to the instructions written on the bag. Bring a medium-sized casserole of cold water to a boil over medium heat, add coarse salt to taste, and 1 clove of the garlic. Drain and rinse the *farro* under cold running water, then add it to the casserole and simmer for 25 minutes, stirrinng every so often with a wooden spoon; by that time, the *farro* should be almost cooked. Drain the *farro* and cool it under cold running water. Discard the garlic clove and transfer the *farro* to a crockery or glass bowl and cover with a wet cotton dish towel. Once the beans are cooked, remove the pot from the burner and let rest, covered, until needed.

Finely chop the remaining garlic, sage, and rosemary with the celery, carrots, parsley, basil, and onion all together on a board. Heat the remaining ¼ cup olive oil in a medium-sized nonreactive saucepan over medium heat. When the oil is warm, add the chopped vegetable-and-herb mixture and lightly sauté for 3 or 4 minutes, or until the onion is translucent. Add the bean mixture with its broth, then add the tomatoes. Season with salt and pepper and simmer for 1 hour, stirring every so often with a wooden spoon to be sure that none of the ingredients sticks to the bottom of the pot. Discard the *pancetta* and then pass the contents of the stockpot through a food mill, using the disc with the smallest holes, into a large crockery or glass bowl.

Transfer the beans back to the saucepan and set over medium heat. Season with salt and pepper to taste. Simmer until the mixture has the consistency of a thin purée. Add the *farro* and simmer until completely cooked, about 10 minutes longer. The consistency should now be rather thick. Serve hot or at room temperature with some olive oil poured over each serving, and sprinkled with freshly ground black pepper.

minestra di farro all'abruzzese

FARRO SOUP, ABRUZZI STYLE

Soak the *farro* in a bowl of cold water for 45 minutes. Bring a large pot of cold water to a boil, add coarse salt to taste, then drain the *farro* and add it to the pot along with the garlic. Simmer for 45 minutes. Drain the *farro*, discard the garlic clove, transfer the *farro* to a crockery or glass bowl, and let rest, covered with dampened paper towels, until needed.

Meanwhile, bring 10 cups of cold water to a boil in a medium-sized stock-pot over medium heat. Cut the onion and the celery into large pieces. Thoroughly rinse the leeks and coarsely chop them. Add the vegetables along with the pork to the pot, and simmer for 15 minutes. Add the tomato paste along with salt to taste and cook for 1½ hours or until the pork is very tender.

Remove the pork and debone it. Cut all the meat into very small pieces.

Pass the soup with all the vegetables through a food mill, using the disc with smallest holes, into a second clean stock-pot. Set the pot over medium heat and add the meat and the *farro*. Simmer for 20 minutes. Taste for salt and pepper and add the hot red pepper if desired.

Let the soup rest at least 5 minutes before serving. Add the olive oil, mix very well, and serve with freshly grated Parmigiano or pecorino romano cheese.

NOTE

In Italy, pig's feet are quite common.

SERVES 6 TO 8

6 ounces *farro* or 1 scant cup

Coarse-grained salt

1 large clove garlic, peeled but left whole

FOR THE SOUP

10 cups cold water

1 medium-sized red onion, cleaned

1 large stalk celery, cut into large pieces

1 medium-sized leek, green part removed

1 pig's foot, cleaned, about 1 pound

2 heaping tablespoons tomato paste

Coarse-grained salt

Freshly ground black pepper to taste

Hot red pepper flakes to taste (optional)

TO SERVE

2 tablespoons extra-virgin olive oil

6 tablespoons freshly grated Parmigiano or pecorino romano cheese

metric conversion chart

The metric weights given in this chart are not exact equivalents, but have been rounded up or down slightly to make measuring easier.

Avoirdupois	Metric
¼ oz	7 g
½ oz	15 g
1 oz	30 g
2 oz	60 g
3 oz	90 g
4 oz	115 g
5 oz	150 g
6 oz	175 g
7 oz	200 g
8 oz (½ lb)	225 g
9 oz	250 g
10 oz	300 g
11 oz	325 g
12 oz	350 g
13 oz	375 g
14 oz	400 g
15 oz	425 g
16 oz (1 lb)	450 g
1½ lb	750 g
2 lb	900 g
2¼ lb	1 kg
3 lb	1.4 kg
4 lb	1.8 kg

VOLUME EQUIVALENTS

These are not exact equivalents for American cups and spoons, but have been rounded up or down slightly to make measuring easier.

American	Metric	Imperial
¼ t	1.2 ml	
½ t	2.5 ml	
1 t	5.0 ml	
½ T (1.5 t)	7.5 ml	
1 T (3 t)	15 ml	
¼ cup (4 T)	60 ml	2 fl oz
⅓ cup (5 T)	75 ml	2½ fl oz
½ cup (8 T)	125 ml	4 fl oz
⅔ cup (10 T)	150 ml	5 fl oz
¾ cup (12 T)	175 ml	6 fl oz
1 cup (16 T)	250 ml	8 fl oz
1¼ cups	300 ml	10 fl oz (½ pt)
1½ cups	350 ml	12 fl oz
2 cups (1 pint)	500 ml	16 fl oz
2½ cups	625 ml	20 fl oz (1 pint)
1 quart	1 liter	32 fl oz

OVEN TEMPERATURE EQUIVALENTS

Oven	F	C	Gas Mark
Very cool	250–275	130–140	½–1
Cool	300	150	2
Warm	325	170	3
Moderate	350	180	4
Moderately hot	375	190	5
	400	200	6
Hot	425	220	7
	450	230	8
Very hot	475	250	9

index

acknowledgments

This book is a happy team effort of the people at Stewart, Tabori & Chang.

First, I must thank Leslie Stoker, a dream publisher, and H. D. R. Campbell, my always sympathetic and helpful editor.

Thanks also to Alexandra Maldonado, designer; Kim Tyner, production; Sarah Scheffel, copy editor; and Liana Fredley, proofreader. Thanks also to my good friends Carole Lalli, who acted as special consultant, and Bernard Jacobson, who knows my books so well that he can find errors I and others have missed.

Thanks to Glenn Wolff for his excellent drawings, and special thanks to photographer Andy Ryan, who found his way into my world of food and played such a crucial role in making this book. And, once again, thanks to Henry Weinberg, without whose help this book could not have been done.

Thanks also to:

Tessilarte of Florence, Italy, for the beautiful linens; Tognana of Treviso, Italy, for the china; Gastronomia Tassini of Florence, Italy, for invaluable help in finding unusual cuts of dried pasta and the Massanera winery in Chianti Classico, Tuscany, for allowing us to photograph the rare "Cinta" striped pigs. Thanks also to Scala/Art Resource, New York, for the beautiful image of Lorenzetti Ambrogio's *Allegory of Good Government, Effects of Good Government in the City*, Palazzo Publico, Siena, Italy.

Edited by H. D. R. Campbell
Designed by Alexandra Maldonado
Graphic Production by Kim Tyner

The text of this book was composed
in Bembo and Avenir.
Printed and bound in Singapore
by Tien Wah Press

SENCA PAVRA OGNVOM FRANCO CAMINI
ELAVORANDO SEMINI CIASCVNO ·
MENTRE CHE TAL COMVNO ·
MANTERRA QVESTA DONA I SIGNORIA
CHEL ALEVATA AREI OGNI BALIA ·